WESTERN CIVILIZATION

An Urban Perspective

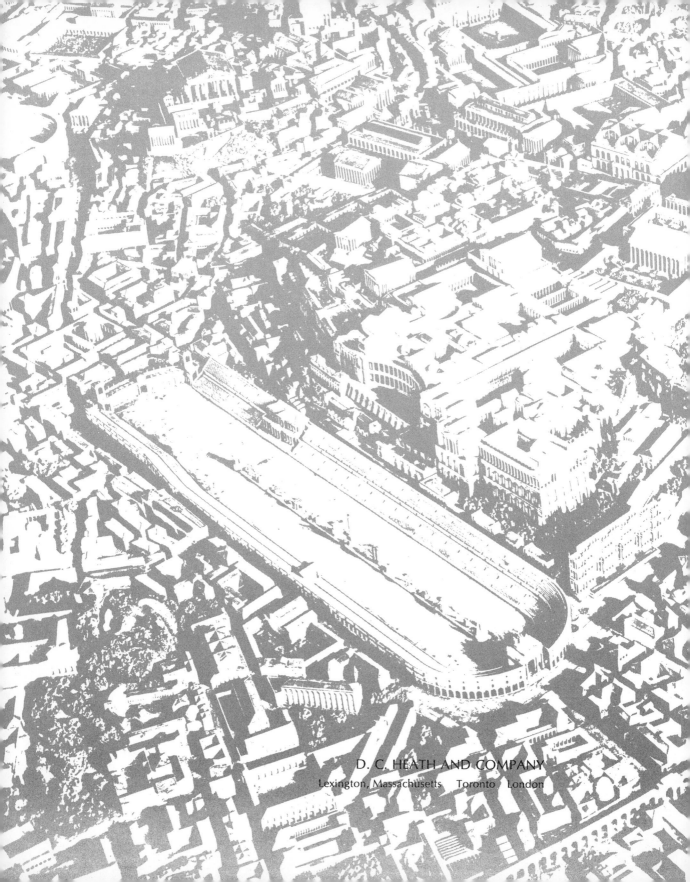

D. C. HEATH AND COMPANY
Lexington, Massachusetts   Toronto   London

WESTERN CIVILIZATION
An Urban Perspective

VOLUME I
From the Rise of Athens through the Late Middle Ages

F. ROY WILLIS
University of California, Davis

Cover illustration: Detail of "View of a City" by Ambrogio Lorenzetti. (Pinacoteca, Siena. Courtesy Art Reference Bureau.)

Title page illustration: Model of 4th-century Rome.

Maps and plans prepared by Richard D. Pusey.

International Standard Book Number: 0–669–89235–1

Library of Congress Catalog Card Number: 72–3834

INTRODUCTION: CIVILIZATION AND THE CITY

Cities have been a major driving force in the development of Western civilization. The highest achievements of man, Sophocles proclaimed in his play *Antigone*, are "language, and wind-swift thought, and city-dwelling habits." The city, from the time of its earliest appearance some five thousand years ago, has focused and magnified man's energies in the task of mastering his environment, enriched his understanding by providing a multiplicity of human contacts, and provided the stimulus to the highest creativity in all forms of science and art. It has at the same time been responsible for many of the darkest features of Western civilization—the spoliation of the environment; the coercion of vast numbers of individuals by government, armies, and economic exploiters; the exclusion of vast segments of the population from intellectual and social advancement; and perhaps even the glorification of war. The city has always been at the extreme of the Western experience.

In recent years, the process of urbanization has been explored with considerable success by a large range of social scientists, including the urban geographer, the political scientist, the sociologist, the social anthropologist, the economist, and the historian. Their findings have thrown great light on such basic concerns as the impact of population growth, the spatial pattern of city development, the occupational structure of cities at varying stages of development, class relationships, family structure and mores, functioning of political systems, and relationship to environment. All of this is enormously helpful to the historian of civilization. But the historian must always remember the one task that distinguishes him from the other social scientists. He must respect the uniqueness of each period of civilization.

This book seeks to meet that challenge by focusing on the achievements of the great cities of Western civilization. Over half of the book is devoted to studies of ten great cities at the height of their creativity. The narrative halts, and we probe into problems of economic and social structure, religion, government and political theory, scientific inquiry, and concepts of beauty and attempts to realize them. In this way, we attempt to combine the findings of the social scientist with the preoccupation of the humanist. The focus on a great city at the moment when it has won a dominating role in a particular period of civilization gives us the opportunity to linger long enough to familiarize ourselves with the city's physical layout, its buildings and its government, its ways of work and of leisure, the thoughts of some of its citizens, and the creation of its artists and writers. For this reason, quotations and photographs are a very important part of the book. Prose quotations are used not only to introduce great writers or statesmen, but to allow the inhabitants of the city to give their own views on the city and its way of life. There is a great deal of poetry too, which is chosen for its historical as well as its literary interest. Reading it, one might bear in mind the whimsical advice of the American poet Marianne Moore:

I, too, dislike it.
Reading it, however, with a perfect contempt for it, one discovers in it, after all, a place for the genuine.[1]

In the same way the photographs, contemporary paintings, etchings, and city plans are intended to build one's familiarity with the contemporary character of the city. Perhaps in a small way they can help the reader feel that kinship with a period in the past that drove Edward Gibbon to write his monumental *Decline and Fall of the Roman Empire*. "It was at Rome," he related in his *Autobiography*, "on the 15th of October, 1764, as I sat musing amidst the ruins of the Capitol, while the barefoot friars were singing vespers in the Temple of Jupiter, that the idea of writing the decline and fall of the city first started to my mind."

Several questions have been asked about each city. The first and most basic is, *How did the city produce its wealth?* The city was a provider of services—religious, governmental, legal, military and commercial; a manufacturer of goods itself, by artisans in the pre-industrial age and by factory production after the industrial revolution of the eighteenth century; and often an exploiter, using military force to acquire economic wealth. Secondly we ask, *What social relationships developed inside this economic system?* We shall be interested in the distribution of wealth, the status accorded to birth or profession, the relationship between classes, the extent of mobility within the social structure, and the distinctive ways of life developed within each stratum of society. Thirdly, we turn to the political superstructure to ask, *How did the citizens conceive the relationship of the individual to the state in theory and carry it out in practice?* Underlying all political systems is a theory or theories of government, though these assumptions are not always explicitly formulated. In times of dissatisfaction with an established political system, theorists construct new formulas based on their own conception of man and the ideal form of state; and as we shall see, these theories are occasionally put into practice, usually as the result of revolution. Political theory will therefore accompany the analysis of the distribution of power within the city and, since most of these cities are also capitals, within the state.

[1] Reprinted with permission of The Macmillan Company from *Collected Poems* by Marianne Moore. Copyright 1935 by Marianne Moore, renewed 1963 by Marianne Moore and T. S. Eliot.

Fourthly, we consider, *How did the city spend its wealth?* The consumption habits of different social classes have been subject to a vast amount of detailed research, and it is increasingly possible to re-create the way of life of the less privileged classes as well as that of the elite. Public expenditure as well as private must be assessed, especially that which is used for the beautification of the city or the improvement of its amenities; but we must also consider the waste of a city's resources, from military adventuring to the ravaging of the natural surroundings. Fifthly, we examine the city's intellectual life, asking, *To what goals was the intellectual activity of its citizens directed?* In cities as multifaceted as these, we must emphasize the most salient features of each city's contribution to the intellectual advance of Western civilization—the contribution of Athens to philosophy and drama, of Rome to law, or of Vienna to music, for example. But in each case the contribution of the environment of the city must be explained: why Paris was a magnet for Europe's theologians in the thirteenth century and for its artists and writers in the late nineteenth century; why tiny Lisbon could attract the continent's cartographers and maritime technologists; why Berlin could be transformed in months from the center of military science to an incubator of avant-garde artistic talent and then in an even shorter time back to its military preoccupations.

Finally, we ask, *How did the achievements of the city, in architecture, art, literature and science, reflect the citizens' conception of man, of God, and of beauty?* This question explains the poetry, sculpture, and buildings abundantly represented in these pages. Much of this creation was the exclusive possession of an elite, but that is hardly a reason for excluding it from a history of civilization. On the contrary, it is one of the brightest features of our century that the creativity of past ages is no longer the preserve of a few. Hence, with no further apology, we shall consider what the Parthenon tells us of the Greek concept of man, how a Botticelli Venus reveals the Florentine conception of the divine, how Newton's laws of motion justify the concept of a naturally ordered universe.

City and countryside, however, cannot be isolated from each other, and should not. As late as 1800, only three percent of the world's population lived in cities of more than 5,000 people; and even in 1950, only thirty percent did so. Throughout the development of Western civilization, most people have lived on the land; the city depends on outside supplies for food. We are therefore concerned throughout the book with the life of the rural population as well as the urban, with agrarian technology and the nature of bulk transportation of agricultural products, with the social structure of the countryside and its impact upon the city, and with the needs, the values, and the aspirations of the inhabitants of the countryside. We must thus consider the farms of the Roman campagna as well as Rome, the decaying aristocratic estates as well as prerevolutionary Paris, the turnips and clover of the agricultural revolution as well as Manchester.

The book is undisguisedly enthusiastic about cities, with a few notable exceptions that will be evident to the reader. I only wish that one could show the same admiration for all man's urban creations that Wordsworth did about London, one bright morning at the beginning of the last century:

Earth has not anything to show more fair:
Dull would he be of soul who could pass by
A sight so touching in its majesty:
This city now doth, like a garment, wear
The beauty of the morning; silent, bare,
Ships, towers, domes, theatres, and temples lie
Open unto the fields, and to the sky;
All bright and glittering in the smokeless air.
Never did sun more beautifully steep
In his first splendor, valley, rock, or hill;
Ne'er saw I, never felt, a calm so deep!
The river glideth at his own sweet will:
Dear God! the very houses seem asleep;
And all that mighty heart is lying still! [2]

---

[2] "Composed upon Westminster Bridge, September 3, 1802."

CONTENTS

9
THE PARIS OF SAINT LOUIS   257

10
THE TRANSFORMATION OF THE
MEDIEVAL SYNTHESIS   291

MAPS

WESTERN CIVILIZATION

An Urban Perspective

1
THE RISE OF ATHENS

Few cities in the whole history of the world have been loved as Athens has; for the reasoned adoration of its own citizens has been shared by generation after generation of peoples who believed themselves to be part of a Western tradition of civilization. Athens during its centuries of greatness was far more than an economic machine, or an imperialist oppressor, or a system of class and racial exploitation, or an educational magnet, or a commercial hub, or a constitutional laboratory, although it was all these things. Athens was an attitude of mind and an achievement of the mind, a unique combination of the physical and the intellectual. And Western civilization has owed an important part of its character, perhaps its finest part, to its nourishment for centuries from the Greek achievement that reached its height in Athens.

There had been rich, powerful, and cultivated cities before Athens—many richer and more powerful. In the cities of the Nile valley and of the Fertile Crescent, which sweeps from the valleys of the Tigris and Euphrates to the shore of the Eastern Mediterranean, an "urban revolution" had begun about 4500 B.C. The Egyptians at Gizeh, Karnak, and Thebes, the Sumerians at Ur, the Akkadians at Babylon, the Assyrians at Nineveh, the Phoenicians at Tyre, the Hebrews at Jerusalem, and the inhabitants of many other cities worked out a new way of life that had profound consequences for the rest of our history. Large bodies of men were organized, often unwillingly, to carry out massive projects for the taming of nature by irrigation or flood control, for defense by erection of city walls and citadels, for war in trained armies, for piety in erection of temples, or for governmental efficiency or glorification through palace building. Differentiation of occupation took place, especially with the rise of commerce and of a merchant class; and social divisions became sharper. Kings and priests united to compel advances in architectural techniques in the building of tomb and temple,

Lion Gate, Mycenae. The main entrance gate in the massive fortifications of Mycenae built around 1400 B.C. (Lawrence Cherney/FPG photo.)

1

palace and citadel, and to develop law that would regulate man's relations to God and to his fellowman. Writing developed from a system of pictures or ideographs until the Phoenicians achieved the alphabet. Astronomy made possible the calendar; arithmetic, geometry, medicine, geography, biology, botany, and geology all made great progress. What had happened, as Lewis Mumford explains, was that the appearance of the city "had resulted in an enormous expansion of human capabilities in every direction. The city effected a mobilization of manpower, a command over long-distance transportation, an intensification of communication over long distances in space and time, an outburst of inventiveness along with a large-scale development of civil engineering, and not least, it promoted a tremendous further rise in agricultural productivity."[1] For all the brutality and egoism of the rulers of these cities, at least some of their inhabitants realized that a new quality of life had been created, and loved their cities for it, as for example this Akkadian:

Come then, O Enkidu, to ramparted Uruk
Where people are resplendent in festal attire,
Where each day is made a holiday.[2]

But, in spite of their intrinsic fascination now that archaeologists have succeeded in making their dead stones speak, the early cities of Egypt and the Fertile Crescent have influenced Western civilization only peripherally. When they were ruined by their rivals, the job of destruction was done really thoroughly. Sennacherib, the Assyrian king, was painstaking in removing Babylon from the map, for example: "The city and [its] houses, from its foundation to its top, I destroyed, I devastated, I burned with fire. The wall and the outer wall, temples, and gods, temple towers of brick and earth, as many as they were, I razed and dumped them into the Arakhtu Canal. Through the mist of that city I dug canals, I flooded its site with water, and the very foundations thereof I destroyed. I made its destruction more complete than that by a flood."[3] With few exceptions, the great buildings disappeared; the major part of the writing, literary or religious, crumbled with the buildings, and within generations often the very language was forgotten. Nevertheless, the influence of the Ancient Near East did survive in those who inherited its achievement—in the material progress of the newer powers like the Carthaginians and the Persians; in a heritage of religion and philosophy that was at the core of much of the West's spiritual development; and in the preparation of the Greeks for the startling advances they were to make in the realization of the potential of the individual human being.

[1] Lewis Mumford, *The City in History* (New York: Harcourt, Brace & World, 1961), p. 30.
[2] Ibid., p. 68.
[3] Ibid., p. 54.

Walls of Tiryns. Constructed about 1300 B.C., these Cyclopean walls of rough-hewn rock encircled the palace or citadel of one of the lesser Mycenaean rulers. Tiryns was captured and laid waste by the Dorian Greeks, probably in the twelfth century B.C. (Author's photo.)

GREECE AND ITS INVADERS

Too much emphasis has been placed on the physical attraction of Greece, mostly by Englishmen and Germans whose misery in the North European drizzle has led them to equate a good climate with civilization. "The preponderance of sunshine," comments one author, "combined with the mildness of winter and the dry warmth of summer, stimulates the energy of the population and encourages an open-air life."[4] "It was perhaps the greatest boon conferred upon Attica by her climate," remarks another, "that her big assemblies could be held in the open air. However democratic the instincts of the Athenian might be, Athenian democracy could not have developed as it did—nor for that matter Athenian Drama—if a roof and walls had been necessary."[5] The scenery too was held to have exercised the same fascination on the wandering tribes from the north, the original Greek settlers, that it does on the modern tourist. "When they emerged at length out of the last rough Balkan defile," wrote Alfred Zimmern, one of the finest Greek scholars, "and pitched camp one evening on level Greek ground between the mountains and the sea, it was the sheer beauty of this new world which made them feel that they had found a home."[6]

It is very tempting to assume that the achievements of the Greeks were determined by this unparalleled setting. But for every beneficial effect of the setting an equally malignant one can be deduced, and the balance of evidence is that the Greeks had to master rather than enjoy their environment.

[4] N. G. L. Hammond, *A History of Greece to 322 B.C.* (Oxford: Oxford University Press, 1967), p. 1.
[5] H. D. F. Kitto, *The Greeks* (Harmondsworth, England: Penguin, 1951), p. 37.
[6] Alfred Zimmern, *The Greek Commonwealth* (Oxford: Oxford University Press, 1931), p. 18.

Minoan Statuette of a Snake Goddess, 16th Century B.C. The Snake Goddess, or perhaps Snake Priestess, was a common figure in the art of Cnossus. She wears the elaborate, flounced dress, with bared breasts, of the royal court. (Courtesy, Museum of Fine Arts, Boston. Gift of Mrs. W. Scott Fitz.)

Minoan Civilization, c. 2000–1400 B.C. Details about the origin of the first settlers in Greece are still open to dispute, although it has been asserted that two waves of invaders, from North Africa and Asia Minor, penetrated the islands in the Neolithic period after 6000 B.C. Whoever they were, by 2000 B.C. these early immigrants had produced a magnificent civilization that we call Minoan, after its mythical king, Minos. The focal point of the Minoans was the palace of Cnossus in North Crete, a sprawling, five-story-tall labyrinth of frescoed assembly halls, storage chambers, lavatories, bathrooms, and colonnaded stairwells. Cnossus ruled Crete and the neighboring islands, and its culture influenced the small towns springing up on the mainland of Greece; and its riches—the vast stores of precious metals and of oil, wine, and grain; the homes and palaces; the pottery thin as eggshell—were a prize for a people strong enough to seize them. The eventual conquerors of Cnossus were the first wave of Greeks, who entered the peninsula around the year 2000 B.C. and probably settled in the mainland towns of Mycenae and Tiryns four hundred years later.

Mycenaean Civilization, c. 1600–1100 B.C. These Greeks were wandering tribesmen, organized in clans under kings. Their language was one of the Indo-European group, and they worshipped male gods of the sky. Fighting on horseback with battle-axes, they had little difficulty in subduing the original inhabitants of the mainland, whom they used as slaves to build the enormous Cyclopean walls of their citadels. After first taking the best that Minoan culture had to offer, and creating a rival Mycenaean civilization, they finally captured Cnossus itself about 1450 B.C., and ruled it until its destruction fifty years later. Mycenae itself, from which the culture received its name, then enjoyed two hundred years of hegemony. During that time, its most grandiose effort was the destruction of Troy on the coast of Asia Minor (c. 1260 B.C.), until it too succumbed to a new wave of Greek invaders, the Dorians (1200–1000 B.C.).

Dorian Invasion, 1200–1000 B.C., and the Dark Age, 1000–800 B.C. What had brought these Dorian invaders into the rockbound land of Greece? First, they were being pushed from behind. The twelfth century was a period of turbulence throughout the Near East. Great empires, like that of the Hittites, were being destroyed by new invaders from Asia; Egypt was under siege; Palestine was being ravaged by the Philistines. Second, they sought plunder, which they found in the Mycenaean cities. They felt little attraction for the palace culture of the Mycenaeans, laid their towns in ruins, and forgot most of their cultural achievements. Third, they came to settle, beginning as nomadic herders and turning later to agriculture on the richer plains. Along the south and east coasts of the Peloponnesus, where the mountain fingers reach to the sea, leaving in their cracks a series of fertile plains, the Dorians founded a series of rough

villages, two of which were to develop into the powerful city-states of
Sparta and Argos. From the Peloponnesus, the Dorians spread across the
southern islands of the Aegean, including Crete and Rhodes, and settled
part of southern Asia Minor.

By the end of the Dark Age (1000-800 B.C.), two hundred years of chaos
about which little is known, the inhabitants of Greece were easily distin-
guishable by the Greek dialect they spoke. In the central highlands of
the Peloponnesus, where three rugged mountain chains and a savage
winter climate discouraged Dorian expansion, the original inhabitants
kept their Arcadian dialect and their claim to have been there before the
birth of the moon. Northern Greece was divided between a pre-Dorian
branch of Greeks called the Aeolians and the last wave of invaders called,
for want of a better label, the North-West Greeks. Finally, the Ionian dialect
was spoken by the lively, versatile people who lived in the central Aegean
islands, the central coast of Asia Minor and in the small peninsula shaped
like a horse's head that juts from the mainland of Greece. The peninsula
was called Attica and its most important town was the Mycenaean settlement of Athens.

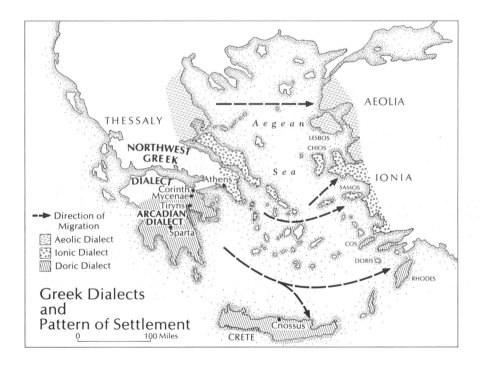

**Greek Dialects
and
Pattern of Settlement**

Physical Character of Attica. The poverty of Attica was its preservation,
as all the ancient writers agreed. "Attica, whose soil was poor and thin,
enjoyed a long freedom from civil strife, and therefore retained its original

inhabitants," the historian Thucydides wrote.[7] The mountains of Attica, once covered with thick forest that was cut down by the early settlers, displayed grey ribs of bare limestone—like a body wasted with disease, Plato commented; and even the plains lacked topsoil. Thus, the first advantages of Attica were that it did not attract invaders, and it did not need large armies of slaves to till the fields. Yet there were natural benefits. The plain around Athens was broad and flat, nine miles by thirteen in size and thus large by Greek standards and divisible into family farms. There was water in a couple of tiny rivers, though they tended to be torrential in winter and almost dry in summer; and hard work made possible market-gardening. The surface of the plain was of high-quality clay, which had superb qualities of color and brightness when turned into the pottery that was one of Athens' chief exports. At the southern tip of Attica, the hills behind Cape Sounion held large deposits of lead and copper; and just at the crucial moment of the Persian invasion at the beginning of the fifth century, an easily exploitable vein of silver was found, which was used to pay for the ships that turned back the Persian invasion. From the

Acropolis of Athens. Easily defensible in times of danger, the rocky plateau was revered as the sanctuary of the Goddess Athena, and thus was the spiritual center of the city. (TWA photo.)

land, the Athenian plain was defended by a semicircle of mountains, broken only by three rough passes that were guarded with border fortresses. Should the invader get past these barriers, the Athenian plain offered a last vital refuge to its inhabitants—a long, anvil-shaped rock three hundred feet high and some nine hundred feet in length, with springs of water, impassable rock faces on three sides, and the protection of the goddess

[7] *Thucydides,* trans. Benjamin Jowett (Boston: D. Lothrop, 1883), p. 2.

Athena. To this Acropolis, the Athenians withdrew in times of trouble. In times of prosperity, however, it was the sea that beckoned. The sea was three miles from the Acropolis; offshore the island of Salamis protected the harbor mouth; and beyond Cape Sounion, lines of islands allowed sailors, who avoided the open sea, to be easily within sight of land the whole way to Asia. The sea provided fish—tunny, anchovy, and sardine; a road to new lands where colonies could be settled in times of over-population; and in imperialist days, the temptation of an empire of islands and coastal ports to an Athens that became too powerful for its own safety.

Class Antagonism in the Countryside, 800–600 B.C. By 800 B.C. the great movement of peoples, both of invaders and of those seeking refuge, had come to an end. Throughout Greece, the control of political power was exercised by the richest of the landowners, who had become a kind of territorial aristocracy replacing the tribal kings, taking to themselves nearly all the duties of governor, judge, jury, bureaucrat, and military overseer. Society was split into two sharply antagonistic classes; and the fascination from a social point of view of the two great works of literature that have survived from the eighth and seventh centuries B.C., the epic poems of Homer, the *Iliad* and the *Odyssey,* and *The Works and Days* of Hesiod, is that they illustrate two differing concepts of society. Probably Odysseus is the most blatant example of the justification of class dominance by the military landowners. When an unpopular warrior called Thersites dared to criticize King Agamemnon, Odysseus beat him black and blue with his staff in front of all the other warriors: "Thersites, this might be eloquence," he shouted, "but we have had enough of it. You drivelling fool, how dare you stand up to the king. It is not for you, the meanest wretch of all who followed the Atreidae to Ilium, to hold forth with the kings' names on your tongue."[8] Hesiod on the other hand, in giving homely advice to his brother on farming, was furious at the "gift-hungry" nobility, whom he likened to a hawk with a nightingale in its claws.

Now I will tell you a fable for the barons; they understand it.
This is what the hawk said when he had caught a nightingale
With spangled neck in his claws and carried her high among the clouds.
She, spitted on the clawhooks, was wailing pitifully, but the hawk in his masterful
    manner, gave her an answer:
"What is the matter with you? Why scream? Your master has you.
You shall go wherever I take you, for all your singing.
If I like, I can let you go. If I like, I can eat you for dinner.
He is a fool who tries to match his strength with the stronger.
He will lose his battle, and with the shame will be hurt also."
So spoke the hawk, the bird who flies so fast on his long wings.[9]

[8] Cited in W. G. Forrest, *The Emergence of Greek Democracy 800–400 B.C.* (London: Weiden-feld and Nicolson, 1966), p. 63.
[9] Hesiod, *The Works and Days,* trans. Richmond Lattimore (Ann Arbor: University of Michigan Press, 1962), p. 43.

Changes in Military Technique, 800–600 B.C. During the next two centuries, the predominance of the aristocracy was undermined by vitally important changes in the methods of fighting and by the development of commerce. For the first two hundred years after the Dorian invasions, the rich nobles developed military predominance, probably because they were owners of horses and the main instrument of fighting was the cavalry.

Combat of Greeks and Amazons. Detail, Athenian Red-figured Pottery, 5th–4th Century B.C. Combats of Greeks with the legendary female warriors of Pontus were used to illustrate the barbarism of the natives of Asia Minor. The Greek soldiers are wearing greaves on their legs and carrying the round shield and thrusting sword of the hoplite. (The Metropolitan Museum of Art. Fletcher Fund, 1944.)

Some time during the seventh century, however, a great change took place in military technique, with significant social and political consequences. The new technique was to arm the infantry in breastplates and helmets of heavy armor, with large strong shields and long spears. These armed men, called hoplites, were trained to attack in coordinated lines, each man's shield protecting the right side of his neighbor and all charging forward in coordination in response to the battle cry or paean of their leader. The phalanx destroyed the predominance of the cavalry and thus of the aristocracy. It introduced a sense of equality of man to man and of solidarity among citizens of one state, for every man was dependent on the man next to him for his own safety. Greek vases of the seventh and sixth centuries B.C. have thousands of pictures of the phalanx—the thrusting spears, the iron helmet with the semicircular protective band, the round shield protecting the whole body from thigh to cheekbone, and the metal greaves that covered the leg from knee to ankle. The vases show, above all, the perfect discipline of the advancing line, firmly in step, rumbling inexorably forward like a wall in motion.

Commercial Revolution and New Wave of Colonization. The phalanx, however, would not have been possible had there not also occurred an economic revolution. The phalanx presupposed the existence of sufficient numbers of what we must call middle-class people who could afford not the highly expensive horse of a cavalryman but the still moderately expensive shield, spear, and helmet of the hoplite. At the same time it presupposed the existence of mining, ore refining, and metalwork on a sufficient scale to provide the equipment for thousands of these soldiers. The economic pattern was fairly simple. Owing to the difficulty of growing grain on the poor soil of Greece, farmers began to concentrate on goods that could be used for export as well as nourishment, notably wine and olive oil. Growing numbers of artisans in the cities produced manufactured goods like vases, cloth, metalwork, and even perfume, for sale abroad. In return, the Greeks imported grain from the Black Sea coast, Asia Minor, and Sicily, and metals from Etruria and Asia. Hand in hand with the development of the export trade was a new wave of colonization from Greece in 750–550 B.C. precipitated by overpopulation in the cities of the Greek mainland. A comparatively small number of mother-cities sponsored colonies, but the colonists were usually joined by the inhabitants of other cities. They settled the islands of the Aegean, the west coast of Asia Minor, the shores of

Temples of Paestum. Founded by Greek colonists from Sybaris about 600 B.C., the flourishing city of Paestum south of Naples contained some of the most beautiful Hellenic temples. In the foreground, the Doric basilica, probably dedicated to Poseidon. (Italian State Tourist Office photo.)

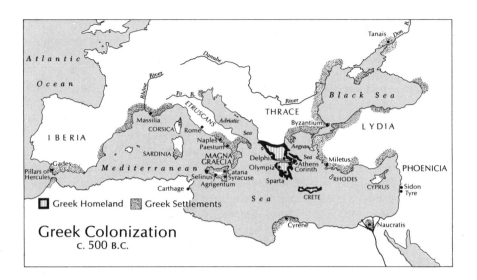

Greek Homeland   Greek Settlements

Greek Colonization
c. 500 B.C.

the Black Sea as far even as the Crimea, the coast of Tunisia, and especially the coast of Sicily and of southern Italy. These colonists founded independent city-states, whose ties with their mother cities were of tradition and of commerce, not of law or of might; and their foundation further encouraged the specialization of trades and the ambition of the middle classes.

Lawgivers and Tyrants, 650–600 B.C.   These military and economic changes made possible a remedy for the grievances that were tearing aristocratic society apart, especially the accumulation of the land in the hands of the aristocrats and the burden of debt on the poor. Occasionally, the warring groups would agree to call in an arbiter or "law-giver," or the newly prosperous groups and the peasantry would throw their support to one man who promised to break the power of the landowners. Tyranny, or one-man rule, became the normal form of government in most Greek states between about 650 and 500 B.C.

It is easy to understand why most Greeks saw the value of the tyrant when one glances at Sparta, the one principal state that avoided having a tyranny. From the time of their conquest of Laconia the Spartans had a society of three classes: the Spartans themselves, the neighbors, or perioikoi, who were a few freeholders not allowed citizenship, and the subordinate population of slaves, called helots. Most of the land was owned by the Spartans and worked by the helots. When the Spartans became too numerous for Laconia, they conquered the neighboring area of Messenia, thereby spreading the control of the Spartan minority so thin that to maintain their predominance, they created a unique system of society. The Spartans devoted themselves entirely to being soldiers, following a system of laws that they believed had been laid down in the ninth century by a mythical lawgiver named Lycurgus. The state took over the total education of a youth from

Spartan Warrior, 6th Century B.C. (Courtesy Wadsworth Atheneum, Hartford.)

age seven to thirty, training him harshly for hoplite warfare. As an adult, he ate with all the other males in common messes, to which he had to contribute from the farm assigned to him. Food was of the most meager and rough kind, especially a famous black broth that horrified more sensitive palates from other cities. The only money permitted was a cumbersome iron "spit." Finally, Sparta had an extraordinary mixture of institutions: two kings, who could thus check each other; five ephors, chosen annually by lot and acting as the real executive; a senate; and an assembly of all the citizens. Sparta went through a period of economic troubles by strengthening the austerity of its social life, so that by the beginning of the fifth century, the Spartans were admired, if not envied, by most other Greeks for their extraordinary devotion to an ideal of discipline and subordination of individual desires. Plutarch tells the story of an old man looking for a seat at the Olympic Games who was being jeered at by those already seated. When he reached the Spartans, every young Spartan and most of the older ones offered him their seats, whereupon the crowd applauded them. The old man commented: "All Greeks *know* what is right, but only the Spartans *do* it."

Hercules Roping the Cretan Bull. Black-figured Amphora, Late 6th Century B.C. The exploits of mythical warriors, such as Theseus and Hercules, provided dramatic subjects for many vase-painters. (The Metropolitan Museum of Art. Rogers Fund, 1941.)

**THE BIRTH
OF ATHENS**

Theseus, Legendary Unifier of Attica.   The whole of Attica was united under Athens, probably peacefully, in a process that took several centuries.   Tradition, however, with more drama than truth, portrayed the unification as the work of one man, the king Theseus, who became a legendary hero in Athens.

His exploits later provided much of the imaginative material for Greek vases, for the statues on the Parthenon, and for the plays of Sophocles and Euripides, and thus fed the imagination of a rationalist Athenian population at the height of its practicality.   Among the many exploits of Theseus, the most famous was his journey to Cnossus to kill the Minotaur, a monster half-man and half-bull, to whom seven Athenian youths and seven Athenian maidens had to be sacrificed annually.   Using a long thread, he found his way through the labyrinth, killed the Minotaur, married Ariadne, who had provided the thread, and later abandoned her. For the Athenian playwrights, Theseus became a convenient mouthpiece for any theme that they wished to present with authentic pedigree; Euripides even used Theseus to explain the advantages of democracy, a theme that would hardly have appealed to the mythical Theseus.

Draco the Lawgiver, 621 B.C.   Following the Dorian invasions, Athens too suffered from the conflicts between the wealthy landowning class and the peasantry and a first attempt to resolve the strife was made by giving Draco power to codify the laws. Draco may not have said that small crimes should be punished by death, and that he had been unable to think of a heavier punishment for larger crimes.   But it is true that the severity of his punishments struck more harshly upon the poorer classes than upon the rich whose property rights he was preserving, and that they so increased the social discontent that Athens was on the verge of bloody revolution by the beginning of the sixth century.

The Reforms of Solon.   The basic trouble was the growing subjection of the poor to the upper class of the "well-born."   Many peasants held their land as sharecroppers and would be sold into slavery for not producing what was owing.   A man could also be sold into slavery for personal debts, since his liberty was accepted as security for his loan.   As a result, there was a widespread demand for an end to sharecropping, for a redistribution of the land, for cancellation of debts, and for the freeing of persons sold into slavery for debt.   Even the upper classes realized the need to face the problem, and in an extraordinary agreement they called in Solon, one of their most admired citizens, with power to remedy the situation.   Solon was a poet, philosopher, and political theorist, as well as a well-to-do merchant with a good understanding of problems of agriculture and of commerce.   He cancelled all debts and all mortgages on land, freed those in slavery for debt, and even bought back from abroad those sold into debt slavery there.   Having restored the freedom of the peasantry of Attica, he set about making a constitution that would break

the political power of the rich. He divided the population of citizens into four classes according to wealth. He permitted all citizens to take part in the assembly and gave it the right to elect a Council of Four hundred, which could act to check the old aristocratic Areopagus, or council of the well born. Even the poorest were given the right to take part in the juries. He finally set out to improve Athenian morality. He controlled the extent of women's wardrobes, ordered fathers to teach their sons a trade, forbade immoral people to speak before the assembly, and punished those persistently idle. Solon was regarded by Athenians as the doctor who helped give Athens the economic and political good health that made its cultural achievement of the fifth century possible.

Perhaps the most moving commentary on Solon's reforms was written by himself:

Aye, many brought I back to their God-built birthplace, many that had been sold, some justly, some unjustly, and others that had been exiled through urgent penury, men that no longer spake the Attic speech because they had wandered so far and wide; and those that suffered shameful servitude at home, trembling before the whims of their owners, these made I free men.[10]

After ruling as Archon for twenty-two years, Solon set off to travel around Egypt and the Near East, enjoining the Athenians to allow ten years in which to test his constitutional reforms. Apparently, Solon continued to

Man and Woman in Oxcart, c. 600 B.C. The simple dignity of the working people is magnified by the so-called geometric style: the rhythm of the statue is based almost entirely upon the crossing of horizontal and vertical lines. (Courtesy, Museum of Fine Arts, Boston. John Michael Rodocanachi Fund.)

[10] Cited in André Bonnard, *Greek Civilization* (London: Macmillan, 1957), I, 110.

give free advice wherever he went, because when asked by the rich king Croesus of Lydia, "Who is the happiest of men?" he replied:

I know God is envious of human prosperity and likes to trouble us; and you question me about the lot of man. Listen, then; as the years lengthen out, there is much both to see and to suffer which one would wish otherwise. Take seventy years as the span of a man's life: those seventy years contain 25,200 days, without counting intercalary months. Add a month every other year, to make the seasons come round with proper regularity, and you will have thirty-five additional months, which will make 1,050 additional days. Thus the total of days for your seventy years is 26,250 and not a single one of them is like the next in what it brings. You can see from that, Croesus, what a chancy thing life is. You are very rich, and you rule a numerous people; but the question you asked me I will not answer, until I know that you have died happily. Great wealth can make a man no happier than moderate means, unless he has the luck to continue in prosperity to the end. . . . Though the rich have the means to satisfy their appetites and to bear calamities, the poor have not, the poor, if they are lucky, are more likely to keep clear of trouble, and will have besides the blessings of a sound body, health, freedom from trouble, fine children and good looks.[11]

Croesus apparently realized the wisdom of this advice when the Persian king was about to burn him alive; for then he sighed, "Ah, Solon! Solon!" and was set free to explain what he meant by his sigh.

Tyranny of Pisistratus and Hippias.   Fortunate in the mediation of Solon, Athens was even more lucky in its tyrants, Pisistratus (c. 605-527 B.C.) and his son Hippias (died 490 B.C.). In the 560s B.C., Athens, far from becoming the harmonious place envisaged by Solon, was split between two factions, the old aristocracy of the plain and the new mercantile middle class of the coast. Intervening in their dispute, Pisistratus put together a third group, the discontented poor and the smaller landholders from "beyond the hills" in Eastern Attica. He displayed considerable bravado as well as a sense of humor in making himself tyrant. On the first occasion, he rushed into the assembly covered with self-inflicted wounds, presumably superficial, and demanded a bodyguard; given the bodyguard, he seized the Acropolis. Driven out later by the factions of the coast and the plain, he returned with a procession led by a very tall, lovely woman whom he had dressed as the Goddess Athena in a complete suit of armor. According to Herodotus, the Athenians, who must have been quite gullible, thought that Athena herself was speaking when the armored beauty told them: "Men of Athens, give kind welcome to Pisistratus whom Athena herself honors above all other men, and is now conducting to her own citadel." Driven out again shortly afterwards, he returned with a strong army and a good supply of silver; and with such effective means, for the next quarter-

---

[11] Aubrey de Selincourt, trans., *The Histories of Herodotus* (Harmondsworth, England: Penguin, 1954), p. 25.

Maidens Preparing for the Dionysian Festival, Athens. Red-figured Pottery Vase, c. 330 B.C. (The Metropolitan Museum of Art. Rogers Fund, 1906.)

century, from 546 B.C. on, Pisistratus and his son gave Athens a period of prosperity that the citizens themselves recognized as a golden age.

Pisistratus allowed the existing constitutional machinery to go on working, intervening only when necessary to make his own policies respected. In a period of calm, the Athenians got used to running the machinery of government that Solon had created. The grievances of the poor farmers were partially removed by grants to them of state lands and of estates confiscated from disloyal aristocrats. Farmers in trouble were granted loans. By planting strategic colonies on the Dardanelles, Pisistratus safeguarded the vitally important route to the southern grainlands of Russia on the Black Sea. Above all, he and his son set out to make the Athenians proud of their own state. Religion was used. Athena's head and her owl appeared on the coinage of Athens, which soon became the most important currency of the Eastern Mediterranean region. Athena was glorified by the embellishment of her temple on the Acropolis, and the Acropolis was turned into the shrine of the city. The Panathenaic Festival, the four-yearly festival in honor of the goddess, was built up into the greatest festival in the life of Athens and a rival to the national festivals like the Olympic Games. Probably the definitive forms of the Iliad and the Odyssey were drawn up for this festival, and the public reading of the poems played an important role in impressing them into the citizens' consciousness. To the tyranny is due also the creation of the festival in honor of the god Dionysus, the god of wine, music, and fertility. For the Dionysian Festival, the first plays, both in tragedy and in comedy, of Greek literature were created. Thus, under Pisistratus, music, drama, and poetry became Athenian institutions, open to the whole body of the citizens, and under constant improvement by the introduction of the competitive spirit that appealed forcefully to the Greeks. By the end of the tyranny, not only was the average Athenian in possession of a law code and constitution with which he was asked to identify, but his very conception of the meaning of Athens was beginning to take on physical connotations, or rather, the physical characteristics of Athens—the Acropolis, the temples, the theaters, the marketplace—were beginning to have emotional appeal.

Theater of Epidaurus. The sacred precinct of Asclepius outside the city of Epidaurus on the Peloponnesus was visited by invalids who wished to receive medical advice from the god. Its theater, built in the 4th century B.C., was the site of regular dramatic festivals. (Author's photo.)

Reforms of Cleisthenes The expulsion of Hippias was followed by a short civil war, in which one aristocratic group led by Cleisthenes won the support of the poorer classes, or *demos,* and succeeded in holding off a Spartan intervention. Cleisthenes then carried out a third remodeling of the Athenian democracy. He made the unit of local government the *deme,* which was the equivalent of a village or city ward, and of which there were about one hundred seventy altogether in Attica. He then divided Attica into three areas, the city, inland, and the coast, and formed ten completely new tribes, each of which was composed of demes picked equally from each of the three new divisions. Deme and tribe were basic to the new Athenian democracy. In the deme, everyone was eligible for office. The small local assemblies became a training-ground for participation in the larger assemblies. Naturalized citizens were admitted through the deme, and became indistinguishable from other citizens, since everyone took his surname from the deme in which he lived. The tribe was now composed of citizens of all parts of Attica, who came to feel a new loyalty to their country as a whole, because these artificially created tribes voted together, for example, in choosing fifty members to represent them in the new assembly of five hundred, or *boule,* and fought together in tribal regiments. The Council of Five Hundred, whose members were chosen by lot, did most of the administration and a good deal of judicial work, while the assembly of all the citizens held ultimate power. Finally, Cleisthenes introduced the institution of ostracism, whereby once a year the assembly could order any one of its leading citizens into exile, honorably, by writing his name on a broken piece of pottery. Six thousand votes were required and a majority of those present. Since this was a large number and required up to twelve thousand people to be present, it needed considerable popular discontent before a man could be exiled in this way.

The Athenian citizens quickly used the power given them by the reforms of Cleisthenes to reject his foreign policy of friendship with the Persian Empire. The great Persian Empire had been built up in less than half a century, but by the beginning of the fifth century it included all the territory from the Eastern Mediterranean and the Black Sea as far as northern India. It was well governed, but Persian overlordship was still unacceptable to the Greek cities of the Ionian coast. In 499, the Ionian cities revolted, and succeeded in burning Sardis, one of the great cities of the Persian Empire. Although aided by Athens, the Ionian rebels were put down after five years of fighting; and the Persian king Darius decided to prevent a second intervention from the Greek mainland by punishing Athens.

THE PERSIAN WARS, 490–479 B.C.

Battle of Marathon, 490 B.C. The Persians did not expect the Greeks to put up much resistance, and Darius sent only a fleet of one hundred ships, carrying about twenty thousand men as well as the former tyrant Hippias, who was to be reinstated in power. Aided only by one other city, the

Athenians met the Persian army on the plain of Marathon. The Athenians had perhaps half the number of soldiers of the Persians. Their hoplites, however, broke through the undisciplined Persian line, and if the traditional figures are to be believed, killed more than six thousand Persians for the loss of one hundred ninety-two Athenians. Three days later, a small Spartan army arrived, found no one to fight, and, said Herodotus, "praised the Athenians and their achievement, and then went home." Many reasons were adduced for the Athenian victory—the lack of large-scale preparations by Darius, the effectiveness of the Athenian phalanx and the skill of its general, the fact that the Athenians were defending their own city—but undoubtedly the sense of defending their new liberties against Persian autocracy played a vital role. In a famous passage, Herodotus characterized the Athenians' spirit after the end of the tyranny:

Thus Athens went from strength to strength and proved, if proof were needed, how noble a thing freedom is, not in one respect only but in all; for while they were oppressed under a despotic government, they had no better success in war than any of their neighbors, yet, once the yoke was flung off, they proved the finest fighters in the world. This clearly shows that, so long as they were held down by authority, they deliberately shirked their duty in the field, as slaves shirk working for their masters; but when freedom was won, then every man amongst them longed to distinguish himself.[12]

Invasion of Xerxes, 480–479 B.C.   The Athenians had won only a temporary respite. Ten years later, Xerxes, the son of Darius, returned with a far larger and better-equipped expedition. To get his soldiers to Greece, he built a bridge of boats across the Hellespont; and he dug a canal across the Mount Athos peninsula to allow his ships to sail safely near the coastline. As the vast army advanced slowly through the north of Greece, the Greek cities there submitted and put their armies at his disposition. So clear was the threat to all the remaining Greek city-states that almost all united in preparation to hold off the Persians in the mountains north of Athens; but the Persians were delayed only for a short while in the pass at Thermopylae by three hundred soldiers under Spartan king Leonidas. Fortunately for the Athenians, they had just used the silver from the newly discovered mines near Sounion to build a new navy of two hundred ships, which now became their final line of defense, the "wooden walls" behind which the Oracle at Delphi had advised them to find safety. The first sortie of the Athenian fleet taught them that they were no match for the Persians except in narrow straits, where the faster Persian ships could not maneuver. This meant that they had to lure the Persians into the waters between the island of Salamis and the Athenian mainland. So, as the Persian army flooded southwards, the whole Athenian population, abandoning Attica to the Persians, fled to the island of Salamis with whatever possessions they could carry with them.

[12] Selincourt, *Histories of Herodotus*, p. 339.

From the hills of Salamis, the Athenians saw their city go up in flames, and the sacred temples on the Acropolis ruined. Perhaps tempted by a trick, perhaps overconfident, the Persian fleet allowed itself to meet the Greeks in the straits at Salamis. Xerxes, sitting on his throne on the shore, saw his ships first rammed, then turn tail, and finally sink in the universal chaos. The next year, the Persians occupying northern Greece were driven out at the battle of Plataea by a large Spartan army.

By the end of 479 B.C., the Persians had withdrawn from the Greek mainland, and all the Greeks exulted in the extraordinary achievement by which so small a people had humiliated the greatest military empire of the time. The Spartans were quietly proud of their achievement. At Thermopylae, they put up an understated memorial to their dead:

Stranger, go to the Spartans and say,
Here we lie, obedient to their command.

The Athenians, however, felt they had made the greatest sacrifices and the greatest contribution for victory. Herodotus expressed it succinctly: "The Athenians through fear of the approaching danger had abandoned their

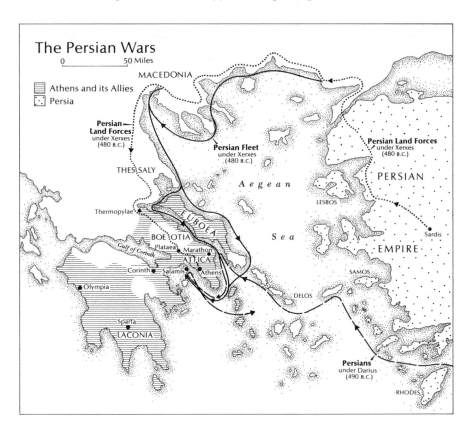

The Persian Wars

country, or if they had stayed there and submitted to Xerxes, there would have been no attempt to resist the Persians by sea, . . . the Spartans would have been left alone to perform prodigies of valor and to die nobly. . . . In view of this, therefore, one is surely right in saying that Greece was saved by the Athenians." [13]

Boat Race. Black-figured Amphora. Greek ships were propelled by banks of oars and a single, large sail. (Courtesy of the Louvre, Paris.)

A more fascinating insight into the attitude of the Athenians can be found in Aeschylus' play, *The Persians.* Aeschylus had fought at Marathon and at Salamis, and had seen the devastation of the Persian occupation of Athens. Yet only eight years later *The Persians* portrays the greatness of the triumph of Athens, not by vilifying the Persians but by ennobling them. The play opens in the palace of Xerxes at Susa, where the chorus of Persian nobles are uncertain of the fate of the vast army that had left for Greece. Slowly the doom is revealed. A messenger arrives, with a long list of Persian leaders killed. Then he describes the ruined navy; then the last battle on land. But it is for the queen to seek out the reasons for this disaster. At first, she displays her ignorance of even the whereabouts of Athens.

Queen: *My friends, where is Athens said to be?*

Chorus: *Far toward the dying flames of sun.*

Queen: *Yet my son lusts to track it down?*

[13] Ibid., p. 460.

Chorus: *Then all Hellas would be subject to the king.*
Queen: *So rich in numbers are they?*
Chorus: *So great a host as dealt to Persians many woes.*
Queen: *Who commands them? Who is shepherd of their host?*
Chorus: *They are slaves to none, nor are they subject.*

Then she cannot understand how the city of Athens could have fallen without the Persians winning a victory.

Herald: *The gods saved the city of the goddess.*
Queen: *What? Athens still stands unsacked?*
Herald: *As long as there are men the city stands.*[14]

After the messenger's description of the losses at Salamis, the chorus brings home to her the meaning of the battle. The Persian power to enforce submission and crush liberty is ended:

They throughout the Asian land
No longer Persian laws obey,
No longer lordly tribute yield,
Exacted by necessity;
Nor suffer rule as suppliants,
To earth obeisance never make:
Lost is the kingly power.

Nay, no longer is the tongue
Imprisoned kept, but loose are men,
When loose the yoke of power's bound,
To bawl their liberty.
But Ajax's isle, spilled with blood
Its earth, and washed round by sea,
Hold the remains of Persia.[15]

Finally her husband Darius himself, from the grave, warns the queen and all Persia with her to leave Greece unmolested in the future, and emphasizes the message of Aeschylus, that the Greeks are the instrument of the gods to punish excessive ambition.

And corpses, piled up like sand, shall witness,
Mute, even to the century to come,

---

[14] David Grene and Richmond Lattimore, eds., *The Complete Greek Tragedies* (Chicago: University of Chicago Press, 1959), I, 228–29.
[15] Ibid. I, 232–33.

Before the eyes of men, that never, being
Mortal, ought we cast our thoughts too high.
Insolence, once blossoming, bears
Its fruit, a tasseled field of doom, from which
A weeping harvest's reaped, all tears.
Behold the punishment of these! remember
Greece and Athens! lest you disdain
Your present fortune, and lust after more,
Squandering great prosperity.[16]

Only by bearing in mind the nobility of this approach can one understand the quality that the Athenians sought to achieve during the next, and greatest, half-century of their history.

SUGGESTED READING

For a brief survey of the "urban revolution" in the Near East, suggestively and provocatively written, consult Lewis Mumford, *The City in History* (1961). A more scholarly treatment is provided by Henri Frankfurt, *The Birth of Civilization in the Near East* (1951) and Jacquetta Hawkes and Leonard Woolley, *History of Mankind,* vol. 1 (1963), the opening volume of a series commissioned by UNESCO. The work of the archaeologists, especially of Schliemann, who discovered Troy, is popularized reliably by C. W. Ceram in *Gods, Graves, and Scholars* (1951), and Leonard Woolley tells in *Digging Up History* (1962) how he dug up Ur. Written records of the Sumerians are widely quoted in S. N. Kramer, *History Begins at Sumer* (1956). The Minoan age in Crete is assessed in R. W. Hutchinson, *Prehistoric Crete* (1962), and the buildings described in J. Walter Graham, *The Palaces of Crete* (1961).

Among the innumerable general histories of Greece, H. D. F. Kitto, *The Greeks* (1963) is a lively, idiosyncratic overview by a British scholar who has devoted his life to Greek literature. Moses I. Finley, *The Ancient Greeks* (1963) is readable, reliable, and too short. Evocation through color photography is successfully practiced by the magazine *Horizon, The Horizon Book of Ancient Greece* (1965); by contrast, N. G. L. Hammond, *A History of Greece to 322 B.C.* (1967) is based on vast research, extremely detailed, and very dull. R. M. Cook, *The Greeks Till Alexander* (1961) is easy to use for individual topics, such as religion or war, but is not integrated as a book. Latest findings of scholarship are surveyed in Victor Ehrenberg, *From Solon to Socrates* (1968), which is hard to read but useful. The classical, rather romanticized account of Alfred Zimmern, *The Greek Commonwealth* (1924) is still worth reading, as is the similarly dated Werner Jaeger, *Paideia: The Ideals of Greek Culture,* 3 vols. (1939–44).

The Mycenaean age is best understood by reading the poems of Homer, especially the *Iliad*, which is well translated by E. V. Rieu (1946); but the recent advances

---

[16] Ibid. I, 249.

made by archaeologists in accurate reconstruction of that age can be admired in John Chadwick's *The Decipherment of Linear B* (1960) which tells how Michael Ventris worked out the Mycenaean script from thousands of clay tablets, and in William A. MacDonald, *Progress into the Past: The Rediscovery of Mycenaean Civilization* (1967). Emily Vermeule, *Greece in the Bronze Age* (1964) is up to date, thorough, and amusing. The finest history of the Dark Age is Chester G. Starr, *The Origins of Greek Civilization, 1100–650 B.C.* (1961).

The political development of the seventh and sixth centuries B.C. is freshly treated in an exciting new analysis by W. G. Forrest, *The Emergence of Greek Democracy 800–400 B.C.* (1966) and quite boringly in A. Andrewes, *The Greek Tyrants* (1956).

2
THE ATHENS OF PERICLES

Looking back in later centuries, Greeks called the period of Athenian greatness between the defeat of the Persians in 479 B.C. and the beginning of the Peloponnesian war with Sparta in 431 B.C. the Pentekontaetia, or "the time of fifty years." Only a special word could describe that unique half-century of human achievement. During the Pentekontaetia, the Athenians had seen the Parthenon and its subsidiary temples rise on the Acropolis. They had turned out by the thousands to see plays like the *Oresteia* of Aeschylus, the *Antigone* of Sophocles, or the *Medea* of Euripides. Socrates had wandered through the streets and colonnades, endlessly talking of the eternal problems of justice and human goodness. Direct democracy had become a way of life, with most citizens participating in the making of the laws and the administration of justice. Whereas few people in history have ever caught what they were pursuing, it can be said for Athens that at no other time have a greater proportion of a city's population come closer to achieving their ideals. The sense of having lived through great events inspired Thucydides to write, in the first paragraph of his history of the Peloponnesian war: "Judging from the evidence which I am able to trust after most careful enquiry, I should imagine that former ages were not greater either in their wars or in anything else."

Yet there was a contrast, which thoughtful Athenians recognized and many deplored, between their ideal of Athens and the material realities of its social and political life. No one was more sensitive than Pericles to the apparent irony of the coexistence of the Athens of the Acropolis and the drama festivals and the democratic assemblies, and the Athens of imperialist expansion and political demoguery and war profiteering. This seeming contradiction, which as we shall see occurs again and again

Parthenon. Athens. The temple to the goddess Athena was the centerpiece of the great reconstruction of the temples of the Acropolis undertaken by Pericles in the mid-fifth century B.C. (David Beal from Black Star.)

in cities at the height of their greatness, between superb achievements of the human intellect and the continuance of social injustice and political self-seeking, was recognized by Pericles as a problem of the utmost importance. But far from separating the ideal Athens from the less satisfactory reality of the city's daily life, as many of the later admirers of Athens have done, Pericles affirmed that both formed a unity. In a concrete sense, the empire, the money-making, the class of slaves were all necessary to provide the citizens with the wealth and the time to create the ideal city. But it was the greatness of Pericles to remind the Athenians that it was the pursuit of their ideal city that mattered, and that without that ideal the rest of the city's activities would degenerate into individual self-seeking. The true well-being of the individual Athenian citizens, he constantly urged, lay in the greatness of their city.

PERICLES AND THE RECONSTRUCTION OF ATHENS

When the Athenians abandoned their city to the Persians and fled to Salamis, they were knowingly sacrificing what was already becoming a beautiful city. The Acropolis was ringed with hewn stone walls and embellished with the two fine temples erected by Pisistratus. The marketplace, or agora, of Solon was lined with temples and public buildings. Elaborate fountains supplied mountain water brought by a long new aqueduct. The Persians left everything in ruins, except for a few houses where their leaders had lodged, and thus compelled the Athenians to rebuild their city.

Fearing both a return of the Persians and a possible attack from their rivals the Spartans, the whole Athenian population set to work in enormous haste pulling down the ruined buildings and using the stone for erection of new walls. According to Thucydides:

In such hurried fashion did the Athenians build the walls of their city, to this day the structure shows evidence of haste. The foundations are made up of all sorts of stones, in some places unwrought, and laid just as each worker brought them; there were many columns too, taken from sepulchers, and many old stones already cut, inserted in the work. The circuit of the city was extended in every direction, and the citizens, in their ardor to complete the design, spared nothing.[1]

After the wallbuilding was complete, however, the rest of the city rose haphazardly, as a confusion of tiny uncomfortable houses of unbaked brick and narrow broiling streets, while the temples on the Acropolis were left in ruins as a reminder of the Persian invasions.

Social Structure and Constitution. For Pericles, the great orator and statesman who dominated Athenian politics and government from 461 to 429 B.C., it was intolerable that the physical beauty of Athens was not commensurate with its political and economic achievements or with its position as the head of a wealthy empire. By the middle of the fifth century, Athens was

[1] *Thucydides,* trans. Benjamin Jowett (Boston: D. Lothrop, 1883), pp. 58–59.

the most powerful city-state in Greece. It had the largest population on
mainland Greece—perhaps a hundred thousand of whom about one-
third were slaves and one-tenth resident aliens. Its economic structure
seemed ideally suited to maintenance of the political system of direct
democracy that Athens had enjoyed since the time of Cleisthenes. The
majority of the citizens were independent small farmers, growing olives,
vines, figs, and a little grain. With the help of two or three slaves, they could
feed their families and share in a small way in the export of oil and wine.
When Pericles introduced payment for service in the administration or
the juries, it became easier for the farmers to take a bigger share in the city's
political life. The citizens who lived in Athens itself tended to be larger
landowners, who could leave a bailiff to manage their estates while they
devoted themselves to politics, or tradesmen and artisans who made and
sold the staple items of the Athenian export trade in manufactures, such as
pottery, woolen textiles, weapons, or silver goods. Among the citizens
of Athens, therefore, there was division by wealth, but the poorer citizen
felt a sense of social independence from the wealthier, since his livelihood
was derived from either his own farm or trade. This feeling was essential,
if all citizens were to meet personally on terms of equality in the assemblies
and juries. The aliens, who were not allowed to own land and were still
liable for taxes and military service, took care of a large part of the city's
commerce and its banking, as well as many menial manufacturing jobs the
Athenian looked down on. The slaves did all the tough painful work in the
lead and silver mines, most of the domestic work not done by women, and
about one-third of the labor on the farms. Although the conditions in the
mines were ghastly, slaves worked beside Athenians in most other jobs, and
there was never a fear in Athens, as there was later in Rome, of slave revolt
or indeed of excessive reliance on slave labor.

The institutions were carefully planned to permit direct participation
by the body of citizens. All were eligible to sit in the *ecclesia,* or assembly,
which met about forty times a year, and was the supreme legislative and
judicial body. Anyone could speak who could make the others listen,
and proceedings were frequently emotional, tempestuous, and chaotic.
The business of the assembly was prepared by the Council of Five Hundred,
whose members were chosen by lot from the ten tribes. The boule members
served in groups of fifty, called the *prytany,* for one-tenth of the year,
maintaining a permanent executive between full meetings of the Council.
Those on the juries, which numbered from 101 to 1001 members, were
also chosen by lot from a list of 6,000 volunteers from the assembly,
while magistrates were elected from the whole assembly and reported directly back to it at the end of their term of office. Thus, because of the use
of election by lot, the majority of citizens, whether they wanted to do so
or not, would have served in Council and would have been directly responsible for the technical administration of the city. The only position where
strong leadership could be perpetuated was the office of general; the ten

generals were elected annually for their competence, and this test applied in no other office in the Athenian state. It was as general that Pericles was able to guide Athenian policy for more than thirty years.

Pericles (c. 495–429 B.C.).   Pericles, a young aristocrat who had taken the leadership of the democratic party in Athens, was a man of broad culture and varied talents. He had studied music, literature, and philosophy. His oratory was so calm and impressive that his nickname was the "Olympian." Although personally incorruptible, he was determined to make permanent the supremacy of the democratic party over the aristocratic supporters of oligarchy; and he slowly introduced the constitutional reforms needed for that goal—abolition of the power of the Areopagus, reduction of property qualifications for office, and establishment of pay for jurors, expense allowance for Council members, and most criticized, pay for soldiers and sailors. The conservatives felt that he had destroyed the moral fiber of Athens; but he had built such strong political support that, by creating democracy, he had brought about one-man rule.

Pericles' ambitions for Athens were unbounded, even by moral scruple, or perhaps he regarded the cause of Athens as the highest morality. By founding colonies he attempted to expand Athenian influence in Italy and the Black Sea, but without much success. His principal effort was to expand, and exploit, the Athenian empire in the Aegean Sea. At the end of the Persian wars, Athens had formed the Delian League as a means of maintaining the protection against Persia that Athens had extended to the Aegean islands and the Ionian cities in Asia Minor. All members were compelled to contribute either ships and men, or money, which was stored in the sanctuary on the island of Delos. The voluntary character of the league soon disappeared. Cities that refused to join or that attempted to leave the league were besieged by the Athenian fleet, disarmed, and forced to pay monetary recompense. Pericles himself was no less aggressive. He attacked Egypt, fought briefly with Sparta, tried to break down the sphere of influence of Corinth, stationed garrisons in the lands of recalcitrant members of the league, and finally in 454 B.C. announced that he was moving the treasury from Delos to the Acropolis in Athens. With the surplus from the treasury, he planned an enormous building program that would make Athens the strongest and most beautiful city of the Mediterranean.

The program Pericles envisaged was to include the reconstruction of the sanctuaries and theater on the Acropolis, of the public buildings in the agora, of the port of Piraeus, and of the defense walls that linked Athens to the Piraeus. Not only would the program bring Athens eternal honor, he told the assembly, according to Plutarch, but it would bring immediate economic benefits. It would provide work for the unemployed, stimulate the economy, and involve the citizen in the life of his polis. "For building," he explained, "we shall need stone, bronze, ivory, gold, ebony, and cypress wood, and to fashion them, carpenters, masons, dyers, goldsmiths, ivory-

Pericles. Roman Copy of a Bust Made in Athens, 5th Century B.C. Pericles, who owed his power to his frequent re-election as general, is wearing the Corinthian-style helmet that pulls down in battle to cover the face. The artist has displayed dignity and authority, but has made no effort to portray Pericles' real appearance. (Photo copyright by the Trustees of the British Museum.)

carvers, painters, and sculptors. Our shipwrights and seamen will work to bring the materials we need from overseas and our wagoners will find employment hauling materials we need for the hinterland. Every auxiliary craft will be stimulated, from metallurgy to cobbling and every trade will be organized under a chief, becoming part and parcel of the services of the state. In a word, all the different needs will be carefully planned and catered for and prosperity will spread to every citizen of whatever age and trade." (Pericles was overly sanguine since many of the artisans had to be brought in from the outside.) Nevertheless, by the end of the century, the work was almost completed, and Athens had achieved the beauty it had been the genius of Pericles to conceive. Contemporaries were well aware of the greatness of what had been accomplished, and they came by the thousands to see for themselves, to wander over the Acropolis, to study in the schools, to attend the theaters, and to watch the Athenians in their assemblies. Perhaps for the first time in history, as Pericles himself noted, a city threw itself open to the inspection of the world, and was proud to do so.

**THE FACE
OF THE CITY**

Most visitors to fifth-century Athens came be sea, to one of the three harbors of the Piraeus. After its reconstruction by the town-planner Hippodamus of Miletus, whom Pericles had called in for the task, the Piraeus had a checkerboard appearance, with warehouses and business offices crowded around the waterfront and the more imposing religious and civic buildings set around the market place in the center of town. It was a pleasant place whose exotic sights and brilliant festivals made an attractive excursion for Athenian citizens. Socrates remarks in the misleadingly simple opening of Plato's greatest book, *The Republic,* "I went down yesterday to the Piraeus with Glaucon, the son of Ariston. I wanted to say a prayer to the goddess, and also to see what they would make of the festival." On his way back to Athens, a slave sent by friends caught at his cloak and begged him to come back to town to see the all-night carnival, with a torch-race on horseback. But within a short time, the Piraeus had become the setting for one of the profoundest discussions of justice, the character of man, and the nature of the state; and the festival had been forgotten.

One road to Athens lay between the Long Walls, tall stone defenseworks six thousand yards in length that linked the walls of the Piraeus with those of Athens but most people preferred the pathway to the north of the Walls, where they could avoid military traffic and enjoy the fields and olive groves that stretched from the little river Cephissus all the way to the suburb of Colonus on the edge of the city. Contrasting with the little farms and the grey-green olive groves, one saw the long, grey outline of the Acropolis of Athens, crowned with its golden complex of temples, high above the orange and white houses of the city. This was the excitement and the charm of Athens, the combination of a countryside teeming with gods and flowers on the edge of the urban clamor. The poet Sophocles, at the age of ninety, turned back to the beauty of Colonus after the horror of the Peloponnesian war:

Of all the land far famed for goodly steeds,
Thou com'st, O stranger, to the noblest spot,
  Colonus, glistening bright,
Where evermore, in thickets freshly green,
  The clear-voiced nightingale
  Still haunts, and pours her song,
  By purpling ivy hid,
And the thick leafage sacred to the God,
  With all its myriad fruits.
  By mortal's foot untouched,
  By sun's hot ray unscathed,
  Sheltered from every blast;
There wanders Dionysus evermore,
  In full, wild revelry,
And waits upon the Nymphs who nursed his youth.

And in it grows a marvel such as ne'er
  On Asia's soil I heard,
Nor the great Dorian isle from Pelops named,
  A plant self-sown, that knows
  No touch of withering age,
  Terror of hostile swords,
  Which here on this our ground
  Its high perfection gains,
The grey-green foliage of the olive-tree,
  Rearing a goodly race:
  And never more shall man,
  Or young, or bowed with years,
  Give forth the fierce command,
  And lay it low in dust.
  For lo! the eye of Zeus,
  Zeus of our olive groves,
  That sees eternally,
  Casteth its glance thereon,
And she, Athena, with the clear, grey eyes.[2]

By contrast with the quiet beauty of these Athenian suburbs, the streets inside the city walls at once brought home the simplicity, and at times the meanness, of everyday Athenian life. All the streets were narrow, winding,

[2] *Oedipus at Colonus*, trans. R. H. Plumptre, cited in Charles A. Robinson, Jr., *Athens in the Age of Pericles* (Norman: University of Oklahoma Press, 1959), pp. 49–50.

Woman Grating Cheese, 5th Century B.C. (Courtesy, Museum of Fine Arts. Boston. Gift by contribution.)

The Agora of Athens
2nd Century A.D.
0 _____ 100 Feet

and dusty in summer and muddy in winter; and the lack of sanitation was evident to even the least sensitive nose. Most of the houses were one-story, with two or three rooms and whitewashed walls of sunbaked brick or even mud and wattle. When there was a second floor, one reached it by an outer wooden staircase. Usually, it would be rented out to a peasant, or occasionally to a visitor from out of town. The walls were so thin that burglars entered by making a hole in the wall rather than trying the door. From place to place, the owner of a house might be seen removing the door or taking off the tile from the roof, the normal method of ousting people who couldn't pay the rent. Smoke poured above the flat roofs of the houses from simple braziers where the women or slaves prepared the meal, or got ready charcoal for heating the inside of the house. The few better-built houses were little more comfortable. Some might have a colonnaded courtyard, and even a few wallpaintings or tapestries. But even the richest homes had little furniture—a few tables, sofas for reclining while eating or for sleeping, a sideboard for jewels or vases. With the rats, flies, and mosquitoes that abounded, it was hardly surprising that the male Athenian spent most of his time out of doors, and even when possible slept on the roof rather than

in the bedroom. It was perhaps symbolic that Athenian doors opened out onto the street, not inwards; and one knocked on going out so as not to hit the people in the street as the door swung open.

Most of the city's activity was concentrated in the *agora*. One passed a stone inscribed, "I am the boundary of the Agora," performed a rite of purification since the agora was a sacred place, and entered an open spacious square. On the north side was an impressive line of government buildings. On the extreme left was the circular tholos, where the fifty pritany on duty ate at public expense before beginning work, and where one-third of them slept every night on constant executive readiness. Next to it was the bouleterion, or council house, where the full five hundred met. Inside, it had a semicircular theater cut in the rock, with a large annex for storage of documents. This council chamber was similar to the parliament buildings of France or to the United States Senate—roofed, with seats for

Foot Race. Detail From Black-figured Amphora, Late 6th Century B.C. The foot race was the main event at the Olympic Games, which were held every four years at Olympia from at least the eighth century B.C. (The Metropolitan Museum of Art. Rogers Fund. 1914.)

Grave Stele of Greek Athlete.
(Turkish National Tourist
Office photo.)

the members, a public gallery, and offices nearby. In spite of the constant assertion that Greek democracy was dependent on meetings in the open air, the basic work of government was done indoors in Athens as it is anywhere else. Next came a small Doric temple of the god Apollo, and finally a fine marble *stoa*. The stoa was essential to Greek city life. It was a colonnade, roofed over, which usually served as entrance to a line of shops and offices. It suited the climate perfectly, providing shade in summer and protection from rain or wind. It was used for gossiping and more serious discussions—in the fourth century, the followers of the philosopher Zeno, who met there, were known as Stoics—for meetings of the Areopagus acting as a court, and for business transactions and banking. Behind this line of buildings, set high on its own pedestal, stood one of the great Doric temples built by Pericles, the Hephaestaeion, which is still preserved in almost perfect condition today.

This superb architectural ensemble looked out over a scene of swirling confusion. Scattered over the agora were altars, shrines, fountain buildings, tiny temples, minor stoas, metalsmiths' fires, fishmongers' stands, and tombs for heroes. Most Athenians thrived on this excitement, notably Socrates, who drew many of his celebrated metaphors from the craftsmen he watched at work there. Others however were less admiring. Aristophanes, the comic playwright, constantly portrayed the agora as a place for decent people to avoid, suggesting that they would do better to go out of town to the gymnasium. "Brilliant and fresh like a flower," one of his characters advises, "you should spend your time in the gymnasium, instead of indulging in the artful chattering of the agora, or undoing yourself in some minor legal affair, full of chicanery, argumentation, and roguery."

THE ACROPOLIS: ATHENIAN ARCHITECTURE AND SCULPTURE

The great rock of the Acropolis was the natural choice for a fortress and sanctuary. It rose about three hundred feet above the city. On three sides, it fell away so sharply that it was impregnable, and could only be reached on the fourth side by a steep winding pathway. For Pericles, it was natural that the most beautiful of the new shrines should be Athena's on the Acropolis. The planner was to be Icthinus, the best architect of his day. The great statue of gold and ivory of Athena was to be sculpted by Phidias, the finest sculptor. To ensure harmony in the architecture and decoration of the building, the supervision of all the work was given to Phidias. The temple to Athena, called the Parthenon, was completed in the astonishing time of only eleven years. The workmen then began the triumphal gateway to the rock, called the Propylaeon, which was almost completed during the Peloponnesian War, when the workmen turned to the two other buildings on the Acropolis, the tiny jewel of the temple of Athena Nike and the temple to Athena and Poseidon, the Erectheion. Work was finished in 395 B.C.

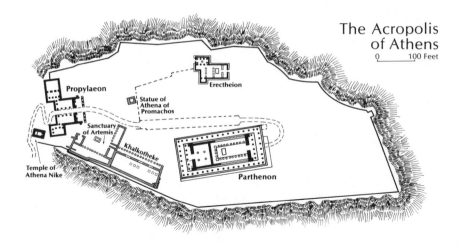

The Acropolis of Athens

0   100 Feet

Propylaeon

Erectheion

Statue of Athena of Promachos

Sanctuary of Artemis

Khalkotheke

Temple of Athena Nike

Parthenon

The Architecture of the Acropolis. The Acropolis was the greatest achievement of Greek architecture and sculpture in the creation of urban beauty and especially in the harmonization of buildings with natural environment. In the spring and autumn, the Acropolis reaches its highest beauty. In the days of early fall, the sky is full of pastel shades, muted grays, creamy blues, and soft pinks, with a mild wind rustling clouds that seem more like the embellishments of a Corot painting than the brazen dome of the Mediterranean sky. Against that pale wash of the fall heavens, the buildings of the Acropolis assume shades of pink and gold of incredible complexity, contrasting with the rough greens and browns of the pine and aloes below. The slope of the cliffside was also used for dramatic effect. The complex of temples on the plateau of the Acropolis was reached by a meandering path up the west slope. As one approached the fortresslike gateway of the Propylaeon, it was impossible to see the Parthenon. The two square porticoes on either

Propylaeon of the Acropolis, Athens. The massive gateway of the Acropolis, built in 337–332 B.C., provided a dramatic entrance to the sacred rock. (Author's photo.)

Parthenon, Athens (David Beal, Black Star.)

side of the gate were bare and unadorned. The gateway itself was narrow, barely six feet across. The excitement grew as one reached the narrow gate, knowing but not seeing what lay beyond. One passed through the heavy Doric gateway, below the four delicate pillars of the temple of Athena Nike. Finally, across the rocky surface of the Acropolis, with its tones of pink and blue, set surprisingly at an angle of some 45 degrees, one saw the glorious west front of the Parthenon.

Since the Parthenon, like all Greek temples, consisted only of one main room, the *cella,* where the statue of the goddess was housed and a secondary room for storage of treasures of the goddess, it appears deceptively simple as architecture. Why do architects regard this as "the most perfect example ever achieved of architecture finding its fulfillment in bodily beauty?"[3] A little knowledge of the technical details of the temple enables one to gain a growing feeling for the achievement.

Many of the elements of the classical Greek temple had been invented centuries earlier. Temples consisting of forests of huge stone colonnades serving as frames for mammoth statues of Pharaohs had been built in Egypt around the fifteenth century B.C. The ground plan had already been used in the palaces of the Mycenaean kings. But in the two centuries before the erection of the Parthenon, Greek architects had advanced far beyond these earlier buildings. Using wood, they had transformed the simplest of building devices, the lintel laid across a post, into the Doric column and entablature. To protect the fragile brick walls of their temple they had surrounded it with a colonnade and covered it with a sloping roof, thereby creating a triangular pediment in the facade of the building, into which sculpture could be inserted. By increasing the size of the lintel, they had

[3] Nikolaus Pevsner, *An Outline of European Architecture* (Harmondsworth, England: Penguin, 1961), p. 10.

left space free for a long decorative frieze. Finally, in the sixth century they had mastered the technique of building in marble and limestone. Final perfection of the style was reached in the Parthenon.

The base of the temple consists of three steps. In Doric temples like the Parthenon, the columns sit directly on the top step. The column itself is composed of a series of circular stones placed one on top of the other and joined through the center by a small square wooden post. The columns are fluted with sharp edges. On the top of the column is placed a simple round capital, on which a series of flat stone blocks are laid to create the entablature. Above the entablature at each end of the building is the depressed triangle of the pediment, the tiny fragment remaining indicative of the place where the Athenians lavished their greatest compositions of sculpture. The three steps at the base lift the temple from the ground, without one's even being aware of their existence, so that the columns seem to rise suspended in the air. The columns themselves, so strong that the heavy weight of the entablature seems slight by comparison, are not crass but delicate in appearance. It was once thought that the curve in the line of the entablature and the bulges in the columns, which are clearly visible to the eye, were

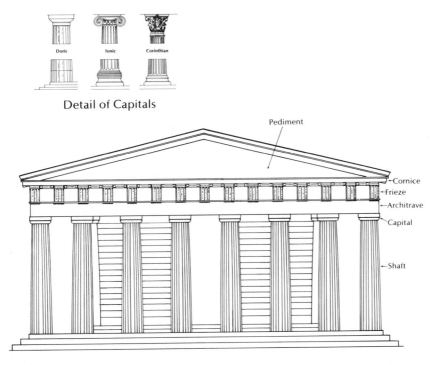

Detail of Capitals

Greek Architecture

deliberately used by the architects to avoid the effects of foreshortening that a perfectly straight building produces. We now feel, however, that the Greeks exaggerated the curves to such an extent that, far from negating illusory optical effects, the curves endowed the architecture with an aspect of lightness.

After creating a totally harmonious building, the architects of the Acropolis proceeded to erect a series of sharply contrasting buildings. The little temple of Athena Nike was built in the second of the classical Greek styles, known as Ionic because it was developed under Eastern influences in the Greek cities of Ionia in Asia Minor. The Ionic style was more delicate and elegant than the Doric. The column was placed on a circular, molded base; it was deeply fluted, and much slimmer than the Doric column; and most important of all, its capital was decorated with two swirls, like rolled up parchment, called volutes. The effect was of softness and charm, contrasting with the robust self-assertion of the Doric colonnade. Finally, a few yards away on the north side of the Acropolis was the Erectheion, set at an angle from the Parthenon, so that the buildings might catch the light at different angles. The Erectheion also contrasts with the Parthenon by the change in the character of the architecture, which is much lighter and more feminine.

Temple of Athena Nike of the Acropolis, Athens.
The delicate little temple was built during a temporary truce in the Peloponnesian War. Its elegant Ionic columns contrast with the power of the Doric Parthenon and Propylaeon.
(Author's photo.)

The Sculpture of the Acropolis. The Porch of the Maidens of the Erectheion provides the odd spectacle of a group of girls acting as the columns of a projecting porch. Yet their flowing garments provide a quick glimpse of the character of classical Greek sculpture. There is perfection of technique in the handling of clothes, and there is deliberate exclusion of all individuality. These women represent all Greek women. There is perfection, and yet something is missing. It was this determination to exclude the emotional and the individual that led English art critic Eric Newton to complain that Greek sculpture had made the mistake of "pursuing an aim that was attainable. Beyond a certain point nothing more could be done. . . . When we see a headless Greek statue, we do not wonder what the head was like: we know that the head would tell us nothing. It would not alter the statue's mood, for the statue has hardly any mood. An armless Greek Venus is not incomplete; it arouses no curiosity as to what she was doing with her arms. We know perfectly well she was doing nothing. She was just being Venus—and even that in the mildest way." [4]

Porch of Maidens, The Erectheion of the Acropolis, Athens. The last of the great temples on the Acropolis completed as part of Pericles' reconstruction, it was used to guard many of the sacred treasures, such as Athena's olive tree and the mark of the trident of Poseidon. (Greek National Tourist Office photo.)

[4] Eric Newton, *European Painting and Sculpture* (Harmondsworth, England: Penguin, 1951), p. 86.

In short, as soon as Greek artists had mastered the technical problems of presenting the human anatomy and clothing naturalistically, they decided on principle not to represent the peculiarities of each individual, even though they were capable of doing so, but to idealize him. The great bronze *Diadoumenos* of Polykleitos, cast in 440 B.C., shows both technical mastery and deliberate abstraction. The face was apparently what all Greeks wanted to look like, and did look like in many statues carved for the next hundred years. The face does not represent emotions, such as determination or excitement but rather qualities of character, such as intelligence or self-control. It is hard to say why the Greeks adopted this method of portrayal during the classical age—perhaps most sculpture was dedicated to the gods, or perhaps the individual was expected to subordinate himself

Diadoumenos of Polykleitos. This Roman copy in marble of a bronze statue cast in 440 B.C. by the Argos sculptor Polykleitos portrays the Greek ideal of manly beauty as embodied in a victorious athlete. (The Metropolitan Museum of Art. Fletcher Fund, 1925.)

to group, or state, or eternal laws of justice. Whatever the reason, when Phidias sought in the frieze of the Parthenon to represent the procession that culminated the great Panathenaic Festival of Athens, he chose to present not one but all Panathenaic processions. For one hundred and seventy-three yards, the stone procession wound around the entablature of the inner cella of the temple—charioteers and prancing horses, maidens bearing the robe of the goddess, young men with sacrifices, and older folk seated to watch. The frieze represented the unity of the Athenian people. The metopes, outside, showed the mythical fights of Greeks with giants, Amazons, and barbarians, the achievement of a united people. The pediments represent the birth of Athena and her contest with Poseidon for possession of Attica, the symbol of the city itself. In this way, the great sculptural achievements of the Parthenon realized Pericles' goal of focusing the patriotism of the Athenian citizen in the love of their goddess and her temple.

Two years after the beginning of the Peloponnesian War, asked to make the customary funeral oration to those who had died, Pericles seized the opportunity to bring home the purpose of what had been achieved: "I would have you day by day fix your eyes upon the greatness of Athens until you become filled with the love of her. And when you are impressed with the spectacle of her glory, reflect that this empire has been acquired by men who knew their duty, and had the courage to do it."

THE DRAMA OF MAN'S FATE

For Pericles, the city was far more than the buildings he was erecting. It was the character of the citizens and of their way of life. After the physical setting, the form of government that allowed all to participate, and the economic prosperity that filled Athens with the products of faraway countries, what most impressed foreigners was the intellectual vigor of the Athenian population. To get the Spartans to act against Athens, the Corinthians insulted them by contrasting their sluggishness with Athenian vivacity:

Have you never considered what manner of men these Athenians are with whom you will have to fight, and how utterly unlike yourselves? They are revolutionary, quick in the conception and in the execution of every plan. . . . Their bodies they devote to their country as though they belonged to other men. Their true self is their mind, which is most truly their own when employed in her service. . . . If a man should say of them, in a word, that they were born neither to have peace themselves, nor to allow peace to others, he would simply speak the truth.[5]

Athens was a city bubbling with talk. Strangers were astonished to be asked the most impertinent, personal questions. They were even more astonished to see leading men called to account before an assembly of thousands who all seemed to have opinions on the matters discussed. Teachers called Sophists were paid handsomely to teach questioning that would find the flaws in an opponent's arguments and even one's own. Thousands sat breathless while their favorite playwrights explored the most difficult questions of human fate: Does duty to the state take precedence over duty to the gods, or one's own conscience? Is a man responsible for acts committed in ignorance? Why do the gods permit so much suffering in the world? From the questions asked in Athens came our modern theater, our logic and metaphysics, our political science and history.

Two superb instruments developed by the Athenians for asking the most profound questions about man and his fate were the theater and the philosophic dialogue. The former reached its height in the tragedies of Aeschylus, Sophocles, and Euripides; the latter in the conversations of Socrates as reported and developed by Plato.

Origin of Athenian Drama. Theater as we know it was invented in Athens at the beginning of the fifth century. Before then there had been epic songs, like those of Homer, and poetry, both performed in public, and religious ritual dances. But the Athenians hit on the idea of letting the playwright take an ancient religious myth and embroider it, presenting his own version of the situations and characters of the myth. At first there was only one actor, who talked to a chorus. Aeschylus added a second actor, and Sophocles a third; by changing their masks and costumes, these actors were allowed to play more than one role. The plays were written for the five-day festival of Dionysus, the god of wine and revelry, which was held in the spring. On the first day there was a procession and the sacrifice of a bull, and a competition for the recital of poems between ten choruses, each of fifty performers. Five comic plays were produced on the second day. On

[5] *Thucydides*, trans. Benjamin Jowett (Boston: D. Lothrop, 1883), p. 44.

each of the last three days one playwright chosen by a jury was permitted
to stage three tragedies. Plays were almost never repeated, so that throughout the fifth century nine new tragedies were produced at each festival. Of
the twelve hundred plays we know were written at this time, only forty-
seven have survived!

Throne of Venus. (Museo Nazionale
alle Terme, Rome. Alinari photo.)

Comedy took the form of a ribald satirical probing of the character of
democracy, of the foibles of rulers, or of the teachings of Sophists. It dealt
exclusively with contemporary vices, personalities, and policies, and only
a self-confident, democratic people could stomach many of the criticisms
hurled at it and its heroes. But it required even greater moral and intellectual stamina to face, year after year, the harsh questions of man's destiny
that were raised by the writers of tragedy. One symptom of the decline of
Athens after the Peloponnesian War was that almost no new tragedies were
written, and contemporary playwrights concentrated on bawdy, mindless
comedy intended to divert the audience from weighty or worrying questions.

Aeschylus (524–456 B.C.). Aeschylus excelled in the dramatic presentation of Nemesis, the vengeance that is dealt out by the jealous gods to men who have transgressed. But he enhanced the tragic impact of his presentation by showing that the punishment either was the result of an action that was both good and bad at the same time, or was the result of a tragic flaw in an otherwise admirable or even awesome character. Aeschylus also made it clear that he did not like this state of affairs, and he raged against the injustice of the gods. The great trilogy of the *Oresteia,* which Aeschylus produced in 458 B.C., illustrates perfectly his technique.

Agamemnon, the first play in the triad, opens with quiet portents of coming doom, which intensify as the play progresses. Clytemnestra is waiting to murder her husband, Agamemnon, on his return from the siege of Troy. The trap has already been laid. Beacon fires will be lighted all the way from Troy across the islands of the Aegean to Argos to tell her when the soldiers will return. Dressed in her finest robes she meets him at the port, and takes him inside the palace to bathe. But the audience is warned by the prophetess Cassandra that she will hack him to death with an axe:

See there, see there! Keep from his mate the bull.
Caught in the folded web's
entanglement she pinions him and with the black horn
strikes. And he crumples in the watered bath.
Guile, I tell you, and death there in the cauldron wrought.[6]

The play ends with Clytemnestra standing with one foot on her murdered husband's body, with her lover by her side; and as the chorus warns that her son Orestes will avenge his father, Clytemnestra turns superbly to her lover and sneers,

These are howls of impotent, bitter rage; forget them, dear, you and I
Have the power; we two shall bring good order to our house at least.[7]

This is the terrible fate that Agamemnon suffers for the sins of his family that go back through generations of murder and sadism. The revenge of the gods is visited on the children as well as on the fathers who commit the sins. Why can this be? asks Aeschylus. He then goes on to show that Agamemnon too is guilty of the crime of *hubris,* of offending against the gods by excessive ambition. He has already made several bad choices. He has gone to war unjustly:

For one woman's promiscuous sake   *Knees grinding in dust,*
The struggling masses, legs tired,   *Spears broken in the onset.*[8]

[6] David Grene and Richmond Lattimore, eds. *The Complete Greek Tragedies* (Chicago: University of Chicago Press, 1959). I, 70.
[7] Ibid., I. 90.
[8] Ibid., I, 37.

**Greek Theatrical Mask for Tragedy,
Boeotian, c. 400 B.C.** Greek dramatic
productions were highly stylized. Actors
covered their faces with masks and de-
claimed their lines without any attempt at
realism. To take the part of another character, they simply changed masks. (Courtesy,
Museum of Fine Arts, Boston. Gift by
Contribution.)

Worse, he has compounded this error by giving in to the blood-lust of the
army leaders, who wanted to get the fleet moving, sacrificing his own
daughter to make the storm cease. Finally, Clytemnestra tempts him to
one last act of sacrilege. She places before the palace a purple carpet whose
use was reserved for those carrying images of the gods; and Agamemnon,
after a brief hesitation, strides across it. He has thus sealed his own doom.

In the second play, Clytemnestra has to be punished even if her husband
was guilty in the eyes of the gods. But the tragedy is that Orestes has to kill
the murderer of his father, knowing that he himself will then be punished
for killing his mother. After he has stabbed her to death, he displays her
body to the chorus, which tries to console him: "What you did was well
done." But they have not understood what Orestes knew all along, that
his punishment must come next in this seemingly endless cycle of killing.
Suddenly, Orestes sees the avenging Furies, and is driven mad:

They come like gorgons, they
Wear robes of black, and they are wreathed in a tangle
Of snakes. . . .
Ah, Lord Apollo, how they grow and multiply
Repulsive for the blood drops of their dripping eyes.[9]

[9] Ibid., I, 130–31.

But Aeschylus refuses to accept this endless violence, and in the final play of the series, *The Eumenides,* or "The Kindly Ones," Orestes, still pursued by the Furies is permitted by the gods to be tried by mortals, by the court of the Areopagus in Athens. When the jury divides equally, Athena herself casts the deciding vote in favor of acquittal. The chain of vengeance is finally broken; the gods come out in favor of justice; the Furies are converted into the Kindly Ones, who will live in Athens and promote respect for marriage. The play ends beautifully with the apotheosis of Athens that has reconciled destiny and justice through the intervention of Athena:

Chorus: *What song then shall I chant over the land?*

Athena: *A song of faultless victory: from earth and sea*
From skies above may gentle breezes blow,
And, breaking sunshine, float from shore to shore;
That corn and cattle may continually
Increase and multiply, and that no harm
Befall the offspring of humanity;
And prosper too the fruit of righteous hearts;
For I, as one who tends flowers in a garden,
Delight in those, the seed that bring no sorrow.[10]

Most experts on Aeschylus lean over backwards to find the ending of the *Oresteia* a stroke of genius; but one knows that the gods have not changed, just as one knows in the earlier trilogy on Prometheus that the Titan who stole fire from the gods will remain nailed to a rock by Zeus until his final destruction. The real answer of Aeschylus to the question of why men seem to be punished by implacable and often unjust gods is that men grow nobler through suffering. Like Prometheus, the man of character accepts his fate and grows stronger by refusing to be cowed. As the thunder crashes around him, Prometheus hurls back threat for threat:

Worship him, pray; flatter whatever king
is king today; but I care less than nothing
for Zeus. Let him do what he likes,
let him be king for his short time: he shall not
be king for long.[11]

Sophocles (496–406 B.C.). Although Sophocles used many of the same stories as Aeschylus, he never attempted to present the tragedy of man as

[10] *Oresteia of Aeschylus,* edited by George Thomson (Cambridge: Cambridge University Press, 1938), p. 343.
[11] Grene and Lattimore, *Complete Greek Tragedies,* I, 345.

a result of the cruelty or lack of feeling in the gods, or of chance. So he did not put on the great spectacles of approaching cataclysm that terrified the audiences of Aeschylus. Sophocles was interested in the character that determined the decisions a man, or woman, made when faced with a moral dilemma. He posed his questions from two points of view: from that of the character of the stage who has to make a decision—for example, Should I obey my conscience or the state?—and from the point of view of the audience—for example, What drives a woman to sacrifice herself and the man she is to marry, in order to satisfy her conscience?

Oedipus the King is the story of a man who, in complete ignorance, murders his father, marries his mother, and on discovering what he has done, gouges out his own eyes. Piece by piece, the evidence is put together before Oedipus. His wife admits that she once exposed her own son by her first husband so he might die. A shepherd confesses that he gave the child to the neighboring king for adoption. A messenger tells Oedipus that he was adopted as a child by that king. His wife tells Oedipus that her first husband was killed on the road by robbers; Oedipus tells her that he killed an old man on the road on his way to Thebes. The queen rushes from the stage and hangs herself. Finally, Oedipus, in a moment of terrible anguish, screams:

O, O, O, they will all come,
all come out clearly! Light of the sun, let me
look upon you no more after today!
I who first saw the light bred of a match
accursed, and accursed in my living,
with them I lived with, cursed in my killing.[12]

What has also been revealed by Sophocles, however, is far more than the web of an archaic murder mystery. It is the imperfection, the violent rage, that Oedipus has never been able to master. On the road to Thebes, he lost his temper when the old man in a chariot hit him with a stick, and knocking the old man from the chariot, Oedipus beat him to death. The man happened to be his father. Twice during the play he threatens to torture old men who refuse to tell him the truth they fear will hurt him. "You blame my temper," says the seer, "but you do not see your own that lives within you." The man who cannot control himself is ready therefore for his final outburst of rage; but this time the victim is himself.

Antigone presents a far more complex set of questions. Antigone's two brothers have fought for the control of Thebes, and killed each other. Creon, the ally of the younger brother, has made himself king, and has ordered that

[12] Ibid., II, 63.

the body of the older brother should not be buried so that, as the Greeks believed, his spirit would be endlessly in torment. His punishment after death would, in Creon's view, preserve civil order. Antigone decides that her moral and religious duty is to bury her brother even though she will herself be executed. For Sophocles, the story is complicated from a psychological point of view. Why does one disobey the state? he asks. The answer seems easy: Because there is a higher law than that of the state. As Antigone explains to Creon:

For me it was not Zeus who made [your] order.
Nor did that Justice who lives with the gods below
mark out such laws to hold among mankind.
Nor did I think your orders were so strong
that you, a mortal man, could over-run
the gods' unwritten and unfailing laws.[13]

Sophocles, however, wants to know why a particular human being has the willpower to follow through the consequences of such an opinion. To make Antigone's case more difficult, she is betrothed to the son of Creon, and by sacrificing herself, she knows she will be causing terrible pain. To explain Antigone's actions, Sophocles presents her as hard and inflexible, "a rigid spirit." She betrays little feeling for her fiancé, Haemon, and scorns the weakness of her sister. One is left with the uncomfortable feeling that Antigone was a woman who welcomed martyrdom as a way of showing how worthless other people were. Sophocles now shows that he is more interested in the man enforcing the questionable decree than in the woman opposing it. Creon believes almost as strongly as Antigone that his decision is morally right, that it is necessary for the well-being of the state for which he is responsible, and that he must sacrifice his niece Antigone and the happiness of his son to maintain the rule of the law. It is the dilemma that all governments, just or unjust, believe they have to face. Creon's first speech explains his concept of the state:

For I believe that [he] who controls the state
and does not hold to the best plans of all,
but locks his tongue up through some kind of fear,
that he is worst of all who are or were.
And he who counts another greater friend
than his own fatherland, I put him nowhere.[14]

Like any state official, he is faced with down-to-earth disrespect, and has to stomach it, when a guard comes to tell him of Antigone's action:

[13] Ibid., II, 174.
[14] Ibid., II, 165.

Guard: *May I say something? Or just turn and go?*

Creon: *Aren't you aware your speech is most unwelcome?*

Guard: *Does it annoy your hearing or your mind?*

Creon: *Why are you out to allocate my pain?*

Guard: *The doer [Antigone] hurts your mind. I hurt your ears.*[15]

When confronted with Antigone, he becomes petty and overbearingly male. "No woman rules me while I live," he snaps. Finally, Creon can stand the pressures upon him no longer, and he gives orders that Antigone shall be freed from the cave where she has been entombed. But Antigone has hanged herself; his son has stabbed himself over her body; and Creon, now seen to be a weak, changeable man, who has not even had the strength to uphold a decree he believed to be just, is broken in spirit. His breakdown is ignominious and pitiable, and he goes off with a whimper:

Servants, take me away, out of the sight of men.
I who am nothing more than nothing now.[16]

Antigone is a great play because it contrasts absolutes, political and moral, but shows that there is no comparable absolute in the human character that carries them out.

Euripides (c. 480–406 B.C.). Euripides faced the basic question, Is there something wrong with our society and with us as human beings? And with a little subterfuge, he gave the answer, Yes, far too many things. Our religion preaches injustice, if not at times flagrant immorality; our wars are cruel and nonsensical; our women are oppressed; our slaves are men like us, and not the debased creatures we pretend them to be. Worse yet, however, in some human beings there are traits of character that will bring inevitable suffering to those around them. The Athenians listened in fascination, but rarely gave him the festival prize; and at the end of his life, annoyed at being twice prosecuted, though unsuccessfully, he went to live in Macedon. After his death, and after the sufferings of the Peloponnesian War, he became the favorite tragic playwright of Athens, because only then had his message been accepted.

The greatest moments in Euripides' plays occur when he shows that love and jealousy can become "blind and irrational forces in human nature," destroying the person in whom they lodge and causing frightening suffering to all whom the person comes near. "Love when it comes in too great strength, has never brought good renown or virtue to mortals." The great example is the play *Medea.* Jason, a nasty boorish fellow, has

---

[15] Ibid., II, 168.
[16] Ibid., II, 203.

been helped to find the Golden Fleece by the barbarian princess Medea, who has borne him two sons. Back home, Jason decides to marry a younger, less exacting woman from his own people, and he has Medea exiled. Medea first breaks into the famous lament on the misery of women:

*Of all things upon earth that bleed and grow
A herb most bruised is woman. We must pay
Our store of gold, hoarded for that one day,
To buy us some man's love; and lo, they bring
A master of our flesh! . . .
Home never taught her that—how best to guide
Toward peace the thing that sleepeth at her side.
And she who, laboring long, shall find some way
Whereby her lord may bear with her, nor fray
His yoke too fiercely, blessed is the breath
That woman draws! Else let her pray for death.*[17]

But Medea is not one to writhe in self-pity. She has a savage strength that compels her to plan revenge. She sends a magic robe as a gift to the would-be bride of Jason, who is immediately burned to death in its folds. With a frightful insight into abnormal psychology, Euripides then changes the traditional legend, has Medea take her revenge on Jason himself by murdering their own two sons. There are few more terrible moments in all literature than when Medea wavers in her resolve to carry through this hideous plan.

O children, my children, for you there will be a city, a home where you will always live, robbed of your mother, while for me there can only be my misery to live with. . . . Never again, from that other life, shall your dear eyes behold your mother. Woe, woe! Why do you look at me like that, my sons? Are you trying to smile at me for the last time? . . . Come, my sons, give me your right hands and let me hold them. O dearest hands, O lips I love, the form and noble features of my children! Go, go away. I've no strength left to look upon my sons: I am borne down by evil. Too well I know what horror I intend, but passion overwhelms my mind, worst cause of man's worst ills.[18]

THE SEARCH FOR REALITY IN ATHENIAN PHILOSOPHY

While the Athenian playwrights were struggling with problems concerning man and the nature of the universe, the Athenian philosophers were seeking a method of inquiry by which an answer to these problems could be found. Philosophy began only in the sixth century B.C., in the Ionian cities of Asia Minor, when, for the first time, men tried to explain the nature of the world without using myths. Instead of saying, "The external world is controlled by gods," the Ionian philosophers asked more scientific questions, such as, Is there a material explanation of the nature of matter? Their

[17] *The Medea*, trans. Gilbert Murray (New York: Oxford University Press, 1912), p. 15.
[18] Cited in *Literary History of Greece* by Robert Flacelière, published by Elek Books Ltd. London, 1962, p. 213.

answers were necessarily less satisfactory than their questions. One philosopher held that water was the basic element; another, air and earth. Soon, however, the philosophers turned from their study of the nature of the material universe to concentrate on the nature of man, and particularly on man's knowledge of right and wrong, and on the type of state in which man can achieve the most ethical way of life.

In Athens, the philosophers most in public view were the Sophists, "the teachers of wisdom" who, for money, taught well-to-do young men the principles of rhetoric and, probably to a lesser degree, of the search for a theory of knowledge. One, who was a friend of Pericles and later exiled for impiety, proclaimed: "Man is the measure of all things, of things that are what they are, and of things that are not what they are not." Another, apparently overwhelmed with the need to rely on man as the source of knowledge, fell back on total skepticism: "There is nothing; even if there is anything, we cannot know it; even if we could know it, we could not communicate our knowledge to anyone else." But the philosopher who most upset traditional Athenian thinking by his questioning was Socrates.

Socrates (469–399 B.C.). The reputation of Socrates has survived unblemished longer than that of any other person in history. In the fourth century B.C., Plato called him "the best and the wisest and the most righteous man of our time." Twenty-four hundred years later, a fine classical scholar could describe him as "the most noble man who has ever lived." Yet the evidence of his life is very sparse. He was the son of a stonemason and a midwife, and he followed both professions. After a little stonecutting, he said, he became a midwife; but "I attend men and not women, and I practise on their souls when they are in labor, and not on their bodies; and the triumph of my art is in examining whether the thought which the mind of the young man is bringing to birth is a false idol or a noble and true creation." In city affairs he did only what he had to, serving as a hoplite and in a few minor city offices. He was ugly and pot-bellied, and looked like a satyr, and could apparently become immobilized for hours in mystical trances. He avowed his own ignorance: "The only thing I know is that I know nothing." Nonetheless, wherever he went, he talked, and his talk began a revolution in philosophy. Part of the effect was due to his personal magnetism; he was like a torpedo-fish whose touch makes a man torpid, said one of the Sophists. But his real contribution was to teach a new method for seeking truth through discussion.

He began by destroying preconceptions. "Justice is nothing else than that which is advantageous to the stronger," an unwary young man tells him at the beginning of Plato's *The Republic*. "I must first learn what you mean," Socrates replies. "As yet I do not know. You say to me that what is advantageous to the stronger is just. Now what do you mean by that, Thrasymachus? For example, you surely do not mean to assert that if Polydamus, the athlete, is stronger than we and it is to his bodily advantage to eat meat, then for us also who are weaker, this diet is advantageous,

Head of Socrates. Carnelian Ringstone, Graeco-Roman Period. (The Metropolitan Museum of Art. Gift of John Taylor Johnston, 1881.)

and consequently just."[19] The second step is inductive inquiry, that is, to take a series of individual examples of something that might be beautiful or just in order to discover what they have in common. What they have in common would then be beauty or justice, and one would thus have reached the third step in the Socratic dialogue, which is definition. The definition that Socrates sought, of the good man, for example, had always a moral purpose. We shall see as we explore the political thinking of later cities that one can crudely classify political philosophers into those who believe in the goodness of man, and who therefore seek a state that will bring out that goodness, and those who believe either in the selfishness or in the morally neutral character of man, whom the state must therefore mold so that he may become good according to that particular state's conception of goodness. Socrates believed in the essential goodness of man. He considered that it was necessary for man to know himself better, to achieve that goodness.

The irony of Socrates' life, and the disgrace of Athenian democracy, are that the philosopher who sought goodness should have been tried and condemned to death for impiety. In 399 B.C., Socrates was accused of corrupting the young and introducing new gods. In his trial, far from defending himself, Socrates asserted that Athens needed him as a "gadfly."

I think that no better piece of fortune has ever befallen you in Athens than my service to God. For I spend my whole life in going about and persuading you all to give your first and chiefest care to the perfection of your soul, and not till you have done that to think of your bodies, or your wealth; and telling you that virtue does

[19] Plato, *The Republic,* trans. A. D. Lindsay (London: Dent, 1948), p. 14.

not come from wealth, but that wealth, and every other good thing which men have, whether in public or private, comes from virtue. . . . Either acquit me, or do not acquit me: but be sure that I shall not alter my way of life; no, not if I have to die for it many times.[20]

The jury was even less impressed by his suggestion that instead of condemning him to death they should give him a state pension. On being condemned, he refused an escape plan dreamed up by his friends, talked to them a long last time about the problem of immortality, drank hemlock, and died in front of them. His death was a measure of the debasement of Athenian democracy under the impact of the Peloponnesian War.

Plato (427–347 B.C.).   In Plato, who was twenty-eight years old at the time of the trial, the views of Socrates achieved a flowering that the master never dreamed of, and would probably have disapproved. With an aristocratic background, the shock of the brutality of the Peloponnesian War, and especially the degradation of Athenian democracy displayed in the treatment of Socrates, Plato was led to reject the polis of Pericles. Although many of his dialogues have left us in an idealized form the splendor of the intellectual sparring of fifth-century Athenians, yet he rejected the political system in which this mental give-and-take thrived. Plato's greatest book, *The Republic,* proclaims the ideal of a city-state that is far closer to the military oligarchy of Sparta than the Athens that Socrates had loved. The purpose of *The Republic* is to define the meaning of justice. At the heart of his argument was his theory of knowledge expounded in the marvelous simile of the cave. Mankind, he says, are like prisoners in an underground cave, chained by their legs and necks, so that they can only see the back wall along which shadows cast by a fire behind them are moving. The prisoners believe that the shadows are real objects because they have never seen anything else. When one of them is released, and goes to the mouth of the cave, he is first dazzled and wants to return to the shadows. Then he becomes used to the light, and perceives the objects that have been casting the shadows. The purpose of education is to bring men out of the cave to a perception of reality. But what does Plato mean by the real objects one finds outside the cave? To understand this we must glance at his theory of "ideas."

What is it that a chair with four legs, and an armchair, and a rocking-chair have in common? They all resemble the idea of a perfect chair, Plato would reply. The idea of a chair exists, for otherwise we would not know that these three objects are all chairs. So also the idea of goodness or justice or of the perfect state exists. These are the real objects to be found outside the cave. Plato felt, however, that not all men were capable of perceiving all reality. Some could get as far as perceiving the

[20] Benjamin Jowett, trans. (1875), cited in G. Lowes Dickinson, *Plato and his Dialogues* (Harmondsworth, England: Penguin, 1950), p. 32.

idea of a chair but were incapable of perceiving the idea of the perfect state. He therefore held that the few who were capable of perceiving all the ultimate ideas should rule the state. Then, they could bring the state in which they were living as close as possible to the ideal state that they alone could perceive. These rulers would of course be the philosophers: "Unless philosophers bear kingly rule in cities, or those who are now called kings and princes become genuine and adequate philosophers . . . , there will be no respite in evil for cities or for humanity." A second group were to be the Guardians, and live much like Spartan soldiers. The rest were to be Workers. To fortify his argument, Plato launched a telling attack on democracy, in which men are free to do what they want. Such a democratic city would be devoted to the pursuit of pleasure and the avoidance of pain, and would inevitably decline into a tyranny. Unfortunately Plato himself ends with the justification of all authoritarian states, that the rulers have the duty to force men to lead good lives for their own benefit. Plato accepted too easily a blanket condemnation of Periclean democracy. Instead of appreciating its vitality, and seeking a method to cure the ills within the political system, he rejected it. As he himself remarked, "Plato was born late in the day for his country."

Aristotle (384–322 B.C.). Aristotle, Plato's most famous pupil, exercised far greater influence than his master, since his views on almost every one of the many subjects he studied came to be accepted as final truth by the medieval Christian Church. Only when Aristotle had been displaced as the ultimate authority was progress possible in medicine, biology, political theory, ethics, and logic. The reasons for the longevity of Aristotle's teachings were their encyclopedic volume and their internal consistency, even more than the fact that they represented the most up-to-date research of the day. Aristotle was an experimenter; he studied embryology by breaking open eggs at regular intervals to inspect the development of the chicken, and he dissected fish and shellfish. But he was above all a collector and classifier. To write a book on politics, he collected 158 constitutions; he broke down his collection of data on living things into a form of classification similar to the modern one that is organized into species and genera. In his logic, he developed a method of establishing truth by the use of classified forms of argument called syllogisms. (Here is one of the most common. "All men are mortal. Socrates is a man. Therefore Socrates is mortal.") The final results of his work were so voluminous and so impressive that he eventually came to be known as The Philosopher.

The Politics provides a good example of Aristotle's method of work, some of his most basic ideas, and examples of his disagreement with Plato. From his classification of the 158 constitutions he had collected, Aristotle determined that there were only three types of state, each of which could be good or bad. Good rule by one man was monarchy; bad, was tyranny; good rule by the few, aristocracy; bad, oligarchy; good rule by the many, polity; bad (usually by the poor or a mob), democracy. Unlike Plato, Aristotle felt that there was no such thing as an ideal state that would suit all men. Observation had shown him that, while the state was the natural unit in which man would achieve the good life, different states suited different people. Tradition and habit molded the citizens in the working of a particular state; education was necessary to train a man in the spirit of the constitution; the most successful state was run by a large middle class whose members possessed a "moderate and adequate property." The ideal in politics as in ethics was the golden mean—a state of moderate size, with sufficient natural resources and a temperate climate, a balanced distribution of age groups, and a wide sharing of wealth. Only then could the citizen pursue one of the few absolutes of which Aristotle approved, "the energy and practice of goodness, to a degree of perfection, and in an absolute mode."

The disillusionment of Aristotle and the outright disgust of Plato with Periclean democracy can, however, only be understood by consideration of the disastrous effects of the Peloponnesian War, which many felt to be the result of the failings of Athenian political leadership.

THE PELOPONNESIAN WAR: THE HUBRIS OF THE PERICLEAN EMPIRE

The Peloponnesian War left Athens its buildings, but impaired its nobility of thought. And for this Pericles must take a large share of the blame. Pericles had argued that the Athenians owed no responsibility to their empire beyond extending protection. They were free to use the tribute as they liked for the glorification and amusement of Athens. They could use their power at sea to enforce obedience in their league, and, worse, they could challenge the land power of the rival Peloponnesian League headed by Sparta. By 431 B.C., Pericles had succeeded in making enemies of every important city in Greece. Moreover, Pericles felt that he had made Athens impregnable. His fleet and colonies controlled the grain route to the Black Sea. Construction of the Long Walls had made Athens and the Piraeus into an enormous fortress. The annual tribute from the empire, which was as great as the revenue of Athens itself, had been used for a vast war treasury. With a land army of over twenty thousand hoplites, and a navy of three hundred triremes, Pericles believed he could neutralize any opponents by land and defeat them at sea.

He had recognized that war was a probable consequence of his policy. "Do not imagine that what we are fighting for is simply a question of freedom and slavery," he told the Athenians at the beginning of the war. "There is also involved the loss of our empire and the dangers arising from the hatred which we have incurred in administering it. . . . In fact, you hold your empire down by force: it may have been wrong to take it; it is certainly dangerous to let it go." The Spartans were finally persuaded by the Corinthians to take the lead in a war against Athens. At first it appeared that there would be a stalemate. Pericles called the inhabitants of the countryside into Athens and abandoned the fields to the Spartans. The Athenian fleet was sent to ravage the coasts of the Peloponnesus. In the pages of Thucydides' account of the Peloponnesian War, which is not only a superb reconstruction of the events but a telling portrayal of the character of men at war, Pericles blossoms into a great war leader. When the headstrong young men would have rushed out of the walls at the sight of the Spartan army burning the fields only six miles from the city, he ignored the anger of the people and forced them to stay with his wise but unpopular strategy. A year later, when the even more disastrous progress of the war led them to blame him personally for their troubles, he appeared before the assembly and called on them to remember their highest traditions:

You, in your private afflictions, are angry with me that I persuaded you to declare war. Therefore you are angry also with yourselves, that you voted with me. . . . I have not changed: it is you who have changed. A calamity has befallen you, and you cannot persevere in the policy you chose when all was well: it is the weakness of your resolution that makes my advice seem to have been wrong. It is the unexpected that most breaks a man's spirit.

You have a great polis, and a great reputation; you must be worthy of them.[21]

Above all, in the great funeral speech that he gave in memory of those who had died in the first year of the war, he reminded Athenians of the ideal of Athens for which they were fighting.

It is true that we are called a democracy, for the administration is in the hands of the many and not of the few. But while the law secures equal justice to all alike in their private disputes, the claim of excellence is also recognized; and when a citizen is in any way distinguished, he is preferred to the public service, not as a matter of privilege, but as the reward of merit. Neither is poverty a bar, but a man may benefit his country whatever be the obscurity of his condition. There is no exclusiveness in our public life, and in our private intercourse we are not suspicious of one another, nor angry with out neighbor if he does what he likes. . . . And we have not forgotten to provide for our weary spirits many relaxations from toil; we have regular games and sacrifices throughout the year; our homes are beautiful and elegant; and the delight which we daily feel in all these things helps to banish melancholy. Because of the greatness of our city the fruits of the whole earth flow in upon us; so that we enjoy the goods of other countries as freely as our own. . . .

We are lovers of the beautiful, yet simple in our tastes, and we cultivate the mind without loss of manliness. Wealth we employ, not for talk and ostentation, but when there is a real use for it. To avow poverty with us is no disgrace; the true disgrace is doing nothing to avoid it. . . . We alone regard a man who takes no interest in public affairs, not as harmless, but as a useless character. . . . The great impediment to action is, in our opinion, not discussion, but the want of that knowledge which is gained by discussion preparatory to action. . . . To sum up: I say that Athens is the school of Hellas, and that the individual Athenian in his own person seems to have the power of adapting himself to the most varied forms of action with the utmost versatility and grace. . . .

[21] Cited in H. D. F. Kitto, *The Greeks* (Harmondsworth, England: Penguin, 1963), p. 142.

*I have dwelt upon the greatness of Athens because I want to show you that we are
contending for a higher prize than those who enjoy none of these privileges, and to
establish by manifest proof the merit of these men whom I am now commemorating.
Their loftiest praise has been already spoken. For in praising the city I have praised
them, and men like them whose virtues made her glorious.*[22]

In 430 B.C., the weakness of Pericles' military strategy was exposed when
plague, probably typhus, brought from Egypt hit the city. During the next
months, about one-third of the population of Athens died in terrible suffering. Thucydides himself caught the plague, recovered, and described it in
the medical terms of his day, with his usual didactic conclusions.

*Internally, the throat and the tongue were quickly suffused with blood, and the
breath became unnatural and fetid. There followed sneezing and hoarseness; in a
short time the disorder, accompanied by a violent cough, reached the chest, then
fastening lower down, it could move the stomach and bring on all the vomits of
bile to which physicians have ever given names. . . .*

*Men who had hitherto concealed what they took pleasure in, now grew bolder.
For, seeing the sudden change—how the rich died in a moment, and those who had
nothing immediately inherited their property—they reflected that life and riches
were alike transitory, and they resolved to enjoy themselves while they could, and
to think only of pleasure.*[23]

Pericles himself died of the plague in 429 B.C. Lacking his resolute leadership, the city divided into warring factions of those who had done well out
of the war, the commercial and manufacturing classes, and those who had
suffered, the aristocrats and the peasants together. Demagogic leaders
appeared, playing on the passions of the assembly. For Thucydides, the
breakdown of morality was complete. The whole of Greece was engaging
in a civil war of city against city and class against class. He used the waves
of murder inside the city of Corcyra as an example of the degradation that
war had brought. "In peace and prosperity," he commented, "both states
and individuals are actuated by higher motives because they do not fall
under the dominion of imperious necessities. But war, which takes away
the comfortable provision of daily life is a hard master, and tends to assimi-
late men's characters to their conditions." By now, neither side was willing
to give up without complete victory. After a long truce, the Athenians
struck out foolishly to conquer the rich city of Syracuse in Sicily, and lost
both fleet and army. Athens itself was seized by an oligarchy that perse-
cuted the leaders of the democratic party, and then by the democrats, who
banished the oligarchs. With political chaos in the city, the Athenians' ability
to fight lessened year by year. The Persians entered the war on the side
of the Spartans; and finally, in 404 B.C., the Athenians fearfully accepted the
peace terms imposed by Sparta: destruction of the Long Walls and the walls

[22] Jowett, *Thucydides,* pp. 117–22.
[23] Ibid., pp. 125, 128.

of Piraeus, surrender of their fleet except for twelve ships, return of the banished oligarchs, and recognition of Spartan leadership. So happy were the people of Athens at the coming of peace that they rushed with great enthusiasm to pull down the walls, to the accompaniment of female flute players. It was a suitably ignoble end to a war that had poisoned the soul of Athens.

SUGGESTED READING

Angelou Procopiou, *Athens City of the Gods* (1964) is a beautifully illustrated history of classical Athens, with emphasis on the physical appearance of the city. R. E. Wycherley explains in *How the Greeks Built Cities* (1962) why Athens looked as it did; this is a clear, layman's account based on the latest documentation, with detailed study of the different parts of the city, such as the agora, shrines, and gymnasium. Roland Martin, *Living Architecture: Greece* (1967) is part of a fine Swiss series, providing a simplified introduction to the technical aspects of Greek architecture by a prime authority. Martin's *L'Urbanisme dans la Grèce Antique* (1956) is the definitive work on Greek town planning. Thin on facts but long on excerpts from primary sources, Charles A. Robinson, Jr.'s *Athens in the Age of Pericles* (1959) is an evocative introduction.

Social life in fifth-century Athens is described in a juvenile way in Marjorie Quennell and C. H. B. Quennell, *Everyday Things in Classical Greece* (1932), which has a few insights, into women's hairstyle, for example; but fortunately Robert Flacelière, *Daily Life in the Athens of Pericles* (1964) is excellent on social structure, education, and details of daily life, and makes fine use of primary sources and photographs.

The economic structure of the city can be pieced together from the old-fashioned H. Michell, *The Economics of Ancient Greece* (1957) or the even more antique George M. Calhoun, *The Business Life of Ancient Athens* (1926), which does have some interesting details on the grain trade. A short but reliable analysis of the economy of the whole Greek world is made by Frank Frost in *Greek Society* (1971). Commerce and industry are treated in the collaborative study edited by Carl Roebuck, *The Muses at Work* (1969). The controversy over the economic value of slavery is illustrated in W. L. Westermann, *The Slave Systems of Greek and Roman Antiquity* (1955) and Moses I. Finley, *Slavery in Classical Antiquity* (1960).

The evolution of Greek architecture can be followed in A. W. Lawrence, *Greek Architecture* (1957) or the rather more complete D. S. Robertson, *A Handbook of Greek and Roman Architecture* (2nd ed., 1954). Eric Newton disparages Greek sculpture quite effectively in *European Painting and Sculpture* (1951), but more appreciative views can be found in R. Lullies and M. Hirmer, *Greek Sculpture* (2nd ed., 1960) and Rhys Carpenter, *Greek Sculpture* (1960).

For superbly literate introductions to Greek literature, see the limpid treatment of C. M. Bowra, *Landmarks in Greek Literature* (1966) and the penetrating analysis of H. D. F. Kitto, *Greek Tragedy* (1955), which perhaps gives too much attention to the form of the tragedies and too little to their meaning. Or better yet, read the tragedies in the translations edited for the University of Chicago Press by David Grene and Richmond Lattimore. Aubrey de Selincourt has a fine new translation of *The Histories of Herodotus* (1954), and Benjamin Jowett's translation of *The Peloponnesian War* of Thucydides is still exciting. A fascinating guidebook of Greece by Pausanias, one of Baedeker's forerunners in the second century A.D., called *Description of Greece*, provides marvelous descriptions of the antiquities that would appeal to a tourist-minded Roman. Greek philosophy before Socrates is discussed in F. M. Cornford, *Before and After Socrates* (1950) and J. Burnet, *Early Greek Philosophy* (rev. ed., 1958), Greek religion in Edith Hamilton, *Mythology* (1942) and W. K. C. Guthrie, *The Greeks and Their Gods* (1950).

Finally, it is instructive to compare Athens with Sparta, by consulting K. M. T. Chrimes, *Ancient Sparta* (1949) or W. G. Forrest, *A History of Sparta* (1968).

Detail, The Altar of Zeus, Pergamum. Erected in 180 B.C. on the slope below the acropolis of the little Hellenistic capital city of Pergamum in Asia Minor, the Altar of Zeus celebrates the victory of King Eumenes II over the Gauls. This detail illustrates the myth of the goddess Athena crushing the giant Alcyoneus. (Art Reference Bureau.)

3
THE HELLENISTIC AGE

The vicious struggles of the Peloponnesian War destroyed the precarious harmony of fifth-century Greece. That harmony had been a balancing of tensions—of city with city, class with class, even philosophy with philosophy; but the wars had bred the intolerance that destroys civic harmony. When Athens surrendered to the Spartan commander Lysander in the spring of 404 B.C., it was a city that had lost confidence in itself.

During the next two centuries, however, the Greeks succeeded in salvaging a good deal from the wreckage of the wars, and with the restoration of political calm displayed continuing virtuosity in the creation of a distinctly different culture, which we call Hellenistic, or Greek-like. This culture, which might have remained an interesting backwater off the mainstream of civilization, was instead spread throughout the Eastern Mediterranean area and the Near East by the conquests of Alexander the Great (356–323 B.C.) of Macedon, and was absorbed by the eternally receptive Romans during their more enduring imperial expansion. The Greek culture that left its lasting stamp upon the Roman Republic was not from the time of Pericles, but that lighter, flashier, more superficial, yet attractive mode of thought created in the renewed vigor that came with convalescence from the Peloponnesian War.

The Greek cities remained blind to the lessons of the Peloponnesian War. Unity had enabled them to hold off Persia at the beginning of the fifth century. Unity, Xenophon told them at the beginning of the fourth century, would enable them to conquer the Persian Empire itself. Xenophon, a young Athenian aristocrat who had studied with Socrates, had turned mercenary soldier in the service of Persia after the defeat of Athens. Leading ten thousand Greek mercenaries on an exciting trek from Babylon across Armenia to the Black Sea, which he described in the great adventure story *Anabasis,* Xenophon became convinced that the weaknesses of the Persian armies were so great that the empire lay open to Greek conquest. Their duty, Xenophon told his soldiers at the beginning of their march, was

ALEXANDER AND THE SPREAD OF HELLENISTIC CULTURE

not "to live in idleness and luxury, and to consort with the tall and beautiful women of these Medes and Persians," but to get back home "to point out to the Greeks that it is by their own choice that they are poverty-stricken, for they could bring their poor here and make them rich." Evidently the dreams of empire were hard for some Athenians to relinquish. Another century passed, however, before the Greek cities followed Alexander into Persia.

Philip of Macedon (Reigned 359–336 B.C.). Instead, the Greek city-states continued their internecine struggles, dominated now by Sparta, now by Thebes. The result of their fighting, Xenophon commented despairingly forty years after the Anabasis, was "the opposite of what all men believed would happen. . . . While each party claimed to be victorious, neither was found to be any better off, as regards either additional territory, or city, or sway, than before the battle took place; but there was even more confusion and disorder in Greece after the battle than before." [1] Both in Greece itself and among the Greek cities on the coasts of Italy and Sicily, political life had degenerated into petty squabbles by the middle of the fourth century B.C. In Greece, the way was open for Macedon; in Italy for the expansion of Rome. Macedon, a large tribal state in the north of Greece, influenced by Greek culture but run despotically by its kings, had both a tougher climate and people than the rest of Greece. The Macedonians were sturdy peasants and mountaineers with little love for the city-states that had treated them for decades as poor relatives in the Greek family. When Philip seized the throne in 359 B.C., he decided to bring Greece under his control by bribery and guile, and if necessary, by force. His citizen army, with an infantry of peasants and cavalry of nobles, was a professional force easily superior to the mercenaries being used by most Greek cities. Moreover, many sincere Greeks were beginning to wonder if Philip might not be their salvation, bringing efficiency and discipline that the bickering city governments could not supply; and many refused to see in Philip, as the great Athenian orator Demosthenes begged them to do, the embodiment of military autocracy. Nor were they stirred by Demosthenes' passionate demand, in his first great attack on Philip, known as the *Philippic:* "Are you content to run around and ask one another, 'Is there any news today?' Could there be any news more startling than that a Macedonian is triumphing over Athenians and settling the destiny of Hellas?" [2] With his victory over the Greeks at Chaeronea in 338 B.C., Philip ended forever the dominance of the polis. The influence of Greek civilization in the future was to be spread by empires—by Alexander and the heirs to his divided empire and by Rome.

Far from destroying Athens, as Demosthenes had forecast, Philip seemed determined to fulfill the hopes of his admirers, "to put an end to the madness and the imperialism with which the Greeks have treated one another, reconcile and bring them into concord, and declare war on Persia." The first

---

[1] Xenophon, *Hellenica* VII, 26–27 (London: W. Heinemann, 1918), p. 227.
[2] *Demosthenes* (London: W. Heinemann, 1930), p. 75.

Alexander's Empire

Extent of the Empire (and dependent states) → Alexander's Route, 334–323 B.C.

troops sent against Persia had already crossed the Hellespont when Philip, at the age of forty-six, was murdered by a disaffected noble; but his twenty-year-old son, Alexander, was immediately acclaimed king. No one could have been better prepared. Aristotle, his tutor since he was thirteen, had given him a broad training in ethics, metaphysics, politics, science, and medicine, as well as a genuine love of Greek poetry. Alexander's favorite poem was the *Iliad,* since it portrayed the exploits of one of his own fabled ancestors, "swift-footed Achilles." He had already subdued an uprising, commanded the left wing at Chaeronea, and governed Macedon in Philip's absence. He quickly put an end to Athens' rejoicing over Philip's death, broke an incipient rebellion of the Greek cities, and within two years was ready to take up again the invasion of Persia.

Conquests of Alexander the Great.   During the eleven years of life he had left—he died in 323 B.C. at the age of thirty-three—Alexander proved conclusively that he was one of the greatest generals who ever lived. Setting out with an army of thirty thousand men and five thousand horses, he took most of Asia Minor within a year; Syria fell in 333 B.C., and Egypt shortly after. Finally, with the whole coast of the Eastern Mediterranean secure, he struck inland to defeat the main Persian army in Mesopotamia. Then the beautiful Persian cities fell to him one by one—Babylon, Susa, Persepolis, Ecbatana. By the spring of 330 B.C., with a sullen army rebellious at campaigning endlessly in the wastes of central Persia and with his empire on the point of revolt, he should have withdrawn to a defensible frontier on the Euphrates. Instead, declaring he was "King of Asia," he plunged deep into Central Asia, past the southern shore of the Caspian Sea, up through Afghanistan near to Bokhara, over the Khyber Pass into northern India, and finally down the Indus River and back to Babylon. On his death he was planning to capture Arabia, as the link of his Indian and Near Eastern provinces. In thirteen years, he had marched twenty thousand miles, won every battle he had fought, caused the death of thousands of soldiers in battle and from disease, and created an empire that stretched from Greece to India. But the fascination of Alexander's career goes beyond the rapidity and scale of his conquests; for like Napoleon with whom he is often compared, Alexander had far-reaching plans for his empire.

Vaulting ambition was undoubtedly his driving force, as his biographer Arrian testified:

Alexander had no small or mean conceptions, nor would ever have remained contented with any of his possessions so far, not even if he had added Europe to Asia, and the Britannic islands to Europe; but would always have searched far beyond for something unknown, being always the rival, if of no other, yet of himself. In this connection I applaud the Indian wise men, some of whom, the story goes, were found by Alexander in the open air in a meadow, where they used to have their disputations, and who, when they saw Alexander and his army, did nothing further than beat with their feet the ground on which they stood. Then when Alexander enquired by interpreters what this action of theirs meant, they replied: "O King Alexander, each man possesses so much of the earth as this on which we stand; and you being a man like other men, save that you are full of activity and relentless, are roaming over all the earth far from your home, troubling yourself and troubling others. But not so long hence you will die, and will possess just so much of the earth as suffices for your burial." On that occasion Alexander applauded their remarks and the speakers, but he always acted diametrically opposite to what he then applauded.[3]

He showed no more understanding for the philosopher Diogenes, who lived in a barrel to show his freedom of material possessions. One of the most famous meetings in ancient history occurred when Alexander, conqueror of half the known world, asked Diogenes what he could do for him only to be told, "Don't block my light."

Alexander however wanted more than territorial conquests. He sincerely felt that he had a mission to bring peace, justice, and unity to this vast war-torn area, a mission implied by his willing acceptance of deification as the son of the god Amon-Re in Egypt and his later attempts to be deified in Greece. He met the racial problem directly, ordering Greeks and Persians to be associated equally in the government and armies of the empire, and encouraging intermarriage. He saw the integrating function of trade, which he tried to develop by creating an empirewide coinage, new sea routes, and great ports like Alexandria at the mouth of the Nile. Above all, however, he believed that his foreign subjects would be best served by exposure to his own native culture, Hellenism. The seventy cities he founded (mostly named Alexandria) were to spread Greek learning and Greek military and administrative skills among the upper classes of Asia and the Near East.

[3] *Arrian* (London: W. Heinemann, 1923–1933), vol. 2, VII, 4–2.1.

At the time of his premature death, however, only Alexander's personality and the power of his troops were holding his empire together. He left no heir and no provision for future administration; and by the end of the century, three of his generals and their descendants had split up most of the empire among them. These three absolute dynasties—the Seleucids in Persia, the Ptolemies in Egypt, and the Antigonids in Macedonia—continued to hold power until they were defeated by Rome, in the second and first centuries B.C.

Alexander at the Battle of Issus, 333 B.C. In this mosaic from Pompeii, which copies a Greek original, Alexander (at the left) is seen defeating the Persian Emperor Darius III (in the chariot). (Museo Nazionale, Naples. Alinari–Art Reference Bureau photo.)

Urban Centers of the Hellenistic Age. In spite of this political disunity, Alexander's empire remained united by what we call Hellenistic culture, a culture that the Romans swallowed whole as they penetrated the area from 200 B.C. on. The pins on which the unifying web was stretched were the cities, which were predominantly of Greek culture and often even of Greek nationality. Here lived the bureaucrats who made the administrative language, the law, the calendar, and the coinage all Greek; many of the mercenary soldiers recruited from Greece and Macedonia; teachers readily employed in hellenizing the local inhabitants, who found it advisable for their own advancement to develop a veneer of Greek culture; and the merchants and bankers who ran the flourishing commerce.

Trade and the cities expanded together, until the great urban agglomerations of Hellenistic days created a totally different way of life from that of the tiny city-states of the classical age. The basis of the trade was the exchange of exotic products of Asia and Africa, such as spices, ivory, incense, pearls, and rare woods; the native manufactures of Syria and Egypt, such as glass, metals, and linen; the pottery, wine, and olive oil of Greece; the wheat of Sicily and Egypt; and slaves. The vast profits to be made from the more exotic products produced some extraordinary voyages of discovery, such as the one of Pytheas that took him all around Britain and up into the North Sea, and of Eudoxus, who sailed the open ocean from the Red Sea to India; the great caravan routes stretched across Afghanistan to India and through the Sudan to Ethiopia; and contact was made even with China. At the nodal points of these routes, several cities became vast boiling caldrons of human activity—Rhodes that dominated the trade of the Eastern Mediterranean; Alexandria, the export center of the Ptolemies; the pink city of Petra in the Jordanian desert; and the Seleucid creations of Antioch and Seleucia in Mesopotamia.

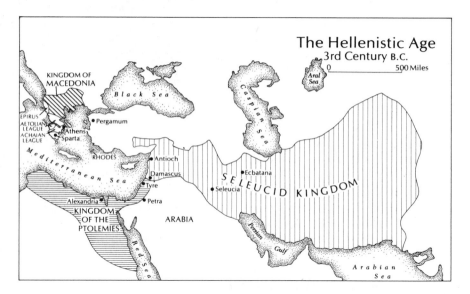

Both the comforts and discomforts of this rich material life formed Hellenistic culture. The cities themselves, existing primarily for trade rather than defense or administration, were no longer built around an acropolis but almost always adopted the more functional rectangular or gridiron plan, sometimes called Milesian, after Miletus where it was first used. To create a whole city in rectangular blocks made colonization, or the expansion of existing cities, easy to carry out, providing the planners ignored any topographical features that interfered with their rectangles. Towns and army camps were laid out on the same basis. Several important changes in the appearance of the city resulted. The street, which in Periclean Athens had been a rough, rambling inconvenience, became uniform in size, averaging eighteen to nineteen feet, although a few main thoroughfares where big

processions took place were considerably wider. The rectangular blocks were ready-made lots for public buildings, such as temples that were no longer to grace high cliffs above the city, the public baths, and especially the marketplace, or agora. In the Hellenistic city, the agora was built with lines of shops on three sides, and often with a long colonnaded porch in front that provided the shopper or talker with shelter from the rain or sun. One of the finest of these, the stoa of Athens, has been recently reconstructed. The rectangular plan also introduced to town planning one of the most characteristic features of the later European city—the vista. Long rows of relatively uniform houses, or the repetitive columns of the stoa arcades, drew the eye into the orderly distance in a search for some grandiose, monumental apotheosis, which the architects were willing and the rulers able to provide.

In these rectangular cities, self-government was almost nil. The absolute monarchs, controlling the public purse, indulged their populations with a spree of public buildings that literally dwarfed that of Pericles. Every city had to have its colonnaded market squares, aqueducts and public fountains, baths, gymnasium, stadium, theater, libraries, and harbor facilities. The rich middle classes were little less lavish. With no time lost on politics or military service, they flung themselves into the making and spending of money. For themselves, they bought ever greater luxuries—improved sanitation, better diet and medical care, sculptured busts of themselves, mosaic floors. But they also made ostentatious public gifts of temples or bridges or public banquets. The cities themselves, as one ancient writer related, were incapable of providing these functions themselves:

The Stoa of Attalos, Athens. Originally built in the mid-second century B.C. and now reconstructed, the Stoa of Attalos dominated the agora, or marketplace, of Athens. (Author's photo.)

The folk of Myme in Aiolis raised a sum of money by mortgaging one of their public colonnades. As the loan was not repaid, the mortgagees took possession of the property, kindly allowing the people to shelter from the rain. As this was announced by a crier shouting "Come under shelter!" a story grew up that the inhabitants were so stupid they didn't know when to seek shelter unless told.[4]

Alexandria under the Ptolemies.   Alexandria was the archetype of the great cosmopolitan city of the Hellenistic age. Founded by Alexander in the inhospitable sands of the Mediterranean shore of Egypt, it sprang into full-blown life when chosen by the first Ptolemy as the burial place for the corpse of Alexander, which he had succeeded in purloining, and as capital of his share of the conqueror's empire. Within seventy years of its foundation, Alexandria was luring Greeks from all over the Eastern Mediterranean to share in the sparkle of its intellectual and social life and the economic opportunities of its commerce and imperial administration. Two great harbors protected by breakwaters were dominated by a lighthouse four hundred feet tall. Alexander's body, wrapped in gold and placed in a coffin of glass, lay with later Ptolemaic rulers in the Royal Tombs beside the marble colonnades of the busy central street. A vast palace, replete with gardens and summer houses where Cleopatra was later to dally with Julius Caesar (and Mark Antony), overlooked the main harbor and the Mediterranean shore; and attached to it was the great intellectual creation of the early Ptolemies, the museum and library. The museum was a kind of research university, staffed by famous scholars who were enticed by large salaries and fine working conditions to carry on their scientific and philosophic work for the enhancement of the dynasty's reputation. At their disposal was the greatest book collection of antiquity, perhaps 700,000 works, which attracted researchers from all over the Mediterranean and beyond. The fabulous wealth of this city was provided, as it had been in Egypt for three thousand years, by the grain harvest of the Nile, now more efficiently exploited than by any earlier pharaoh. The Greeks who flocked to serve the Ptolemies found no barriers to advancement such as had been imposed in the smaller city-states of the Hellenic age by democratic controls, family exclusiveness, or restricted economic opportunity. Alexandria thus became the intellectual and commercial hub of the Eastern Mediterranean, the model of urban organization that was followed by all the other great cities of the Hellenistic age and whose influence can be seen in the character of the other great cosmopolitan cities that rose later, Rome and Constantinople.

Hellenistic Culture.   For learning and art, the outpouring of royal and bourgeois patronage was a great stimulant. In the new libraries, scholars worked on textual criticism of the Greek classics, and issued carefully

[4] Strabo, cited in Jack Lindsay, *The Ancient World* (London: Weidenfeld and Nicolson, 1968), p. 155.

Plan of Alexandria, 16th Century. This city plan is taken from the great series of drawings called *Civitates Orbis Terrarum* (cities of all the lands of the earth), which portrayed almost every city in Europe and several in Asia and Africa.

revised texts of the great writers. In the museums, important advances were made in science and mathematics; Hellenistic scientists laid the basis of plane and solid geometry, surmised that the earth moved around the sun, measured the earth's circumference with an error of only 200 miles, and came near to discovering the circulation of the blood, among other achievements. Aristotle and Theophrastus, Euclid and Archimedes, Hipparchus and Ptolemy laid down the scientific theories that, accepted by medieval Christianity as dogma, remained unchallenged and largely undeveloped until the sixteenth century. Only creative literature fell behind. Drama was rough and dirty, involving the stereotypes of slaves, prostitutes, cuckolds, and misunderstood youth. Poetry was stiff and elegiac, although occasionally a moving lyric survived, including that best known of all Hellenistic poems:

They told me, Heraclitus, they told me you were dead,
They brought me bitter news to hear, and bitter tears to shed.
I wept as I remembered, how often you and I
Had tired the sun with talking and sent him down the sky.
And now that you are lying, my dear old Carian guest,
A handful of grey ashes, long long ago at rest,
Still are they pleasant voices, they Nightingales awake,
For Death, he taketh all away, but them he cannot take.[5]

[5] "Heraclitus," by William J. Cory, in Arthur Quiller-Couch, ed., *The Oxford Book of English Verse 1250–1918* (Oxford: The Clarendon Press, 1939), p. 768.

Sculpture, like everything else in the Hellenistic age, often reflected this down-to-earth quality, the abandonment of the idealization of the classic age. Realistic or sentimental figures of dogs, babies with toys, drunken old women, fishermen, and the like were popular for homes. Portrait sculpture sold by the ton. There were so many public statues in Rhodes that old ones had to be removed to make room for new ones. Kings usually wanted to look like Alexander, young, tough and brilliant; but some were content to look tough and mean. The set pieces on a larger scale, celebrating the gods or the victories of the cities, also displayed an emotional idealism that at times can create in the onlooker the physical pangs of a sword between the shoulder blades or a noose around the throat.

Within this prosperous city world, however, there were many dangerous signs of discontent. Some were disgusted at the obsession with money. "When I saw people's lives wholly absorbed in moneymaking," a character remarks in one comedy, "when I watched them scheming and calculating, by Hephaistus, I grew bitter. Not one of them, I thought, has any true kindly feeling for another. This idea struck me down." Children were disgusted with their parents and their superficial ideals. One daughter remarks:

All this pedigree stuff is killing me, mother. Don't keep bringing it up at every word, if you love me. People who have no good quality in themselves, all take refuge in family monuments, their pedigrees. You reel off a list of grandfathers, and that's all you have to say. We can take for granted that they exist. We can't be born without them. Some folk, through a change of home or a lack of friends, can't give the names; but are they any worse-born than the others? The man whose natural bent is to goodness is the nobly born one, even if he's a black African.[6]

As for the parents, perhaps in despair with the younger generation, they were refusing to have more than one or two children; and infanticide, especially of girls and usually through exposure, was extremely common.

Thus, over all this busy life loomed the specter of unknown but ever threatening calamity, the dark forces prowling outside the little circle of civilization. The old city cults and the worship of the Olympian gods degenerated into dry routine; and emotional outlets were found in the worship of the mystery religions. The alienated—slaves, foreigners, women, freedmen, out-of-luck businessmen—began to form private groups of one hundred to two hundred members. They often met secretly, in the dark, for the worship of the gods of the East—the Egyptian god Serapis; the star-worship of Babylon; Dionysus, the god of natural fertility, who was now treated as a glorification of the many-sidedness of life; and Fortune, the goddess who watched over man's fate. All the religions had in common a rejection of the crass material life of the city, of the injustice and violence and impersonality on which it was based, and all sought to give the individual a meaning for his life in the identification with a wider power than himself.

[6] Lindsay, *Ancient World,* p. 158.

Skeptics, Cynics, Epicureans, and Stoics. Even the philosophers of the Hellenistic age sought to provide an answer to the alienation with politics and the city, and a guide to spiritual survival in a hostile world. The most blunt answer was given by the Skeptics, who told the individual to be indifferent to everything, since nothing could be known, and by the Cynics who dressed in filthy rags, lived in the streets on handouts, and deliberately shocked the conventional not only with their questioning but with their public behavior, which included defecation and more. Epicurus (342–271 B.C.), the founder of Epicureanism, was far less severe with the material world. He accepted man's need for pleasure but held that reason should dictate which pleasures he should seek, so that he would achieve the ideal of imperturbability, or absence of displeasure. Man should not embark on the usual sources of mental anguish, such as marriage or moneymaking, but live, like Epicurus himself, in a little vegetable garden surrounded by a group of like-minded friends, in the conviction that man can carve out a peaceful life for himself in a purely mechanistic world.

Head of Epicurus. This life-sized bust is a good example of the Hellenistic sculptor's desire to display the human qualities of the person portrayed. (The Metropolitan Museum of Art. Rogers Fund, 1911.)

Zeno (335–263 B.C.), who taught, while walking up and down in the Painted Stoa in Athens, disciples later called Stoics, was far more demanding. The universe was rationally organized, he felt, and man had to understand how he fitted into the pattern. To live in accordance with this "law of Nature," a man had to realize that all men were brothers, sharing in a living community both with nature and with mankind. He should follow the cardinal principle of wisdom, which was to have complete control over his material self, and to seek temperance, courage, and fairness. The wise man, it turned out, had to be "a monster, passionless, pitiless, perfect; he would do good, but without feeling for others, for his calm must remain unruffled. . . . Unhappiness usually arose from wanting something you had not got or could not get; the way to be happy, then, was to want what you got, that is, to go in accord with the Divine Will."[7]

Here, then, was a complex civilization, rich in material things, vastly inventive intellectually, yet disturbed by fears for its own spiritual health. At this point, in the last two centuries before Christ, it was faced by Rome, a new puritanical, military power, supremely confident in its own virtues and goal, prepared to gobble up the inheritance of Alexander and to digest the whole rich meal of Hellenism.

TARQUINIA AND THE ETRUSCAN INHERITANCE

Until recently, the birth and early growth of the city of Rome was treated by historians as a unique phenomenon, the tale of a people of giants marked by geography or racial genius or historical necessity for an unparalleled rise to greatness and for an equally impressive decline and fall. As Livy remarked at the beginning of his history of Rome, "If any people should be permitted to consecrate its own origins and attribute them to the gods, the military glory of the Roman people is such that when they call Mars their father and the father of their founder, the nations of men might as well put up with it as calmly as they endure Rome's domination." Divine intervention apart, we now know that the Latin people, an Indo-European group who had penetrated into Italy during the Bronze Age (c. 1500–1000 B.C.), were influenced during the crucial centuries from about 800 to 500 B.C., when they were creating the city-state of Rome, by the higher civilization to the south of the Greek colonies in Italy and to the north by the still mysterious Etruscans. During this period, a relatively unified cultural area existed in the whole of western Italy, from the Po down to Sicily; and Rome began its history with a cultural inheritance ready-made.

Greek Settlement in Italy. The Greek colonies, founded mostly from 750 to 600 B.C., stretched like inset pearls along the glorious coast of southern Italy and Sicily. Lovely in themselves, with temples and theaters that rivaled those of Athens, these cities beamed throughout Italy the brightness of Greek art and learning. Although they conquered them, the Romans never ceased to admire these Greek cities so miraculously planted on Italian soil.

[7] W. W. Tarn and G. T. Griffith, *Hellenistic Civilization* (London: E. Arnold, 1961), pp. 333–34.

Virgil even gives Aeneas a glimpse of the transcendently lovely temples of
Agrigento and Selinunte on the Sicilian coast, as he sails to found Rome:

Thence Pachynus' cliffs and jutting rocks
We round the point, and lo! before our eyes
Stands Camarina, that the Fates forbade
E'er to disturb; and then the plains of Gela,
Gela, named from its river's furious stream.
Then lofty Acragas [Agrigento] displays afar
Her mighty walls, where long ago
High-mettled horses were reared. Then with favoring breeze
Palmy Selinus [Selinunte], leaving thee, I thread
The Channels dangerous with sunken reefs
Of Lilybaeu, till I come at last
To port at Drepanum on that joyless shore.[8]

What does it matter if the temples Virgil describes were built after Aeneas
had supposedly passed by? Virgil was creating a past that would be an
emotional cement for the Roman people; and Agrigento's glory remains
to this day.

The Temple of Concord, Agrigento. (Italian State Toruist Office photo.)

[8] Kathleen Freeman, *Greek City-States* (New York: Norton, 1950), p. 84.

Etruscan Economy and Society.   The Romans were far less grateful to the Etruscans, although their debt to them may well have been greater. No one is sure where the Etruscans came from, or even if they came by land or sea; but they probably conquered the rolling hill country between the Arno and the Tiber, which is called Etruria, between 800 and 600 B.C. and captured the infant city of Rome; and for brief periods they even extended their control to the Po valley and the Bay of Naples.

Although they were small in number and lived as a landowning aristocracy controlling, and highly unpopular with, the native populations, they rapidly became wealthy; and wealth, combined with regimented manpower, paid for their cultural achievements. Fortunately for them, Etruria contained almost all of Italy's mineral resources—copper, zinc, tin, lead, and especially the iron of Elba; fertile soil and an equable climate gave them fine harvests of wheat, olives, and grapes; and a powerful fleet made them not only trading partners but maritime rivals and occasionally predators of the Greeks and Phoenicians. The wealth of the towns was proven by excavation that brought out quantities of gold and silver and jewelry, as well as huge numbers of vases imported from Greece, and by the grandeur of such city walls as still remain. But it is only when one visits the well preserved "cities of the dead" that one realizes the powerful influence that the advanced culture of the Etruscans must have exerted on the Romans during the century of Etruscan rule (traditionally dated 616–510 B.C.), in which they converted Rome from a collection of villages into a genuine city.

Etruscan Cities.   The Etruscans lived in cities, for pleasure and for protection. Most of their cities stood high on defensible hilltops, ringed by sharp ravines and with uninterrupted views on all sides over the land they dominated and the plains from which invaders would appear. They had fine gates and walls, efficient drainage channels, porticoed temples with projecting revetments of brightly colored terra cotta, and tightly packed houses of brick and wood. But, one ravine away, paralleling the town of the living, the Etruscans built an ever expanding city of the dead, a necropolis; and in these acres of tombs we have rediscovered much of their lost civilization.

The little town of Cerveteri about 25 miles from Rome was the most powerful Etruscan city in 600 B.C., with a population of 25,000, three distinct harbors, and a necropolis that covered 140 acres. The original road of hewn boulders, with deep indentions left by the wheels of the funeral processions, still leads through the huge, beehive-shaped mounds in which the Etruscan dead expected to enjoy unrestrained luxury for all eternity. The tombs were carved in solid rock, often several rooms deep, with molded doorways, beamed ceilings, and stone beds around the walls. Here the dead were laid, reclining, on their funeral couches, dressed in their finest clothes and jewelry, with all they might need: silver bowls, bronze vases,

The Necropolis of Cerveteri.
The city of the dead at Cerveteri (Caere) covers 140 acres.
Its beehive-shaped tombs were carved from solid rock.
(Italian State Tourist Office photo.)

jars of honey and eggs, bronze beds, and even triumphal chariots. And on the walls, painted on a thin stucco base, were superbly vigorous scenes of everyday life, or of the last ceremonies of the funeral itself. D. H. Lawrence described the impression these paintings make on us today, and the greatness of the artists' achievement, after visiting Tarquinia (see color insert):

The walls of this little tomb are a dance of real delight. The room seems inhabited still by Etruscans of the sixth century before Christ, a vivid, life-accepting people who must have lived with real fullness. On come the dancers and music players, moving in a broad frieze towards the front wall of the tomb, the wall facing us as we enter from the dark stairs and where the banquet is going on in all its glory. Above the banquet, in the gable angle are the two spotted leopards, heraldically facing each other across a little tree. And the ceiling of rock has chequered slopes of red and black and yellow squares, with a roof-beam painted with coloured circles, dark red and blue and yellow. So that all is colour, and we do not seem to be underground at all, but in some gay chamber of the past.

The dancers on the right wall move with a strange, powerful alertness onwards. The men are dressed only in a loose coloured scarf, or in the gay handsome chlamys draped as a mantle. The subulo plays the double flute the Etruscans loved so much, touching the stops with big, exaggerated hands, the man behind him touches the seven-stringed lyre, the man in front turns round and signals with his left hand, holding a big wine bowl in his right. And so they move on, on their long sandalled feet past the little berried olive trees, swiftly going with their limbs full of life, full of life to the tips.

This sense of vigorous, strong-bodied liveliness is characteristic of the Etruscans, and is somehow beyond art. You cannot think of art, but only of life itself, as if

Etruscan Tomb Sculpture, Cerveteri. The Etruscan dead were often portrayed reclining in life-like posture on the top of their coffins. (Photo courtesy of the Louvre, Paris.)

this were the very life of the Etruscans, dancing in their coloured wraps with massive yet exuberant naked limbs, ruddy from the air and the sea light, dancing and fluting along through the little olive trees, out in the fresh day.[9]

Here then were a people who had not only mastered the Greek styles of sculpture in their own terra cotta and bronze, but had even enlivened it with a fierce realism of their own or a primitive impressionism recently revived by twentieth-century Italian sculptors. Their wall painting achieved a color and passion that is not found again until Pompeii, and their technique in the minor arts of working ivory, gold, and jewels has never been surpassed. They developed granulation, for example, by which tiny gold balls two hundredths of a millimeter in size were soldered to a jewel. Their architecture and town building, their technical advances in agriculture, and their widespread commercial contacts—all made the Etruscans ideal teachers for a people that could learn fast. In their early days, the Romans were voracious students.

REPUBLICAN ROME AND ITS IMPERIAL CONQUESTS

Origins of Rome. In the eighth century B.C. Rome was a few scattered villages of thatched wooden huts inhabited by several hundred shepherds of a mixed Indo-European stock. Five hundred years later, the Romans were in control of all Italy up to the Po. Of their position by the mid–second century, the Greek historian Polybius pointed out, "The Romans have sub-

[9] From *Etruscan Places* by D. H. Lawrence. Originally published by The Viking Press, Inc. in 1932. All rights reserved. Reprinted by permission of The Viking Press, Inc.

jected to their rule not portions, but nearly the whole of the world, and possess an empire which is not only immeasurably greater than any which preceded it, but need not fear rivalry in the future." This empire was the conquest of a single city; and part of the fascination of Roman history lies in the double question of how the Romans did it, and even more intriguing, why they did it? "Who is so worthless or indolent," Polybius asked, "as not to wish to know by what means and under what system of government the Romans in less than fifty-three years have succeeded in subjecting nearly the whole inhabited world to their sole government—a thing unique in history?" [10]

Looking back, the Romans themselves decided that their heroic ancestry had got them off to a triumphant start. According to the hallowed legend that Virgil immortalized in the *Aeneid,* Trojans led by Aeneas fled after the fall of their city to the Greeks, and after many tribulations, settled in the hills of Latium. Several generations later, the daughter of one of Aeneas' descendants bore twins to the god Mars (which surprised no one since Aeneas himself had been the son of the Goddess Venus); their names were Romulus and Remus. The twins were thrown in the Tiber by their great-uncle, but after being washed up on the Palatine Hill, they were looked after by a she-wolf until adopted by shepherds. The Roman historian Livy has a lively story of how the pair as adults appealed to omens to decide who should be the founder of Rome:

Remus was the first to receive an omen; he saw six vultures. He had just pointed it out, when Romulus saw double the number. Each was proclaimed king by his own side. Remus based his claim on priority, Romulus on the larger number of birds. They argued, came to blows; tempers were roused and degenerated into blood-lust. Remus was killed during the fighting. On the other hand, according to more popular tradition, Remus, to make fun of his brother, jumped the newly built walls at one bound and Romulus, angered, killed him, adding: "So shall perish all who attempt to pass over our walls." Thus, the power fell into Romulus' hands alone, and after its foundation the town took the name of its founder. [11]

Archaeologists have not found any evidence of the arrival of seaborne emigrants from Troy or from Greece; but they have agreed that the traditional founding date of 753 B.C. is nearly correct. The legends, however, came to have a power of their own, giving the Romans a common pride in their divine origins and their heroic ancestors and a desire to emulate the first Romulus's gifts as warrior and statesman; and they gave the Romans their own hallowed places, mostly grouped around the Palatine Hill, where a civic religion could be fostered—the she-wolf's cave, the fig tree where the twins were fed, the sacrosanct line where, in Etruscan fashion, Romulus had ploughed the boundary furrow.

In reality, early Rome owed much of its prosperity to its location. The

---

[10] Polybius, *The Histories* (London: W. Heinemann, 1922–1927), I, 1, 7–8, p. 7; I, 1, 5, pp. 3–5.
[11] Cited in Raymond Bloch, *The Origins of Rome* (New York: Praeger, 1966), p. 48.

seven tiny hills of Rome lay in the middle of a coastal plain, fringed by a circle of volcanic hills. The plain was well watered, and suitable for pasture and tilling; along the coast and on the hillsides there was timber for building; the river Tiber was navigable with difficulty as far as Rome, which was the lowest point for fording and bridging the river. The steep slopes of several of the hills, especially the Capitol and the Palatine, made them easily defensible. And best of all, the site commanded the principal routes throughout central Italy, giving Rome a strategic and commercial importance it never lost. Any topographical map shows how the contorted mountain chains of Italy must have dictated the routes that men should follow, and directed travel through Rome, a fact that the Romans enhanced through their road system. Romulus, Cicero concluded, "must at the very beginning have had a divine intimation that the city would one day be the seat and hearthstone of a mighty empire, for scarcely could a city placed upon any other site in Italy have more easily maintained our own present widespread dominion." [12]

The Cloaca Maxima, Rome. The oldest of all Roman engineering works, this great sewer was built in the sixth century B.C. to drain the Forum. Water running off the Capitol and Palatine hills was fed into the Tiber through this outlet, which is still in use today. (Alinari photo.)

The natural advantages of the site were reinforced by its intermediate position between the Etruscan and Greek civilizations; and the Romans profited from being part of the cultural and commercial boom that enriched all of western Italy from the eighth to the fifth centuries. By 500 B.C., Rome

[12] Cicero, *De Re Publica* (London: W. Heinemann, 1928), II, v, 10, p. 121.

had become, under Etruscan rule, a fairly prosperous city. Its huts had
disappeared; and temples with polychrome terra cotta friezes and substantial homes graced the hills. A defense wall, six miles long, of cut stone and
earth surrounded the settlements; and the earliest surviving Roman monument, the great sewer called the Cloaca Maxima, had drained the low-lying
land between the Palatine and the Capitol hills; and this area, called the
Forum, had been paved. Traders were bringing in the finest of Greek goods.
A powerful army, based on legions, fighting in phalanxes, had been created.

Foundation of Roman Republic.   At that point, around the turn of the sixth
century, vast political upheavals swept through the world of the central
Mediterranean. In Rome, the power of the king was replaced by an aristocratic, or patrician, form of government, in the hands of a jealously restricted
group of landowning elders who had usually sat in the highest advisory
body of the kingdom, the senate. In a short time, the patricians worked out
an effective form of constitution to replace the kings. The core of the system

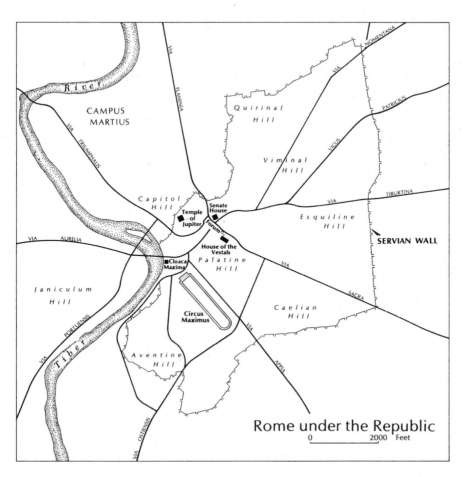

Rome under the Republic

0   2000 Feet

was the election annually by the patrician assembly of two consuls as the highest executive; and the consuls were allowed to veto each other's decisions, as a clumsy system of checks and balances. Other officers were added later as needed—a praetor to supervise justice; quaestors for financial affairs; aediles for markets and roads; and many others. The main assembly, the senate, though advisory in theory, was extremely powerful since it included the wealthiest members of the oligarchy, all of whom had large numbers of dependents, called clients. With the early decline of the power of the curiate assembly, which was supposed to represent the whole citizen body, the key problem facing the oligarchy was to make constitutional provision for the peaceful expression of the will of the nonpatrician, or plebeian, majority of the population. This internal political struggle was closely affected by the wars of conquest and the economic system that grew up during them.

Roman Conquest of Italy.   The Romans easily persuaded themselves that their early wars were necessary for their own or their neighbors' protection. "According to Livy," Edward Gibbon remarked, "the Romans conquered the world in self-defense." This was probably true of their early wars. At first, the Romans drove up into the surrounding hills, where they brought the local tribes under their control. Interrupted by an incursion of Celts or Gauls from the north, who even sacked Rome and left it in ruins in 396 B.C., they picked off the Etruscan cities one by one; and around 340 B.C. they turned to the assault of the coastal plain around the Bay of Naples. In these campaigns, they reorganized their legions for hill fighting, replacing the clumsy phalanx with mobile groupings that could operate independently, and that were armed with javelins for hurling and short swords for hand to hand combat; and they built superb all-weather roads of shaped lava blocks to enable the rapid movement of troops southward. With this means, they sought empire, first in Italy and then in the Mediterranean. The area round Naples was in their hands by 282 B.C.; then, using the excuse that a small Greek city had asked for their aid, the Romans drove their legions even further south to complete the conquest of the peninsula, defeating the coastal cities, the inland tribes, and the elephants of the king of Epirus, who had unwisely chosen to use the confusion of battling alliances as the chance to hack out a dominion in Italy for himself. This king, Pyrrhus, who won so many inconclusive, "Pyrrhic," victories that he exhausted his resources in men and money and elephants, finally withdrew to Greece in 275 B.C. leaving Rome victorious.

The mainland of Italy was not governed by Rome as an empire, but a subtle system called the Roman confederacy was created to hold the defeated peoples under control. About half the population in Italy were classified as "allies," who were nominally autonomous except in foreign policy, but who provided troops for the Roman army. The rest were either full or half (nonvoting) citizens. The Romans thereby avoided the formation of a united opposition to their rule; and in most cases, the peoples of Italy grate-

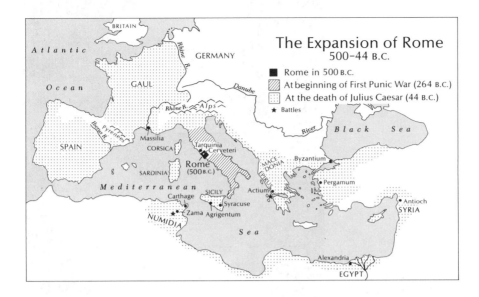

The Expansion of Rome
500–44 B.C.

■ Rome in 500 B.C.
▨ At beginning of First Punic War (264 B.C.)
▫ At the death of Julius Caesar (44 B.C.)
★ Battles

fully accepted the blessing of internal peace and the conveniences of a common currency, written law, and language. Nevertheless, the hard-bitten Romans trusted little in the gratitude of the defeated, especially after they had stripped them of most of their valuables and one-third of their land. To ensure loyalty and at the same time to resettle Latin farmers and reward soldiers, the Romans founded new cities, called colonies. One of the first was a new port for Rome itself, Ostia. Others followed along the coast; and much larger cities, of up to six thousand people were planted at strategic crossroads, mountain passes, fords, or frontiers. From this point, Rome became a city-building empire, thereby transforming the face of Europe.

Acquisition of a Mediterranean Empire.   With Italy secured, Rome moved rapidly against its only rival in the Western Mediterranean, Carthage. This city on the coast of North Africa near Tunis had been founded a little earlier than Rome as a Phoenician colony, by the city of Tyre. Profiting from their superb location at the narrow central straits of the Mediterranean and their skill as sailors and merchants, the Carthaginians had expanded their own colonies and direct military control to large parts of the Western Mediterranean by the third century. In particular, they held Sicily and Sardinia, granaries that Rome coveted. With typical enterprise, the Romans decided to become a sea power, built themselves a fleet of quinquiremes equipped with a nasty spiked gangplank for grappling enemy ships and putting legionaries on their decks, and won a series of naval battles. It still took twenty-three years of exhausting fighting, however, before the Carthaginians handed over Sicily. By then they were so worn down that, faced by a rebellion of their own mercenaries aided by Rome, they gave up Sardinia and Corsica as well three years later.

Scipio Africanus (237–183 B.C.).
Scipio, one of the greatest of Roman generals, was given the surname Africanus after he defeated the Carthaginian general Hannibal at Zama on the North African coast in 202 B.C. (Museo Capitolino. Alinari photo.)

The acquisition of these islands marked a vitally important change in Roman policy. Instead of their being offered the position of allies, like many states of peninsular Italy, they were made into overseas provinces that were governed directly by Roman officials, and they paid tribute, usually one-tenth of their wheat harvest, directly to Rome. Rome had ceased to extend the confederacy, and had created the pattern for the acquisition of an empire and its spoils.

New annexations extended the imperial system for the next two hundred years. Carthage remained the immediate enemy, since under vigorous new leaders it had acquired new wealth in the mines of Spain; and matching Rome's feat of creating a navy to defeat Carthage by sea, it was forming a new army to attack Rome by land. This Second Punic War (218–202 B.C.) fascinated Polybius by its dramatic fusion of the whole Mediterranean world. "Previously the doings of the world had been, so to say, dispersed," he wrote. "But ever since this date history has been an organic whole, and the affairs of Italy and Africa have been interlinked with those of Greece and Asia, all leading up to one end. . . . The Romans, feeling that the chief and most essential step in their scheme of universal conquest had now been taken, were first emboldened to reach out their hands to grasp the rest and to cross with an army to Greece and Asia." [13] Victory was again

[13] Polybius, *The Histories,* I, 3, 3–6, pp. 7–9.

costly for the Romans, because the Carthaginian general Hannibal brought his army and even his elephants across the Alps to defeat several Roman armies in Italy itself. Although he laid waste much of central Italy, he failed to take Rome; and when the Romans counterattacked at Carthage itself, he returned home to be defeated at the decisive battle of Zama (202 B.C.). The Romans then annexed Spain, and at once began exploiting its rich resources of copper, gold, silver, lead, and iron.

No other war was so costly or so risky. The Hellenistic monarchies, which were Rome's next prey, were torn by internal dissensions and their armies were no match for the Roman legions. After half a century of wars, during which the Romans showed surprising reluctance to annex the states they defeated, they finally lost patience. In 146 B.C., the Romans annexed Macedon, punished the Greeks for revolt by destroying Corinth, and completed the ruin of Carthage by leveling the city and spreading salt on its site. The Carthaginian territories, roughly the area of modern Tunisia, were made into the Roman province of Africa. The Seleucid kingdom, after numerous defeats by Rome, was finally overthrown in the middle of the first century; and the kings of Pergamum were so terrified by fear of internal revolution that they donated their kingdom to Rome. Rome thus acquired the richest part of Asia Minor, which became its sixth province, Asia. The rest of the republic's conquests were mostly cleaning-up operations, to protect what had already been taken—southern Gaul to link Spain and Italy; Syria to protect Asia Minor; northern Gaul, to subdue its dangerous tribes. The last of the great Hellenistic monarchies, Egypt, finally fell to Rome in 30 B.C., completing Rome's possession of the whole shoreline of the Mediterranean. The territory it then held was more than one hundred times larger than at the beginning of the wars with Carthage; and its problems had correspondingly increased.

THE ECONOMICS OF EMPIRE BUILDING

The acquisition of empire transformed the economic basis of the city of Rome, revolutionized its social structure, and changed for the worse the Romans' image of themselves. Throughout the history of the republic, leading Romans preached a civic ethic of service and self-denial that they thought derived from the honest peasant farmers they honored as their ancestors. Livy, writing his history of Rome at the time of Augustus, sought "to turn [his gaze] away from the troubles which our age has been witnessing for so many years . . . absorbed in the recollection of the brave days of old." His reader should imagine the change in Rome, "how, with the gradual relaxation of discipline, morals first gave way, as it were, then sank lower and lower, and finally began the downward plunge which has brought us to the present time, when we can endure neither our vices nor their cure." [14]

[14] Livy, *History* (London: W. Heinemann, 1919), preface, 9–10, pp. 5–7.

Economic Power of the Patrician Class.   The economic base of Roman life at the beginning of the Republic (c. 500 B.C.) was of necessity quite simple. Rome controlled only about 400 square miles of territory, and already the population was too large for the land available. Famines were frequent, and the hunger for wheat became a fixed goal of all Roman policy. There were very few slaves until the beginning of the overseas wars of conquest—perhaps less than twenty thousand in 500 B.C. and double that a century later. It is amazing that none of the Roman historians who deplored the corruption of the moral standards of the city thought to connect it with the introduction of enormous numbers of slaves after the wars with Carthage. The bulk of the Roman population, even of the city itself, engaged in small-scale agriculture, feeding their own families; and it was part of the accepted belief of Roman patricians that small farmers possessed the Stoic virtues of thrift and frugality that the state should encourage and were, moreover, ideal soldiers. Yet the patricians were also interested in increasing the size of their own estates, giving themselves not only larger income to spend on life in the city but greater political leverage within the senatorial oligachy; and they tended to gain ever greater shares of the small holdings, especially when the continuous wars often compelled the new draftee to sell his land for a song, as well as to take for themselves a large part of the lands confiscated in the conquest of peninsular Italy. In short, there was a social conflict based on rivalry for land at the heart of the confrontation of patrician and plebeian that was evident at the beginning of the fifth century. In this conflict, the small holders and the expropriated farmers were joined by the remaining freemen of Rome—the artisans, such as woodworkers and builders, the small shopkeepers, the traders, and the manual laborers.

The victories over Carthage ensured the predominance of the patrician class, who had become agricultural capitalists on their huge estates, or latifundia, and began the process of converting the frugal farmer into the debauched proletarian of Augustan days. The acquisition of the great wheat-producing regions of Sicily, Sardinia, North Africa, and Spain made it unprofitable to grow cereals in central Italy, especially as the wheat of the conquered regions was exacted as tribute and sold by the government below the market price or given away free. Hannibal's sixteen-year campaign in Italy itself drove many more peasants off the land, and the government distributed the vacant lands in large estates to those with the capital to care for them. Finally, the victories over Carthage and the Hellenistic monarchies brought vast numbers of slaves into Roman possession, and thereby transformed the whole character of Rome.

Impact of Slavery.   Probably seventy-five thousand prisoners were put on sale after the First Punic War, and afterwards the numbers increased rapidly, supplied not only from conquests of the campaigns and by pirates but even from the children of desperate peasants. By the time of Augustus, it has been calculated, one quarter of Rome's one million population were slaves; and they were permitted to wear the same clothes as freemen so that they would not realize their own numbers. The great slave markets, like the island of Delos or Capua near Naples, put on sale slaves of every nationality and ability, Nubians and Syrians and Gauls, poets and business-men and dancing girls. They were publicly displayed beneath a sign announcing their origin and special talents, and like animals could be thoroughly inspected by prospective buyers. Prices varied according to supply and the qualifications of the slave; but they were low enough for many well-to-do Romans to own four or five hundred. Most of the slaves were put to work on the large estates, which shifted over from wheat production to cattle rearing, market gardening, and oil and wine production. The owner usually stayed in Rome, and left it to his overseer to squeeze the profits from the land. The result was misery for the slaves. They lived in huge barracks surrounded by armed guards, could be chained, tortured, or even killed, and had no hope for anything but backbreaking work until they were dead.

Cato's description of how to get the most profit out of your slaves was famous in Rome for its moderation:

For laborers, 4 pecks of wheat in winter months; $4\frac{1}{2}$ in summer. For overseer, house-keeper, foreman and head-shepherd, 3 pecks. The chain-gang should get 4 pounds of bread daily in winter, 5 when they start digging the vines till the figs begin to ripen, then back to 4 again.

Keep all windfall olives you can. Then keep the ripe ones for which only a small yield can be got. Issue them sparingly so as to last as long as possible. When they're finished, give the slaves fish-pickle and vinegar. A peck of salt should suffice for each man for a year.

A tunic $3\frac{1}{2}$ feet long and a blanket-cloak every other year. On issuing tunic or cloak, take back the old one to make rough clothes. One good pair of clogs every second year.[15]

Part of the fear in which Romans came to live from the second century on was the knowledge that in the fields and mines of Italy among the hundreds of thousands of enslaved human beings many were reaching that point of desperation where they would risk torture and cruxifixion to destroy their odious captors.

The small holders, dispossessed by the growing estates, poured into the cities, especially into Rome. Here again they found much of the manual work and even many of the manufacturing and commercial jobs being carried on by slaves. Almost all domestic service and even the provision of supplies for the wealthy homes, like bread or cloth, were carried out by the household slaves. Greek slaves acted as household tutors; Phoe-nicians or Syrians engaged in commerce for their owners and were given a share of the profits as an incentive. Even the state used large numbers of "public slaves" as petty bureaucrats or in provision of services like

[15] Cited in Lindsay, *Ancient World,* p. 184.

the baths or aqueducts. With this type of competition for jobs, the city proletariat became increasingly dependent on handouts of food by the government and by aspiring politicians and generals. Their volatile discontent added a further element of uncertainty to the fear of slave revolt.

Between the proletariat and the well-to-do, Rome did develop a fairly substantial lower middle class, however. Its basis was the large numbers of shopkeepers, bar-owners, tailors, bakers, and so on whose shopfronts still open onto the excavated streets of Pompeii or Ostia. There was nothing that could be called industry in the city, since Romans bought what manufactured goods they wanted from other parts of Italy, but there was local small-scale production for the needs of the growing city, such as pottery, tiles, and bricks, textiles and shoes, and woodwork. In these trades the artisan class managed to preserve a precarious existence. It was however in commerce and banking that real wealth was to be made.

The House of Mosaics, Herculaneum. The home of a well-to-do Roman was usually built around an open courtyard, or atrium, in the center of which was a fountain and reflecting pool. Herculaneum was buried in the eruption of Vesuvius in 79 **A.D.** which also destroyed neighboring Pompeii. (Italian State Tourist Office photo.)

Structure of Roman Commerce. Rome's commerce was constructed on an unfavorable balance of trade. It produced little to sell—some pottery, oil and wine, and a few metal goods. Rome was a consumer on a scale hitherto unknown. The most significant of its imports was wheat, which it largely acquired free of payment as tribute from the conquered provinces, although it even bought wheat from Egypt before that country was expropriated. The uneasy peace within the streets of Rome depended on the regular arrival of the wheat convoys from Sicily or Africa, for any delay could bring the city poor to starvation. The shipping of this tribute in cereals to Rome was contracted out by the state to private citizens, called publicans, who were also entrusted with operating the state-owned mines, collecting rent from the public lands, constructing public works, and especially collecting taxes. They were able to form joint-stock companies, in which many poorer citizens invested with considerable success. The Roman state was itself thus the principal importer, paying for its purchases with tribute, taxation, customs dues, the sale of slaves, and the products of its mines. But the empire had also brought vast wealth in gold and silver to other groups. Many people were growing wealthy from landed estates and from taking positions within the provincial governments. A year's service as provincial governor was regarded as the opportunity to amass a personal fortune, although the rapacity was less great in the early days of empire. Successful generals were permitted to pocket a share of the booty they exacted, and they in turn made large distributions to their soldiers. The prosperous trading class, called equestrians because they could afford to equip themselves as cavalry, not only engaged in banking at high rates of interest and took a share of the profits made by the publicans, but also were permitted minor administrative plums themselves, such as the governorship of Judaea. The equestrians frequently became wealthier than senators. In short, Rome's oligarchy drew from the land of Italy, the bodies of its slaves, and the conquered territories of empire an abundance of ready cash that they spent in providing themselves with all the luxuries of the known world.

To grace their tables they bought fish from Spain and the Black Sea; cattle from Sicily, Spain, and Gaul; geese from Belgium; figs, dates, pomegranates and nuts from Asia Minor and Syria; ginger, cinnamon, and myrrh from Arabia; and cheese and poultry from Gaul. Huge sums were paid for a special sturgeon. To make the home a match for his menu, the wealthy Roman brought statues from Greece, marbles from Africa, rare woods from Lebanon and Syria, granite and porphyry from Egypt. For adornment, silk was obtained from China, through India or Persia, and after manufacture in Greece, was sold in Rome to the leaders of fashion. The Mediterranean became a single commercial unit, patrolled with increasing effectiveness by the warships of Rome, and from the Mediterranean the trade routes branched out through the empire to Britain, Germany, Parthia, China, India, Arabia, and Ethiopia. "By the lowest reckoning," Pliny complained, "India, China, and the Arabian peninsula take from

Street in Pompeii. The principal streets of Pompeii were about twenty feet wide, with raised sidewalks. The lower floors of the buildings were occupied by stores, artisan workshops, wine parlors, or bakeries; the upper floors, with sleeping quarters. (Italian State Tourist Office photo.)

our empire 100 million sesterces every year—that is the sum which our luxuries and our women cost us.'' It was hardly surprising that vast tensions were building within this empire and particularly in the city of Rome itself that were to erupt with enormous force from 133 B.C. on and eventually destroy the republic itself.

THE CITY DURING THE DESTRUCTION OF THE REPUBLIC

The narrative of the so-called Roman Revolution in the years from the murder of the aristocratic reformer Tiberius Gracchus in 133 B.C. to the establishment of imperial rule by Augustus in 27 B.C. is a confused sequence of obscure names and frequently resultless bloodletting. But if one concentrates on the central experiences of the city, several vital features stand out. First, the acquisition of empire produced extremes of wealth and poverty of a magnitude previously unknown in Rome; and the result was a slow sapping of the civic morality, or at least of the publicly displayed rectitude of all classes of society. Second, the constitutional process disintegrated into a series of struggles among major family groupings within the oligarchy for control of power. And third, the manipulation of violence, either through the pressure of the city mob or of legions loyal to a single general, became the principal instrument in the transfer of power. This unfortunate combination of corruption, family ambition, and violence destroyed the republican form of government.

Economic and Social Tensions. Many of Rome's social problems had arisen from the acquisition of empire. From the empire came much of the wealth of many of the older senatorial families and of the newer men of the business class called the equites, usually as the result of war booty, indemnities, payments both legal and illegal to imperial administrators, and tax collecting. The empire provided many of the luxuries, which more austere Romans felt were weakening the self-control of the city's noble youth. From the empire came the slaves who drove the free peasantry from the land of Italy and the educated urban citizens from the professional jobs as secretaries, doctors, and teachers in the cities. Thus the economic spoils of empire created for the Roman ruling class a range of new, profound problems.

Cato the Elder (234–149 B.C.). To Cato and conservatives among the oligarchy who supported him, the most deleterious effects of the new wealth were the decay of the ancient standards of probity of the ruling class. Cato was an unpleasant newcomer in Roman politics, a rough blunt farmer from the hills near Rome with a genius for scathing oratory. Throughout his political career he campaigned against the superficial luxuries he claimed were weakening ancient Roman virtue; as censor, he taxed luxury goods at ten times their market value, fined senators for flouting laws against public extravagance, and tried unsuccessfully to tighten sexual morality. Achieving little in his campaign for universal frugality, he turned his barbs against those who were seeking to introduce Greek culture and ways of life into Rome. Latin was better than Greek, he said; Roman religion sounder than Greek philosophy; his own prescriptions better than Greek medicine. Rome, he declared, would lose its empire when it became infected with Greek letters. Although he set an example as consul in Spain by refusing to fill his own pockets, leading a life of ostentatious simplicity, he did make a fortune from farming from careful management by squeezing every possible scrap of work from his slaves. Since his appeals for a changed morality went largely unheeded, it was not surprising that he was still prosecuting his enemies in the courts at the age of eighty five with undiminished acerbity. Later critics of the oligarchy's morality had no more success. His great-great-grandson, Cato the Younger (95–46 B.C.), was soon shunted aside when he preached his implacable ancestor's message. Another great admirer of Cato the Elder, Cicero (106–43 B.C.), after distinguishing himself by denouncing individual wrongdoers among the senators, finally retired to write a justification of the Roman oligarchs as he thought they were in the earlier days of the Republic. His *De Re Publica,* copying the form of Plato's *Republic,* argued that the Romans had already achieved a fine constitution early in their history: "The greatest number of votes belonged, not to the common people but to the rich, and put into effect the principle which ought always be adhered to in the commonwealth, that the greatest number should not have the greatest power." But, he warned, the rich should remember that "unless there is in the State an even balance of rights, duties, and functions, so that the magistrates have enough power, the counsels of the eminent citizens enough influence, and the people enough liberty, this kind of government cannot be safe from revolution."[16]

Slave Revolts. In the most immediate sense, there was the everpresent fear of a slave revolt that would find its fighting power among the most oppressed segments of the slave population and its leadership among the best treated. A great series of slave uprisings did begin in the estates of Sicily in 135 B.C. and culminated in the outbreak led by the gladiator Spartacus in 73–71 B.C. The Sicilian uprising was led by an ingenious prestidigitator who, to keep up his followers' enthusiasm, combined religious exhortation with the trick of breathing fire out of his mouth. The slaves seized the central part of the island, organized an army, and even issued their own currency. They were finally starved into surrender. Sporadic uprisings took place every few years until, in 73 B.C., a group of seventy-eight slaves broke free from a gladiators' school in Capua and established themselves on the slopes of Vesuvius. Joined by runaway slaves, the army headed by Spartacus soon numbered seventy thousand men and was easily able to defeat the armies Rome sent against it. When the slave army finally tried to cross the Alps to disperse to their homes, a Roman army blocked their way. Spartacus turned south, and terrified Rome with threat of attack, but he was pinned down and defeated. He himself was killed in battle; six thousand slaves who were captured were crucified along the Appian Way between Rome and Capua. Their bodies were a warning not only to other slaves but a reminder to the Romans of the great fear with which they had to live: "Every slave we own is an enemy we harbor."

No slave revolt could long triumph against the power of the Roman armies. Far more serious problems were undermining the social structure of Rome. The plight of the independent peasant, who was being forced to sell his lands to the rich for large-scale production by slaves worried the more perspicacious of Rome's rulers. This policy was increasing the unemployed and discontented proletariat not only of Rome but of many cities of Italy and Gaul and was reducing the number and health of the farmers from whom the bulk of the Roman armies had been drawn. Moreover, Rome's allies in Italy itself were becoming increasingly dissatisfied with their treatment, both the economic demands being made on them and the interference in their internal political affairs by an increasingly insensitive Roman government. Reformers like the Gracchi brothers realized that the misery of the independent peasantry and the resentment of the allied people in Italy had to be remedied together if Rome was to be secure in its own peninsula.

The Roman Oligarchy. The ruling class that faced these problems was a tightly knit oligarchy whose main constitutional instrument was the senate, the three hundred members of which were mainly drawn from the landed

[16] Cicero, *De Re Publica*, II, xxii, 39, p. 149; II, xxxiii, 57–58, p. 169.

aristocracy but whose decisions were controlled by an inner group of little more than twenty families. The constitution itself, as Ronald Syme has pointed out, was "a screen and a sham"; these great families merely used it for their own purposes. They possessed far-reaching networks of influence based on family relationships, wealth, and carefully cultivated ties of clientage, known as *amicitia,* that enrolled in their support vast numbers of lesser men throughout the landowning and business classes. Occasionally, the great families would admit into their ranks a *novus homo,* a new man whose family had never produced a consul; and they would replenish their finances by ties with the business class of equites whom they satisfied with the provision of a business environment conducive to the making of money, the grant of tax-farming privileges, or the profits of financing state commerce or military operations. The great families employed agents, often freedmen, to scatter bribes, manage elections, and organize physical intimidation; and they ensured the collaboration of spiritual forces by filling the priesthood with their own men. After 130 B.C. the great families divided into two factions, the Optimates and the Populares. These groups did not represent a division between the well-to-do and the poorer, dissatisfied classes, as has frequently been claimed; as recent historians have shown, both groups were members of the same class. The division was a battle between family groupings, not a fight between ideologies and especially not a class war. The Optimates were united by the determination to preserve the oligarchic system without primary economic or social reforms, and since they succeeded in gaining control of the senate, they came to be thought of as the senatorial party. The Populares, a word that means "demagogue" and was applied to them by their enemies, were other members of the inner group of families who turned to the tribunate and the popular assembly for support because their opponents had won control of the senate; their leaders must be divided between those like the Gracchi, who were sincere reformers, and those like Marius, who were self-seekers courting the people to break their rivals inside the oligarchy. Thus the great struggles of the last century of the republic have to be seen, not mainly as battles of principle, but as skirmishes among the leading families of a restricted oligarchy. The Gracchi brothers were from the Cornelii family, the grandsons of Scipio Africanus, who defeated Hannibal; Sulla, who controlled Rome on behalf of the Optimates in 83–79 B.C., based his strength on the Metellii family; and Julius Caesar came from the ancient Claudian family.

The Reform Program of the Gracchi. The character of the struggles within the oligarchy was changed by the resort to violence. At first, the violence was deployed by the controlling faction of the senate against would-be reformers. In 133 B.C., Tiberius Gracchus was elected tribune of the people. He had decided, when passing through Tuscany where he "observed the dearth of inhabitants in the country, and that those who tilled the soil or tended its flocks there were imported barbarian slaves," that Rome's main problem was the expulsion of the peasant-farmer from the land. His solution was simple: limit the holdings of public land to 500 acres, compensate present owners for amounts above that confiscated, and redistribute the land to the city poor in twenty-acre farms. What worried the senators, however, was not only the proposed agrarian reform but the revolutionary oratory with which Tiberius began to inflame the city proletariat:

The wild beasts that roam over Italy have every one of them a cave or lair to lurk in; but the men who fight and die for Italy enjoy the common air and light, indeed, but nothing else; horseless and homeless they wander about with their wives and children. . . . They fight and die to support others in wealth and luxury, and though they are styled masters of the world, they have not a single clod of earth that is their own.[17]

When he illegally stood for reelection as tribune, a group of senators and their hangers-on, armed with clubs, beat him and three hundred of his supporters to death in the assembly, and threw their bodies into the river. A decade later, his younger brother Gaius Gracchus revived and extended the reform proposals. The senate sent armed forces against him and his followers who had barricaded themselves on the Aventine Hill. In a pitched battle fought in the heart of Rome, Gaius's forces were overwhelmed. Gaius had his own slave kill him; but his head was cut off and brought to the senate, which had promised to pay its weight in gold. The head was surprisingly heavy, and it was found that the aristocrat claiming the reward had filled it with lead. In this unsavory fashion, the Optimates repelled a moderate effort to repopulate the countryside and get the mob out of Rome.

Legions as Instrument of Political Change.   Far more significant was the eruption of the legions into Roman politics. Around 100 B.C., the whole character of the Roman army was changed by the reforms of Marius, an ambitious self-made general from a poor farming family. Marius created a new military force by calling for volunteers from the whole citizen body and not merely the propertied classes. He paid them well, organized them into groups of ten-cohort legions of 6000 men each, and provided generous bonuses of land and money; and his example was followed by other generals. These professional legions, composed mostly of the city proletariat, owed little allegiance to the state. They followed their general loyally, for booty; and they were as prepared to attack Rome as its enemies. Marius threw in his lot with the opposition to the Optimates, who picked their own man, a poverty-stricken aristocrat, Sulla, for the military operations in northern Asia Minor and in Greece that Marius had hoped to command. When Marius attempted to use the assembly to get himself the command, Sulla set an ominous precedent by marching on Rome and seizing the city. After Sulla had left for the front, Marius returned, re-established his political alliances in the city, and permitted his soldiers to

---

[17] *Plutarch's Lives* (London: W. Heinemann, 1914–1954), VIII, 7, p. 163; IX, 5, pp. 165–67.

Roman Legionary, 2nd Century. The principal unit of the Roman army was the legion, composed of about 6000 men, mainly foot-soldiers. The legionary wore a metal helmet and tough leather cuirass and carried a round shield and short thrusting sword. In the wars with Carthage, up to 23 legions were put into battle at one time. (Photo copyright by the Trustees of the British Museum.)

murder large numbers of the Optimates who had opposed him. Decapitated heads were displayed on the speakers' platform in the Forum; bodies were left in the streets to be torn to pieces by birds and dogs; and Marius, apparently crazed with his new eminence in bloodshed, presided over the slaughter, giving summary judgments that were at once carried out before him. In the words of the historian Appian, "Neither reverence for gods, nor the indignation of men, nor the fear of odium for their acts, existed any longer among them. After committing savage deeds, they turned to godless sights. They killed remorselessly and severed the necks of men already dead, and they paraded these horrors before the public eye, either to inspire fear and terror, or for a godless spectacle." [18] Sulla returned three years later to carry out a similar butchery; but he followed it with a reform program aimed at restoring law and order based on the power of the senate—ending the free supply of grain, filling the assemblies with his supporters, and enacting a law that no bill could be considered by the assembly without the senate's agreement. But his main efforts were to compensate his army through confiscated property; for behind the senatorial restoration were the bloodstained swords of the legions, the one constant factor in these civil wars.

[18] *Appian's Roman History* (London: W. Heinemann, 1912–1913), I, 71, p. 133.

Julius Caesar (100–44 B.C.).   In the end, victory in Rome's internal political struggles went to the general who could command the finest military strength, backed by wealth and family alliances. Julius Caesar combined these assets. His patrician ancestry reached so far back that he was, he claimed, descended from Aeneas and hence from the goddess Venus. In a fairly conventional early career, he had worked his way through the lower offices of the Republic until, in Spain, he had formed the first important army on whose personal loyalty he could rely. According to the historian Suetonius, he was already burning with ambition: "He saw a statue of Alexander the Great in the Temple of Hercules and was overheard to sigh impatiently: vexed, it seems, that at an age when Alexander had already conquered the whole world, he himself had done nothing in the least epoch-making."[19] To gain the financial support he needed, he struck up an alliance with the wealthy financier Crassus, who fed him the money for organization of magnificent games in Rome and for the bribery necessary to get him elected chief priest of the state religion, and in 59 B.C., consul. By then he had an unsavory reputation for debauchery, bribery, unsuccessful sedition, and pandering to the poor; but he was also building up a political alliance system of his own within the oligarchy, composed of several ancient families excluded by the dominant Optimate group in the senate, ambitious bankers from the equites class, and younger aristocrats eager for rapid advancement. The governorship of Gaul (northern Italy and southern France) proved him to be a superb general, a masterful propagandist in his description of his own triumphs in his book *The Gallic Wars,* and a successful fortune seeker. In nine years he conquered northern France and Belgium, invaded Britain, although he withdrew almost at once, and welded his armies into the most effective fighting force in the Roman Empire. In 49 B.C., he led his forces across the river Rubicon into Italy to strike directly against his Optimate opponents who controlled the senate. In four years of fighting, he defeated the armies raised by the Optimates' leader, Pompey, destroying them one by one in Spain, North Africa, and Greece. By 45 B.C. he was master of the Roman state.

Caesar apparently had serious plans for dealing with Rome's problems. In the three years during which he was dictator, although occupied with the war against the supporters of Pompey, he almost doubled the size of the senate to dissipate its power and bring in the business classes. He attacked the land problem by founding new overseas colonies, and redistributed state lands in Italy. To control the Roman proletariat, he reduced the free grain supplies, provided work on public buildings, and organized huge free entertainments. He even attempted to cut down on corruption in the government of the empire, and he seems to have planned a vast series of campaigns to round out the empire in Europe and Asia. His senatorial

Gold Coin with Head of Julius Caesar, 46 B.C. (The Metropolitan Museum of Art. Gift of Joseph H. Durkee, 1899.)

[19] Suetonius, *The Twelve Caesars,* trans. Robert Graves (Harmondsworth, England: Penguin, 1969), p. 12.

Bust of Marcus Brutus. Brutus, a member of one of the great patrician families of Rome, was thirty-four when he led the assassination plot against Julius Caesar. He committed suicide two years later, in 42 B.C., after his forces were defeated at the battle of Philippi. (Museo Capitolino. Alinari photo.)

opponents, however, fearing the final destruction of their political power if he remained longer at the head of the state, organized his assassination. He was stabbed to death on March 15, 44 B.C., the Ides of March, while attending the senate, unarmed and without his guards.

The murder of Caesar did not restore the power of the Optimates, as the conspirators had hoped. The Roman mob rose in fury against the conspirators, who went into hiding; and when Caesar's body was brought to the Forum for cremation, Suetonius wrote, "two divine forms (perhaps the twin brethren Castor and Pollux) suddenly appeared, javelin in hand and sword at thigh, and set fire to the couch with torches. Immediately the spectators assisted the blaze by heaping on it dry branches and the judges' chairs, and the court benches, with whatever else came to hand. . . . Veterans who had assisted at his triumphs added the arms they had then borne. Many women in the audience similarly sacrificed their jewelry together with their childrens' golden buttons and embroidered tunics." [20] In this universal grief, Caesar was recognized to have become a god; and the precedent for deifying emperors was established. Caesar's obvious successor was his lieutenant, Mark Antony, a fine general but a poor statesman, who might well have taken over the empire with the connivance

[20] Ibid., p. 47.

of the frightened senate had he not been challenged by Caesar's eighteen-year-old adopted son, whom Caesar's will had named as heir—Caius Julius Caesar Octavian, later to become the Emperor Augustus. Supported by Caesar's veterans, Octavian first accepted the support of the Optimates against Antony, but then broke with the senatorial conservatives and defeated their remaining forces at Philippi in Macedonia. Finally he engaged in a new civil war with Antony and his ally, Cleopatra of Egypt. His victory in the naval battle of Actium (31 B.C.) off Greece, followed the next year with the dual suicide of Antony and Cleopatra, finally brought an end to the century of civil chaos that had begun with the murder of Tiberius Gracchus. Octavian returned to a Rome in political, social, moral, and physical degradation.

SUGGESTED READING

The culture of the Hellenistic age is analyzed briefly but profoundly by W. W. Tarn and G. T. Griffith, *Hellenistic Civilization* (1961) and by Michael Grant, *The Ancient Mediterranean* (1969). The basic study of the economic structure of the Eastern Mediterranean is still M. I. Rostovtzeff, *Social and Economic History of the Hellenistic World* (1953), while the changed character of city life is explained in A. H. M. Jones, *The Greek City from Alexander to Justinian* (1940). The exploits of Alexander the Great permitted Plutarch, *Life of Alexander* (many translations), to draw many obvious moral lessons. More documented modern treatments, which of necessity lack the emotive appeal so essential to appreciation of Alexander's extraordinary ambitions, are W. W. Tarn, *Alexander the Great* (1948) and A. R. Burns, *Alexander and the Hellenistic Empire* (1947).

During the First World War, the English novelist E. M. Forster wrote a delightful guidebook to Alexandria which has been republished, as *Alexandria: A History and a Guide* (1961). The fullest scholarly treatment is André Bernand, *Alexandrie la Grande* (1966).

An excellent introduction to the Etruscan society is provided by Raymond Bloch, *The Etruscans* (1958), which is well illustrated, and by Massimo Pallottino, *The Etruscans* (1955). The finest word pictures of the tombs are still those of D. H. Lawrence, *Etruscan Places* (1957), even if some of the information is out of date. Lovely reproductions grace Raymond Bloch's *Etruscan Art* (1959); P. J. Riis, *An Introduction to Etruscan Art* (1953), by a Danish scholar, is quite useful.

Short essays on several of the Greek cities in Italy combine literary with archaeological documentation in Kathleen Freeman's *Greek City-States* (1950), while fuller treatments are J. J. Dunrabin, *Western Greeks* (1948) and A. G. Woodhead, *Greeks in the West* (1962). Greek influence on Roman civilization was obvious to Petronius, *Satyricon* (many translations) as well as to Cato the Elder; and the Roman fascination with the Greek achievement is best illustrated in the search for the Hellenic past in Pausanias' *Description of Greece*. Greek conceptions of the city-state had profound influence on the Roman idea of the city "not as a political or legal institution, but rather as a design for a society in which men could live together," as Lidia Storoni Mazzolani shows in her book, *The Idea of the City in Roman Thought* (1970).

Raymond Bloch, *The Origins of Rome* (1960) takes the history of Rome from Romulus to the founding of the republic, while the character of republican politics, especially the nature of oligarchic family alliances, is explored at length in the magistral *Roman Revolution* (1939) of Ronald Syme, and in less compass in H. H. Scullard's *From the Gracchi to Nero* (1959). Lily Ross Taylor focuses on an even shorter period of political infighting in *Party Politics in the Age of Caesar* (1949). Syme summarizes his views on the failure of the republic in *A Roman Post-Mortem* (1950). The most impressive account of Caesar as a military leader is Julius Caesar, *The Conquest of Gaul* and *The Civil War* (many translations), but for more colorful detail one should not miss Suetonius, *The Twelve Caesars* (1969) as translated by Robert Graves. Finally, for the survey of Rome's early centuries that provided the picture of their own history possessed by the educated of imperial Rome, see Livy, *The Early History of Rome* (1965) and *The War with Hannibal* (1965), both of which are translated by Aubrey de Selincourt.

4
THE ROME OF AUGUSTUS

City growth is a capricious process, and like the sorcerer's apprentice, quickly gets out of hand. Rome's expansion had gone through four phases. As we saw in the last chapter, it had been founded, in the eighth century B.C., as a tribal village of wooden huts spreading across the summits of the Palatine and Capitol hills. As the Romans conquered the neighboring tribes and established control over a hinterland extending from the Bay of Naples to the Arno River, Rome was converted into a small metropolis, with a wall of hewn tufa, temple complexes on its hills, a central Forum crammed with buildings for administrators and priests, and an unplanned sprawl of tenements, villas, baths, theaters, and shops. The confusion was usually explained by the fact that the citizens were given one year to rebuild the city after its destruction by the Gauls in 390 B.C. They were in such a hurry, the historian Livy commented, that they did not bother to lay out streets, and the city resembled a "squatters' settlement rather than a planned community." With the acquisition of empire, from the third century B.C., Rome reflected the tastes, power, and imperial spoils enjoyed by its dominant aristocratic families, who ran their empire with no clear sense of economic rationale or administrative responsibility. Beautiful aristocratic homes, constructed around gracious open patios decorated with fountains and Greek statues, were built on the Palatine. Delicate temples in the Hellenistic style were erected beside the river. Warehouses and shops expanded to deal with the rising commerce of the empire. More ominously, the city's slums expanded to accommodate the thousands of dispossessed farmers whose lands had been taken over by Rome's aristocrats; and the city's arenas grew to provide the free games with which the poor were distracted in their idleness. Rome was not yet a beautiful city, however. Augustus felt that "the City was architecturally unworthy of her position

The Forum, Rome. From the Capitol Hill, the viewer gazes down into the Forum, toward the three Corinthian columns of the Temple of Castor and Pollux. To the left are the three delicate pillars remaining of the diminutive Temple of Vesta, while the Sacred Way crosses out of the Forum through the single span of the Arch of Titus. (Italian Government Travel Office photo.)

as capital of the Roman Empire, besides being vulnerable to fire and river floods,'' and he began its monumental rebuilding. In this fourth phase, the city became a true imperial capital, because Augustus gave Rome the administrative capacity to govern a world empire and he and his immediate successors gave it an architectural grandeur worthy of its imperial position.

To a few, this Rome of Augustus was decidedly unappealing. The satirist Juvenal complained:

Here in town the rich die from insomnia mostly,
Undigested food, on a stomach burning with ulcers,
Brings on listlessness, but who can sleep in a flophouse?
Who but the rich can afford sleep and a garden apartment?
That's the source of infection. The wheels creak by on the narrow
Streets of the wards, the drivers squabble and bawl when they're stopped,
More than enough to frustrate the drowsiest son of a sea cow.
When his business calls, the crowd makes way, as the rich man
Carried high in his car, rides over them, reading or writing,
Even taking a snooze, perhaps, for the motion's composing.
Still he gets where he wants before we do; for all of our hurry
Traffic gets in our way, in front, around and behind.
Somebody gives me a shove with an elbow, or two-by-four scantling.
One clunks my head with a beam, another cracks down with a beer keg.
Mud is thick on my shins, I am trampled by somebody's big feet.
Now what?—a soldier grinds his hobnails into my toes.[1]

Most inhabitants of Rome, however, like New Yorkers today, loved their city in their loathing, and could not be persuaded by any blandishment to prefer the healthy boredom of the fine provincial cities. Rome possessed an indefinable magnetism. Once out of its noise and smells, Romans looked back on it with nostalgia. "From my own [country] home, I turn to the sights of splendid Rome," the poet Ovid wrote, "and in my mind's eye, I survey them all. Now I remember the forums, the temples, the theaters covered with marble, the colonnades where the ground has been levelled— now the grass of the Campus Martius and the views over noble gardens, the lakes, the Waterway, the aqua Virgo."[2]

THE AUGUSTAN POLITICAL SETTLEMENT

The political heart of the Roman republic lay where the Roman Forum met the base of the Capitol Hill, around the spot from which all mileages were counted, the umbilicus of the Roman Empire. The Curia, where the senate usually met, was one of the most venerated of Roman buildings, con-

[1] *The Satires of Juvenal,* trans. Rolfe Humphries (Bloomington: Indiana University Press, 1958), p. 42.
[2] Ovid, *Letters from Pontus* I. 8. 33–38, cited in Donald R. Dudley, ed., *Urbs Roma* (Aberdeen: Phaidon, 1967), p. 5.

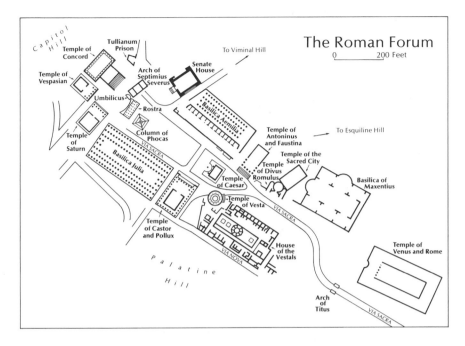

The Roman Forum

stantly destroyed by fire and immediately rebuilt. It had a simple floor of
white marble, and three rows of uncomfortable marble seats for the senators,
an extraordinarily small and simple hall for the main assembly of a world
empire. Just beyond the doorway of the Curia was a small paved space,
occasionally covered with an awning, called the comitium, where assemblies of the people met. Here vast crowds gathered for the voting, which
was often tumultuous and violent, and hundreds with no legal right to vote
frequently participated. Overlooking the comitium was a long stone platform about eight feet in height decorated with rostra, or beaks, of warships
captured in the fourth century B.C. From this vantage point, with his back
to the Capitol Hill and with the Senate House on the left, with his supporters grouped around him, a well-trained orator could dominate the
crowds massed below. The power of Rome was concentrated in this small
area until Augustus established the Principate, and even afterwards lip-
service was paid to the hallowed status of this seat of republican government.

Constitution of Roman Republic. For the first four hundred years of the
republic, a rough-and-ready form of democratic aristocracy had func-
tioned in this tiny place, where patrician and plebeian had reached a workable compromise without interference of forces from outside the city. The
senate, although in theory a consultative body, had supreme control over
finances and most legislation, and its families provided the majority of
leading magistrates. But the power of the people was also recognized,

especially after they had blackmailed the senate on one occasion by leaving the city en masse in a *secessio,* a kind of sit-out. The tribunes chosen by the people could veto acts of the other magistrates; all laws had to be passed and all magistrates elected by the comitia centuriata, one of the popular assemblies; and there was a genuine belief that government power, or *imperium,* could only be conferred by the people's acclamation. It might easily appear that the system was a hoax, an inexpensive method for an oligarchy to keep the masses cooperative; but at least during the years of expansion, when the populace could be recruited into the army, and was, if it turned rambunctious, the system worked. By the time of the Gracchi, however, the poorer classes had such economic grievances that they were alienated from the traditional constitution, and in the first century, a new and more potent influence for change had been the bloody intervention of the armies responsible only to their generals. A return to monarchy would have been one solution out of the constitutional chaos, as Julius Caesar had foretold. But as Brutus and his associates demonstrated, in Rome there would always be many willing to kill and to die for the traditional republic. Augustus had to come to terms with tradition.

Roman Political Theory.   The success of Augustus owed much to the character of Roman theorizing about the state. The Romans did not produce ambitious blueprints for the construction of ideal states, such as appealed to the Greeks. With very few exceptions, Roman theorists ignored, or rejected as valueless, intellectual exercises like Plato's *Republic,* in which the relationship of the individual to the state was worked out painstakingly without reference to particular states or particular individuals. The closest the Romans came to the Greek model was in Cicero's *De Re Publica,* and even here Cicero had his own patrician state clearly in mind rather than hypothetical men emerging blinded from imaginary caves. Roman thought about the state was concrete, even when it involved religious and moral concepts. The first ruler of Rome, Romulus, was held to have received authority *(imperium)* from the gods, and specifically from Jupiter, the "guarantor" of Rome. All constitutional development was a method of conferring and administering the imperium. Very early it was believed that only the assembly of the fathers, the family heads who founded the original senate, possessed the religious character necessary to exercise imperium, because its primal function was to consult the gods. Being practical as well as exclusive, the senators moved on to share out the imperium, holding that their consuls would possess it on alternate months, and later extending its possession to lower officials. But the important achievement was to create the idea of continuing state authority only temporarily embodied in certain upper-class individuals and only conferred when the mass of the people concurred. The system grew with enormous complexity, as new offices and assemblies were created and almost none discarded. In Roman thinking, the individual had a role in a specific state that had developed in time in a particular political form sanctified by the gods. Total demolition

Bust of Augustus. The emperor is wearing the wreath of bay leaves granted a successful general as a supreme accolade. In imperial times, the emperor himself and not his generals was honored with the ceremonial procession of the triumph; the general was regarded only as a deputy for the emperor. (Museo Toloso, Rome. Alinari photo.)

of an existing state, or at least of the existing Roman state, would not be just an act of madness or impiety; it would be impossible. The whole argument of the only important books of political theory that the Romans have left us, Cicero's *De Re Publica* and *Laws,* was the need to preserve the continuity of a great tradition: "On the customs and men of old, the Roman state is founded."

The Senate under Augustus. Augustus satisfied the Optimates in part by restoring the old constitutional forms. "After I had brought to an end the civil wars . . . , having attained supreme power by the consent of all, I transferred the state from my own power to that of the Roman Senate and People," he observed later. He carefully preserved all the republican magistrates' positions, even though he held a large number of them himself. He often attended the senate meetings and, according to Suetonius, allowed a considerable freedom of abuse there:

Augustus's speeches in the House would often be interrupted by such remarks as, "I don't understand you!" or "I'd dispute your point if I got the chance." And it happened more than once that, exasperated by recriminations which lowered the tone of the debates, he left the House in angry haste, and was followed by shouts of: "You ought to let senators say exactly what they think about matters of public importance." [3]

He even succeeded in gaining the collaboration of the leaders of the senatorial oligarchy by sharing with them the fruits of office, especially of provincial office. He left eight rich provinces under direct control of the senate. About one hundred of the six hundred senators were abroad on provincial administration at any time, and thus able to enjoy the perquisites of their position. The sons of twenty senators each year were appointed to the senate by Augustus, a form of patronage that gave him great leverage on the leading families. He was thus able to ensure that the senate should request him to go on administering the state as *princeps,* or first citizen, and *imperator,* or commander-in-chief. The forms were undisturbed, but Augustus in fact held the reins of command.

Any spark of independence in the senate quickly died out. New men personally indebted to the emperor were appointed. Men who spoke out unwisely lost all chance of advancement and might even be tried for treason. The precedent for the senate's self-abasement was set when it proclaimed Augustus *Pater Patriae* (Father of his country).

Instead of issuing a decree or acclaiming him with shouts [the senate] chose Valerius Messala to speak for them all when Augustus entered the House. Messala's words were: "Caesar Augustus, I am instructed to wish you and your family good fortune and divine blessings; which amounts to wishing that our entire city will be fortunate and our country prosperous. The Senate agree with the People of Rome in saluting you as Father of your country." With tears in his eyes, Augustus answered —again I quote his exact words: "Fathers of the Senate, I have at least achieved my highest ambitions. What more can I ask of the immortal gods than that they may permit me to enjoy your approval until my dying day." [4]

Such affecting scenes were less common under the later emperors. Again and again, the senate assembled to ratify the army's or the guard's choice of an emperor, or to vote condemnation for treason on the flimsiest charges. Their prestige gradually diminished until the historian Tacitus finally washed his hands of them: "All readers of the history of these terrible times in my pages or another's may fairly take it for granted that the gods were thanked for each instance of banishment or murder ordered by the emperor. Indeed, such occasions, once the sign of public rejoicings, now marked only public disasters. But I shall still record senatorial decrees that plumbed new depths of sycophancy, or established new records of servility." [5]

---

[3] Suetonius, *The Twelve Caesars,* trans. Robert Graves (Harmondsworth, England: Penguin, 1969), p. 81.
[4] Ibid., p. 83.
[5] Cited in Donald R. Dudley, *The World of Tacitus* (London: Secker and Warburg, 1968), p. 123.

The collapse of even the semblance of independent political life in Rome
was symbolized by the encroachment into the Forum itself of the monstrous
brick arches needed to hold up the increasingly grandiose palaces on the
Palatine; and many a senator, crossing the black volcanic paving on his
way to a yet more demeaning debate in the senate, must have looked up at
the grotesque statues of the deified emperors and the towering marble porticoes of the palace, and sighed for the virtue of an earlier Rome.

Augustus (Reigned 27 B.C.–A.D. 14). In the days of the republic, the Palatine Hill was already regarded as one of the pleasantest places to live in
Rome; and a number of leading citizens had spacious homes there, where
they could enjoy views over the Forum to the Alban hills or across the river
to the cypress-covered slopes of the Janiculum Hill. Augustus himself was
born on the Palatine, and he returned to live there as emperor, buying a
house on the very edge of the hill next to the traditional site of Romulus's
cabin. Beside his home he built the finest temple in Rome, dedicated to the
sun god Apollo, who had helped him defeat Antony's patron god, Neptune,
in the sea battle at Actium. Perhaps Augustus had the Parthenon of Athens
in mind, or perhaps through Apollo worship he was laying the basis for a
new state religion. The magnificent portico of colored Numidian marble,
with the enormous statue of Apollo as the restorer of peace, towered above
the city as a harbinger of a new age of imperial peace and glory. Contem-

**THE VIEW
FROM THE
PALATINE**

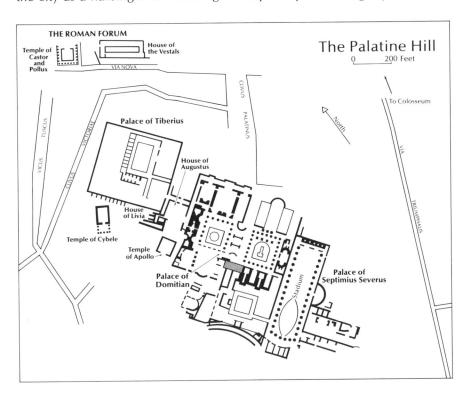

Rome in the 4th Century. On this model of Imperial Rome, the palaces of the Palatine Hill can be seen above the vast oval of the Circus Maximus. In the left center, the complex of temples on the Capitol Hill; in the right center, the Colosseum. Two of the city's aqueducts cut through the close-packed apartment buildings.

poraries were certainly impressed. "You ask why I come so late?" the poet Propertius gushed. "Great Caesar has opened the golden portico of Apollo: a glorious sight, with its columns of African marble, between which sit statues of the many daughters of old Danäus. And there in the middle rose the temple with its shining marble, which Apollo loves more than his home in Ortygia."[6]

In knowing contrast to such splendor, Augustus's home was modest. We can still see its small, painted rooms, set around a little courtyard, almost bare of marble and mosaic. Augustus slept in the same bedroom in this house for forty years, even though the Roman winters did not suit him; and when he wanted to work on secret state papers or to be alone, he retreated to a little study at the top of the house overlooking the whole city. His way of life was as simple as his house. His clothes were usually woven and sewn by the womenfolk of his house; he drank little, and was forgetful about his food. In this unpretentious setting, Augustus developed into the greatest emperor Rome was ever to know; and it pleased him especially that the senate decreed that the title *Pater Patriae* should be inscribed over the doorway of this home.

[6] Propertius, *Elegies* II, 31, cited in Dudley, *Urbs Roma*, p. 155.

Augustus's great achievement was to restore peace at home and abroad. With the treasure of Egypt and a loyal experienced army, Augustus could act from strength. He settled part of the army on the land, but maintained a legionary force of 125,000 men and a personal guard in Rome of 4,500. He developed an imperial bureaucracy, but decentralized the administration of the empire to bring more effective rule to the provinces. On most of the borders of the empire, Augustus was content to hold firm, using negotiation whenever possible to prevent war. On the northern frontiers, however, there was continuous fighting, mostly in Germany and along the Danube; but after several defeats, he had to be satisfied to establish the frontier along the Rhine and Danube rivers. Finally, the coming of internal peace brought economic prosperity. The great altar built by Augustus to celebrate his achievements was an Ara Pacis, an altar of peace, showing the victory of the Pax Augusta (the Augustan Peace) over war. Augustus permitted almost total freedom of trade and industry within the empire, allowing the great capitalists of republican days to continue amassing fortunes and encouraging the smaller men of the provincial cities to emulate them. Italy in particular boomed economically during the Augustan age. Its large agricultural estates were managed on a scientific basis, and brought wealth to their owners who usually resided in the cities rather than on their estates. Oil and wine were sold in the cities, and formed the main items of export trade. But Italy was also transformed into a manufacturing center at this time. Pottery, bronze, glassware, jewelry, even woolen cloth were made for export, while many smaller cities like Pompeii developed workshops to provide the agricultural implements, clothing, and pottery required by their local markets. The booming economy in conditions of peace was a big reason why contemporaries agreed with the poet Horace that Augustus was a Savior of the Empire, a Mercury or Apollo or Hercules.

Even Augustus, however, did not appeal to everyone, as the historian Tacitus showed a century later:

When he had seduced the army by gifts, the common people by the provision of cheap food, and everyone by the blandishments of peace, then little by little he began to enlarge his powers, to encroach upon the proper functions of the Senate, the magistrates and the laws. No one opposed him. Men of spirit had died on the battlefield, or in the proscriptions. The remainder of the aristocracy were rewarded by wealth and position in proportion to their readiness to accept servitude.[7]

The Julio-Claudian Emperors, 14–68. The administrative structure created by Augustus had a solidity that enabled it to function in subsequent years with relative smoothness in spite of the personal deficiencies of the next four emperors. For almost half a century, the Roman provinces remained unaffected by the oddities of the Julio-Claudian dynasty, while in Rome itself the Augustan age's creativity in art and literature, architecture and engineering, and jurisprudence continued with little interruption.

Augustus unwillingly recognized his stepson Tiberius (reigned 14–37)

[7] Cited in Dudley, *World of Tacitus,* p. 77.

as his successor; for at fifty-six Tiberius was moody, brusque, tactless, and implacable. His mother Livia, the wife of Augustus, still tried to dominate him; and the desire to get out from under her scrutiny provided a motive to Tiberius for building a vast new palace on the Palatine, stretching across the hill from Augustus's home to the cliffs overhanging the Forum. From the dining room, he enjoyed a view of the Temple of Jupiter on the Capitol Hill; and in the dark recesses of this palace his enemies were murdered. Thus Tiberius was the first emperor to have a real palace, with huge numbers of reception rooms, offices, kitchens, and baths. Tiberius governed from Rome, sternly and efficiently, for nine years; but then, wearying of the city, he retired to the island of Capri, where he had built a sumptuous villa on the tall cliffs overlooking the Bay of Naples. Roman society buzzed with scandal about the orgies of this sixty-seven year old pervert, and finally concluded that the old man had gone mad. In 37, he was smothered with his bedclothes by the prefect of the guard.

His successor, Caligula (reigned 37–41), demanded deification at the age of twenty-five, and would sit in the Temple of Castor and Pollux, between the statues of the divine twins, "offering himself for the adoration of visitors to the Temple." He finally built a bridge across from the Palatine Hill to the Capitol Hill where, Suetonius reported, he would have conversa-

Bust of Caligula. Roman sculptors displayed great skill in the delineation of character in the portrait bust. The petulant tyranny of Caligula is unerringly portrayed without, apparently, the emperor being aware of it. (Museo Nazionale, Rome. Alinari photo.)

tions with the statue of Jupiter, "pressing his ear to the God's mouth, and sometimes raising his voice in anger. Once he was overheard threatening the god: 'If you do not raise me up to Heaven, I will cast you down to Hell.'" His extravagances dictated his policy—war in Mauretania to seize its royal treasury, conspiracy trials for confiscation of rich men's property, heavy taxation on everything and everyone. Caligula was stabbed to death by the praetorian guard, which then picked his successor, a pedantic student of Etruscan history, Caligula's uncle Claudius. Claudius (41–54) surprised everyone by bringing a little sanity back into the government. He set up ministries headed by Greek freemen to carry on the imperial administration; citizenship was extended to many outside Italy; and he conquered most of England. His fifth wife, however, fed him poisoned mushrooms; and like Caligula, he died in the palace of Tiberius, in agony. Nero (54–68) was dissatisfied with everything he inherited, his palaces not least. He murdered his wife and mother and Claudius's son, and married his mistress. He cast away the last remnants of Roman dignity, and horrified the senate by performing in the public theaters and arenas as a musician, poet, actor, and charioteer; and he compelled senators to do the same. He threw off the guidance of his tutor, the philosopher Seneca, who had given him five efficient years of government at the beginning of his reign, and eventually had him commit suicide for conspiracy.

The Great Fire of 64 and Nero's Rebuilding. The Roman population had no hesitation in attributing the Great Fire of 64 to Nero himself, who, it was thought, wanted the fame of founding a new city of Rome. This fire, probably the worst in Rome's history, began in shops where the Palatine overhangs the great chariot arena, the Circus Maximus, spread through the nearby slum districts, climbed the Palatine and consumed its palaces, temples, and libraries, and was halted on the sixth day just before it could destroy the Forum and the Capitol. The populace was in total panic. In Tacitus's words:

All movement was blocked by the terrified, shrieking women, by helpless old people or children, by those who sought safety or tried to help others—some carrying invalids, others waiting for them to catch up, some rushing headlong, others rooted to the spot. When people looked back, outbreaks of fire threatened them from the front or the flanks. When they reached a neighboring quarter, that too was alight. . . . Finally, utterly at a loss as to what to avoid, or where to go, they filled the streets, or collapsed in the fields. . . . A widespread report had it that as the city was burning Nero entered his private theater and sang "The Fall of Troy," comparing the modern with the ancient calamity.[8]

With two-thirds of the city destroyed, Nero began rebuilding on an ambitious scale. For the first time, Rome had a city plan. Heights of houses, width of streets, building materials, and street layout were prescribed by

[8] Cited in Dudley, *Urbs Roma*, p. 19.

The Colosseum, Rome. The Colosseum, an amphitheater constructed by Vespasian on the ruins of Nero's Golden House, seated up to 50,000 spectators. Its floor could be flooded for miniature naval battles, but most spectacles were battles of gladiators among themselves and with wild animals. (Italian Government Travel Office photo.)

the government. The combination of large tenement houses, monumental areas, and parks was unchanged for the rest of imperial history. But for Nero the crowning achievement of the reconstruction was to be his own palace, the Golden House, of which a few fragments remain. For a site he cleared 125 acres in the heart of Rome, stretching from the Palatine across the site of the future Colosseum. It roused mixed feelings in all who saw it, but it was at least symbolic of how much the empire had changed in fifty years. According to Suetonius:

A huge statue of himself, 120 feet high, stood in the entrance hall; and the pillared arcade ran for a whole mile. An enormous pool, more like a sea than a pool, was surrounded by buildings made to resemble cities, and by a landscape garden consisting of ploughed fields, vineyards, pastures and woodlands where every variety of domestic and wild animal roamed about. Parts of the house were overlaid with gold and studded with precious stones and nacre. All the dining rooms had ceilings of fretted ivory, the panels of which could slide back and let a rain of flowers or of perfume from hidden sprinklers, shower upon his guests. The main dining-room was circular, and its roof revolved slowly, day and night in time with the sky. Sea water, or sulphur water, was always on top of the baths. When the palace had been decorated throughout in this lavish style, Nero dedicated it, and condescended to remark, "Good, now I can at last begin to live like a human being." [9]

He had little time to enjoy it. He not only had squandered the revenues of the state but had caused too many powerful people to be in danger themselves. Plots against him in Rome culminated in a revolt in the army in

[9] Suetonius, *Twelve Caesars,* pp. 224–25.

Spain, which marched on Rome. Lacking all support Nero took a dagger and remarking, ham actor to the end, "What an artist dies in me!" had to be helped to make his suicide effective.

The Flavian Emperors (69–96). In the chaos that followed Nero's death, several army commanders and the praetorian guard attempted to control the succession. The final victor was Vespasian, the commander of the army in the Near East, who sent a deputy to conquer Rome for him while he held up the Roman food supply from Egypt. The Flavian family (Vespasian, reigned 69–79, and his two sons, Titus, reigned 79–81, and Domitian, reigned 81–96) could not work fast enough to remove all traces of Nero. Much of the Golden House was smashed down. Earth was poured into its rooms to make a vaulted foundation for a new baths; the statues were transferred to a temple in the Forum; the lake was filled in, and the largest amphitheater in the world, the Colosseum, erected in its place. And on the Palatine, the Flavians built yet another palace, that took up the rest of Palatine Hill beyond the palaces of Augustus and Tiberius. Private homes were again razed and the area became a palace compound; and any future expansion had to be made by building enormous brick arches out from the sides of the hill to hold the new buildings. Domitian probably outdid Nero, with fountains, lakes, porticoes, domed dining halls, private arenas, and large baths for his concubines. Martial even wrote a poem declaring that if he received two invitations to dinner on the same night, from Domitian

Girls in Bikinis, Piazza Armerina, Sicily. This lively scene depicting an athletic contest is part of a large mosaic floor known as the "Room of the Ten Girls" in an imperial villa. (Italian Government Travel Office photo.)

and from the gods, he would reply: "Please find other people who would like to be guests in heaven; I prefer my Jupiter here on earth."

For a while the solid achievements of the Flavians kept the populace quiet. The senate was replenished with provincial families of sound abilities and mores; the army was satisfied with successful campaigns in Scotland and the Near East; and the frontier regions, with their borders secure, experienced new prosperity. Finances were restored, as provincial well-being enabled the imposition of new taxes. There was even the beginning of a state-financed system of education. Domitian, however, succumbed to the conspiracy complex that sooner or later affected all masters of the Palatine. He had the palace walls lined with polished, translucent stone so he could watch for assassins; and he embarked on a sadistic purge of suspected opposition. Cruelty provoked conspiracy; and Domitian in his turn was murdered in his own palace, in a plot headed by his wife and his own servants and backed by senators. Of the first ten emperors of Rome, seven had been murdered or had committed suicide!

The Five Good Emperors (96–180). Fortunately for Rome and its empire, for the next century it was governed by the so-called Five Good emperors, of whom three were unexceptional and two were great. Their rule provoked one of Edward Gibbon's most famous, and uncharacteristically appreciative, judgments: "If a man were called upon to fix the period in the history of the world during which the condition of the human race was most happy and prosperous, he would without hesitation name that which

Trajan Hunting Wild Boar. When Constantine erected his arch of triumph near the Colosseum, he economized by incorporating in its decoration earlier bas-reliefs from the dismantled arches of other emperors, such as this vigorous scene from the early second century. (Alinari photo.)

Marcus Aurelius Entering Rome in Triumph. (Museo Nuova nel Palazzo Conservatori, Rome. Alinari photo.)

elapsed from the accession of Nerva to the death of Aurelius. Their united reigns are possibly the only period in which the happiness of a great people was the sole object of government.'' [10]

However, although most of the empire did not feel it, there was almost constant war. Trajan (reigned 98–117) embarked on two great wars of aggression, against the Dacians in what is now Rumania, and in Armenia and Mesopotamia. With the spoils from both, he indulged in a new building spree in Rome, not on the Palatine but mostly in functional buildings, like aqueducts, bridges, harbors, and especially his great Forum. But the wars of the later emperors were all defensive. A strong wall was built in Britain to keep out the marauding Scots; an earthen rampart cut across Germany to bar the Germanic tribes; and the bloodiest fighting, in Palestine, occurred when provincial and religious opposition to Rome united in the Jews. And the whole reign of Marcus Aurelius (161–180), who preferred

---

[10] Edward Gibbon, *The Decline and Fall of the Roman Empire* (many editions), chap. 3.

philosophy to war, was a long struggle to fend off attacks along all the frontiers in Europe and Asia. The defense, however, was successful, and was the foundation of the domestic achievements of these years.

Perhaps the most striking change was the new prominence of the provinces. Two of the emperors were born in Spain, the family of another had migrated from southern France. All were prepared to extend the privilege of citizenship more widely. Closer supervision, especially as the result of widespread tours by several of the emperors, helped cut corruption and emphasize efficiency. A workable compromise was reached by using the local upper classes to govern for Rome, or by permitting self-governing cities of the Hellenistic world to retain many of their privileges; and these groups frequently became the missionaries for Rome. One popular Greek philosopher, living in Asia Minor, praised Rome in effulgent terms:

The coasts and interiors have been filled with cities, some newly founded, others increased under and by you. . . . As on holiday, the whole civilized world lays down the arms which were its ancient burden, and has turned to adornment and all glad thoughts—with power to realize them. All the other rivalries have left our cities, and this one contention holds them all, how each city may appear more beautiful and attractive. . . . Cities gleam with radiance and charm, the whole earth has been beautified like a garden. . . . Thus it is right to pity only those outside your hegemony—if indeed there are any—because they lose your blessings.[11]

After Marcus Aurelius, the great days of the imperial rulers were over. Certain danger signals finally appeared: voluntary limitation of population, plague brought in by the armies, financial weakness in the provincial government and dwindling funds in Rome, growing strength in the attacks on the frontiers, and a general lethargy in the Roman ruling class. It is symbolic that the only important buildings constructed in Rome for the next two-and-a-half centuries were two public baths, a shopping center, and a massive fortified wall. Commodus (reigned 180–192), the son of Marcus Aurelius, provided twelve years of indolent self-indulgence, in which he displayed his prowess as an archer, as an animal wrestler, and as a sadist. He was strangled by the praetorian guard while he was taking a bath in the palace. The throne was seized after further civil war by the commander of the armies on the Danube, Septimius Severus (reigned 193–211), a man of Carthaginian origins. Septimius was a soldier's emperor who devoted most of his reign to unproductive wars. His building was done largely in his native Africa, and he recruited the praetorian guard, many senators, and most of his administrators from the provinces. The city of Rome was losing its primacy. His son, Caracalla (reigned 211–217), deprived Roman citizenship of most of its value by giving it to all freemen in the empire, built the largest baths in the world, invaded Parthia, and was murdered during the campaign. From then until the establishment of a taut,

---

[11] Cited in Michael Grant, *The World of Rome* (Cleveland: World Publishing Co., 1960), p. 52.

Arch of Septimius Severus, Rome. Originally, arches of triumph were temporary structures erected for the victory procession of a Roman general. Many Roman emperors, however, erected one or more in stone, to illustrate their own victories. (Italian Government Travel Office photo.)

oriental-style despotism by Diocletian, there was almost uninterrupted chaos. Every emperor was picked by the army or the praetorian guard, and usually murdered by them. Thirty-seven emperors in all were proclaimed but only Aurelian made any mark—by building the great wall that helped prolong the city's safety. Order was eventually restored by two emperors from Illyria, which is now part of Yugoslavia: Diocletian (reigned 284–305), who built his home at Spalato (Split) on the Dalmatian coast, and Constantine (reigned 306–337), who officially moved the capital to Constantinople. After the third century of chaos, we must look elsewhere, to Constantinople, for the continuance of Roman civilization. In Rome, we can only trace the stages of decline.

The most rapturous acclamation of Rome's emperors was provided by its poets, its most scathing indictment by its historians. Both saw themselves fulfilling an important political role in imperial society; and it is for this reason that one understands better the triumphant creation of the greatest writers of Latin literature by considering them in the political context in which they wished to work rather than exiling them to some Parnassus where the reality of Roman life cannot reach.

THE POLITICAL MESSAGE OF ROME'S POETS AND HISTORIANS

The Poets of the Augustan Age. Virgil (70–19 B.C.), the greatest Latin poet, had begun his career with rhapsodies to the life of the countryside, first to the shepherd's idyll in the well-watered meadows of the Po valley where Virgil himself grew up, and then to the practical problems of farming itself. Virgil's *Georgics*, thought by some to be the finest poem ever written, talks about the diseases of cattle and the varieties of soil; but the poet, through his elegance and deep humanity, has transformed the theme into a call to the debased city to restore itself with rural values, the only remedy Virgil can see to the barbarism of the civil wars, and moreover to be aware of the loss all were suffering in the ruin of the Italian countryside.

This was the life which once the ancient Sabines led,
And Remus and his brother; this made Etruria strong,
Through this, Rome became the fairest thing on earth.[12]

In the *Aeneid,* on which he spent the last ten years of his life, he narrowly avoided writing a poem of political propaganda in support of Augustus. What saved him was his worship of Rome and of its traditional *virtus.* For the century past, *virtus* had come to mean winning personal fame as a form of immortality, as *virtú* was to mean again at the Italian Renaissance. Virgil brought back the virtue that demands *pietas,* to do one's duty to the gods, one's own country, and one's family; and, while idolizing Augustus in the poem, he set him a high standard to follow at the same time. The *Aeneid* is a hard poem for modern readers to enjoy, with its endless references to abstruse mythology, its insufferable gods and senseless killings. But one has to see the sensitive, sick poet struggling to set standards for an empire he regards as an essential stage in the slow climb of mankind toward a universal good or even a universal divinity; and at times one glimpses a quick way into the heart of a good man's thought, as when Aeneas suddenly experiences the pity of war:

Yes, Aeneas drove his strong sword
Right through the young man's body, and buried it there to the hilt.
It penetrated his light shield, frail armor for so aggressive
A lad, and the tunic his mother had woven of pliant gold,
And soaked it with blood from his breast.
Then the soul left the body,
Passing sadly through the air to the land of shadows.
But when Aeneas beheld the dying boy's look, his face—
A face that by now was strangely grey—he felt pity for him,
And a deep sigh escaped him.[13]

Virgil had brought the Roman state back to the eternal needs and duties of man. It was not political philosophy, but it came close.

[12] Virgil, *Georgics* II, 531–34, trans. in Gilbert Highet, *Poets in a Landscape* (London: Hamish Hamilton, 1957), p. 69.
[13] Cecil Day Lewis, *The Aeneid of Virgil* (London: Hogarth Press, 1952), pp. 232–33. Reprinted by permission of Hogarth Press and A. D. Peters and Company.

Even Horace (65–8 B.C.), the other great elegiac poet of the Augustan age, had a sharp political content in much of his poetry, and again the theme was the return to the old values and through them to internal peace. At its most blatant, it became: "I will fear neither civil war nor violent death while Caesar rules the earth." At its most scathing, it involved a splendid denunciation of the distasteful Roman population, as in his *Satires* and some of his *Odes:*

The fickle crowd, the false swearing courtesan,
They all move back, these friends, when our casks are drained
Of wine, and only dregs are left; too
Crafty are they to share our misfortunes. . . .
Alas, for shame, these wounds and these brother's woes!
From what have we refrained, this our hardened age?
What crime is left untried? From what, through
Fear of the gods, has our youth held back or
Restrained its hand? [14]

To Horace, the answer was for youth to dedicate itself again to the service of the state, in which alone the individual can achieve virtus. He ended with the most foreboding of sentiments, to be repeated for hundreds of years on countless gravestones: *Dulce et decorum pro patria mori.*

Seemly and sweet is death for one's native land
For death pursues the man who would flee from him,
Nor spares the knees and shrinking back of
Those of our youth unprepared for warfare. [15]

Horace will, however, be better remembered for the delicate complexity of his new poetic forms; in the Odes he worked out an intricate craftsmanship for adapting Greek meters to the more unbending Latin tongue. For fear of tying him to nothing but riling or exhortation, one should at least taste the humor he could bring to a love poem. Here, a lover is shut out by his mistress:

Though you dwelt by the Don, Lisa, and drank of it
And were wed to a harsh husband, you still might weep
To expose me, outstretched prone by your cruel doors,
To Aquilo's native winds.

She ignores his gifts, his prayers, and his pallor, however.

Lady, you are no more soft than the rigid oak,
Neither are you at heart gentler than Moorish snakes;

[14] From *The Odes of Horace,* by Helen Rowe Henze. Copyright 1961 by the University of Oklahoma Press, p. 67.
[15] Ibid., p. 119.

Not forever will my body be lying here
And enduring the rain of heaven! [16]

The Didactic Message of Rome's Historians. The historians found no such distraction in their pursuit of the city's lost virtues. Livy (59 B.C.–A.D. 17) belonged in the tradition of ancient historians who felt that a history book should not only relate facts but be great literature. Livy wrote a *History of Rome* in 142 books, all of which celebrate the virtus of earlier Romans, whose simple conception of the individual's role was to achieve glory by performance of great deeds on behalf of the state, in peace or war: "War no less than peace has its rules and we have learned to wage both with justice no less than courage. . . . I will conquer by Roman methods, by virtus, by labor and by arms." Morals, according to Livy, declined when riches began to abound, and it was the duty of the Augustan age to restore the moral tone. There is no lament for the loss of liberty in Livy, but for the loss of duty; and Livy's ideals, which were studied from his *History* by successive generations of the Roman elite, however little followed in practice created an idealized standard of political conduct to which all would pay lip service.

It was, however, by Tacitus (c. 56–123), the most subtly vindictive of all historians, that the emperors themselves, including Augustus, were tested and found wanting. His two great works, the *Annals,* on the Julio-Claudian emperors, and the *Histories,* on the Flavians, are a scintillating condemnation of one-man rule. "As I see it," he wrote, "the chief duty of the historian is this: to see that virtue is placed on record, and that evil men and evil deeds have cause to fear judgment at the bar of posterity." His excoriation reached its peak in his treatment of Tiberius, who symbolized in his view the almost inevitable degradation of monarchy into tyranny. Unlike the later sadists and madmen, such as Caligula and Nero, Tacitus saw in Tiberius a slow but relentless corruption by exercise of power. His last summation of Tiberius's career is a masterpiece of malice:

As a private citizen, or holding military command under Augustus, his conduct and his reputation were excellent. While Drusus and Germanicus lived, craft and equivocation provided a screen of virtues. While his mother was alive, Tiberius still showed good and bad qualities; while he had Sejanus to love (or fear), his cruelty was appalling but his perversions remained hidden. In his last phase, there was a great eruption of crime and vice: set free from shame and fear he stood out at long last in no other character but his own. [17]

But did Tacitus have an alternative to offer? He dismissed political theory very briefly. A mixed constitution in which the masses, nobility, and individuals share power, he wrote, "is easier to command than to create; or,

[16] Ibid., p. 139.
[17] Cited in Dudley, *World of Tacitus,* p. 82.

if created, its tenure of life is brief." If the masses dominated, one should "study the character of the masses and the methods of controlling them," a strikingly modern concept. If the nobility were in power, one needed "the most exact knowledge of the temper of the senate and the aristocracy." It was this form of government, refreshed by an infusion of new men like himself from outside Rome, that Tacitus approved. But such a restoration of the aristocratic republic was impossible, he saw, and as a result his history of one-man rule could be nothing but a long condemnation: "A series of savage mandates, of perpetual accusations, of traitorous friendships, of ruined innocents, of various causes and identical results—everywhere monotony of subject, and satiety." This was mock modesty, of course. The venom of Tacitus is still fresh on the page today.

If the political theorists of imperial Rome left little of lasting value, the exponents of civil law were extraordinarily fecund. The establishment of social order through a just set of rules and procedures for their administration was a permanent goal of the systematic Roman mind. And they succeeded so well that their concepts are still basic to the law of much of the Western world.

**ATTORNEYS
AND
JURISCONSULTS**

In Rome, the center of judicial life was in two splendid basilicas, the Basilica Aemilia and the Basilica Julia, built on each side of the open courtyard of the Forum where the assemblies of the people met. These two vast buildings were similar in size and decoration. Around the outside ran a two-story portico, lined with small shops. The Basilica Aemilia, we know, had a huge central nave, twelve yards wide and over eighty yards long, paved with colored marbles and lined with columns of African marble carved in spirals of acanthus leaves; and the Basilica Julia, begun by Julius Caesar and finished by Augustus, was even more colorful. Most of the meetings of the most important jury took place there. These cases, dealing with disputes over wills and inheritances of the rich and noble, led to some of the greatest legal battles; and spectators would pour in to listen and comment. Pliny described one case in which he appeared:

One hundred and eighty judges [jurors] were sitting, that being the total of the four panels. A huge number of counsel were engaged on either side: the benches were crowded: and the court, broad as it was, was encircled by a crowd of spectators standing several rows deep. Add to this that the tribunal was crowded, and the galleries were packed with men and women; they hung over in their eagerness to hear (which was hard) and to see (which was easy).[18]

The case was enough to attract a crowd—an eighty-year old patrician had disinherited his daughter after falling hopelessly in love with a younger woman who apparently had married him for the money. With Pliny's help the stepmother's plans were foiled.

[18] Cited in Dudley, *Urbs Roma,* p. 86.

In this supercharged atmosphere, in which every citizen was frequently called on to share in the burden of the law, as judge, juryman, or witness for his friends, and many indulged in litigation as a matter of habit, the Romans hammered out a consistent, effective body of law.

Evolution of Roman Law.   Law in Rome, as in many primitive cultures, was originally a set of customary rules whose existence from time immemorial was simply assumed; and it was the job of the king, then of the consuls, and even later of the emperors, to make them known in specific cases.   Law could therefore evolve as the rules were interpreted to meet changing circumstances.   In the middle of the fifth century B.C. a first attempt was made to write down the laws, in the Twelve Tables, which were put up for everyone to see in the Forum near the speakers' platform.   The Tables were still those of a rural society with strong religious sanctions frequently involving ritual punishments.   For stealing crops by night, the criminal was beaten to death with rods!   But during the republic a vast amount of legislation was enacted by the senate and the assemblies; the decisions of the magistrates and especially of the praetors, who were to supervise justice, became more highly developed; and a number of experts, called jurisconsults, gave opinions that slowly evolved into a complex body of legal commentary that in practice came to be accepted as law.   A serious attempt to bring order to this growing mass of complex rules was made in the second century B.C.; but the emperor Hadrian inaugurated the finest period of Roman jurisprudence by ordering the codification of the praetors' law in a perpetual edict to be observed by all magistrates.   By the end of the second century A.D., Rome already had its legal textbooks for budding lawyers, and one way to advancement as a lawyer was to publish learned commentaries on the law.

Character of Roman Law.   All this development would not concern us greatly if the Romans had not developed good law.   The laws of the Assyrians or the Babylonians strike us as quaint and crude.   The Romans, however, seriously tackled the problem of regulating disputes that arose between persons living side by side in a complex society, and they established many principles of lasting value.   It is important to distinguish some of the differences from our way of thinking.   All men were not equal before the law.   A man's rights were dependent on his status—slave, born free, freed, Roman citizen, resident alien, child under guardianship, and so on.   Slaves were not persons and lacked legal rights, even though the emperors began to lay down some rules for their physical protection. Fathers of families exercised defined powers over their children that lasted throughout life, and in theory until Hadrian's reign the father had the right of life and death.   There was little freedom of political action or guarantee of free speech, and most of the rights zealously preserved and for which there was a genuine legal remedy were the property rights of the upper

Bust of Hadrian. This bronze bust was found in the River Thames under London Bridge. Hadrian inspected the imperial defenses in Britain in 122, and ordered the erection of a stone and earthen rampart across northern England to block the incursions of the Scots. (Photo copyright by the Trustees of the British Museum.)

classes. What the Roman lawyers achieved was first the recognition that all men of the same status enjoyed equal rights under the law; and under the influence of Stoicism in the second century, they were moving toward the idea of *ius gentium,* an "international law" achieved by human reason and applicable to all men. They had recognized the idea that guilt as well as consequences of an act should be considered in determining punishment, and that it was better for the guilty to go free than the innocent suffer. And by the development of private property law, to which most of their efforts were directed, they provided the mechanism for the complex economic and social structure of an empire of seventy million people. The law that was elaborated in Rome in the second century was developed in Constantinople under Justinian in the sixth century, passed on to the Catholic Church in the canon law, applied through most of Europe in the Middle Ages, and absorbed into the present law of many countries of continental Europe and of their former colonies overseas.

Posterity's admiration was not however shared by all Roman citizens! One will that has survived begins: "I, Lucius Titus, have written this my testament without any lawyer, following my own natural reason rather than excessive and miserable diligence." It is hard for a layman to love the law, even for a Roman layman.

Neptune Mosaic, Herculaneum. Neptune, associated by the Romans with Poseidon, the Greek god of the sea, was frequently portrayed in mosaic on the walls of private homes, perhaps because the Romans had originally considered him the god of fresh water rather than salt water. (Italian Government Tourist Office photo.)

PRIESTS AND PHILOSOPHERS

Roman State Religion.   Temples, not law courts or parliament chambers, dominated the heart of Rome.   Religion—and superstition—was all-pervasive. From the early days, Romans had enjoyed the company of their own comfortable, household gods, which were disembodied spiritual forces that accompanied all their daily actions. Vesta protected the hearth, Janus the doorway, the Penates the storeroom, and hundreds of others watched over stump, rivulet, rainstorm, or planting. Peasants had to look after their own gods; and the Roman state immediately saw the benefits, and the necessity, of a state religion. In its origins, the state religion undoubtedly represented the feeling of the government that among its many duties, one of the most important was to maintain the harmony between human beings and the divine order; this was a complicated task involving specialists employed by the state to master the difficult formulas that assured the city's well-being at the hands of the gods. Receptive as ever, the Roman state took all the native, anthropomorphic spirits and gave them official status. Vesta became the goddess of the common hearth of the whole Roman people, and a perpetual flame was kept burning in her temple in the Forum as a symbol of the Roman home. From the Etruscans, the Romans took the mighty triad of Jupiter, Juno, and Minerva. Jupiter, the most powerful god in Rome, was the god of light, thunder, and rain, the source of state authority, and the special guardian of Rome itself. Juno was a kindlier creature, the goddess of women and all their manifold activities, especially weddings and childbirth. Minerva was the goddess of arts and crafts, which came to include musicians and actors, and to even to extend to all wisdom.

The first large temple erected on the Capitol Hill was for these three deities, the so-called Capitoline Triad; and for the rest of Roman history all solemn religious processions as well as the triumphs of victorious generals wound their way across the Forum along the Via Sacra (Holy Road) and up the side of the Capitol Hill to the seat of Jupiter and his accompanying goddesses.

Other gods were added as they made themselves useful. Two divine youths on horseback were seen to intervene decisively in the Romans' victory over the Etruscans in 496 B.C., and simultaneously announce the victory in Rome. A temple was at once erected to the divine twins, Castor and Pollux, across the street from Vesta's hearth. Acquaintance with the Greek cities of the south, perhaps through the Etruscans, led to the absorption of most of the Greek gods, especially of Apollo, whose invaluable capacities included archery, medicine, music, prophecy, philosophy, and purification. He helped fend off plague, and won the battle of Actium for Augustus. To simplify matters, most Roman gods were assumed to be different from Greek gods only in name—Neptune was Poseidon, Mercury was Hermes, Minerva was even Athena. The state religion, for all its staid moralistic character, permitted some extraordinary innovations. In the third century, the worship of Cybele, a goddess from Asia Minor was permitted, even though her rites were carried out by eunuch priests who in a frenzy of blood lust provoked by wild ritual dances cut themselves all over with knives. Cybele's stone was brought to the Palatine Hill, and a temple erected, a few yards from the site of Augustus's future home.

A large priesthood administered the state religion. At its head was the *pontifex maximus,* elected by the people, who picked another eight members of the principal college of priests. But there were many other colleges for separate functions, like blessing foreign relations, or bringing in the New Year by dancing. The priests alone knew the ritual formulas, drew up the calendar of religious festivals, and told whether a particular day was auspicious for public business. Indeed, a well-placed bribe to a priest could close down the law courts when an inconvenient charge had been brought. The most pervasive influence of the priests however was through augury; for while many religions have specialized in consoling for past misfortune, the Roman priesthood could predict the future. The art had been a long time in the fashioning, possibly since the Babylonians; but the augurs claimed to be able to tell from the flight of birds or the appearance of the entrails of a sacrificed animal, whether a particular action would have a favorable outcome. The liver in particular was an infallible portent. Almost every natural phenomenon, however, had to be watched, for the Roman moved in a world full of supernatural powers. Julius Caesar should have known better than to go to the senate on the Ides of March, since he had dreamed the night before that he was sailing in the clouds to shake hands with Jupiter, and a little wren, with a sprig of laurel in its beak, had been torn to pieces by a pursuing group of birds in the Pompeian Assembly room. Caesar had been warned directly by the augur Spurinna that he was in danger until the Ides of March were over. Suetonius recorded the famous scene as Caesar entered the senate: "Several victims were then sacrificed, and despite consistently unfavorable omens, he entered the House, deriding Spurinna as a false prophet. 'The Ides of March have come,' he said. 'Ay, they have come,' replied Spurinna, 'but they have not yet gone.'"

Similarly unfortunate signs preceded the murder of Claudius, as Tacitus records:

A series of prodigies in the following year indicated changes for the worse. Standards and soldiers' tents were set on fire from the sky. A swarm of bees settled on the pediment of the Capitoline temple. Half-bestial children were born, and a pig with hawk's claws. A portent too was discerned in the losses suffered by every official post: a quaestor, aedile, tribune, praetor, and consul had all died within a few months. Agrippina was particularly frightened—because Claudius had remarked in his cups that it was his destiny first to endure his wife's misdeeds, and then to punish them. She decided to act quickly.[19]

No less important for the safety of the city were the vestal virgins, who kept alive the sacred flame of the hearth and looked after other precious objects, including a statue that had fallen from the sky at Troy and been brought to Rome by Aeneas. The vestals, usually six in number, had been chosen at an age between six and ten, and devoted thirty years of virginity to their priesthood. If they ceased to be chaste, they were buried alive. During their priesthood, they lived together in a lovely colonnaded home just below the Palatine Hill, in the heart of the Forum, amid fountains and reflecting pools. They had special seats at all state functions, including the gladiatorial games; and at the end of thirty years were given a large dowry and permitted to marry. Most did not.

This whole apparatus of official religion was welcomed, even by nonbelievers, as the cement of the state, the supernatural stimulus to patriotism. Augustus deliberately turned it to his own advantage. He became pontifex maximus himself, repaired the ruined temples, built new ones to gods related to himself, such as Apollo, and sought to revive the veneration for the old religion that had lapsed during the civil wars. He set an important precedent, however, by erecting a temple to the *deified* Julius Caesar, on the spot where his body had been cremated. Emperor worship became an important asset both to future emperors and to the cohesion of the state. Augustus refused to be considered a god during his lifetime, but was deified after his death, as most other emperors were, except those the senate specifically condemned. It thus became possible to name as traitors to the state any religious sect, like the Christians, that refused to worship at the shrines of the divine emperors.

[19] Tacitus, *Annals* I, 28; XII, 64, cited in Grant, *World of Rome,* p. 46.

THE ROMAN GODS

Official State Religion

CAPITOL TRIAD

> Jupiter: *God of day, controller of thunder and lightning, guardian of Rome. Greek Zeus.*
>
> Juno: *Wife of Jupiter, goddess of women. Greek Hera.*
>
> Minerva: *Patroness of arts and crafts, wisdom, doctors, and musicians. Greek Athena.*

Mars: *God of agriculture, then of war, special protector of Rome. Greek Ares.*

Saturn: *God of newly sown seed, then of agriculture. Greek Cronus.*

Venus: *Goddess of fertility. Greek Aphrodite.*

Ceres: *Goddess of harvest, and of plebeians. Greek Demeter.*

Apollo: *God of emperors. Greek Apollo, name unchanged.*

Mercury: *God of merchants and robbers. Greek Hermes.*

Diana: *Goddess of light, moon, women, and hunting. Greek Artemis.*

Castor and Pollux: *Divine twins, associated with sons of Zeus and Leda. Protectors of Rome and patrons of equites.*

Household Deities, or Numina

Janus: *God of beginnings, guardian of the doorway.*

Vesta: *Goddess of hearth.*

Di Penates: *Keepers of the storehouse, deities of the home.*

Di Manes: *Kindly shades, spirits of ancestors.*

N.B.   Varro said the Romans had thirty thousand gods!

Worship of Dionysus, Isis, and Mithras.   This state religion was not exclusive. The Roman state had no objection if its subjects wanted to worship other religions as well. From the second century B.C., many did, seeking an emotional release that the ritualized official religion could not give. Many simply practiced magic. To hurt your enemies, it was quite common to stick nails in images of them, or to burn part of their clothes. Others followed astrology, worshipping the sun and moon, studying the influence of the seven planets, and especially the twelve signs of the zodiac. But from the second century B.C. outbreaks of religious emotionalism began to occur on such a scale that the senate clamped down on their excesses. Among the first to be introduced was worship of the Greek god Dionysus, who was identified with the Roman god of the vine, Bacchus. The initiates indulged in wild orgiastic rites, in which they submitted to thrashing for purification, and even at times went so far as human sacrifice. The great attraction was the promise of happy afterlife for all the miserable of this earth. The appeal of the worship of the Egyptian goddess Isis, which was the most popular of all Roman religions in the first two centuries of the Empire, was its promise of immortality through union with the divine. Isis, a sweet dignified woman, enjoyed musical processions, with slow lines of linen-clad priests intoning hymns and playing flutes and tambourines. She was the universal mother, the shield against demons, and the pardoner of the penitent. Her attraction is most graphically portrayed in Apuleius's novel, *The Golden Ass,* the picaresque masterpiece by an African lawyer. Lucius, roaming the world in search of magic, unfortunately uses the wrong ointment in a witch's house, and is turned into an ass. After innumerable adventures, most of them unpleasant, he gallops off to the sea and falls asleep by the shore.

Not long afterwards I awoke in sudden terror. A dazzling full moon was rising from the sea. It is at this secret hour that the Moon-goddess, sole sovereign of mankind, is possessed of her greatest power and majesty. She is the shining deity by whose divine influence not only all beasts, wild and tame, but all inanimate things as well, are invigorated, whose ebbs and flows control the rhythm of all bodies whatsoever, whether in the air, on earth or below the sea.

Lucius begs Isis to end his sufferings, restore him to human shape, and send him back home, or else give him the gift of death.

I had scarcely closed my eyes before the apparition of a woman began to rise from the middle of the sea with so lovely a face that the gods themselves would have fallen down in adoration of it. . . . Her long thick hair fell in tapering ringlets on her lovely neck, and was crowned with an intricate chaplet in which was woven every kind of flower. Just above her brow shone a round disc, like a mirror, or like the bright face of the moon, which told me who she was. Vipers rising from the left-hand and right-hand partings of her hair supported this disc, with ears of corn bristling beside them. . . . All the perfumes of Arabis floated into my nostrils as the Goddess deigned to address me: "You see me here, Lucius, in answer to your prayer. I am Nature, the universal mother, mistress of all elements. . . . Weep no more, lament no longer; the hour of deliverance, shone over by my watchful light, is at hand."[20]

The softness of Isis came up against a tough competitor in the first century A.D., when the cult of Mithras was brought into Italy, probably by soldiers who had served in Asia Minor. Mithras was an Iranian god, born in a cave in the rocks at the will of the sun god. His greatest deed was to slay a bull after a tremendous struggle by plunging a knife into its throat, whereupon the earth was fertilized, plants grew to nourish man, and the first human beings were born. As the story became more elaborate, Mithras fought the

Head of a Roman Priest of Isis, 2nd Century A.D. (Los Angeles County Museum of Art. William Randolph Hearst Collection.)

[20] Apuleius, *The Golden Ass,* trans. Robert Graves (Harmondsworth, England: Penguin, 1950), pp. 268–70.

perils that plague the earth, overcoming the evil spirit, and finally ascended
to heaven in the sun's chariot. The devotees usually met in an underground cave such as the one found beneath St. Clement's in Rome, which
represented the cave where Mithras was born and where a statue of Mithras
killing the bull was placed. Only men could join. Vicious initiation tests,
including torture, were applied. Strict rules of personal conduct had to be
observed. It was a soldier's religion, and shrines to Mithras have been
found in all the garrisons of the Empire.

Victory over all the other emotional religions would eventually go to
Christianity. (See Chapter 5.) But when the empire was at its height, the
Christians were regarded by most Romans as a small, unappealing group
of fanatics. Cybele, Isis, and Mithras held the field.

Epicureanism and Stoicism.   There was always a small intellectual elite
who regarded the state religion with approval only because it kept the
common people obedient. "The whole base throng of gods assembled by
a superstition coeval with time," wrote Seneca the Younger, "we must
worship without forgetting that we do it to set an example, not because they
exist." And the elite was equally repelled by the emotionalism, and also by
the lack of class barriers, in the newer religions. They therefore turned to
philosophy for guidance, with the same pragmatic genius they brought to all
their activity. The Romans wanted something they could use, and their
philosophers provided it. Once more, however, they appropriated ideas
developed by that far more creative people, the Greeks, and made them
practical. Lucretius (96–55 B.C.) took the ideas of Epicurus, and created
the classic statement of Epicureanism, his long poem, *De Rerum Naturae*
(On the Nature of Things). Fear, he argued, was destroying men's lives,
especially such unwarranted fear as terror of the gods (who had no relationship to men) or of death (which was not followed by an afterlife). The only
reality was physical sensation, the greatest happiness the experience of
unspoiled nature—trees, grass, streams, moonlight, birdsong. In the
operation of nature, mechanistically conceived as a constant flow of atoms,
he saw the boundaries of man's existence. The implication for one's daily
life were obvious: ignore religion, shun moral causes, avoid involvement,
seek mental peace and quiet. It is the passion with which Lucretius recom-
mends dispassion that makes him a great poet, and gives his verse such a
modern flavor.

*Do you not see that nature is clamoring for two things only, a body free from
pain, a mind released from worry and fear, for the enjoyment of pleasurable sensa-
tions? So we find that the requirements of our bodily nature are few indeed, no
more than is necessary to banish pain. . . . Nature does not miss luxuries when
men recline in company on the soft grass by a running stream under the branches
of a tall tree and refresh their bodies pleasurably at small expense.*[21]

[21] Lucretius, *De Rerum Naturae* II, 16–21, 23, 29 ff., trans. R. C. Trevelyan, cited in Grant, *World of Rome*, p. 19.

Roman governments were of necessity unfriendly to the spread of such debilitating ideas among a people with an empire to conquer and administer. The Greek Epicureans had been expelled from Rome in the second century B.C. for enticing the youths away from the military exercises of the Campus Martius, and in the time of Augustus's religious revival it was unwise to announce one's admiration of Lucretius. He was forgotten until the Italian Renaissance rediscovered his power; but he has never been so thoroughly appreciated as in the twentieth century.

Stoicism, especially as expounded by Seneca (2 B.C.–A.D. 65), became the commonly accepted belief of the Roman upper classes in the second century A.D. Seneca, born in Spain, had moved to Rome where he had a career of sensational variety: philosophical study in the best literary circles, serious illness and years of convalescence in the hothouse atmosphere of Alexandria, promising political career interrupted by banishment to Corsica, return as tutor to the future emperor Nero followed by five years' guardianship, in which he ran the Roman Empire as a philosopher-king, dismissal, conspiracy, and state-ordered suicide. A career, in short, that required more than a normal dose of Stoicism. In all these vicissitudes, Seneca developed a noble message for the man who must face the worst of life's challenges. The two most important things a man possessed could not fall into the control of others. Money, goods, office, power, could all be taken away, and one should not become attached to them. But one's own mind and universal Nature, a kind of divine providence that existed in all things, could not be affected by the actions of others. Moreover, Nature or Providence was benevolent to man. It recognized an essential equality and brotherhood in all human beings, even in slaves: "We are members of one great body. Nature has made us relatives. She planted in us a mutual love, and fitted us for a social life. . . . You must live for your neighbor if you would live for yourself."[22]

In all the inhumanity of Roman life, into which we are about to plunge, the words of the Stoics blow like a clean breeze from the country. It was a pity that their ideals were not more practiced.

BREAD AND CIRCUSES

The Everyday Life of the Proletariat. For the great mass of Rome's inhabitants, slave or free, everyday life was a harsh struggle for survival in conditions of noisome squalor. The great intellectual achievements in law or literature and the physical achievements in engineering or architecture brought few benefits to the poor. Most Romans lived in blocks of tenement houses, six to ten stories high, housing up to two hundred people in narrow, cubicle-like rooms. Water available at city fountains had to be carried through the streets and up long flights of stairs; garbage and sewage was flung in unsanitary heaps at the bottom of stairwells. Great outbreaks of typhoid, typhus, and cholera were inevitable in these

[22] Ibid., p. 196.

conditions, and serious plagues broke out at least two or three times a century. Malaria was ever present even until the end of the nineteenth century. Until Augustus ordered cremation, dead bodies of people and animals were piled in enormous pits on the edge of the city, poisoning the air and feeding the epidemics. Ordinary comforts were few and far between. Sleep itself was hard to obtain, since the streets reechoed all night to the sound of carts that had been forbidden to circulate in the narrow thoroughfares of the city during the day. Perhaps one-fifth of the city's population, that is, up to two hundred thousand people, relied on government handouts of bread for their main sustenance, while thousands of others sought support as clients of the great families. The destitute arrived in the morning at their patron's house with a basket, to pick up the food he would hand out; but most patrons came to prefer a small payment of six and a half sesterces. Work itself was in short supply for the freemen of the city's vast proletariat, especially as their numbers were constantly augmented from the countryside and the demobilized armies.

The Public Games. In these circumstances, the proletariat turned for entertainment to the free public games that, by the middle of the first century, were being held on 93 days a year. At first the games had been intended as a salutary display of public punishment of criminals, who were thrown to wild animals; but the games increased rapidly in complexity and expense. Theatrical performances were given, on a competitive

Air View of the Ruins of Pompeii. Pompeii, a flourishing port city on the Bay of Naples, was buried in a layer of cinders and ashes twenty feet deep by the eruption of Vesuvius in 79 A.D. Preserved almost intact for eighteen centuries by the volcanic ash, Pompeii now provides extraordinary insight into the character of Roman urban life. (Italian Government Travel Office photo.)

The Arena of Verona. Roman provincial cities were provided with all the amenities of the capital itself. Verona has the remains of a large theater as well as this well-preserved arena, built in the first century. (Italian Government Travel Office photo.)

basis as in Athens; but the size of the theaters, which accommodated only about twenty thousand people, show that they were not the chief magnet for the crowds; and almost no new tragedies were written after the time of Claudius. Far more popular were the chariot races, the most important of which were held in the vast Circus Maximus below the Palatine Hill. This oval arena seated two hundred fifty thousand people; and the emperor attended the games from a high balcony that Augustus had erected on the side of the Palatine Hill. The crowds followed the exploits of the popular charioteers with a passion that Pliny the Younger found execrable: "Such favor, such weighty influence, hath one worthless [charioteer's] tunic—I say nothing of the vulgar herd, more worthless than the tunic—but with certain grave personages. When I observe such men thus insatiably fond of so silly, so low, so uninteresting, so common an entertainment, I congratulate myself that I am insensible to these pleasures." The attraction of the gladiatorial games was even more debased, however. Teams of gladiators, consisting mostly of slaves and the most desperate of the poor, were trained by contractors and hired out for the games both in Rome and the provincial cities. They used specialized weapons. Samnites carried a sword and shield, Thracians a dagger and buckler, others called *retiarii* specialized in net and trident. Sometimes they fought with animals, the more exotic the better. Some provinces saw whole species wiped out to provide Rome's amusement. The hippopotamus disappeared from Nubia, the elephant from North Africa, and the tiger from Hyrcania. Augustus boasted that he gave twenty-six shows of African animals, in which thirty-five hundred were slaughtered. Often the gladiators fought in duels to the death. But the slaughter was soon extended to include the massacre of such undesirables as arsonists and Christians. One of the most impressive of all Roman buildings, the Colosseum, was erected by Vespasian and Titus for these games. It could seat forty-five thousand people, who were protected from rain or sun by a huge canvas awning. Its equipment provided for every kind of spectacle, from a sea battle with real ships to the slaughter of five thousand animals in one day.

It was this city, "Babylon, the harlot of the seven hills, the great city that holds sway over the kings of the earth," that the Christian John assigned to damnation in the book of the Apocalypse:

Her sins are piled as high as heaven, and God has not forgotten her crimes. Pay her back in her own coin, repay her twice over for her deeds! Double for her the strength of the potion she mixed! . . . The kings of the earth who committed fornication with her and wallowed in her luxury will weep and wail over her, as they see the smoke of her conflagration. They will stand at a distance, for horror at her torment, and will say, "Alas, alas for the great city, the mighty city of Babylon! In a single hour your doom has struck!" The merchants of the earth also will weep and mourn for her, because no one any longer buys their cargoes, cargoes of gold and silver, jewels and pearls, cloths of purple and scarlet, silks and fine linens; all kinds of scented woods, ivories, and every sort of thing made of costly woods, bronze, iron, or marble; cinnamon and spice, incense, perfumes and frankincense; wine, oil, flour and wheat, sheep and cattle, horses, chariots, slaves, and the lives of men. "The fruit you longed for," they will say, "is gone from you; all the glitter and the glamor are lost, never to be yours again!"[23]

SUGGESTED READING

Augustan Rome is successfully re-created in two short studies, Henry T. Rowell's *Rome in the Augustan Age* (1962), which deals at length with the physical appearance of the city and Thomas W. Africa, *Rome of the Caesars* (1965), which prefers to let the city come alive through an extremely variegated group of its citizens, including a wizard. The ancient historians themselves, however, are a splendidly entertaining introduction to their city, especially Suetonius (cited in chap. 3); Tacitus, in Michael Grant's translation, *The Annals of Imperial Rome*

[23] *Revelation of John*, 18: 5–23, cited in Thomas W. Africa, *Rome of the Caesars* (New York: Wiley, 1965), p. 20.

(1959); Donald R. Dudley's *The World of Tacitus* (1968) is exciting reading, while his *Urbs Roma* uses quotations from the ancient writers as background for good photographs of the imperial city. Juvenal's scathing comments are well translated by Rolfe Humphries in *The Satires of Juvenal* (1958). Many translations are available of the bawdy but revealing novel of Petronius, *The Satyricon,* and of *The Golden Ass* of Apuleius with its great evocation of the goddess Isis.

Augustus's account of his own exploits, which was carved on a number of temple walls in different parts of the empire, can be read in *Res Gestae Divi Augusti* (1924), translated by Frederick W. Shipley. The major documents of his reign are collected by V. Ehrenberg and A. H. M. Jones, in *Documents Illustrating the Reigns of Augustus and Tiberius* (2nd ed. 1955). The better biographies of the emperors include T. Rice Holmes, *The Architect of the Roman Empire* (2 vols., 1928–31) and John Buchan's very popular *Augustus* (1937); D. Earl, *The Age of Augustus* (1968); F. B. Marsh, *The Reign of Tiberius* (1931); J. P. V. D. Balsdon, *The Emperor Gaius* (1934) on Caligula; V. Scramuzza, *The Emperor Claudius* (1940); M. Hammond, *The Antonine Monarchy* (1959).

The administration of the empire is analyzed in several sound studies by A. H. M. Jones, including *The Cities of the Eastern Roman Provinces* (1937), and *The Later Roman Empire, 284–602* (1964), and in G. H. Stevenson, *Roman Provincial Administration* (1949). J. P. V. D. Balsdon, *Rome: The Story of an Empire* (1970) is comprehensive, up-to-date, and very well illustrated. Studies in depth of individual provinces are often the most revealing of the pitfalls of imperial expansion, as well as Rome's great achievement in stamping its own character on distant peoples. See especially Sheppard Frere, *Britannia* (1967); J. Wilkes, *Dalmatia* (1969); O. Brogan, *Roman Gaul* (1953); D. Magie, *Roman Rule in Asia Minor* (1950); and the classic study published originally in 1886 by Theodor Mommsen, *The Provinces of the Roman Empire* (1968).

The economic structure of the empire is described in another classic work by M. Rostovtzeff, *Social and Economic History of the Roman Empire* (1957). For the more important aspects of Roman commerce, see J. Innes Miller, *The Spice Trade of the Roman Empire* (1969); M. P. Charlesworth, *Trade Routes and Commerce in the Roman Empire* (1926); and Tenney Frank, ed., *Economic Survey of Ancient Rome* (1933–40), especially volume 5. The military forces are portrayed in G. Webster, *The Roman Imperial Army of the First and Second Centuries A.D.* (1969) and C. G. Starr, *The Roman Imperial Navy, 31 B.C.–A.D. 324* (1960).

Fortunately, excellent translations are available of the major Roman poets. Among them are Rolfe Humphries's edition of Virgil, *The Aeneid* (1951) or the looser translation by the English poet C. Day Lewis (1952); and Helen Rowe Henze's version of Horace, *The Odes* (1961). The best introduction to Roman poetry is Gilbert Highet's *Poets in a Landscape* (1957), a sensitive re-creation of the environment of the Augustan age. The visual achievements of the Roman architect and engineer can be assessed in M. Wheeler, *Roman Art and Architecture* (1964) and H. Kähler, *The Art of Rome and Her Empire* (1963).

Rome's religious beliefs are described in detail by H. J. Rose, *Ancient Roman Religion* (1949) and R. M. Ogilvie, *The Romans and Their Gods* (1969), while the mystery religions are the subject of F. Cumon's *Oriental Religions in Roman Paganism* (1956).

The influence of Roman society on the evolution of its law is traced in J. Crook, *Law and Life of Rome* (1967). F. Schulz, *A History of Roman Legal Science* (1946) stays more closely to his brief.

Finally, Jérôme Carcopino's *Daily Life in Ancient Rome* (1940) provides a fascinating glimpse into the down-to-earth realities of Roman life, and Michael Grant's *The World of Rome* (1960) brings new life to a masterly synthesis of imperial politics and society.

5
WESTERN EUROPE ON THE THRESHOLD OF THE MIDDLE AGES, 300-600

The three centuries following the reign of Diocletian were not marked by the decline and fall of the Roman Empire. They were the period when the western part of the Roman Empire passed out of the control of Rome and when Rome itself ceased to be an imperial capital. The richest, most populated, and most cultured part of the Roman Empire, however, that is to say its eastern half, remained prosperous and powerful, and retained control of approximately the same territory as under Augustus until the Moslem conquests of the late seventh century. What one saw in these three centuries was therefore the continuation of the Roman Empire from a new capital, namely Constantinople (see Chapter 6). In the western part of the empire, while the control of Rome and the distinctive characteristics of Roman society were slowly dissipating, two vital new influences were introduced, giving rise to a distinctively new society and culture, which we call medieval. Those two influences were the rise of the Catholic Church and the invasion and settlement of the barbarian tribes. These centuries saw the formulation, in the eastern part of the empire, of the type of government, the economic and social system, the religious orthodoxy, and the cultural principles that transformed the Graeco-Roman culture of the eastern Roman Empire into a distinctively different society and culture, which we call Byzantine.

In looking at this period, which has traditionally been treated as the coming of the Dark Ages, we must therefore avoid two dangerous distortions of focus. One is exclusive concentration on the western part of the Roman Empire, because this leads us to accept the view of universal decline, whereas the most important section of the empire was going from strength

Carved Doors, Santa Sabina, Rome. 5th Century. (Alinari photo.)

to strength. The other is the notion of a sudden cataclysmic decline into barbarism in the west. The Germanic tribes brought far more than flame and sword to Europe. They brought new constructive ideas—for example, the ability to colonize the forest lands of central Europe and Britain—and a respect for Roman culture. And the Catholic Church prospered in the absence of Roman imperial authority, so that by the end of the fifth century it had established the basis of a new unity of thought, a capable administration, and a prestigious role in the new society.

THE CRISIS OF THE THIRD CENTURY

The crisis of the Roman Empire from which both medieval and Byzantine civilizations finally emerged began in the third century. The period of the Roman peace, that had begun with Augustus and survived through the reign of Marcus Aurelius, ended with Aurelius's mistake in naming his own son Commodus as emperor (reigned 180–192). The brutality and incompetence of Commodus, which led to his own murder, flung the empire back into the same sort of troubles that it had undergone in the last century of the republic. During the third century, all the causes of the decline of the western part of the Roman Empire became blatant, and though they were diagnosed and temporarily checked by the authoritarian reforms of the emperors Diocletian and Constantine at the end of the century, these deep-seated sources of decay proved fatal in the fifth century to the continuance in western Europe of the Roman Empire. As a result, in the fifth century, western Europe, including Rome, ceased to be a part of the Roman Empire.

Political and Economic Problems of the Empire. The most obvious cause of decay in the empire was the breakdown of the constitutional system invented by Augustus. Augustus had struck an uneasy compromise with the senators and knights, that is, with the aristocracy and the gentry, giving them a privileged status in a society governed by a largely civilian bureaucracy under an absolute emperor, in return for their collaboration in commanding the army and governing the provinces. During most of the third century, however, the army chose and overthrew the emperors, especially during the fifty-year period of military anarchy from 235 to 284, during which all but one of the twenty-six emperors that reigned died violently. One emperor supposedly advised his sons, "Stick together, pay the soldiers, and forget everything else." The emperors resembled the soldiers who picked them—tough, cruel, venal, reckless, and short-sighted. The army too had ceased to be Roman. It was recruited mostly from the frontier provinces, where the veneer of Roman culture was most superficial, or from among the barbarian tribes who were threatening the empire in the north and northeast. The army exhibited corruption by forcing into power generals who were incompetent to run the central government, and overthrowing those few who were competent before they could enforce a consistent policy. They also added to the economic distress by demanding a larger and larger share of the state's revenues in wages and special gifts, and allowed internal order to break down. Even within the empire no individual felt safe. "Behold the roads closed by brigands, the seas blocked by pirates, the bloodshed and the horror and the universal strife," wrote Saint Cyprian. "The world drips with mutual slaughter, and murder, considered a crime when perpetrated by individuals, is regarded as virtuous when committed publicly."

Provincial government broke down with the collapse of the imperial authority. The success of the empire in romanizing the western provinces had been due above all to the planting of cities, where a wealthy middle class had gladly taken over the duties of municipal administration. The grant of citizenship to almost all free-born provincials had, however, made Roman citizenship less of a privilege for the provincial elite, who were also alienated by growing taxation and administrative interference from Rome. So in the third century the urban middle class became increasingly unwilling to work for the central government in the collection of taxes, or to use their own wealth to beautify their cities or run public games and festivals. The decline of the provincial cities, on whose prosperity the Roman peace had largely depended, was accelerated by the debasement of the currency and by a general breakdown of trade. Long-distance commerce with the East—the purchases of jewels and spices from India, and silk from China especially—was decreased in volume by chaotic transport conditions and lack of money for payment. Manufacturing in the old established cities was reduced, for example in glass and pottery, with the foundation of industries in the northern provinces, such as Gaul, Britain, and Germany. No effort was made to develop a market among the poorer classes, or beyond the frontiers of the empire. It was a luxury trade that declined, however, since the goods manufactured in Italy itself, such as pottery, cloth, or weapons, were mostly small-scale craft products. The real surplus of manufactured goods was produced in the eastern sections of the empire, in cities of Asia Minor and Syria, that manufactured bronze, pottery, linens, ornaments, paper, and glassware; and this trade continued within the eastern section during the western part's decline. Also, plague that was brought into the empire by the Germanic tribes, as well as the older established curse of malaria, cut the population of both city and country by perhaps as much as a third.

When the western section of the empire ceased to be a civilization of cities, the imperial government was unable to find an alternative source of strength in the countryside. Most of the agricultural land had been divided up into huge estates, and small peasant farmers who had been the strength of the early Roman republic had virtually disappeared. The estate was an almost completely self-sufficient and self-governing unit. It manufactured all its own tools and clothes. It even had its own prison. The best part of the estate was kept by the landowner for himself and worked by slaves. But most of the land was leased to tenants, called *coloni,* who paid part of the harvest and certain personal services to the landlord. Under the colonate, there was no improvement in farming tools or methods, nor any production for open market; and a form of class inferiority had been institutionalized that had turned the Roman Empire into a rigid and static "caste system." One might add that the fall in agricultural production in the third century has also been attributed by some historians to a change in climate, a reduction in rainfall supposedly producing drought and impoverishment of the soil; but satisfactory proof of this has not yet been adduced.

Reforms of Diocletian. The western section of the empire was thus in such trouble that it might well have fallen to the barbarian tribes at the end of the third century had its decline not been arrested by the emperors Diocletian (reigned 285–305) and Constantine (reigned 306–337). Diocletian was a highly experienced soldier and administrator from a poor family in Spalato in what is now Yugoslavia. Although made emperor by his troops he at once distinguished himself from his predecessors who had taken power in the same time-dishonored way, by destroying this system. He threw out the little that was left of the liberal character of the principate of Augustus, and copied the Persian system of ceremonial monarchy. He wore Persian royal robes, scarlet boots, and a purple robe embroidered with gold. He forced even his most important subjects to prostrate themselves and kiss the hem of his robe. To keep an aura of mystery around himself, he appeared in public only on specially staged ceremonial occasions. To the dignity of empire he added the sanctity of theocracy. He called himself Jovius, or son of Jupiter, and declared his powers to be derived not from the Roman people but directly from the gods. Although retaining primacy himself and thus perpetuating the unity of the empire, he divided it for administrative purposes into two sections, taking the eastern part himself and giving the western part to his best general, who also took the title of Augustus. Later, however, he appointed as well two junior emperors, called caesars. In this way the empire was divided into four parts, although Diocletian retained supreme control. This complicated system broke down after his death, but Diocletian was faced by only two revolts during his reign, and was even able after twenty-one years of rule to retire peacefully to his own palace at Spalato.

It was not, however, the ceremonial changes so much as the administrative and military reforms that broke the political power of the army. Diocletian put an end to the system whereby military officers frequently moved into civil service positions, and he made the army a purely professional body, which he doubled in size to about four hundred thousand men. He also doubled the number of provinces, so that the smaller units could be kept under control and made more quickly responsive to his wishes. The small provinces were regrouped into larger units, called dioceses, and at the head of each diocese was a *vicarius,* a kind of prefect. Thus Diocletian's solution to the constitutional problem was an absolute

Bust of Diocletian. Diocletian's tough and uncompromising policy restored the effectiveness of the central government of the Roman empire. (Museo Capitolino, Rome. Alinari photo.)

emperor governing through an efficient bureaucracy on a reorganized provincial basis. It worked so well that it became the basis of the organization of the Byzantine Empire, and was absorbed into the structure of the Catholic Church in the west.

Secondly, Diocletian turned to the economic problem. Instead of trying to change the agricultural system, he decided to perpetuate the social system built upon it. To stop inflation, he fixed maximum prices for food, raw materials, and textiles, and also maximum wages. In a preamble to the law, Diocletian denounced "the tradesmen who were constantly raising prices." "Who is so dumb-witted, or so devoid of human feeling that he cannot have known or noticed that all salable objects, offered for sale or traded in towns, have increased so much in price that unbridled greed is no longer restrained even by superfluity in the market or a good harvest?"[1] Large sections of the population were tied to a hereditary profession. Sons of soldiers had to be soldiers. Gold miners' sons had to be gold miners. Even town councillorships were hereditary. But most important of all, Diocletian ordered the peasantry to stay in the places where they were registered, which meant that he bound them to the soil. In these ways, Diocletian did not reverse the economic decline and start the state toward new economic progress, but he at least stopped the decline.

---

[1] Cited in Joseph Vogt, *The Decline of Rome: The Metamorphosis of Ancient Civilization,* trans. Janet Sondheimer (London: Weidenfeld and Nicolson, 1967), p. 77.

It was an attempt to stabilize the existing situation in the Roman Empire. Diocletian, however, had made one significant error of judgment. In 303, he began to persecute the Christian Church, in the hope of wiping it out; and he failed. The next strong emperor, Constantine, reversed the policy completely by accepting conversion himself, and giving official toleration of the religion in the empire. Christianity could then make its contribution to the end of the Roman Empire in the west, a contribution that, as we shall see, has been evaluated in the most diverse ways, from Gibbon's conviction that by Christianity "the attention of the emperors was diverted from camps to synods" to St. Augustine's view that Christianity was the only good thing left in the declining Roman Empire.

CHRISTIANITY:
FROM CHRIST
TO CONSTANTINE

The Origins of Christianity. Augustus had been ruling in Rome for over twenty years when sometime between 8 and 4 B.C., in a small town called Bethlehem in the obscure province of Judea, a young Jewish couple named Joseph and Mary registered their first child, Jesus, who had just been born in a stable while they were in town for the tax census. Thirty years later, the young man Jesus began his meteoric three-year career as a religious and social reformer with the first of his attacks on the scribes and Pharisees who dominated the application of the Judaic religious laws. He was a sensational speaker, with the capacity to reach the uneducated in his audience with the telling of parables and the direct simplicity and kindness of his character. People attributed miracles to him, which enhanced his fame. Above all, however, he claimed to have a unique relationship to God, to be the son of God, and alone to be able to reveal the truth about the Father. Hence, his followers declared that he was the Messiah, the Savior, or Christ, whom the Jewish people had traditionally expected to come to bring them prosperity on this earth. Jesus himself was careful to point out that although he had come to save them, he was far from being the kind of savior they had been expecting. How different they would later realize after he had been crucified.

In A.D. 29 he led his followers to Jerusalem for the celebration of the Passover, the feast of Jewish independence. In the superheated climate of a city thronged with Jews from all over Palestine, the nervous Jewish government tried him before the Jewish ecclesiastical court and found him guilty of blasphemy and deserving of the death penalty. After some hesitation, the Roman governor, Pontius Pilate, agreed to his death, and his crucifixion was carried out by the Roman occupation troops. His disciples were flung into dejection. During the next forty days, however, they later claimed, Christ's physical body disappeared from the tomb and Christ himself appeared visibly to them on several occasions to tell them to go out as witnesses and representatives of him throughout the world. On the fortieth day after his resurrection from the tomb, his disciples believed that they saw him ascend to heaven. Jesus, in short, had had only three years to preach his gospel, had died a horrible and ignominious death, and would probably have been quickly forgotten if a handful of people had not been convinced by what they believed was supernatural experience after his death that he was indeed what he had claimed to be, the son of God.

Jewish Influence on Christianity. The survival and future spread of Christianity is partly explained by the fact that Jesus was Jewish. The Jews were a Semitic people, small in number, who had moved from the Fertile Crescent into Egypt around 2000 B.C. After seven hundred years, they were led by their leader, Moses, into the area of Palestine, where they established a kingdom whose height of prosperity and culture was reached in the reign of Solomon in the tenth century B.C. However, the tribes of the north and south of the kingdom quarreled, and created two new kingdoms, Israel in the north and Judah in the south. Their internal quarrels left the Jews open to easy conquest by the great kingdoms of the Near East: the Assyrians conquered Israel and the Babylonians, under Nebuchadnezzar II, removed most of the Jews from Judah into captivity in Babylon. When the Persians conquered Babylon, the Jews were allowed back to Jerusalem, where they enjoyed nominal independence until falling under Roman rule in 63 B.C. Their discontent with Roman rule led to constant troubles that culminated in a vast rebellion in A.D. 70, and the Romans decided to drive them out of Palestine altogether. During this disturbed history, which is not much different from that of any of the smaller peoples who were unfortunate pawns of the great military empires of the Fertile Crescent, the Jews had developed a unique religious tradition; and Christianity was to absorb many of its ideas. The most important was the belief in the coming of the Messiah, although there had been a good deal of debate over the kind of savior he would be. Most Jews had put such expectation of material prosperity in the coming of the Messiah that they could not accept Jesus as the Messiah. Secondly, the Jews believed that they were the chosen people of God, exclusively marked out for salvation, which could be immortality of the spirit or even resurrection of the body. The idea of immortality was connected with the idea of a kingdom of heaven, in which the everlasting values of goodness were observed, in which as a result the guilty were punished or perhaps from which the guilty were banished, and in which the virtuous were rewarded. Third, there was monotheism, the belief that there was only one God, who was personal and who intervened directly in human history. This forced the Jews to reject all forms of polytheism as practiced in the Graeco-Roman religions, and made it impossible for them to accommodate themselves with Roman ease to the undemanding state religious ceremonies. It also posed great problems for the Christians themselves in the future. They had to decide how, for example, Christ could be treated as divine if there was only one God, that is, the relationship of Father and Son in a monotheistic system. Finally, from an organizational point of view, the Jews also left a great contribution to the early Christians:

the habit of meeting privately in special buildings, called synagogues, for reading the scriptures and listening to a talk on their meaning. In these synagogues, the Christians first organized.

Christ had added through his teaching, however, certain doctrines of great power. First, his social message was simple and direct, as the Sermon on the Mount shows. All individuals were important in God's eyes, the poor more than the rest. All should be kindly and forgiving toward each other. Charity, self-control, and humility were desirable virtues. These views were preached by other great religions; to these ethical views, however, Christ added the claim that his father, God, had sacrificed him, his only son, to redeem the world of sin. Belief in him was necessary for this redemption. Ethics was no longer enough for personal salvation, nor indeed was a belief in God alone. There had to be a commitment to Christ, a man who lived in a particular time and place and yet was the Savior of all mankind, irrespective of time and place.

The Early Church. The immediate question for Christ's followers was whether this religion was a reformed type of Judaism that would appeal largely to Jews or a new form of religion open to everyone, and therefore probably unappealing to most Jews. The question was settled when the early Christians asked whether converts to Christianity would be required to accept circumcision and the ritual requirements of the Mosaic law. Christianity's greatest missionary, Saint Paul, settled the matter, and with it the future of the Christian Church, by declaring that the spirit was more important than the letter of the law, and that circumcision and the Jewish culinary laws were not needed for non-Jews. Saint Paul himself carried the message to the Gentiles, traveling for more than thirty years throughout the Eastern Mediterranean area to found little communities of Christians. He preached in synagogues and marketplaces, and sent long epistles to help the people understand the meaning of Christianity. He was finally arrested for provoking a riot, and after months of imprisonment sent to Rome for trial, as was his right as a Roman. He was probably acquitted after long imprisonment in Rome, and he spent the next years of his life helping to establish the Christian community in the capital.

By the reign of Nero, the Christians were established throughout the empire. They were still a fairly undisciplined group, with many fanatics and a large following among the poor and the slaves. To the dignified Tacitus, they were repellent:

Their founder, one Christos, had been put to death by the procurator Pontius Pilate in the reign of Tiberius. This checked the abominable superstition for a while, but it broke out again and spread, not merely through Judaea, where it originated, but even to Rome itself, the great reservoir and collecting-ground of every kind of depravity and filth.[2]

[2] Cited in Donald R. Dudley, *The World of Tacitus* (London: Secker and Warburg, 1968), p. 166.

For Nero, they were an obvious scapegoat to blame for the burning of Rome; and in the great persecution Saint Paul was arrested again and beheaded outside the walls. A church, San Paolo alle Tre Fontane, now stands where his head was supposed to have bounced three times, causing hot, tepid, and cold fountains to gush from the ground. On the same day, Saint Peter, who had been the principal companion of Jesus and had in fact been told by him that he was the rock on which Christ would build his church, was also executed in Rome. Peter, after taking part in the founding of the Christian community in Antioch, had moved to Rome as head of its Christian congregation. When the persecutions began, legend relates, he fled from Rome along the Appian Way, but two miles out, at the point now called Quo Vadis, he met Christ hurrying in the opposite direction. "Lord, where are you going," he asked. (*"Domine, quo vadis?"*) "I am going to Rome to be crucified again," said Christ. Peter returned in Christ's place, and at his own request, was crucified upside down, and buried in a little Christian graveyard on the Vatican hill, which in the fourth century was used as the site for one of the principal Christian churches, Saint Peter's. By killing Peter, the first Pope, and Paul, the greatest Christian missionary, Nero had unwittingly strengthened the Roman Christian congregation's claim to superiority over the other congregations associated with Christ's original apostles. These were Antioch, with Saint Peter; Jerusalem, with Saint James; and Alexandria, with Saint Mark.

The Chalice of Antioch, Early Christian Metalwork, 4th to 5th Century. (The Metropolitan Museum of Art. The Cloisters Collection, purchase, 1950.)

For the next two hundred fifty years, the Christian Church went under-ground. Veneration of the martyrs was used to help propagate the faith. Four accounts of the life of Christ, called gospels, written by Matthew, Mark, Luke, and John, who had all known him, a description through the *Acts of the Apostles* of the spread of the Church after Christ's death, Paul's commentary on Christian doctrine, and a few other books were generally recognized as divinely inspired, and read in Christian worship as the New Testament of the Bible. Greek philosophy was slowly harmonized with Christian teachings, as intellectuals of the church attempted to provide the new religion with a developed philosophical foundation. Organization remained elementary because of the persecutions; but within the local churches a professional hierarchy of bishop, priest, and deacon had been established. By the end of the third century, Christianity had progressed so far that persecution was ineffective against it. Perhaps one in ten of the population of the empire was Christian, but the Church had a solid basis not only among the poor of the cities, but among the peasantry, the army, and the educated upper classes. As early as 200, the Christian writer Tertullian warned that the Christians could paralyze the state by passive resistance alone: "We could take up the fight against you without arms and without commotion, merely by passive resistance and secession. With our numbers, the loss of so many citizens in the far corners of the earth would be enough to undermine your empire, our mere defection would hit you hard. Imagine the horror you would feel at finding yourselves thus deserted, in the uncanny stillness and torpor of a dying world. You would look in vain for your subjects—the enemy at your gates would be more multitudinous than the population of your empire."[3] It was hardly sur-prising that eventually a Roman emperor would decide to enlist the Chris-tians on his side.

ORGANIZATION OF THE CHURCH IN THE WEST

The Conversion of Constantine. After Diocletian had retired to his palace on the Dalmatian coast, his plans for assuring an easy transition of power quickly went awry, with his junior emperors and their sons fighting each other for supremacy. In twenty years of bitter fighting, control of the whole empire was won by Constantine, a violent-tempered, ruthless, but farsighted general from Niš, in southern Yugoslavia. Constantine believed that the turning point in his struggle for empire was the Battle of the Milvian Bridge, that occurred just outside Rome. According to his biographer and friend, Eusebius, on the day before the battle:

Being convinced that he needed some more powerful aid than his military forces could afford him, on account of the wicked and magical enchantments which were so diligently practised by the tyrant [his rival Maxentius], he began to seek for Divine assistance. . . . He considered therefore on what god he might rely for pro-tection and assistance. . . . While he was thus praying with fervent entreaty, a most marvellous sign appeared to him from heaven. . . . About mid-day, when the sun

[3] Vogt, *Decline of Rome*, p. 69.

*was beginning to decline, he saw with his own eyes the trophy of a cross of light
in the heavens, above the sun, and bearing the inscription, CONQUER BY THIS. At
this sight he himself was struck with amazement, and his whole army also, which
happened to be following him on some expedition, and witnessed the miracle.*[4]

Constantine instructed his soldiers to put a monogrammed cross of Christ
on their shields, won the battle with ease, and immediately afterwards
declared his own conversion to Christianity.

In Rome, where the Christians had had only graveyards in the catacombs
but no church above ground, he permitted the construction of a fine new
basilican church at the Lateran, and the next year he joined with the
ruler of the eastern part of the empire in granting toleration to the Christians.
The transformation of Rome into the Christian city we know today was
pushed rapidly. Constantine's mother went to Jerusalem, and brought
back the Holy Staircase that Jesus had supposedly mounted in the house
of Pontius Pilate, and also some pieces of the cross on which Christ was
crucified. Constantine began a new church, San Paolo fuori le mure,
on the spot where Saint Paul was buried, and on top of Saint Peter's tomb
on the Vatican Hill he began the first great church of Saint Peter's. This

[4] Eusebius Pamphilus, *The Life of the Blessed Emperor Constantine* (London: Samuel Bagster,
1845), pp. 25–27.

Arch of Constantine, Rome.
(Italian Government Travel
Office photo.)

vast church, with five naves and eighty-six marble columns taken from imperial buildings, covered with frescoes and mosaics, was to be the principal church of the pope until the fifteenth century. Rome too was to bear a few marks of Constantine's own fame. He built himself a triumphal arch between the Colosseum and the Forum, decorating it with sculptures taken from earlier arches; and he used the same parsimony in dedicating the partly finished Basilica of Maxentius on the edge of the Forum to himself. Although its wonderful arches were used as a source of building brick throughout the Middle Ages, the three remaining arches of one aisle were an inspiration to the greatest architects of the Renaissance and even today astound onlookers with their size and grace.

Constantine was not satisfied with transforming Rome, which in spite of all his buildings still looked like a pagan city. His desire to create a new Christian capital for the empire coincided with his conception of the administrative need for a capital more realistically located in the eastern part of the empire. He won the final battle against his rival for control of the empire at Scutari on the Bosphorus in 324, and at once began the conversion of the little Greek town of Byzantium on the opposite European shore into his new capital city of Constantinople, or New Rome. Six years later, the new capital was consecrated, and the center of government transferred there. Constantine was thus responsible for two vital changes in the history of the empire—the acceptance of Christianity as the religion of the emperor and the transfer of the capital from Rome to Constantinople.

The Elaboration of a Christian Theology. During the fourth century, Christianity became the sole tolerated religion of the empire and began to fashion a theology that would take account of its supreme position inside the empire. Constantine had continued to tolerate the pagan religions, and was only baptized on his deathbed. After an attempt by the emperor Julian to take the empire back to paganism, Theodosius I (reigned 379–395) declared Christianity the sole religion and reversed the established procedures by persecuting pagans who would not repent and destroying their books and temples. The Church too had its problems of defining the nature of the faith that was to unify the empire spiritually. Most of the theological infighting was centered around Constantinople and the Eastern churches, especially the great patriarchates of Antioch and Alexandria, with the pope of Rome standing on the sidelines and intervening as a kind of impartial outsider, and the emperor ordering agreement from his position as a deeply concerned insider. This important process of formulation of Christian theology took two forms. On the one hand, there were the writers called the Fathers who were accepted by the Church as official exponents of its doctrines. Most of them were from the eastern part of the empire and wrote in Greek, but in the fourth century the West produced three Latin Fathers of great influence—Saint Ambrose, of Milan; Saint Jerome, of Aquileia in central Italy; and Saint Augustine, of Hippo in North Africa. The future character of Christianity was shaped by the deep grounding of all these writers in Greek philosophy, especially in Plato's works, although they used pagan writing in their work to make Christianity comprehensible and even acceptable to the well-educated of their own day. Through them, many of the habits of thought of the Hellenistic world entered even into the theology of Christianity. Saint Jerome, for example, saw the entry of the Goths into Italy as a repetition of the troubles of fifth-century Greece: "The Roman world is falling yet we hold up our heads instead of bowing them. What courage, think you, have the Corinthians now, or the Athenians, or the Lacedaemonians or the Arcadians, or any of the Greeks over whom the barbarians bear sway? I have mentioned only a few cities, but these once were the capitals of no mean states." [5] To Saint Augustine above all, the Latin church owed the basis of its theology for the next thousand years, and many of his ideas passed over into the Protestant churches through Luther and Calvin.

Augustine had come to a sense of sin the practical way, and his *Confessions* is an edifying illustration of this. From the sense of sin, he derived man's need of salvation by direct intercession with God. In the *Confessions*, he related how "the flesh wrestled with the spirit in Augustine."

Thus was I sick and tormented, reproaching myself more bitterly than ever, rolling and writhing in my chain till it should be wholly broken, for at present, though all but snapped, it still held me fast. And Thou, O Lord, went urgent in my inmost heart, plying with austere mercy the scourges of fear and shame, lest I should fail once more. . . . [Augustine hears a voice telling him to pick up the Bible and read.] I caught it up, opened it, and read in silence the passage on which my eyes first fell, "Not in rioting and drunkenness, not in chambering and wantonness, not in strife and envying: but put ye on the Lord Jesus Christ, and make not provision for the flesh to fulfill the lusts thereof." . . . As I reached the end of the sentence, the light of peace seemed to be shed upon my heart, and every shadow of doubt melted away. [6]

After this conversion, Augustus was baptized, and within eight years had been appointed Bishop of Hippo. From Hippo (Carthage), he surveyed the cataclysm of the Germanic invasions falling on the Roman Empire, and he died while the Vandals were besieging his own city. The message he preached to those suffering from the ending of a comfortable urban life they had grown to take for granted was that God had created two cities: one, the city of this earth, and another that could be called by the name of his great book, *The City of God*. The urban image was central to his theology, because he was determined to show that Rome had passed from a city-state to a cosmopolitan capital of an empire to a final and higher membership in the universal city. The earthly city, he argued, was the product

---

[5] Cited in Bertrand Russell, *History of Western Philosophy* (London: George Allen and Unwin, 1947), p. 363.
[6] *The Confessions of St. Augustine,* trans. C. Bigg (London, 1897), VIII: 11, 12.

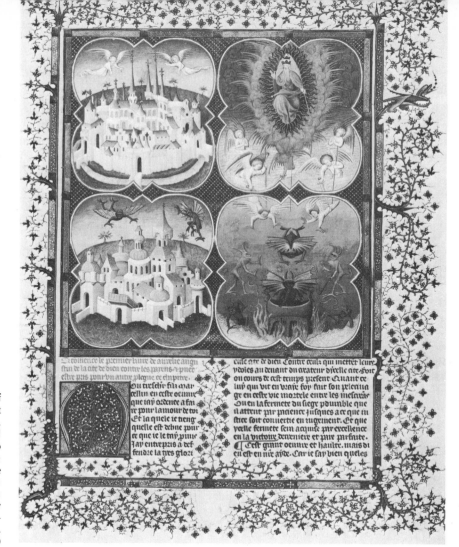

St. Augustine, The City of God. This French manuscript of about 1410 illustrated St. Augustine's great theological treatise. On the left, two earthly cities, one of the blessed and one below for the sinful. On the right, the city of God and below the regions of the eternally damned. (Philadelphia Museum of Art. Photo by A. J. Wyatt, Staff Photographer.)

of man's selfishness; and even at its best, when it sought earthly peace, civic obedience, and social harmony, its aim was merely things helpful in this life. The heavenly city was different in origin, since it was created by love of God, even in conflict with one's self-interest; and it was different in purpose. On this earth, it consisted of "citizens out of all nations . . . a society of pilgrims of all languages," who achieved earthly peace by faith in God and not for their material betterment; in the spiritual life beyond this earth, those who have lived righteously will receive their reward. "There the virtues shall no longer be struggling against any vice or evil, but shall enjoy the reward of victory, the eternal peace which no adversary shall disturb. This is the final blessedness, this the ultimate consummation."[7] Saint Augustine's own personal experience of the struggle of good and

[7] St. Augustine, *City of God* (London: Dent, 1945), II, 245.

evil and his determination to incorporate the contributions of even such non-Christian philosophies as Neoplatonism greatly enriched the complete philosophy of history and the full statement of the Christian faith that he conceived.

While the fathers were defining Christian theology in their writings, the churches in the East were hammering out the principles of Christian orthodoxy in their condemnation of heresies. The questions troubling Christians in the eastern part of the empire were mainly concerned with the nature of Christ, specifically the problem of how he could be both human and divine. The intellectual problem was exacerbated by rivalries between the great patriarchates of Constantinople, Antioch, and Alexandria. Generally the theological school of Antioch would develop a new interpretation of the Scriptures, which would be opposed on theological grounds by the churchmen of Alexandria and frequently on political grounds (that is, to maintain its supremacy within a unified church) by the patriarchate of Constantinople. The heresies also became identified with movements of the provinces to break away from the fiscal burden of rule from Constantinople and with nationalist movements, especially in Syria and Egypt. Finally, outstanding Church leaders sought to advance their own personal power by espousing or extirpating one or another interpretation of Christ's nature. Trouble began when Arius, a priest from Alexandria, claimed that Jesus was created by his Father and was not equal with him. The rapid spread of this doctrine, Arianism, with its threat to Christian unity, outraged the new convert Constantine, who ordered the calling of the first ecumenical council, a meeting of all the bishops of the Church, in Nicaea. The council condemned the doctrines of Arius, and the orthodox position was stated for the benefit of the faithful in the Nicene creed, which is still used by the Roman Catholic, Greek Orthodox, and some Protestant churches:

We believe in one God the Father All-sovereign, maker of heaven and earth, and of all things visible and invisible;

And in one Lord Jesus Christ, the only-begotten son of God, Begotten of the Father before all the ages, Light of Light, true God of true God, begotten not made, of one substance with the Father. . . .[8]

Unfortunately, this statement did not settle the Arian question, since Constantine himself began to incline toward Arianism, and missionaries who went out shortly after converted the Goths and Vandals to Arianism. A new council was called at Constantinople in 381, which blasted Arianism again. This shifted the dispute to the relationship of the human and divine in Christ's nature, which pitted Nestorius, patriarch of Constantinople against Cyril, patriarch of Alexandria. Cyril was an unscrupulous, brilliant fanatic, with a justified reputation for organizing anti-Semitic riots,

[8] Henry Bettenson, ed., *Documents of the Christian Church* (New York: Oxford University Press, 1947), p. 37.

who found distasteful the claim of Nestorius that Christ had two distinct natures, divine and human, which were separate within his own person. By emphasizing the human nature of Christ, Nestorius was making it difficult for those who had begun to venerate the Virgin Mary as mother of God, since according to Nestorius, she was merely the mother of the human but not of the divine part of Christ, which had a father but no mother. The Council of Ephesus in 431 was presided over by Cyril, who kept out the supporters of Nestorius by the simple expedient of locking the doors early, and thus enabled his own supporters to declare Nestorius a heretic. Nestorius was finally exiled to Egypt, and Nestorian Christian churches grew up there beyond the boundaries of the empire and in the province of Syria, whose disaffection prepared it for an equable acceptance of the Moslem armies two centuries later.

When a new synod was called at Ephesus in 449 to crush Nestorianism further, the Alexandrian priests persuaded it to adopt a new interpretation, Monophysitism, which held that Christ had a single divine nature that encompassed his human nature. This heresy in its turn was rejected by the Fourth Ecumenical Council at Chalcedon, which ended the ambitions of the patriarch of Alexandria. But the council indicated the arrival of a new challenger to the power of the patriarch of Constantinople, by approving a compromise text that was suggested by the pope of Rome, Leo the Great. Monophysitism, however, was adopted on a large scale in Egypt and Syria and even by the emperor's opponents in Constantinople. The gains from attempts to extirpate heresy have always been questionable. As a result of the decisions of these ecumenical councils, Syria and Egypt, the two richest sections of the Roman Empire, became supporters of heretical branches of Christianity, Nestorianism and Monophysitism, and seized any chance to break away from the empire, while two of the most powerful of the barbarian peoples, the Goths and Vandals, adopted the equally heretical Arian form of Christianity and fought for it passionately when they invaded western Europe.

Up to this point, the pope in Rome and patriarch of Constantinople were more or less in agreement as to what in theory constituted orthodox Christianity. In administration the Church was a hierarchy headed by the five patriarchs, of Rome, Constantinople, Alexandria, Antioch, and Jerusalem. Although the supremacy of Rome in *honor* as the original capital of the empire and the seat of the descendants of Peter was recognized, its claim to administrative supremacy in the whole Church was ignored. From the fourth century on, however, the power of the pope of Rome increased enormously. His most important advantage was actual possession of the city of Rome. After Constantine, the empire when unified was governed from Constantinople. When it was divided into two parts, the western section was ruled from Ravenna, or Milan, or even Trier. The pope was thus forced to exercise not only religious duties but to take on various political tasks as well, including the job of protecting the city of Rome from the barbarian invaders. In the west, moreover, the pope had no rival, like the warring patriarchs of the East. He was the recipient of vast donations, which the emperor permitted the Church to retain in perpetuity. During the invasions of the barbarians, which destroyed the military hold of the emperor on Italy, first during the Gothic invasions in the fourth and fifth centuries and again during the Lombard invasion in the sixth century, the pope's independence of action was increased. The success of the missionary movements sent out by the pope to convert the barbarians vastly increased the number of Christians recognizing the supremacy of the Latin Church. Between the fifth and eighth centuries, the peoples converted included the West and East Goths, the Irish, the Anglo-Saxons, the Franks, the Lombards, and the Saxons. Thus, little by little, the popes gained the basis of wealth and power that led them to the assertion of their primacy in the Christian Church and to a permanent break with the patriarch of Constantinople. Although the division of Christianity into a Latin, or Roman Catholic, Church and a Greek Orthodox Church was recognized officially by both churches only in 1054, the separation of the churches was evident as early as the sixth century, especially during the papacy of Gregory the Great.

Gregory the Great (590–604). Gregory was an autocratic Roman aristocrat who served as prefect of Rome and as papal ambassador to the court of Constantinople, which he despised. He had not wished to be pope, and accepted his choice by acclamation reluctantly. But at a time when the Church was faced with the enormous problems provoked by the Lombard invasion, he brought to the papal duties enormous energy and also administrative and scholarly talent. Unaided by the imperial representative in Ravenna, he negotiated peace with the Lombards, who were threatening to seize Rome; and he even succeeded in converting some of them from Arianism to acceptance of the Nicene Creed. He established strict standards of administration throughout the Church, and put his instructions into a widely used book called *Pastoral Rule*. He required clerical celibacy, and demanded high standards of financial incorruptibility in the clergy. For the layman, he poured out his advice in hundreds of simple, outspoken letters, which he sent to lords, barbarian princes, and even to ladies of the Byzantine court, as well as in stories of the miracles of the saints.

The life Gregory held up as a standard was that of Saint Benedict, the founder of the order of monks to which Gregory belonged. In his dialogues, Gregory gives us a glimpse of the asceticism that was at the origin of the monastic movement:

A certain woman there was which some time he had seen, the memory of which the wicked spirit put into his mind, and by the memory of her did so mightily inflame with concupiscence the soul of God's servant, which did so increase that, almost overcome with pleasure, he was of mind to have forsaken the wilderness.

But suddenly, assisted with God's grace, he came to himself; and seeing many thick briers and nettle bushes to grow hard by, off he cast his apparel and threw himself into the midst of them, and there wallowed so long that, when he rose up, all his flesh was pitifully torn; and so by the wounds of his body, he cured the wounds of his soul.[9]

He saw that the message of Christ was preached to the heathen, as when in 596 and 601 he sent Saint Augustine of Canterbury on a successful mission to convert the Anglo-Saxons in England. He felt that in theology he should explain the role of unquestioning faith in the achievement of salvation; and his writings earned him the recognition as last of the great church fathers in the West. Finally, he faced the problem of the relative standing of the pope in Rome and the patriarch of Constantinople, by refusing to recognize the patriarch's claim that his title was "ecumenical" or "worldwide." He thus established the precedent of the separation of the two churches. By the time of his death, Gregory had established the papacy as a finely honed administrative machine, a spiritual body of great prestige and influence, and as an independent center of power in western Europe.

Saint Benedict and the Benedictine Order. With Saint Benedict, a third important feature entered medieval Christianity, to complete its basic triad—an orthodox theology based on the Scriptures and elaborated by the fathers; the supremacy of the pope of Rome in the Latin, or western, section of Christendom; and the organization of monks into disciplined orders of great attractive and expansive power.

The first monks were simply ascetics who wandered off into the deserts of Egypt and Syria to get away from the corruption of civilized life and to devote themselves to the mortification of the flesh and the struggle with their own evil desires. Many showed great ingenuity in finding ways to mortify their bodies; Saint Simon Stylites sat on top of a pillar! Saint Pachomius in the fourth century persuaded dirty, lice-ridden hermits that the Christian life required not only cleanliness but hard work; and he organized his followers into little communities that cooperated in agricultural labor. In this form, monasticism spread to the West, but it remained chaotic and, many clergymen felt, a refuge for fanatics whose excesses brought the Church into disrepute. A form of organization that could bring the monasticism within the discipline of the Church without destroying its ascetic purpose was provided by Saint Benedict of Nursia. Benedict, born near Rome to a wealthy provincial family, had fled from the temptations he had at first enjoyed in the city; and by the age of twenty, following the hermits' example, he had spent three years in a totally secluded life at the bottom of a cave, where he too had wrestled with the temptations of the body. From this experience, he decided that "idleness is enemy of the soul"

[9] Cited in Russell, *History of Western Philosophy*, p. 399.

**The Monastery of Monte
Cassino.** The monastery
established by St. Benedict
in 529 was the most influential
center of Western monasticism for over five centuries.
(Italian State Tourist Office
photo.)

and that what monasticism needed was less contemplation and more work.
Gathering together those disciples who had been impressed by his appren-
ticeship in the cave, he took them south to the flat-topped mountain,
Monte Cassino, that commands the long valley linking Rome to Naples.
He lived here for the next twenty-three years until his death in 543, making
of the abbey of Monte Cassino the model for future monasteries throughout
the west. The way of life of the monks was prescribed in great detail in
his "Rule," which required three vows: poverty, chastity, and obedience
to the abbot. Excess was to be avoided. Clothes were to be simple but
warm. Two cooked dishes were to be served at the evening meal. Most
of the day was to be spent in manual work, but time was set aside for reading of sacred books or lying quietly on one's bed. The monks were to sleep
together in dormitories, the younger ones spread among the older: "And
when they rise from the service of God, let them gently encourage one
another because the sleepy ones are apt to make excuses." Guests, and
especially the poor and pilgrims, were to be welcome at the monastery
at all times. The rule, in short, prescribed a simple, disciplined, but not
excessively hard way of life for his monks. It was the work of a practical
man experienced in the everyday problems of running communal living,
as can be seen in the article, "Whether all ought to receive necessaries
equally."

*As it is written: "It was divided among them singly, according as each had need"
(Acts 4:35.): whereby we do not say—far from it—that there should be respect
of persons, but a consideration for infirmities. Wherefore he who needs less, let
him thank God and not be grieved; but he who needs more, let him be humiliated
on account of his weakness, and not made proud on account of the indulgence*

that is shown him. And thus all members will be in peace. Above all, let not the evil of grumbling appear, on any account, by the least word or sign whatever. But, if such a grumbler is discovered, he shall be subjected to stricter discipline.[10]

In the centuries of turmoil that followed, thousands of men sought in the Benedictine monasteries an oasis of quiet and security, so that within four centuries several hundred monasteries had been founded throughout western Europe. At first they served as agricultural colonies, opening up land that had never been colonized; but later they became centers for the preservation of learning, through the establishment of libraries, the copying of Latin books, and even through provision of schooling for the lay nobility. Medieval Christianity would have been completely different without the contribution of the monastic orders, whose success was attributable in large measure to Saint Benedict.

THE GERMANIC INVASIONS

The purpose of the great defense walls of the Roman Empire, the *limes* that ran across central Germany, Hadrian's Wall in England, and the fortifications along the Danube, and also most campaigns fought in Europe from the time of Augustus, had been to protect the area of "civilization" within the empire from the "barbarians" outside. In Scotland and Ireland, the barbarians were Celtic, an artistic, warlike, and highly emotional people, who for several centuries had been withdrawing ever further northwards to the coastal fringes of northwestern Europe from the lands they had once held in France and Germany. On the continent between the Rhine-Danube frontier, Scandinavia, and the Black Sea, lived the Germanic tribes. In spite of the danger they represented to the empire, these tall fair-haired warriors, dressed in skins and draped in gold armbands and chains, fascinated the urbanized Romans. Tacitus claimed to see in them a noble simplicity and vigor that had been lost by the effete Roman of his own day. The way of life of all the Germanic tribes, at least before the influence of Rome affected those closest to the empire, was fairly similar. They had begun to give up a nomadic life and to settle in small village communities separated from each other by the forest. Their political institutions were primitive but important for the future. Law was administered through a tribal court, called a moot, in which all the warriors of the community judged complaints brought by one member of the tribe against another. The court usually settled the matter either by allowing the defendant to take an oath of innocence provided he was supported by friends who swore to his reliability, or by putting the defendant to ordeal. In this case, he might be made to walk through fire. If he were innocent, his wounds would begin to heal in a few days. Here in germ was the doctrine of trial by one's peers that was to appear in its most famous form in the English Magna Charta. The chief was also chosen by the warriors for his fitness to lead them in war; the warriors in

[10] Bettenson, *Documents of the Christian Church*, pp. 169–70.

turn swore personal allegiance to the chief, and became a member of his *comitatus*, or group of warrior companions. Elective monarchy was thus accompanied by the principle of personal loyalty to one's lord that became one of the primary social bonds in medieval European society. Beyond these facts, little is known about the German tribes before they began to press again on the weakening Roman Empire in the late fourth century.

The first Germanic people to penetrate the frontiers of the empire were the West Goths, who were given permission to live south of the Danube in 376 by the emperor Valens of Constantinople. The Goths had originally lived in southern Scandinavia and around the Baltic. But moving south in the second century they had split into two groups, the East Goths, or Ostrogoths, who had remained in southern Russia to live off the land as an army of conquerors, and the West Goths, or Visigoths, who drove the Romans out of Dacia, or modern Rumania. The Goths were receptive to Roman ways of life, developed a taste for Roman luxuries, and adopted the Arian form of Christianity. Many were recruited into the Roman army, and even took offices of state in Constantinople itself. Thus, when the westward drive of a Mongolian people called the Huns from the steppes of Russia overwhelmed the East Goths, the emperor was not unwilling to permit the West Goths to move into the empire to defend its Danube border. Apparently outraged at the treatment they had received from imperial officials, the Visigoths took up arms against the emperor, who was defeated and killed at the battle of Adrianople in 378. His successor attempted to buy off the Visigoths, who themselves did not relish an attack on the fortifications of Constantinople. Under their young, ambitious king, Alaric, they gladly ravaged the cities of Greece before moving northward to garrison Illyricum (modern Yugoslavia). Alaric had thus been diverted to the borders of Italy, where the western emperor had sought a luxurious seclusion behind the marshes of Ravenna, leaving the rest of the country almost defenseless. Alaric campaigned for several years throughout central Italy, accepting bribes to stay away from the terrified Roman population. But in 410, he shocked the whole civilized world by sacking Rome itself. It was nine hundred years since a foreign invader had broken through the walls of Rome. "The world sinks into ruin," wrote St. Jerome. "Yes! but shameful to say our sins still live and flourish. The renowned city, the capital of the Roman Empire, is swallowed up in one tremendous fire; and there is no part of the earth where Romans are not in exile." Fortunately, Jerome was exaggerating. Few people were killed; the houses of nobles were plundered. The Forum was set ablaze, but all the churches were spared. Alaric even organized a fine procession to Saint Peter's to present the treasures he had saved for the pope. Alaric died shortly afterwards, and a river was temporarily diverted to provide a secure grave for him in its bed. The Visigoths then moved on to southern France and Spain, where they finally settled.

Even before the Goths sacked Rome, another Germanic tribe, the Van-

Barbarian Warrior. 4th to 5th Century. This gold figure probably represents a Frankish warrior in armor. (Courtesy of the Dumbarton Oaks Collection, Washington, D.C.)

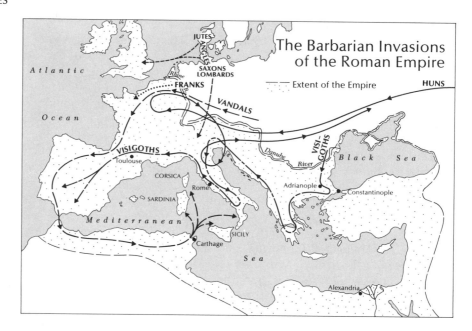

The Barbarian Invasions
of the Roman Empire

dals, had pushed into the empire over the Rhine. Crossing France, they settled for a short while in Spain, from which the Visigoths expelled them. They then crossed the Straits of Gibraltar, conquered the rich province of North Africa, built themselves a fleet, and in 455 sacked Rome with greater thoroughness than the Visigoths. They took the treasures from the emperor's palaces on Palatine Hill and even the tile from the roofs of the temples, and returned with their spoil to their new capital of Carthage, where their kingdom lasted less than a century.

The Huns, who had set in motion this vast movement of peoples, moved westward from the center they had established in the plains of Hungary. Both Romans and Germans were terrified of these savage warriors whose only interest was plunder and bloodshed. Joining momentarily together in 451, the Romans and Visigoths defeated the Hun leader, Attila, at the battle of Châlons; and within a couple of years the Huns had withdrawn from Europe. Their disappearance, however, only facilitated the entry into the empire of several more Germanic tribes: the Ostrogoths, the Franks, and the Anglo-Saxons.

Once they had broken loose from Hun control, the Ostrogoths moved slowly toward northern Italy. Their leader was Theodoric, one of the most talented leaders of all the Germanic peoples. He had spent ten years in Constantinople as a hostage, knew both Latin and Greek, and had developed a profound admiration for the ancient civilization he had been forcibly acquainted with. He had not, however, lost his tribal skills, for after conquering most of northern Italy, he demonstrated his ability with the broadsword by slicing in two his rival for control of Italy; he also showed his ruthlessness by exterminating the rival's family. Theodoric then showed more constructive statesmanship. From 493 till his death in 526, he governed Italy and large parts of the Balkans as the regent of the emperor in Constantinople and as King of the Goths, establishing both in title and in actuality a successful policy of racial coexistence. The Goths took one-third of the land and houses and all military duties. The Romans kept the rest, and devoted themselves to peaceful pursuits. Gothic law applied to Goths, Roman law to Romans. Intermarriage was forbidden. Although Theodoric was an Arian Christian, he tolerated the Catholic religion and even the Jewish and other faiths. "Religion is not something we can command," he said. "No one can be forced into a faith against his will." He showed great concern for Roman culture. He restored monuments that had fallen into ruin, including the Colosseum in Rome, where circuses were still presented. But it was at the capital of Ravenna that the Ostrogothic king showed the heights of civilization that could be achieved with the fusion of Germanic and Roman skills.

Ravenna had been made the capital of the western part of the Roman Empire because of its excellent harbor and because it was protected by wide marshes. It was a city of islands, canals, bridges, and causeways, looking across lagoons to the Adriatic Sea. Here Theodoric found that the Roman artists had brought to perfection one of the most demanding and uncompromising of all artistic forms, the art of mosaic; and it was for this achievement that his Ravenna would be principally remembered. In mosaic the artist must set enormous numbers of tiny bits of marble, enamel, glass, and colored stone into damp cement. He cannot produce those subtleties of expression possible in an oil painting, but must seek an overall effect usually visible only from a distance. But in return he is able to use the play of light not only upon the many different angles of the tiny mosaic stones but within the mosaic itself. In Ravenna, the artists were developing new materials for this art, applying gold leaf to glass cubes and covering them again with a thin film of glass, using metallic oxides to produce variations of color, or employing mother of pearl to produce just the right effect of creamy perfection. In the windows, they often used thick sheets of alabaster, so that the entering light already had a soft opacity before playing upon the planes of yellow marble and the complexity of the mosaic surface. In Ravenna too they constructed buildings as though they were containers for mosaics, with bare walls designed to permit the artist to create the largest and most complex compositions yet attempted in this exacting form of art. One last advantage is still evident today. The process is almost permanent. Unlike frescoes, which fade fairly rapidly, many of the mosaics in Ravenna have required no restoration, and shine as brightly today as in the sixth century.

The building that turned Theodoric to the use of mosaic for his churches and palaces was the tiny mausoleum of Galla Placidia, probably the tomb of an emperor's daughter who had been married to a Visigothic prince.

The Mausoleum of Theodoric, Ravenna. Inspired by the Mausoleum of Galla Placidia, Theodoric's tomb is topped by a monolithic rock weighing three hundred tons brought from Istria on the opposite shore of the Adriatic. (Italian State Tourist Office photo.)

Christ as the Good Shepherd. Mausoleum of Galla Placidia, Ravenna. This early fifth-century mosaic, depicting one of the scenes most favored by artists of the early Christian Church, shows Christ without a beard in reminiscence of the young Apollo. (Italian State Tourist Office photo.)

The architecture was simple, a cross of unadorned brick with very small windows. Its mosaics however are the loveliest possible introduction to the art that was the glory of Ravenna and later of Constantinople itself. The mosaic over the entrance to the mausoleum represents the good shepherd, a kindly protector, not feeding his sheep but patting them benevolently on the nose. He is dressed in a stunning robe with red piping and deep blue stripes that could appear unchanged at a present-day fashion show. In the center of the tiny chapel, one turns to look upward to the dome, the Dome of Heaven, lit up by almost eight hundred golden stars; these become smaller as the dome rises, increasing the sensation of the swirling distance in which a gold cross symbolizes Redemption.

Theodoric took the skilled mosaic craftsmen and used them to decorate one of the most beautiful basilicas in Europe, Sant' Apollinare Nuovo. The church consists of a central aisle, with a narrow nave on each side separated by a line of columns, with a small semicircular apse at the east end. As one steps inside the central nave one at once feels the rushing, forward motion built up by the long line of columns surmounted by the figures in the mosaics above. On each side, there are twelve columns of Greek marble, topped by delicately carved capitals. The mosaic carries on the forward motion of the pillars. On the north side is a procession of twenty-two virgin martyrs, preceded by a very lifelike group of the three Wise Men bringing gifts to the Madonna and the child Jesus. Again the clothes are amazingly modern. The three kings seem to be wearing stretch pants decorated with the most imaginative designs in orange and deep vermilion. Indeed, King Caspar seems to be wearing a pair of leopard-skin tights. We are a long way from the impersonality of Greek sculpture, and the three men, one brown-bearded, one white-bearded, and one clean-shaven, are hardly idealized pictures of piety. On the opposite side of the church, above a line of twenty-two male martyrs, there is a whole panoply of scenes, each one worth looking at in detail. Perhaps most moving of all is the scene of the paralytic being lowered from a roofless building on ropes to be healed by Christ below.

The Three Kings. Sant' Apollinare Nuovo, Ravenna. After the Byzantine conquest of Ravenna in 539, the mosaic artists completed the decoration of Sant' Apollinare Nuovo begun under the Ostrogoths. Here the three kings bring their gifts to the infant Christ. (Alinari photo.)

Interior Sant' Apollinare Nuovo, Ravenna. (Alinari-Art Reference Bureau.)

After visiting Sant' Apollinare Nuovo, one understands why Romans who had seen Ravenna under Theodoric stopped calling the Goths barbarians.

Theodoric died in 526. His successors lacked his skills, and in less than forty years, the Ostrogoths were driven from Italy by the army of the Byzantine emperor; they moved north of the Alps, and rather surprisingly disappeared from history. Thus, the Visigoths, the Ostrogoths, and the Vandals, who were largely responsible for the disappearance of the Roman Empire in the West, left little lasting trace. The Franks and the Anglo-Saxons, however, were to become the principal creators of medieval civilization.

The Franks lived between the North Sea and the upper Rhine, and they never gave up this territory but expanded from it both westward and eastward. Most of France was in the hands of the Visigoths and another Germanic tribe, the Burgundians, when the Franks began their conquests in the fifth century. Under their powerful king, Clovis (481–511), they defeated both the Visigoths and the Burgundians, and established control over most of modern France. The crucial event in the reign of Clovis occurred in 496, during one of his many battles. Apparently influenced by his wife, who was Catholic, Clovis promised to give up his paganism and to become Christian if he were victorious. He kept his promise, and took three thousand of his warriors with him to be baptized in the local shrine. By his conversion to Catholicism, Clovis accepted the ecclesiastical structure of Gaul based upon the original Roman administration, won the alliance of the Catholic clergy, and took for the Frankish armies the task of crusader against non-Catholic barbarians. At the same time, he made possible the intermingling of the Germanic tribesmen with the original romanized population of France. Once the religious barrier was removed, intermarriage was permitted. The Germanic language slowly gave way to the rough Latin that was to turn gradually into French. The constitutional ideas of Romans and Germans were combined, usually to the benefit of the absolutism of the Germanic kings. Roman agricultural practices were taken up by the Germans, who contributed their ability to open up the heavy clay soils that appeared once the forests had been cleared. What distinguished the Frankish kingdom was not the height of its culture. Clovis was no Theodoric, and his capital city of Paris was no Ravenna. The Franks were creating a new people whose culture would be a genuine fusion of Roman and Germanic elements.

Whereas in France, the original romanized inhabitants vastly outnumbered the invading Franks, in England the Germanic invaders, the Angles, Saxons, and Jutes from North Germany and Denmark, drove most of the original Celtic inhabitants to Cornwall, Wales, and Scotland in the far western regions of the British Isles. The invaders, whom for convenience we call the Anglo-Saxons, ignored most of the Roman achievements they found. They disliked the land already being farmed, which was mostly light chalky soil on the hilltops, and preferred the clay lands of the river vallies. They paid no attention to Roman law, but introduced a wholly Germanic tribal system of government. They arrived as pagans, and were converted only at the end of the sixth century by St. Augustine's mission sent directly from Rome. The Anglo-Saxons thus received what romanization they had from the Catholic Church. From the Roman Empire itself, they acquired only the roads. By contrast even with Clovis's Paris, life in Anglo-Saxon England was rough, drab, and dangerous.

Under the impact of these Germanic invaders, the control of the Roman Empire in Western Europe disappeared. The last emperor in the West was the boy ruler Romulus Augustulus, who was killed in 476 by the Germanic chieftain Odoacer. Odoacer however did not declare that he had put an end to the Roman Empire in the West. He sent the insignia of the emperor back to Constantinople with the message for them that the empire needed only one emperor, and that he would act as the representative of Constantinople in Italy. Odoacer felt, in short, that he had reunited the Roman Empire. However, the Roman Empire in the West had fallen. Britain, France, the Low Countries, Spain, North Africa, and Italy itself were all in the hands of Germanic invaders, whether or not those invaders paid lip service to the emperor in faraway Constantinople.

SUGGESTED READING

Edward Gibbon's *Decline and Fall of the Roman Empire* (1776–88) can be sampled in all its suggestive grandeur in the abridgement by D. A. Saunders (1952). Several excellent shorter and more modern introductions to the problems of Roman decline can supplement the diapasons of Gibbon and correct his attribution of guilt. R. F. Arragon, *The Transition from the Ancient to the Medieval World* (1936) emphasizes economic decay in the late empire, but is useful on the cultural heritage bequeathed by Rome. H. T. L. B. Moss, *The Birth of the Middle Ages, 395–814* (1935) is vividly written and still valuable, especially on relations of barbarian invaders and romanized populations. Although A. H. M. Jones's *The Decline of the Ancient World* (1966) is palpably a summary of a larger book, it is a good analytical summary of the problems of the empire as a whole. Hugh Trevor-Roper ventures enthusiastically and successfully out of his own field of specialization in modern history to provide a very stimulating survey in *The Rise of Christian Europe* (1965); and Solomon Katz's *The Decline of Rome and the Rise of Medieval Europe* (1955) is reliable, short, and soundly documented. Joseph Vogt, *The Decline of Rome: The Metamorphosis of Ancient Civilization* (1967) translated by Janet Sondheimer, is an important work of scholarship on the third, fourth, and fifth centuries, fascinating to expert or beginner.

On the rise of Christianity, see the basic account from the Christian point of view by Kenneth S. Latourette, *A History of Christianity* (1953). The most important primary sources on the church are gathered in Henry Bettenson, ed., *Documents of the Christian Church* (1947). For Constantine's conversion, one can consult Eusebius, *Ecclesiastical History: The Life of the Blessed Emperor Constantine* (many translations available), which is an important biography by a friend and admirer exclusively in search of the Christian faith displayed by his hero; or the short and lively *Constantine and the Conversion of Europe* (1949) by A. H. M. Jones. Charles N. Cochrane, *Christianity and Classical Culture: A Study of Thought and Action from Augustus to Augustine* (1957) is a rather difficult study of intellectual changes brought to Graeco-Roman civilization by early Christianity; it gives a parallel in intellectual history to the political and economic changes emphasized in the surveys mentioned above. The most important of the Church fathers, St. Augustine of Hippo, wrote a revealing autobiography, *Confessions* (many translations) and the masterpiece of political and theological theory, *The City of God* (many translations).

On the barbarian invasions, Ferdinand Lot's classic study, *The End of the Ancient World and the Beginnings of the Middle Ages* (1961), translated by P. Leon and M. Leon, has been brought up to date in bibliography and introduction by Glanville Downey. On England, see F. M. Stenton, *Anglo-Saxon England* (2nd ed., 1947); on France, see S. Dill, *Roman Society in the Last Century of the Western Empire* (1966), or the contemporary account of Gregory of Tours, *History of the Franks* (several translations); for a general survey of the new kingdoms, see M. Wallace-Hadrill, *The Barbarian West, 400–1000* (1952) or A. R. Lewis, *Emerging Medieval Europe, A.D. 400–1000* (1967).

Finally, for a fascinating change of viewpoint, see the decline of Rome as viewed from Constantinople in Walter E. Kaegi, Jr., *Byzantium and the Decline of Rome* (1968), which makes great use of contemporary writings, especially Zosimus's eyewitness account of the court of Ravenna.

6
THE CONSTANTINOPLE OF JUSTINIAN

For more than a thousand years, Christian Constantinople was the richest, most beautiful, and most cultivated city in Europe; and for several centuries, it had no rivals anywhere in the world in wealth, power, or culture. Throughout its history, from its foundation by the emperor Constantine in 324 to its capture by the Turkish sultan Mohammed II in 1453, foreigners came and marveled at its beauty. When the Crusaders reached Constantinople in 1204, they were dazzled by its magnificence (but not deflected from their desire to sack it). The French chronicler of their expedition commented:

Indeed you should know that they gazed well at Constantinople, those who had never seen it; for they could not believe that there could be in all the world a city so rich, when they saw those tall ramparts and the mighty towers with which it was shut all around, and those rich palaces and those tall churches, of which there were so many that nobody could believe their eyes, had they not seen it, and the length and breadth of the city which was sovereign among all others.[1]

The appearance of this splendid city and the character of its civilization were established by the end of the reign of the emperor Justinian (527–565). Constantinople enjoyed by then the three bases of its future prosperity and endurance. It was a great military bastion; it was the center of world commerce; and it enjoyed a political and ecclesiastical constitution of great resilience. In this situation of prosperous safety, the city had become the

[1] G. de Villehardouin, *Chronicle of the Fourth Crusade,* trans. Frank Marzials (London: Dent. 1908), p. 31.

Santa Sophia, Constantinople. Built 532–537. Moslem plaques and interior decoration were added, but no structural changes made, after the church was converted to a mosque in 1453. (Bruno Barbey/Magnum.)

home of a new form of culture, which we call Byzantine, and which can still be admired in the buildings, paintings and mosaics, histories, and poems that have fortunately survived.

CONSTANTINOPLE AT THE ACCESSION OF JUSTINIAN

When Constantine began casting around, "on the command of God," for a place where he could found a new Christian capital for the Roman Empire, he knew only that it would have to be somewhere to the east of Rome. He toyed briefly with the idea of putting it in the inaccessible mountains of Yugoslavia, at his birthplace of Niš, began a few buildings at Troy, and finally decided to build it at the point where the waters from the Black Sea flowed through the narrow channel of the Bosphorus into the Sea of Marmara. Even then it took a flight of eagles to give him supernatural warning not to build on the Asiatic shore, but to choose the triangular peninsula on the European shore where Greek sailors from Megara in the seventh century B.C. had founded the colony of Byzantium. The site had only one principal disadvantage, its climate. In the summer it was hot and muggy. In the winter and spring a north wind blew from the plains of southern Russia across the Black Sea and rushed with gale force down the seventeen-mile funnel of the Bosphorus. The wind not only chilled the citizens of Byzantium but often prevented sailing ships from rounding the tip of the city to enter the superb natural harbor of the Golden Horn, a deep sheltered bay at the north of the city, seven miles long, whose existence was one of the primary reasons for Constantine's choice of the site. But all other factors were overwhelmingly favorable.

Advantages of Constantinople's Site. Constantinople lay at the intersection of two of the greatest routes of the ancient world. It controlled the trade route that led from the wheatfields of southern Russia, which had fed Athens, through the Bosphorus and the Sea of Marmara to the narrow channel of the Hellespont and out into the Aegean, and on to the cities of Greece and Italy or down the eastern shore of the Mediterranean to Syria and Egypt. It sat on the short ferry crossing on the quickest land route from Europe to Asia, and thus was ideally located to become the trading center for the exchange of European goods and money for the products of India and China. Fishing was good around its shores. Fresh water was abundant in the hills to the north. On both the European and the Asian shores the land was well suited to wheatfields and vineyards. And it was beautiful. The gentle hills on either side of the Bosphorus combined the startling colors of the Mediterranean landscape—the dark green of juniper and pine, the sharp brown of outcropping rock—with a more northern effulgence of meadow grass and wildflowers where the streams burst out into the Bosphorus. As in Hong Kong and San Francisco of later date, wherever one looked there were vistas of blue waters, over the rooftops or at the ends of streets that seemed to dip into the bay. The sixth-century his-

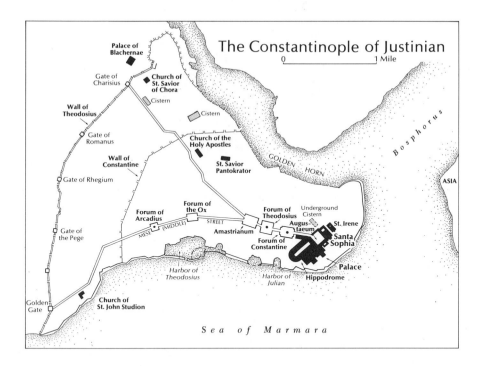

torian Procopius broke off his description of the buildings of Justinian, to which we shall return, to "say a few words about the glory which the sea adds to Byzantium":

The two seas which are on either side of it, that is to say the Aegean and that which is called the Euxine [Black Sea], which meet at the east part of the city and dash together as they mingle their waves, separate the continent by their currents, and add to the beauty of the city while they surround it. It is therefore encompassed by three straits connected with one another, arranged so as to minister both to its elegance and its convenience, all of them most charming for sailing on, lovely to look at, and exceedingly safe for anchorage. . . . The sea encircles the city like a crown, the interval consisting of the land lying between it in sufficient quantity to form a clasp for the crown of waters. This gulf [the Golden Horn] is always calm, and never crested into waves, as though a barrier were placed there to the billows, and all storms were shut out from thence, through reverence for the city. Whenever strong winds and gales fall upon these seas and this straits, ships, when they once reach the entrance of this gulf, run the rest of their voyage unguided, and make the shore at random; . . . when a ship is moored there the stern rests on the sea and the bow on land, as though the two elements contended with one another to see which of them could be of greatest service to the city.[2]

[2] Procopius, *The Buildings of Justinian* (London: Palestine Pilgrims' Text Society, 1896), pp. 24–25.

Bust of Constantine. This colossal head was part of a seated statue placed in the Basilica of Maxentius, which Constantine renamed after himself. (The Metropolitan Museum of Art, Bequest of Mary Clark Thompson, 1926.)

Constantine's City Plan. Constantine himself laid out his new city. The Greeks had settled only the tip of the peninsula, around a little hill they had made their Acropolis, which later became the site of the imperial palace. Constantine, with his spear in his hand, walked westward with his architects and planners, until the new Rome, like the old Rome, enclosed seven hills. When his planners expressed surprise at how far he was walking before marking the line for the defense wall, Constantine replied: "I shall keep on until He who is going before me stops." Like Romulus, he knew he was tracing a sacred boundary. The parallels with Rome did not stop there. The Acropolis became another Palatine Hill, from which the courtyards, gardens, colonnades, and churches of the scattered palace buildings descended in a series of terraces to the water and the private harbor of the emperor. In front of the Great Palace was a large square called the Augustaeum, the heart of the empire, like the Forum in Rome; and here was built the milestone, or Milion, from which, like the umbilical stone in Rome, all mileages in the empire were calculated. At the southwestern corner of the Augustaeum was a huge arena, the oval Hippodrome, which combined the functions of the Roman Colosseum and the imperial chariot ring. Between the palace and the Hippodrome, Constantine again copied Rome by building a senate house. Having thus established the center of his city, Constantine laid down the plan of its streets. Leading out from the Augustaeum was the main street of the city, Middle Street, or Mese, which was paved with large stone blocks. On either side, using a structure like the stoas of Athens, Constantine erected roofed colonnades covering the sidewalks and the shop entrances. Immediately beyond the palace of the governor of the city, the Praetorium, the street entered the hexagonal Forum of Constantine, conceived as the commercial heart of the city. In the center of the forum, Constantine erected a tall column of porphyry, on which he placed a statue of Apollo with his own head substituted for that of the god. Later emperors carried on many of these ideas. The more ambitious would build new forums named after themselves, along the main street, just as earlier emperors had done in Rome. Theodosius I, whose column had spiral reliefs, imitated Trajan's column. Arcadius built his forum near the wall, and set there one of the tallest columns in the city, one hundred forty feet high. Theodosius II found that in only a century the population had outgrown even the area planned by Constantine, and he enlarged the city by building new land walls one mile beyond those of the city's founder.

Constantinople as Fusion of Classical and Christian. Constantine had, however, done more than lay down the ground plan of the city. He had established the character of Constantinople as a combination of classical and Christian. To complete the capital within six years, he had ransacked the Eastern Mediterranean for its artistic treasures. From Delphi he brought the pillar of bronze that the Greek states had set up to commemorate their final victory over the Persians, and put it in the middle of the Hippodrome. From Ephesus, Rhodes, Athens, and Rome itself he brought statues and temples, thereby setting the city's taste in sculpture with the highest examples of ancient art. He also helped himself to Christian relics. At the base of his column in his Forum, he deposited what he believed to be the crosses of the two thieves crucified with Christ, part of the bread with which Christ had fed the five thousand, and one of Noah's tools used in building the Ark. He set the example to future emperors of the acquisitive passion that led to the eventual location in Constantinople of the Crown of Thorns, the Lance, most of Christ's cross, and a phial of Holy Blood. But the mark of the Christian capital was to be its churches, which were to distinguish the new capital clearly from the pagan temples of old Rome.

On the fourth side of the Augustaeum, Constantine built the Church of the Holy Wisdom, or Santa Sophia, the city's cathedral, where the emperor was to be crowned and the patriarch was to conduct the major services. Near the wall he built a second large church, a shrine to the Holy Apostles. Since he was himself known as the thirteenth apostle, he thought it suitable that he, and future emperors, should be buried in this church; and until the sack of the city by the Crusaders in 1204, one emperor after another was entombed there in a huge sarcophagus of porphyry. This habit of building a shrine where generations of rulers could lie together in sumptuous death was followed by the French kings in the Abbey of St. Denis, by the English in Westminster Abbey, and the Russian tsars in the Cathedral of the Archangel in the Kremlin. A mausoleum of this kind became a necessity for any self-respecting ruling family, so that even the dukes of tiny Burgundy had to have their own sanctified necropolis; and as late as 1888,

**S. Mary Pammakaristos,
Constantinople.** This late
Byzantine church was built
on the ruins of the Church
of the Holy Apostles, which
was destroyed during the sack
of the city by the Fourth
Crusade in 1204. (Turkish
State Tourist Office photo.)

the emperor of a highly industrialized Germany sought respectability
among his peers by burial in his own sepulcher in the park of the Char-
lottenburg palace in Berlin.

To people his city, Constantine provided the same inducement that had
filled Rome with a mob of dispossessed—free bread and circuses or at
least chariot races. To bring scholars, he built libraries, for storage and
study of Greek manuscripts; and a knowledge of Greek and Latin was the
key to rapid advancement inside his court and administration. Army recruitment brought vast numbers of Isaurians from Asia Minor and Illyricans
from the Balkans and many other nationalities including even the Germanic
tribes. Commercial advantages shared with all citizens of the empire
brought Syrians and Egyptians, Armenians and Jews; and to persuade the
highest ranks of the Roman aristocracy to move with him, Constantine
created a new senate and, it was said, built homes that were exact replicas
of the houses the aristocrats had had in Rome itself. Of all the great cities
created by the vision and obstinacy of an absolute ruler, only St. Petersburg
could rival Constantine's creation; and St. Petersburg was a capital for
less than two hundred years.

By the year 330, Constantine was satisfied that his city was ready. On
May 11, he dedicated it as New Rome. A solemn procession made its way
from the Augustaeum, down the Mese, into the Forum of Constantine, where
his statue was hoisted to the top of its enormous column, on which was
inscribed: "Oh, Christ, ruler and master of the world. To you now I dedi-

cate this subject city, and these scepters and the might of Rome. Protect her; save her from all harm.''

In 518, the rich prize of Constantinople fell into the hands of a rough, illiterate general from a peasant family in Illyrica, who had used bribes, given him for use on behalf of another candidate, to make himself emperor of Byzantium. Justin I (518–527) was then sixty-eight years old, in bad health, unskilled in government, and in brief, unfit to be emperor. Fortunately he had a nephew he had brought up almost as a son, to whom he gave the best classical and theological education available in Constantinople, and whom he pushed ahead rapidly through the ranks of the emperor's bodyguard. In gratitude, the young man copied his uncle's name, called himself Justinian, and governed from behind the throne throughout the whole of his uncle's reign. Constantinople was thus dominated from 518 to 565 by Justinian, a man who added robust health to his many other achievements.

Character of Justinian.   Justinian was unusually qualified to be emperor. He had served in the army. He knew the technique of war and the qualities that make great commanders. During his uncle's reign he had learned the intricacies and the intrigues of Byzantine politics, without having to take personal responsibility for his decisions. His education had given him a wide background in classical learning and the ambition to patronize its practitioners, whatever their background. In spite of the occasional savageries in which he indulged, he had a deep love of the Christian Church and less fortunate fascination with the complexities of theological dispute. Speaking Latin in a capital where most people talked Greek, he was convinced of the necessity of maintaining the link of the Latin and Greek parts of the empire. And as an upstart, one generation removed from the poverty of the Dalmatian swineherds, he believed that human talent should be recognized without regard to the niceties of aristocratic upbringing. Here lay his greatest skill—to be able to pick brilliant people to serve him in the vast enterprises he had conceived for his empire. To take care of the codification of the laws, he singled out Tribonian, a lawyer from Asia Minor who was working his way up through the bureaucracy, and who developed into one of the most subtle legal minds of all time. To command the armies in the reconquest of the West, he chose one of his youngest generals, Belisarius, a man like himself from a peasant family in Illyrica. And as his wife, he picked Theodora, the daughter of a bearkeeper in the Hippodrome, an actress with a reputation for bewitchment, literal and metaphorical; and with this brilliant forceful woman he shared not only a lifelong if turbulent love affair but also the decision-making of empire. Theodora frequently abused her powers. She could make or break the highest public officials. Her inordinate love of ceremonial, her passion for debasing highborn aristocrats, and her countermanding of imperial orders bred hatred and disorder in the administration. But on most crucial matters her advice to Justinian, whether or not he followed it, was sound. She wanted him to accept Monophysitism, or at least come to a compromise with it, not only because she believed in it herself but because such a course might weaken the disaffection of Syria and Egypt. She finally persuaded Justinian to get rid of the unpopular finance minister, whose extortion brought the mob of Constantinople into open revolt in 532. After her death from cancer in her early fifties, Justinian began to lose himself in ever more intricate theological expositions that satisfied no one but himself.

Empress Theodora and Her Ladies. San Vitale, Ravenna. The empress appears in her ceremonial robes and crown, against an elegant background that probably represents her rooms in the palace. (Italian Government Travel Office.)

Justinian came to the throne with a clear, ambitious program of securing, quite deliberately, his own place in the history of the Roman Empire. He wanted to reunite the Latin-speaking and Greek-speaking parts of the empire by conquering the barbarians who had illegally entrenched themselves in his rightful dominions in western Europe and North Africa. Secondly, he wanted to make the empire economically prosperous and politically and legally efficient. And third, he wanted to patronize a new golden age of literature, art, and architecture, of which the most impressive feature would be a series of great churches scattered throughout his empire.

Justinian's War Goals. Justinian had no qualms about being constantly at war. He had received from the earlier emperors a city that was already superbly fortified; and he did little to enable the city to withstand a siege beyond keep the great land and sea walls in good repair and build magnificent underground cisterns. A small navy was maintained, which was sufficient to give superiority in the Black Sea and most of the Mediterranean then and for the next century. But to embark on a program of reconquest, he had to have a large enough army to hold firm on the eastern frontier against Persia and to defeat the Germanic warriors, whose whole economic organization was planned to enable them to embark instantly on war. He was fortunate in having a large treasury built up by his uncle's frugal predecessor and an army of one hundred fifty thousand men. The army had a tradition of scientific management and the study of military theory; and in the armored horse and rider, called the cataphract, it had the foremost military weapon of the sixth century. Justinian was also aided by the fact that the Byzantine and Persian empires were both so well matched that neither could conquer the other. In sensible days, the two empires concluded truces that varied from a five-year breathing space to the Perpetual Peace of 532, which lasted eight years; they even shared the financing of border fortresses. Justinian was even prepared to pay tribute to the Persians to buy peace on his eastern border. Unfortunately for him, his reign coincided with that of one of the greatest Persian emperors, Khusru I, who hoped to profit from the disloyalty of Armenia and Syria and the absence of Justinian's finest troops in the West. To Justinian's fury, therefore, most of his reign he was forced to waste troops and finances in forcing back the incursions of the Persians, who at one time penetrated far enough into the empire to sack Antioch, the richest city of Syria.

Campaigns in Western Mediterranean. In the respite brought on by the Perpetual Peace of 532, Justinian struck westward for the first time, at the Vandal kingdom of North Africa. His advisers were appalled at the expense, at the long sea voyage, and at the strength and skill of the enemy. He raised only fifteen thousand men, but it took five hundred ships to transport them. Luck was on his side, however. Rule in North Africa had been seized by a usurper who was disliked by both his fellow Vandals and the native Libyans. The Ostrogoths allowed Belisarius to land in Sicily, so that he was able to invade Tunisia from Sicily. He was thus able to revive his forces among the rich cities of southern Sicily before making the short sea trip to Carthage. Within a few days of landing, Belisarius had defeated the Vandal ruler and was in possession of Carthage. By the spring of 534, the North African coast was under the control of Belisarius, who was back in Constantinople within a year of his departure. Victories of this kind had been rare in recent Roman history, and Justinian decided to celebrate with a triumph as grand as anything out of the Roman past. The procession set off from Belisarius's own house, and passed through the streets of Constantinople to the Hippodrome, where the emperor and empress awaited it. The display of captives and spoils outshone anything seen in Rome, or to be more accurate, it included much of the spoil that had already been seen in Rome. There was not only the Vandal king and a well-picked group of the handsomest blonde warriors of the Vandals. There were all the treasures the Vandals had brought back from their sack of Rome in 455, including jewelry, gold dinner services, chariots, and so on. Finally there was even the treasure of the Jews that had been displayed by the emperor Titus in his triumph after he had sacked Jerusalem in 70.

In 535, Belisarius was sent back to Sicily, this time with orders to defeat the Ostrogothic rulers and bring the whole peninsula under the control of Constantinople. The situation again seemed hopeful. The great ruler Theodoric was dead, and rivals were fighting for the succession. The native Roman population was prepared to throw off the rule of the Ostrogoths, as heretic Arians and alien invaders. The Catholic Franks were willing, for a price, to invade from the North. The early campaigns went well. Although he only had eight thousand men, Belisarius took first Sicily, then Naples, and finally Rome itself. There, however, he was besieged by the Goths for more than a year. "After sixty years," wrote Procopius in his history of these campaigns, "Rome was again brought under the Romans." The result, however, was misery for its citizens. The Goths cut the aqueducts, and for the first time since their construction, water stopped running into the great baths of Caracalla and Diocletian. A surprise attack by the Goths on the mausoleum of Hadrian was repelled only when the Roman soldiers tore down the statues on the tomb and dropped them on their attackers. For lack of food and water, plague broke out. The city was finally relieved by another army sent from Constantinople. Belisarius drove north to capture Milan in 539, and at last in May 540 he crossed the marshes to enter the Ostrogothic capital of Ravenna. The war was not over, however. For the next twelve years the Goths tried to drive out the imperial armies. Rome changed hands four times, suffering further devastation each time. But in 552, the last remnants of the Ostrogoths were retreating to oblivion across the Alps. The Gothic war that restored Italy to the empire had been a long struggle of sieges that had left the cities in shambles and the people in starvation. It did not, however, deter Justinian from sending another force against the Visigoths in Spain, which succeeded in bringing the southwest under the rule of Constantinople for seventy years.

Procopius attempted fairly successfully to copy Herodotus and Thucydides in his description of these wars. He had seen the fighting, and could describe in detail the battles and sieges. He was a subtle observer who could characterize men like the Vandal king or his hero Belisarius, in their reactions to misfortune or victory. But he did not conceal the total waste of the whole enterprise. Justinian spread hatred of his rule among the provinces of the East by the extortions necessary to pay for these wars. He had failed to realize that when Rome conquered the East it was seizing rich provinces whose wealth would support the less productive West and the city of Rome, whereas when the East conquered the West it was simply winning new financial responsibilities. Above all, he could not understand that the future of the West lay in the fusion of Germanic invader with the romanized population of western Europe. Europe did not gain from the disappearance of the Visigoths, the Ostrogoths, and the Vandals, but might have profited greatly by their further domestication. In any case, their disappearance merely opened the way for the less civilized Franks and Lombards in Italy, and for the Arabs in North Africa and Spain. Justinian was a great ruler in spite of his wars, and not because of them.

THE ECONOMIC BASIS OF CONSTANTINOPLE'S PROSPERITY

War had made Rome prosperous; war added nothing to Constantinople's wealth, which was the product of healthier factors. Constantinople never led the kind of parasitic existence that Rome did. Although the customs duties provided a large share of the empire's income—a straight ten percent duty was applied on all imports and exports—Constantinople created its own wealth by its services as the world's greatest trading center and by its own manufacturing.

Commerce of Byzantine Empire. The basis of international trade in the sixth century was the exchange of goods between Asia and Europe, although a small amount of trade between Europe and North Africa also existed. The most prized item of international commerce was Chinese silk, whose secret had been guarded by the Chinese emperors for three thousand years, in part by imposing the death penalty on anyone guilty of trying to export the eggs of the silkworm. Only limited quantities of silk were exported, and enormously high prices were paid by such fashionable customers as Cleopatra of Egypt, who would wear nothing else, and aristocrats who found wool abrasive next to the skin. To season the food of the well-to-do, especially the dried meats and salt fish that were the staple of European diet through all the winters of the Middle Ages, came the spices of southeast Asia and India—pepper, cloves, nutmeg, aloes, cinnamon, camphor, balsam, and musk, as well as sugar and ginger. India also supplied pearls and jewels, and ivory, used by the Byzantine craftsmen for church ornaments, furniture, book covers, and reliquary cases. Southern Russia continued to send wheat, furs, salt, and slaves. Syria shipped its manufactured goods such as textiles, enamels, and glassware that were highly esteemed in China, to which they were transshipped. The Balkans supplied flax and honey. The barbarian invasions did not provoke a complete breakdown of West Europen trade, as was once assumed; but Italy and France continued to send to Constantinople their manufactured goods, including textiles and weapons. While Constantinople itself was a large customer for these imported goods, especially raw materials for its textile and metal workers, the great bulk of these wares were reexported, Eastern goods to the Mediterranean basin and northern Europe, and to a much smaller extent, European, Syrian, and Egyptian goods to the East. The basis of Constantinople's wealth was its position as middleman, in a commercial situation where the extraordinary difference in price between original sale and final purchase permitted enormous profits to be made without any danger of losing customers. There was never any danger that a glut in supplies would drive down prices, especially as both the Chinese and the Byzantines were careful to maintain supplies low in the most profitable of all trades, the sale of raw silk and silk textiles.

It was vitally important to Constantinople that secure and rapid trade routes should be kept open. Vast difficulties faced the merchant making the long journey by land from China to Europe, a trip that under ideal circumstances took 230 days. The greatest difficulty was the existence of the Persian empire, which straddled all except two of the routes from the East; for the Persians used their favored geographical position to impose very large tolls for passage of goods across their territory, and in times of war would cut off the trade entirely. Nevertheless, the easiest trade route passed from Constantinople along the southern shore of the Black Sea to the port of Trebizond, skirted the southern slopes of the Caucasus Mountains as far as the Caspian Sea to reach the great oasis cities of Samarkand and Bokhara before crossing central Asia to enter China just south of the Great Wall. It was possible to avoid the Persians by going north of the Caspian Sea, across the steppes of Russia, crossing the Black Sea to the port of Cherson on the Crimean peninsula. Justinian spent much time and money to persuade the inhabitants of the plains of Turkestan to permit caravans to use this route, but without much success. The sea route was also a way of avoiding the Persians. Ceylon acted as the shipping point for all Asian goods, which then passed along the shore of Arabia to the Persian Gulf, and then, if relations with the Persians were good, up the Euphrates to Antioch in Syria. If relations were bad, however, the shipping could pass along the coast of Arabia and up the Red Sea to enter the Byzantine empire in the Nile valley. Again, however, the lack of many Byzantine ships in the Red Sea and difficulties with the kingdom of Ethiopia made it generally more profitable to pay the price the Persians were demanding. Constantinople was linked with the West by the old land route across the Balkan peninsula, the Roman Via Ignatia, and with central Europe and France by a longer and less safe route that followed the Danube River. Most European goods, however, came from the Mediterranean ports of Marseilles, Syracuse, and especially Salonica. Justinian, as emperor, did not make the mistake made by later rulers, of discouraging the citizens from trading outside the boundaries of the empire themselves; but even so the greatest volume of the shipping trade was in the hands of foreigners, most of whom came all the way to Constantinople itself to sell their goods. Special provision was made in Constantinople for lodging these foreigners, who were expected to stay apart from the native population in segregated national compounds, so that the police and customs officials could keep an eye on their activities. The great storehouses for imported goods were down at the harbor on the Golden Horn, but much of the buying and selling took place in the pandemonium of Middle Street.

An unusual insight into the experiences of the Byzantine merchants who ventured into the Indian Ocean is given in the strange book, *The Christian Topography*, of Cosmas. As part of his attempt to prove that the earth was flat, Cosmas, a sea captain who became a monk, described his own observations of the countries where he traded, especially Ethiopia and Ceylon. On the silk trade, he commented:

If Paradise did exist in this earth of ours, many a man among those who are keen to know and enquire into all kinds of subjects, would think he could not be too quick in getting there: for if there be some who to procure silk for the miserable gains of commerce, hesitate not to travel to the uttermost ends of the earth, how should they hesitate to go where they would gain a sight of Paradise itself? Now this country of silk is situated in the remotest of all the Indies, and lies to the left of those who enter the Indian sea, far beyond the Persian Gulf, and the island called by the Indians Selediba [Ceylon]. . . . He who comes by land from Tzinitza [China] to Persia shortens very considerably the length of his journey. This is why there is always to be found a great quantity of silk in Persia. Beyond Tzinitza there is neither navigation nor any land to inhabit.[3]

He also described how in Ethiopia the merchants bargained with the natives for gold.

[The merchants] take along with them to the mining district oxen, lumps of salt, and iron, and when they reach its neighborhood they make halt at a certain spot and form an encampment, which they fence around with a great hedge of thorns. Within this they live, and having slaughtered the oxen, cut them in pieces, and lay the pieces on the top of the thorns, along with the lumps of salt and the iron. Then come the natives, bringing gold in nuggets like peas, . . . and lay one or two or more of these upon what pleases them—the pieces of flesh or the salt or the iron, and they retire to some distance off. Then the owner of the meat approaches, and if he is satisfied he takes the gold away, and upon seeing this its owner comes and takes the flesh or the salt or the iron. If, however, he is not satisfied, he leaves the gold, when the native seeing that he has not taken it, comes and either puts down more gold, or takes up what he has laid down, and goes away. Such is the mode in which business is traced with the people of that country.[4]

[3] Cosmas Indicopleustes, *The Christian Topography*, trans. J. W. McCrindle (London: Hakluyt Society, 1897), pp. 47–49.
[4] Ibid., pp. 52–53.

At the end of the book, he described the strange Indian animals and plants he had seen: the rhinoceros ("His skin, when dried is four fingers thick, and this some people put, instead of iron, in the plough, and with it plough the land"); the giraffe; the hippopotamus ("It had teeth so large as to weigh thirteen pounds, and these I sold here"); and cocoanuts ("Their taste is sweet and very pleasant, like that of green nuts. The nut is at first full of a very sweet water which the Indians drink, using it instead of wine"). Finally, he described the bustling trade of Ceylon.[5]

In this island they have many temples, and on one, which stands on an eminence, there is a hyacinth [ruby] as large as a great pine-cone, fiery red, and when seen flashing from a distance, especially if the sun's rays are playing round it, a matchless sight. The island being, as it is, in a central position, is much frequented by ships from all parts of India and from Persia and Ethiopia, and it likewise sends out many of its own. And from the remotest countries, I mean Tzinitza and other trading places, it receives silk, aloes, cloves, sandalwood, and other products, and these again are passed on to marts on this side, such as Male [Malabar coast of India], where pepper grows, and to Calliana [near Bombay], which exports copper and sesame-logs, and cloth for making dresses, for it also is a great place of business. And to Sindu [mouth of Indus] also where musk and castor is produced and androstachys [spikenard], and to Persia and the Homerite country, and to Adule. And the island receives imports from all these marts which we have mentioned and passes them on to the remoter ports.[6]

Manufactures of Constantinople.   Industry in Constantinople was stimulated by this international trade. Possibly Justinian's most lasting contribution to the city's prosperity was to persuade two Nestorian monks to smuggle back from China in their hollow staves several silkworms and the seeds of the mulberry tree. The industry was planted in Syria, and from then on the need to import from China fell. The production of silk fabrics was a state monopoly, and the workshops were in the palace grounds, in a building called the House of Lights because it was lit up all the night. Superb quality of design and color was achieved. Designs were of animals, pagan and religious stories, and abstract patterns, often of Persian origin. Violet, peach blossom, and deep purple were the favorite colors, although later gold and silver threads were added. The silk cloth of Constantinople was so highly prized in western Europe for kings and aristocrats and especially for the vestments of the clergy that it became the city's most profitable manufacture.

The most prosperous artisans concentrated on luxury goods. The goldsmiths worked gold, silver, pearls, and jewels, to produce jewelry for personal adornment, frames for icons, covers for relic boxes, tableware for sacred or culinary use, and all the badges and insignia required for the imperial ceremonies. Trade and manufacture thus provided employ-

---

[5] Ibid., pp. 358–62.
[6] Ibid., pp. 356–66.

THE FUNCTION OF
THE PRE-INDUSTRIAL CITY

The city was created to provide services that the village could not. The religious function was primary. Often the earliest cities were not cities of the living but of the dead, as in the Egyptian tomb-cities built by the Pharaohs or the necropolises of the Etruscans where the dead caroused for all eternity in sumptuously decorated underground houses, like this Tomb of the Leopards from Tarquinia.

The temple, in which ceremonies for the glorification or propitiation of a god or gods were performed by a priestly caste, provided a holy nucleus around which the city clustered for spiritual protection.

In Catholic Spain, the great cathedrals expressed the pervasive dominance of the Church over the urban community, as can be seen in the *View of Toledo* in the sixteenth century by El Greco.

Photoresearchers/Fritz Henle.

In many cases, patriotism to the city was linked to worship of the city's gods, and erection of a great temple served to swell the pride and confirm the loyalty of the citizens. After the defeat of the Persian invasions in 480 – 479 B.C., Pericles induced the Athenians to build the great complex of temples on the Acropolis and to dedicate the most beautiful, the Parthenon, to their city's goddess Athena.

The Florentine city government sought to express a similar civic pride when they began construction of their Cathedral in 1294, which they hoped would surpass "anything of the kind produced in the time of their greatest power by the Greeks and Romans."

The city was the seat of secular as well as ecclesiastical power. The palace, at first secondary in grandeur to the temple, slowly came to supersede it, as the ruler's services expanded to include political, legal, social, and even cultural leadership. In the tiny principality of Urbino the greatest monument was the ducal palace, which housed the most cultivated court of Renaissance Italy.

The dominance of secular power reached its culmination when the ruler chose to become the creator of a totally new capital city, as when the Emperor Constantine (shown above in a tenth-century mosaic from the Cathedral of Santa Sophia) created Constantinople, or when Tsar Peter I ordered the construction of St. Petersburg.

For the average citizen, however, his city was a creator of economic wealth, and he himself was classified by his position in its economic structure. Except in the very largest cities, the principal occupation remained agriculture. Even in fifteenth-century Paris, as the manuscript page for October from the *Book Of Hours of the Duke of Berry* shows, peasants plowed to within yards of the city walls and the royal palace of the Louvre.

Almost as important as agriculture were the various handicrafts or artisan trades necessary to feed, clothe, and house the city's population, and to supply the needs of the countryside. Along the streets of Pompeii in the first century, bakers sold their goods from open stalls, like the one illustrated in this fresco from the so-called *House of the Baker in Pompeii,* which differed little from the cobbler's stall of fourteenth-century Siena from Ambrogio Lorenzetti's allegory of *The Effects of Good Government in the City.*

Almost invariably, however, economic power and social predominance lay in the hands of a restricted class, the manipulators of wealth and patrons of culture whose self-reliant features bear a strong resemblance whether in a terra cotta of *Lorenzo de' Medici* by Andrea del Verrocchio (top), a detail from Hans Holbein the Younger's *Portrait of a Member of the Wedigh Family* (bottom), or a fresco of a citizen of Pompeii (right).

This multiplication of activity within the restricted area of the pre-industrial city increased the range of human contacts, stimulated individual creativity, and enhanced the quality of daily life. In spite of all discomforts, the citizens of the great pre-industrial cities shared an undisguised enthusiasm for the privilege of living in their city, an enthusiasm they expressed in elaborate religious festivals such as *The Procession of the True Cross* in Venice, by Gentile Bellini or more boisterous secular shows such as *The Race of the Palio in the Streets of Florence* depicted by Giovanni di Francesco Toscani.

Byzantine Silk, Alexandria. 6th to 7th Century. (Courtesy of the Dumbarton Oaks Collection, Washington, D.C.)

ment for a good part of the city's population. Constantinople differed from Rome in that its poorer classes could find work in the artisan shops, as porters or longshoremen, as shopkeepers in the bazaars or in the other trades fostered by the city's growth, such as the building trade or food suppliers. Moreover, in contrast with the situation in medieval western Europe, it was no disgrace for an aristocrat, or an emperor for that matter, to engage in trade in order to make money. On the contrary, it was admired. One empress ran a perfume factory in her own bedroom. The aristocrats had to go to a shop in the palace grounds to buy their silk. It is still disputable whether the intricate regulations with which the emperors bound up every aspect of economic life acted as a hindrance or as a stabilizing factor in the development of commerce. The state's bureaucrats were everywhere ensuring that niggling regulations were respected. The state set wages and prices and supervised quality. It laid down strict rules as to what could be imported—soap for example was forbidden— and what could be exported—nobody could export ceremonial robes, raw silk, raw materials needed by the artisans, salt fish, or gold. All trade was in the hands of guilds, who were regulated minutely; there were five guilds in the silk industry alone. Probably these regulations prevented great fluctuations of economic growth and decline; and it is indisputable that until the twelfth century Constantinople remained the center of world trade. Its predominance was symbolized, and in part maintained, by the use of the Byzantine coinage based on the gold coin known as the solidus, or noumisma, throughout Asiatic as well as European commerce. Its reliability remained unchallenged until the twelfth century, when the emperors foolishly debased its value. It would be hard to find another great commercial city whose currency has kept its value for six centuries.

Weakness of Byzantine Agriculture.   Byzantine agriculture did not share the prosperity of its commerce. The tax on land was so great and so mercilessly extorted that many peasants fled from the land into the cities. It was hard to make a profit from wheat since the state insisted on providing cheap bread for the cities. Worse, however, the aristocracy and the commercial middle class sought to buy up big estates, and frequently did so by force. Justinian himself protested in vain:

We are almost ashamed to refer to the conduct of these. Men of great possessions, with what insolence they range the country; how they are served by guards, so that an intolerable crowd of men follow them; how daringly they pillage everybody, among whom are many priests, but mostly women. . . .

What can be more trying than the driving-off of oxen, horses, and cattle in general, or even (to speak of small matters) of domestic fowls . . . whence a multitude appeal to us here, hustled from their homes, in beggary sometimes to die here. [7]

The emperors made constant efforts to preserve the character of the free villages, at the same time undermining their independence by their fiscal exactions. Nevertheless, in spite of all difficulties, the more fertile agricultural areas continued to produce a surplus: wheat in Asia Minor, wine and oil in Greece, cotton in Syria, timber in the Balkans. It is doubtful whether the Byzantine empire knew the agrarian poverty that appalled visitors to the same areas in the late nineteenth century.

**THE EMPEROR
AS THE
GUARANTOR
OF STABILITY**
The symbol of the third basis of Constantinople's greatness, the political counterpart to its military and economic power, was the vast equestrian statue of Justinian in the center of the Augustaeum. The statue stood on the top of a tall column of cut stone, bound in brass, which rose on a huge rectangular base that was used for seats by the citizens. Procopius described it graphically:

This brass is in color paler than unalloyed gold; and its value is not much short of its own weight in silver. On the summit of the column there stands an enormous horse, with his face turned towards the east—a noble sight. He appears to be

[7] Cited in Jack Lindsay, *Byzantium into Europe* (London: Bodley Head, 1952), p. 128.

walking, and proceeding swiftly forwards; he raises his left fore-foot as though to tread upon the earth before him, while the other rests upon the stone beneath it, as though it would make the next step, while he places his hind feet together, so that they may be ready when he bids them move. Upon this horse sits a colossal brass figure of the Emperor, habited as Achilles, for so his costume is called; he wears hunting-shoes, and his ankles are not covered by his greaves. He wears a corslet like an ancient hero, his head is covered by a helmet which seems to nod, and a plume glitters upon it. . . . He looks towards the east, directing his course, I imagine against the Persians; in his left hand he holds a globe, by which the sculptor signifies that all lands and seas are subject to him. He holds no sword or spear, or any other weapon, but a cross stands upon the globe, through which he has obtained his empire and victory in war; he stretches forward his right hand towards the east, and spreading his fingers seems to bid the barbarians in that quarter to remain at home and come no further.[8]

Constitutional Position of Byzantine Emperor. Justinian was determined, in short, to carry on the political ideal established by Constantine and his successors of the Christian emperor who on behalf of God rules both state and church. Without altering the essential character of this system in any way, Justinian used his half-century of rule to establish it even more firmly. He reorganized the provincial administration to lessen corruption, and divided the imperial bureaucracy in the palace, making its chiefs directly responsible to the emperor. Through his changes he was able to ensure that no minister could ever aspire to the powers of a prime minister but that in fact the emperor would always be the head of his own government. While accepting the difference in duties of the civil and ecclesiastical authorities, he made clear, by his punishment of heresy, his interference in doctrinal disputes, and his control of church appointments, that he was the ultimate authority over the church. "Nothing will be a greater matter of concern to the emperor than the divinity and honor of the clergy," he informed the patriarch, "the more as they offer prayers to God on his behalf. . . . We therefore have the greatest concern for the true doctrines of the God-head and the dignity and honor of the clergy." But the two actions of totally different character that most contributed to the political stability were his codification of the laws and his defeat in 532 of the attempt by the factions of the Hippodrome to overthrow his rule.

Codification of the Law. Justinian's codification of the laws affected the lives of more men than any of his other deeds. Justinian's law code continued in force in Constantinople until 1453. It was regarded as the basis of the law of the Holy Roman Empire set up by Charlemagne in western Europe in 800. Many of its conceptions were embodied in the canon law of the Roman Catholic Church. After the discovery of a complete manuscript of the most important section of the law, the *Digest,* at Pisa in the eleventh century, study of Roman law became the basis of all legal

[8] Procopius, *Buildings of Justinian,* p. 2.

faculties in the European universities. Napoleon's law code, the Code Napoleon, drew heavily on Justinian's; and many other nations modeled their codes on Napoleon's, including, for example, the Italians, the Belgians, and most Latin American states. The only Western countries little influenced by Roman law were England, and its former colonies, where common law based on Germanic tribal practice was established early.

Less than six months after becoming emperor, Justinian ordered a commission of ten lawyers headed by Tribonian, of the imperial civil service, and Theophilus, a professor of law at the University of Constantinople,

Justinian Offering Money to the Church. San Vitale, Ravenna. Although the emperor occupies center stage in this sixth-century mosaic, the powerful archbishop of Ravenna, Maximianus, who commissioned the mosaic, is the only person whose name is inserted. (Alinari photo.)

to draw up a codification of the law, that is, a collection of laws then in force that would supersede all codes. As an efficient man, Justinian was appalled at the confusion existing in the laws, many of which were out of date, contradictory, or repetitive. As emperor, he was aware that the continuous existence of Roman law for almost a thousand years had been one of the great bonds guaranteeing the permanence of the Roman state, and incidentally linking the eastern and western parts of the empire together. The new code, called the Codex Justinianus, was ready in just over a year. It was a fine clear summation, of which any emperor could have been proud. But it only whetted Justinian's legal interests. The writings of the legal experts called jurisconsults had also come to have the force of law. Justinian decided that these writings too should be drawn up in an authoritative form. This work was more necessary than the collection of the laws, in that the writings of the jurisconsults were even more contradictory and hard to find (unless like Tribonian one owned a large library of scarce law books oneself), and to consult them was more time-consuming. Another commission headed by Tribonian set to work and produced first a collection of Fifty Decisions, corrected where necessary, which were for the use of judges. With this out of the way, the commission began to draw up its *Digest,* or summation of the jurisconsults' writings from the first to the fifth century. Although they had allowed ten years, the commission finished its work in three. It consulted 2,000 books by 39 authors, classified the quotations from their writings that were to have the force of law into separate "titles," each of which dealt with a different point of law. The greatest of the Roman legal writers, Ulpian, was quoted 2,464 times. Since the commission's work had made the original Codex Justinianus outdated, Tribonian and his group revised the code itself. Thus the great work of clarification of the law for which Justinian is remembered was all carried out between 527 and 534, an amazingly short time for so complicated a task. From then on, all new laws, or *Novels,* issued by Justinian, were written in Greek rather than the Latin of the earlier compilation, a most important milestone in Constantinople's loss of contact with the Latin West.

Justinian took a great interest in the training of young lawyers in the universities, and he himself wrote the preface to the handbook he commissioned as the basic introduction to their studies. In it he explained what he had tried to achieve.

In the name of Our Lord Jesus Christ . . . to the youth desirous of studying the law. . . . Having removed every inconsistency from the sacred constitutions hitherto inharmonious and confused, we extended our care to the immense volumes of the older jurisprudence, and, like sailors crossing the mid-ocean, by the favor of heaven, have now completed a work of which we once despaired. When this, with God's blessing had been done, we called together Tribonian, master and ex-quaestor of our sacred palace, and the illustrious Theophilus and Dorotheus, professors of law . . . and specially commissioned them to compose by our authority and advice a book of Institutes *whereby you may be enabled to learn your first lesson in law no longer from ancient fables, but grasp them by the brilliant light of imperial learning. . . .*

Receive then these laws with your best powers and with the eagerness of study, and show yourselves so learned as to be encouraged to hope that when you have encompassed the whole field of law you may have the ability to govern such portions of the state as may be entrusted to you.

Given at Constantinople, the 21st day of November in the third consulate of the Emperor Justinian, ever August.[9]

---

[9] Cited in P. N. Ure, *Justinian and His Age* (Harmondsworth, England: Penguin, 1951), pp. 142–43.

However, nothing illustrates better Justinian's legislation and the modernity of some of his concerns than his *Novels*. He had arms legislation: "Arms are to be manufactured only in state arsenals and for state purposes and on no account to be sold to private individuals." He had a wage freeze: "Artisans, laborers, sailors and the like are forbidden to demand or accept increases of wages. Offenders are to pay the treasury three times the amount concerned." And he would not allow real estate speculators to ruin the views in Constantinople.

In this our royal city one of the most pleasing amenities is the view of the sea; and to preserve it we enacted that no building should be erected within 100 feet of the sea front. This law has been circumvented by certain individuals. They first put up buildings conforming with this law; then put up in front of them awnings which cut off the sea view without breaking the law; next put up a building inside the awning; and finally remove the awning. Anyone who offends in this way must be made to demolish the buildings he has put up and further pay a fine of ten pounds of gold.[10]

Political Factions of the Hippodrome. If the law was the greatest contribution to continuity in Byzantine life, the activity of the factions of the Hippodrome was its most disruptive force. The Hippodrome was a huge oval arena at the south of the Augustaeum, built of brick and covered with marble. Thirty tiers of seats could accommodate a crowd of forty to sixty thousand. On the side next to the palace was the imperial box, which the emperor and his court entered by a closed passageway. In the center of the arena was a raised barrier decorated with famous monuments, including a great obelisk brought from Egypt, which is still standing there today. While fights of gladiators with wild animals, boxing and wrestling matches, and acrobats were presented, the main spectacle was the chariot race, of which twenty-four were presented in one day's spectacle. The Constantinople crowd had a passion for the sport. Charioteers and horses became public heroes. Emperors and even patriarchs would breed their own horses for the races. Statues were erected to the charioteers, with occasionally poignant inscriptions, such as "Since Constantius has entered the house of Hades, the racecourse is dark with mourning faces." What made this emotion politically dangerous, however, was that the crowd was split into two organized factions, or demes, called the Blues and the Greens. They became so powerful that the government found it wise to organize them, giving them the duties of a local militia for city defense, of a ceremonial escort, and of entertainment for special festivals. The factions gloried in their role as the one democratic element in the city. A new emperor would come to the Hippodrome to be acclaimed. The factions made demands for the redress of grievances during the race days, and even engaged in a

[10] Ibid., p. 164.

Blue Mosque and the Ruins of the Hippodrome. On the opposite side of the Hippodrome, facing Santa Sophia, the Ottoman emperors erected the Blue Mosque, so called because it is entirely covered inside with translucent blue tiles. The link between Santa Sophia and the great Ottoman mosques of the fifteenth and sixteenth centuries is evident in the use of a great dome superimposed upon four half-domes and in the placing of the windows. (Turkish State Tourist Office photo.)

kind of dialogue with him on those occasions. The emperors found it judicious to side with one faction against the other; but befriended by an emperor or not, the factions were a dangerous element to any emperor. The young men of the factions roamed the streets at night, beating up enemies and stealing from all. They ignored the prohibition on possession of weapons, and fell on each other in the Hippodrome, often fighting to the death over the result of a chariot race. Justinian attempted to curb both factions at once, and thereby united them against him.

Nika Riots. In 532, the city prefect ordered the execution of seven faction members, both Blue and Green, for a riot in which several people had been killed. Two of the rioters, though hanged, survived and were taken to a church sanctuary, outside which the prefect posted troops. At the chariot races shortly afterwards, the factions demanded that Justinian pardon the two men, and when he ignored them, raised the seditious cry, "Long live the humane Greens and Blues," and "Nika" or "Conquer." That evening the factions besieged the prefect's palace and prison, freed the prisoners, and set fire to the building. From there, they moved on down Middle Street to the Augustaeum, starting more fires as they went. In the main square, they burned the palace gatehouse, the senate building, and finally the church of Santa Sophia. Although Justinian dismissed his most unpopular ministers on the mob's demand, the incendiarism continued.

Justinian was besieged in his own palace, while the two factions united in agreeing on a new candidate for emperor to replace Justinian. Justinian again appeared in the royal box, holding a copy of the Gospels in one hand, and promised amnesty and satisfaction of all demands. The rioters refused. Justinian returned to the palace, his nerve broken, and ordered ships to be prepared for his escape. At that point Theodora made her most famous intervention, which is usually credited with saving Justinian his throne.

While it is not proper for a woman to be bold or to behave brashly among men who themselves are hesitant, I think the present crisis hardly permits us to debate this point academically from one perspective or another. . . . For my part, then, I consider flight, even though it may bring safety, to be quite useless, at any time and especially now. Once a man has come into the light of day it is impossible for him not to face death; and so also is it unbearable for someone who has been a ruler to be a fugitive. . . . So now if it is still your wish to save yourself, O Emperor, there is no problem. For we have plenty of money, the sea is there, and here are the ships. Nevertheless, consider whether, once you have managed to save yourself, you might not then gladly exchange your safety for death. But as for me, I take pleasure in an old expression that royal rank is the best burial garment.[11]

Justinian sent two forces, composed mostly of Goths, to the Hippodrome where the crowd was acclaiming their new candidate. There, the troops massacred thirty thousand people. The next day, their candidate was executed. Leading aristocrats implicated were exiled. And the bodies of the slain were laid in a mass grave near a city gate that was henceforth known as the Gate of Death. The factions were not destroyed, but they never again combined together in this way against the emperor. Future troubles were sporadic and usually unorganized. But the heart of Constantinople was a mass of burned ruins. To Justinian, however, the destruction had given him the opportunity to outdo Augustus, who had found Rome brick and left it marble. Justinian expected the rebuilding of the city to usher in a second golden age of Roman culture.

JUSTINIAN AS PATRON OF A NEW GOLDEN AGE

Character of Byzantine Literature. As an emperor who wanted to be remembered as the patron of a golden age of culture, Justinian was fortunate in the intellectual character that had already been imprinted on his city. Schools for both boys and girls were good; and at Justinian's accession, the great universities of the Hellenistic age, Antioch, Beiruth, Alexandria, Gaza, and Athens, and also the newer university of Constantinople, were flourishing. Constantinople was steeped in Greek culture. For example, children from the age of six studied the classics, especially Homer, whose works every educated person knew by heart. Later studies could include rhetoric, law, or philosophy; and nonspecialists often also studied physics

[11] Procopius, *History of the Wars*, I, xxiv, 32–37, cited in John W. Barker, *Justinian and the Later Roman Empire* (Madison: University of Wisconsin Press, 1966), pp. 87–88.

and medicine. At the same time, theological works of the Greek fathers were read side by side with the pagan classics, so that a student in Byzantium gained a thorough grounding in both Christian and pagan Greek achievements. Constantinople was felt to have the task of preserving the heritage of Greek culture. The fine libraries containing manuscripts of classical authors were patronized by the state, the church, and private families; and the continuing study of these manuscripts was indicated by the large number of dictionaries, lexicons, grammars, anthologies, and encyclopedias that were written. Preserving and keeping alive the study of the works of classical Greece was of great importance to the Western tradition of classical culture. With the revival of interest in Greek culture in the Italian Renaissance of the fifteenth century, the students had to turn to Constantinople for their manuscripts and teachers. Unfortunately, this great admiration of classical achievements had the effect of stifling originality in Byzantine literature; and even the best works of Justinian's age were deliberate continuations of writing traditions already established, to the copying of the style of individual authors. Hence, the writers of Byzantium during its whole history produced no novels, no good plays, and almost no original poetry; and even theology, which through the sixth century profoundly considered the widest philosophical questions, descended into polemics whose intricacies have little lasting interest. The creative writing of Constantinople thus was canalized in two separate forms. Great writing was produced when the genuine religious feeling of orthodox Christians could break past the polemics, in hymns that are still in use today, for example, or in books of devotion. In history and biography, the age of Justinian came closest to rivaling the classical Greek writers so much admired. The long line of historians goes from Eusebius, the biographer of Constantine, through the fifteenth-century historians who chronicled the fall of the empire; and the foremost of all these historians was Procopius of Caesarea, who has already been quoted several times in this chapter.

Byzantine Historians. Procopius studied Greek literature at Gaza, and law, probably in Constantinople. In 527, he was appointed to travel as the secretary and legal assistant of Belisarius in his campaign against the Persians in Syria. He followed him from Syria to the Vandal wars in North Africa and to the Gothic wars in Italy. Procopius saw that he had the chance to emulate his two heroes, Thucydides and Herodotus. He too lived in a great age and was to be an eyewitness to the wars that would change its character. He modeled himself consciously on the methods and style of Thucydides; and when he first began writing the history of the wars, in 545–50, he copied the very first paragraph of *The History of the Peloponnesian War:* "Procopius of Caesarea wrote the history of the wars which Justinian, emperor of the Romans, waged against the barbarians both of the East and of the West . . . that the long years might not for lack of record, consign mighty deeds to oblivion, and altogether blot them out." [12]   Thucydides served Procopius well. The reconstruction of the battles is vivid and exciting. Procopius's character studies, especially of Belisarius, are subtle and far ranging. And for all his aim to produce a panegyric of Justinian's great achievement, Procopius showed honesty, as for example, when he comments on the end of the Gothic wars. After describing how the Goths murdered all the Romans they came upon in their flight to the Alps, he adds: "Then indeed it was most plainly shown that when men are doomed to disaster even what seem to be successes always end in destruction, and that when they have got their heart's desire such success may bring ruin in its train. Thus for the senate and people of Rome this victory proved to be still more the cause of ruin." [13] It was discovered after Procopius's death that he had also written a secret history of the reign of Justinian, in which he used a skill at scurrilous invective he had hidden in his public work to blast the emperor as a blood-thirsty monster and his wife, Theodora, as a scandalous, rapacious, and sadistic adventurer. Untrustworthy as the *Secret History* may be, it provides fascinating antidote to the official panegyrics as well as a useful glimpse into the dark corridors of the Great Palace. And even in the *Secret History*, the comments of the man who has seen the ravages of war have the ring of truth:

That Justinian was not a man, but a demon in human shape, as I have already said, may be abundantly proved by considering the enormity of the evils which he inflicted upon mankind. . . . He so devastated the vast tract of Lybia that a travel-ler, during a long journey, considered it a remarkable thing to meet a single man; and yet there were eighty thousand Vandals who bore arms, besides women, children, and servants without number. . . . The natives of Mauretania were even still more numerous, and they were all exterminated, together with their wives and children. This country also proved the tomb of numbers of Roman soldiers and of their auxiliaries from Byzantium. . . . In time of peace or truce, [Justinian's] thoughts were ever craftily engaged in endeavoring to find pretexts for war against his neighbors. In war, he lost heart without reasons, and, owing to his meanness, he never made preparations in good time; and, instead of devoting his earnest attention to such matters, he busied himself with the investigation of heavenly phenomena and with curious researches into the nature of God. [14]

The other historian of Justinian's age, Agathias, is better remembered for his elegiac poetry. Like all the bureaucrats, lawyers, businessmen, and courtiers of Constantinople, he wrote short, charming epigrams in a Greek style that went back a thousand years. A famous collection of thirty-seven hundred of these poems called the Palatine Anthology, which

[12] Ure, *Justinian and His Age,* p. 18.
[13] Ibid., p. 172.
[14] Procopius, *The Secret History of the Court of Justinian* (Athens: Athenian Society, 1896), pp. 149–51, 154.

was made in the tenth century, is still much admired by students of Greek poetry; and in this anthology, about one-tenth of the poems were written by the upper crust of Byzantine society. Here are two examples:

You roll your eyes, dark fire's similitude;
Lips tipped with rouge ambiguously protrude;
In fits of giggles toss your glossy hair,
And flaunt your swaggering hands. I'm well aware.
But in your stiff heart swollen pride bears sway;
You have not softened, even in decay.

"Anacreon, you overdrank and died." "But I lived well;
You also, though you may not drink, will find your way to hell." [15]

Justinian's Building Program. Significantly enough, two of the most famous pieces of Byzantine writing, one in prose and one in verse, were called forth not by love or drink or war but by a building, the great church of Santa Sophia. In 559–60, Justinian ordered Procopius to write an account of the buildings he had erected throughout the empire, "lest posterity beholding the enormous size and number of them, should deny their being the work of one man." Justinian's building program exceeded that of any previous Roman emperor. Like other emperors, he had a program of public works—bridges, roads, border fortresses, walls, aqueducts,

[15] *Translations from the Greek Anthology,* trans. Robert A. Furness (London: J. Cape, 1931), pp. 80, 83.

The Cisterns of Constantinople. To safeguard the water supply of the peninsula-city, Justinian constructed several vast, covered cisterns. Water was brought into the city from the small hills to the northwest by aqueducts that ran below the surface of the ground. (Turkish State Tourist Office photo.)

Church of St. Savior in Chora, Constantinople. Although much altered during the later Byzantine empire, this church dates back to the fifth century. Its chunky, indented façade and high, small domes are typical of the new style of ecclesiastical architecture adopted in the late sixth century, when the outer façade was divorced from the design of the interior. (Turkish State Tourist Office photo.)

cisterns, warehouses, public baths, and law courts. As a Christian ruler, he built works of charity such as asylums, hospitals for the incurably ill, orphanages, schools, and monasteries. Since both he and Theodora loved the waterfront of Constantinople and its nearby straits, he constructed churches at the finest viewpoints, and provided promenades beside the water for the citizens to enjoy. "Those who take their walks [at the new church of Anaplus]," wrote Procopius, "are charmed with the beauty of the stone, are delighted with the view of the sea, and are refreshed with the breezes from the water and the hills that rise upon the land." The Great Palace too was greatly extended, especially with the building of a new entrance hall called the Chalke, which was gorgeously decorated with mosaics of his triumphs in Africa and Italy. It was in church buildings, however, that Justinian exceeded himself. Procopius describes huge programs of church building in Mesopotamia and Syria; in Palestine, where Justinian paid special attention to Jerusalem; and in Armenia, the Crimea, the Balkans, Egypt, and North Africa. And though Procopius failed to describe Italy, Justinian built some of his finest churches in Ravenna. In Constantinople itself, however, the emperor's church building became a mania. He had already rebuilt seven churches before becoming emperor, and had probably given orders for construction of a new Santa Sophia before the Nika rioters helped him by burning the old one down. In all, he built or rebuilt thirty-four churches in Constantinople.

San Vitale, Ravenna. Constructed under Justinian in 538–547, San Vitale is one of the most subtle spatial compositions in all church architecture. It combines the straight lines of the outer octagonal walls with the undulations of seven circular interior arcades. (Alinari photo.)

Santa Sophia. Justinian's church of Santa Sophia is the single finest achievement of all Byzantine civilization, and the only building so far mentioned
in this book that rivals the Parthenon. (There will be more to mention, but
not many.) Moreover, it still exists, almost exactly in the form in which it
was completed in 537, five years after Justinian put his engineer-architects,
Anthemius and Isidore, to work on its construction. Santa Sophia deserves
a prolonged visit, even in these pages. Justinian spared no expense to
build the Great Church, as it came to be called. The basic construction was
the normal Roman use of brick and stone set in thick layers of cement. Almost no attempt was made to embellish the outside, of which the structural
features were left to speak for themselves—the huge projecting buttresses
on the north and south, the undulating rise of the superimposed domes on
east and west. Inside, however, every available space was covered with
carefully worked sheets of marble, fitted so skillfully as to blend one into
the other and to emphasize the distinctive veins in each piece. In the
Homeric form of epic poem that one of Justinian's court officials, Paul the
Silentiary, wrote to celebrate Santa Sophia, he described the marbles:

*Yet who, who even in the measures of Homer shall sing the marble pastures gathered
on the lofty walls and spreading pavement of the mighty church? Those the iron
with its metal tooth has gnawed—the fresh green from Carytus, polychrome marble
from the Phrygian range, in which a rosy blush mingles with white, or it shines*

*bright with flowers of deep red and silver. There is a wealth of porphyry too,
powdered with bright stars, that has once laden the river boat on the broad Nile.
You would see an emerald green from Sparta, and the glittering marble with wavy
veins which the tool has worked in the deep breast of the Iassian hills, showing
slanting streaks blood-red and livid-white. From the Lydian creek came the bright
stone mingled with streaks of red. Stone too there is that the Libyan sun, warming
his golden light, has nourished in the deep clefts of the hills of the Moors, of crocus
color glittering like gold; and the product of the Celtic crags, a wealth of crystals,
like milk poured here and there on a flesh of glittering black. There is the precious
onyx, as if gold were shining through it; and the marble that the land of Atrax yields,
not from some upland glen, but from the level plains; in parts fresh green as the sea
or emerald stone, or again like blue cornflowers in grass, with here and there a drift
of fallen snow—a sweet mingled contrast on the dark shining surface.[16]*

A vast empire has never been praised in quite this way for the varieties of
stone it is capable of producing! But the passage is worth rereading, because the architecture of the Roman Empire, West and East, of medieval
Italy, and of the Italian Renaissance, cannot be understood unless one shares
to some degree this feeling for the variety, and surprisingly enough, the
emotional appeal of marble.

[16] Cited in Philip Sherrard, *Constantinople: Iconography of a Sacred City* (London: Oxford
University Press, 1965), p. 27.

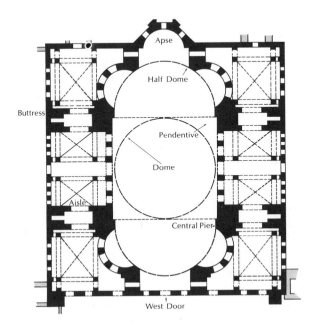

Ground Plan of Santa Sophia

The altar was a table of gold, with an inlay of precious stones, sheltered by a vast conical canopy of silver. Byzantine textiles of silk, gold and silver, embroidered with scenes of the life of Christ and the charitable deeds of Justinian, hung around the altar. Hanging chains of beaten brass, fitted with silver disks and thousands of candleholders of fine glass held cups of burning oil by night, so that the church itself acted as a beacon to mariners coming up the Bosphorus. And all this richness of decoration was lavished on a church of enormous size, 220 feet long by 107 feet wide in the central nave, with the dome 180 feet above the floor. But the decoration, so unlike the Parthenon, would not alone have accounted for the impressiveness of this building. Its designers combined technical mastery of building skills— they were mathematicians as well as architects—with artistic subtlety of the highest form. Let us glance both at the plan and at the photographs of the interior of Santa Sophia here and on pages 164, 192, and 193 to try to grasp what they were trying to achieve.

The plan shows that the architects combined two basic church forms: the rectangular basilica that we already saw in Sant' Apollinare Nuovo in Ravenna, and the centrally planned church. The distinction between these two types of churches is basic to all Christian architecture. The basilica is a rectangular building with the altar placed at the east end and the congregation, seated or standing, facing lengthways down the building. It can be made in the form of a cross when a transept is inserted near the east end. The centrally planned church began with mausoleums, in which the grave was placed in the middle of a circular or octagonal building. Often the church took the form of a Greek cross, that is a cross with arms of equal length, with a vaulted dome placed where the four arms of the cross met. The plan of Santa Sophia shows that the building is almost a square, if one looks at the outside walls. In the center of the square is a dome built upon four enormous piers. So far, the building is centrally planned. However, to the east and west of the central dome are two half-domes, also rising from the four central piers, while to the north and south of the dome, two aisles have been built. The plan shows therefore that the architects deliberately created two different kinds of feeling for space inside the building. There is the longitudinal, or forward, drive, produced by the side aisles and by the rectangular share of the central space. Entering at the main west door, one expects one's glance to be directed toward the far east end of the building, as in a basilica. But the dome creates an entirely different feeling. The culminating point of the building is not the east end, but the center of the great dome. One's eyes automatically look up and around the dome, and one feels the urge that the architects worked to inspire—to move forward to the very center of the building. Then, one stands before the very dome of heaven, and all around in exciting symmetry are displayed the images of the beauty, grandeur, and harmony of God's universe. The great dome united all worshippers in a community under God. The photos show what the ground plan does not, that the

architects succeeded in making the dome appear to float, unconnected with the huge pillars that support it. "From the lightness of the building," wrote Procopius, "it does not appear to rest upon a solid foundation, but to cover the place beneath as though it were suspended from heaven by the fabled golden chain." [17] The device used by the architects was the pendentive. Once they had built the four huge round arches in a square, on top of the four central piers, they had to figure out how to rest the dome upon these arches, transferring the weight of the dome from there to the piers. To do this they filled in the space between the edges of the round arches

Interior, Santa Sophia, Constantinople. Great variation in lighting is achieved by the forty-two windows in the base of the dome and by the opening up of the solid masonry of the wall. (Turkish State Tourist Office photo.)

[17] Procopius, *Buildings of Justinian*, p. 9.

and the base of the dome with masonry, creating a spherical triangle called a pendentive, which looks weightless but in fact transfers the weight of the dome away from the round arches to the piers. Secondly, the architects pierced the base of the dome with forty-two windows, not only enhancing the impression of the separation of the dome from the rest of the building but permitting the constant play of sunlight, which is one of the most superb characteristics of Santa Sophia. "It is singularly full of light and sunshine," Procopius commented. "You would declare that the place is not lightened by the sun from without, but that the rays are produced within itself, such an abundance of light is poured into this church." Thus the appearance of the building was constantly changing as the shafts of sunlight shifted in its many windows; and "No one ever became wearied of this spectacle." This display of light was essential to a church dedicated to the second person of the Trinity, the abstract Wisdom of Christ. "Whoever enters there to worship perceives at once that it is not by any human strength or skill, but by the favor of God that this work has been perfected; his mind rises sublime to commune with God, feeling that He cannot be far off, but must especially love to dwell in the place which He has chosen; and this takes place not only when a man sees it for the first time, but it always makes the same impression upon him, as though he had never beheld it before." [18]

Justinian, like Pericles, knew what he had created; and according to a tenth-century description that still rings true, he exclaimed, after walking the length of the church to the altar on the day of the church's dedication, "Glory be to God, who has thought me worthy to finish this work. Solomon, I have outdone thee!"

CONSTANTINOPLE AFTER JUSTINIAN

While a new form of civilization was being created in western Europe during the Middle Ages, two great and totally different civilizations continued to flourish on the European continent and at times to influence the development of medieval Christendom—the Byzantine civilization on the southeastern tip of Europe and the Moslem civilization on the southwestern, in Spain and Portugal. Moslem Spain will be discussed in the next chapter. Let us glance briefly here at the fortunes of Constantinople after Justinian's death.

By the mid–sixth century, the character of the Byzantine monarchy, the sources of its military and economic strength, the nature of the Greek Orthodox Church, and even the appearance of Constantinople had been given a definitive form. In spite of the evolution of eight centuries, the Byzantine empire in the fifteenth century was recognizably the same society as that under Justinian. One can realize the amazing achievement of continuity this is if one contrasts Victoria's England with that of William the Conqueror, which also represents the evolution of eight centuries, or even if one contrasts Rome at the time of Justinian with Rome at the time of Michelangelo.

---

[18] Ibid., pp. 6–7, 11.

Justinian's policy of reconquest in western Europe had weakened the empire in men and money; but the remaining resources of the empire were gathered for a long and ultimately victorious war against the Persians, which destroyed the Sassanid empire but left the Byzantine monarchy too weak to save large parts of its own empire from the many new waves of invaders that were threatening. All the territory taken by Justinian in Italy, except Ravenna and the south coast, was taken by a new Germanic tribe, the Lombards, in the seventh century. The Visigoths soon regained control of southern Spain. Slavs and Bulgars penetrated the Balkans and settled. But above all, the Arab followers of Mohammed seized half of the Byzantine empire—between 634 and 647, they took Syria, Palestine, and Egypt, whose inhabitants, weary of taxation and persecution for heresy, made no effort to oppose them. In 670–697, they took North Africa, the first of Justinian's conquests, and moved on from there into Spain. Their fleet raided the Sea of Marmara, and on several occasions their armies reached the walls of Constantinople itself. They were finally driven back after the siege of 717–718 by a new dynasty of Byzantine emperors, the Isaurians (717–867). The Isaurians reestablished the empire's finances, or at least of what was left of the empire: Asia Minor, the Balkans, and the southern tip of Italy. The new stability encouraged the appearance of a new period of cultural achievement through the late ninth and tenth centuries.

The Macedonian dynasty (867–1081) brought a new wave of economic prosperity, favored by developing trade relations with the new states of western Europe. It spread the Greek Orthodox religion to the Bulgars, the Russians, the Croats and Serbs. Its newly built fleets again controlled the waters around the empire. Constantinople's artisans in silk and metalwork again dominated the European market. From the end of the eleventh century, however, the slow but seemingly inexorable downfall of the empire began. The Normans drove the Byzantines out of Sicily and southern Italy by 1071. The Crusaders struck two damaging blows. First, after sacking Constantinople during the Fourth Crusade in 1204, they enabled the Venetians and other Italians to set up almost a stranglehold on Constantinople's trade. Second, the opening of new trade routes between western Europe and the Near East through Palestine broke Constantinople's monopoly of the Asiatic trade. When, after sixty years, a Greek emperor finally drove out the "Latin emperors" imposed by the Crusaders, he took possession of a ruined, starving, and depopulated city. The Byzantines therefore lacked the strength to hold out against the Ottoman Turks, the last of a series of Turkish tribes who had been moving westwards through central Asia since the tenth century. Throughout the fourteenth century, the Ottoman Turks, who had taken possession of all the Arab lands of the Near East, moved to encircle Constantinople. From Anatolia, they attacked the Balkans, taking Adrianople in 1347. They transformed the tiny city into their new capital, at a distance of only fifty miles from Constantinople. By 1390, they held all the Balkans and had reached the Danube. They besieged Constantinople in 1397, again in 1422, and began their final assault in April 1453.

Sultan Mohammed II, by Gentile Bellini. This fine example of Venetian portraiture was painted twenty-seven years after Mohammed II's capture of Constantinople in 1453. (Turkish State Tourist Office photo.)

More than seventy thousand picked Turkish troops armed with gigantic cannon besieged a city held by only seven thousand soldiers. Few documents are more moving than the last letter sent by the last East Roman emperor, Constantine XI, to his assailant, Sultan Mohammed II:

As it is clear that you desire war more than peace, since I cannot satisfy you either by my protestations of sincerity, or by my readiness to swear allegiance, so let it be according to your desire. I turn now and look to God alone. Should it be his will that the city be yours, where is he who can oppose it? If he should inspire you with a desire for peace, I shall be only too happy. However, I release you from all your oaths and treaties with me, and, closing the gates of my capital, I will defend my people to the last drop of my blood. Reign in happiness until the All-just, the Supreme God, calls us both before his judgement seat.[19]

The city fell at dawn on May 29 when the Turks finally succeeded in getting a small group of men over the top of the land walls. At midday the young sultan rode with his court through a city given over to pillaging, across the forums along Middle Street, to the Church of Santa Sophia. There he dismounted, picked up a handful of soil which he scattered on his head to humble himself before his god, and in Santa Sophia, he listened to the first Moslem prayer recited from the pulpit. He then moved on to the Great Palace, where, seeing the cobwebs spreading across its ruins, he murmured the lines of an old Persian poem: ''The spider has woven his web in the imperial palace, And the owl has sung a watch-song on the towers of Afrasiab.'' At the age of twenty-three he had destroyed an empire that had lasted for 1,123 years.

[19] Sherrard, *Constantinople,* pp. 127–28.

SUGGESTED READING

Philip Sherrard has combined superb photography with a wealth of contemporary quotations to create a marvelously poetic but historically valid portrait of the city in *Constantinople: Iconography of a Sacred City* (1965). Glanville Downey, an outstanding Byzantine historian, makes many provocative judgments but succeeds very well in re-creating the character of the age in *Constantinople in the Age of Justinian* (1960). For the building programs of the emperors and their significance, one should consult Michael Maclagan, *The City of Constantinople* (1968) or John E. N. Hearsey, *City of Constantine 324–1453* (1963). Dean A. Miller's *Imperial Constantinople* (1969) is well documented but marred by jargon. Cyril Mango, *The Brazen House: A Study of the Vestibule of the Imperial Palace of Constantinople* (1959) demonstrates the archaeological methods by which knowledge of the imperial palace and its surrounding buildings has been obtained.

For the life of Justinian, John W. Baker, *Justinian and the Later Roman Empire* (1966) is solid, with emphasis on military and religious questions, and contains a good list of primary sources. P. N. Ure, *Justinian and His Age* (1951) is unbalanced and opinionated, but makes very rich use of contemporary writings.

There are many excellent surveys of Byzantine history. Charles Diehl, *Byzantium: Greatness and Decline* (1957) is a first-class summary by a French historian, even if slightly outdated in places. It contains an indispensable bibliography by Professor Peter Charanis for additional study. Steven Runciman, the doyen of British historians of Byzantium, provides an elegant study, which packs an incredible amount of information into a short space, in *Byzantine Civilization* (1956). His earlier *The Byzantine Empire* (1925) still makes good reading. For a narrative with emphasis on religious problems, see Joan Hussey, *The Byzantine World* (1957); for cultural background, see Speros Vryonis, Jr., *Byzantium and Europe* (1967); for political intricacies, see George Ostrogorsky, *History of the Byzantine State* (1956), translated by Joan Hussey. Jack Lindsay, *Byzantium into Europe* (1952) makes use of wide knowledge of primary sources, especially literature, and brings such topical studies as Faction and Circus to life. Tamara Talbot Rice, *Everyday Life in Byzantium* (1967) is quite scholarly and gives many fascinating details. For example, she points out that one of the most popular imports from Asia in the sixth century was sets of chessmen and checkers.

André Grabar has written two gorgeously illustrated books on Byzantium's art: *Byzantium from the Death of Theodosius to the Rise of Islam* (1966), which covers architecture, painting, sculpture, sumptuary arts, and art industries, and *Byzantine Painting* (1953), which includes studies of the mosaics of the Great Palace and such later Byzantine mosaics as St. Mark's in Venice and the Palatine Chapel in Palermo. David Talbot Rice, *The Art of Byzantium* (1959) is short and well illustrated with color photos of paintings and metalwork.

Once again, the ancient writers are the most vivid. Procopius's *The Secret History of the Court of Justinian* has attracted many translators; the Palestine Pilgrims' Text Society put *The Buildings of Justinian* (1897) in the hands of its peregrinating members. The Hakluyt Society of London published *The Christian Topography of Cosmas Indicopleustes* for its armchair travelers. Robert A. Furness has translated selections from *The Greek Anthology* (1931). Ernest Barker, *Social and Political Thought in Byzantium* (1957), covers the whole sweep of the city's political science.

7
THE EARLY MIDDLE AGES, 600-1000

During the five centuries following the disappearance of the Roman Empire in the West, a flourishing city life continued to exist only at the extremities of the European continent, in the Byzantine empire and in the Islamic caliphate of Spain. In the rest of Europe, city life slowly decayed under the impact of several waves of invasions—first, the Germanic tribes and the Huns, then the Moslem Arabs, and finally the Magyars and Vikings. In the violent and precarious life during the invasions, central administration broke down, ending the role of the cities as political centers. Trade routes were obstructed, and long-distance commerce greatly restricted, so that the cities gave up most of their commerce and manufacturing, except for the local market. The process was gradual but except for the brief slight resurgence under the Carolingian Empire of Frankish ruler Charlemagne (reigned 768–814), inexorable. The inhabitants of most of Europe fell back on the village as the nucleus of their economic and social life. By the tenth century, this village economy, known as manorialism, was the predominant form of economic life on most of the continent; and as the agricultural historian Georges Duby has recently pointed out, the student of the period does not have "to consider the problem, so pressing in succeeding times, of the relationship between town and country." The city had temporarily given precedence to the village.

Mohammed and the Religion of Islam. Arabia did not figure large in the history of civilization before the sixth century, except to send wave after wave of Semitic invaders from its forbidding deserts and mountains to seek a better life among the cities and irrigated plains of the Fertile Cres-

MOHAMMED AND THE CIVILIZATION OF ISLAM

The Mosque, Cordoba. The mosque of Cordoba was begun in the eighth century and enlarged several times by later caliphs. Eight hundred and fifty columns of marble, jasper, and porphyry topped by alternating bands of red brick and white stone create the impression of a luxuriant forest of stone. (Spanish National Tourist Office photo.)

Detail of Wall Panel, The Alhambra, Granada. The words of the Koran and non-representational design, often of intricate geometrical patterns, formed the basis of the stucco decoration that covered the walls of Moslem palaces. (Spanish National Tourist Office photo.)

cent. Most of its inhabitants were desert nomads, except for small numbers of sophisticated traders who grouped in cities in the oases along the caravan routes. Mohammed was born in Mecca, the most important of these trading cities, and spent his early life in the caravan trade, traveling widely through Arabia and probably north into Palestine and Syria, where he became acquainted with the beliefs of both Christians and Jews. He was an astute businessman, married the wealthy widow whose business he had managed, and might have led a wholly unexceptional life had he not begun at the age of forty to see visions. Mohammed believed he saw the Angel Gabriel, who ordered him to reveal the will of God, in part by "reciting" the words of God revealed to him in his visions. These revelations continued for twenty years, and were collected in the Moslem holy book, the *Koran*. The message Mohammed had to teach was very simple. There is only one god, Allah, who can never take human form; he will judge all mankind in a terrible Day of Judgement; while awaiting that day, men must lead a decent life along the lines indicated by Allah's last and greatest prophet, Mohammed.

Mohammed preached the new faith, which he called Islam, or "abandonment" to the will of God, among the people he knew in Mecca. But most of the city's leaders attacked him for his opposition to their polytheism, especially as the great black meteorite in the center of the city was the main goal of pagan worship in Arabia. In 622, however, Mohammed was invited to mediate the disputes of feuding tribes in Medina, the second largest city of Arabia, and he decided to take "flight," or *hegira,* there. All Moslem history has since been dated from the Hegira, because in Medina, Mohammed was able to give Islam a political base. As chief magistrate of Medina, Mohammed elaborated the rules that were to govern the daily life of believers in Islam, and laid down five basic requirements for all believers: ritual prayer five times a day; belief in one god, Allah; fasting from dawn to dusk during the month of Ramadan; a pilgrimage at least once in a lifetime to Mecca; and almsgiving. To support the overcrowded community of Medina, Mohammed sent marauding parties to raid the caravans passing to Mecca; and after several indecisive battles, he led a successful expedition to capture Mecca in 630. War against the pagans was justified as *jehad,* or holy war, for the conversion of the unbelievers. By the time of Mohammed's death in June 632, Moslem rule extended over two-thirds of Arabia, and had reached the southern edge of Palestine.

The Expansion of Islam. After the Prophet's death, Islam was faced by two great difficulties. An enduring method of regulating the succession to Mohammed had to be found; and if expansion was to continue, the military strength would have to be raised to defeat the two great empires, Byzantine and Persian, that held Islam penned up in the Arabian peninsula. Mohammed had left the basis of the new religion—the sayings revealed to him by Allah, that were to be collected in the *Koran;* his own sayings, called the *hadith,* dealing with the detailed rules for everyday conduct; and the *sunna,* or custom, a description of the life of Mohammed himself, which set an example for the faithful. But Mohammed had ignored the problem of making permanent in a political form the theocracy of Islam. His closest companions settled the question temporarily by appointing Abu Bakr, one of his oldest and most trusted followers, as his "successor," "deputy," or "representative," that is, as *caliph.* During

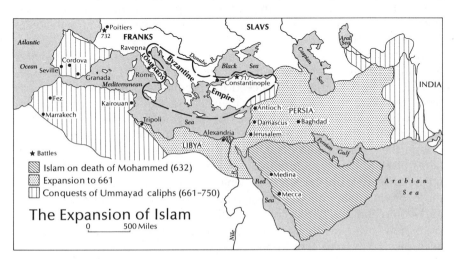

The Expansion of Islam

0   500 Miles

★ Battles

Islam on death of Mohammed (632)

Expansion to 661

Conquests of Ummayad caliphs (661–750)

his two-year rule, Abu Bakr was preoccupied with crushing the revolts of the Arab tribes, who felt that Mohammed's death had dissolved the political control of Islam. The second caliph, Omar (reigned 634–644), settled both basic problems. He regulated the claims of the army by listing the soldiers on the *diwan*, a payment sheet naming the contribution they were to receive from the public treasury instead of conquered lands. He increased the state domain by confiscating land conquered, and the state treasury by imposing tribute on those who surrendered voluntarily to his armies. Above all, he turned the Bedouin tribesmen under their superb Arab generals against disaffected provinces of the Byzantine and Persian empires. With little opposition from the inhabitants, the armies of Islam destroyed the great cavalry of Byzantium and Persia, riding nimbly around them on their desert ponies; and before Omar was assassinated, they had captured Palestine, Syria, Mesopotamia, Persia itself, and Egypt.

The Ummayad and Abbasid Caliphates. The death of Omar marked the end of the first great period of Islamic expansion. A vast migration of Arabs into the conquered territories took place, perhaps half a million establishing themselves throughout the Fertile Crescent and in Egypt. Overpopulation in Arabia that had been a significant factor in the military expansion was thus relieved, and also the endurance of Arab control of this empire was assured. Unlike Justinian's conquests, the conquests of Islam were to be lasting because they involved not only conversion to the religion of Islam but also the bodily settlement of a new ruling class. Omar's successor, Othman, of the Ummayad family, was a kindly, pious man unresistant to the demands of his near relatives and unsuited to the rigorous demands of the caliphate. When he too was murdered, Ali, son-in-law of Mohammed, was named caliph, but his succession precipitated civil war when the Ummayad governor of Syria, Muawiya, revolted. Ali in turn was murdered, and Muawiya restored stability to the Moslem empire.

The caliphate remained in the hands of the Ummayad family for almost a century, in spite of revolts of the Shi'ites who held that only the descendants of Ali had the right to succeed the prophet and that the Ummayads were usurpers. The Ummayads revived the expansionist drive, using it to whip up religious fervor and the unifying desire for booty. They were foiled in several attempts to capture Constantinople, but they did extend their control into central Asia and western India, along the coastlands of North Africa, and into Spain. It is often suggested that the Arabs intended to link up the forces driving from the west through Spain with those driving into the Byzantine empire somewhere in central Europe, thus completing the Arab control of the whole Mediterranean. But they were now overextended. When the Byzantine armies used Greek fire, an explosive mixture shot through copper tubes, the Moslems abandoned the attempt to capture Constantinople in 717; and in 732, defeated near Tours by the cavalry of the Frankish leader Charles the Hammer, they withdrew to south of the Pyrenees. In this way, the Arabs established the northwestern and northeastern boundaries of their conquests, which would not be surpassed until the empire of Islam was taken over by the Seljuk Turks; and the caliphs settled down to digest their conquests.

The Ummayads had recognized that the center of Islamic power was no longer Medina, by moving their capital to Damascus in Syria, where, under Byzantine influences, they sponsored a vast building program and encouraged artists, artisans, and scholars in the creation of Islam's own culture as well as in the study of early cultures of the Eastern Mediterranean. The Ummayads did not survive to see the height of the cultural boom they had inaugurated. They were overthrown in 750 by the Abbasid family, the descendants of the uncle of Mohammed, who transferred the capital from Syria to a newly founded city, Baghdad in Iraq. The only member of the Ummayad family to escape the Abbasid sword fled to Spain, where he was recognized as the rightful emir. During the next two centuries, Islam saw an extraordinary intellectual boom whose centers were the two capitals of the rival caliphates, Abbasid Baghdad and Ummayad Cordoba. Both eventually exerted a beneficial effect on the development of Western culture, the lesser center, Cordoba, probably exercising a greater influence because of its geographical accessibility.

Under the Abbasids, the character of Islamic rule changed. The caliph withdrew into oriental seclusion, with all the pomp and ritual of the Persian and Byzantine courts. He abolished the distinction between Arab Moslem and non-Arab Moslem, making all eligible for office in the royal bureaucracy and for a share in the duties and profits of the army. Moslem life was thus open to the influences of the earlier civilizations— of the conquered territories, Byzantium and Persia, and even of Greece. Possession of the Fertile Crescent brought great economic resources in agriculture, in cereals, olives, and dates. The outer provinces of the empire in Africa and Asia supplied gold and silver, copper, iron, and precious stones. New crops were introduced, such as sugar cane and cotton from India; and silk manufacture was continued in Syria, where Justinian had started it. Captured Chinese soldiers introduced the art of papermaking, which soon spread throughout the empire. Islam too now controlled the great trade routes between Asia, Africa, and Europe, including the Red Sea, Persia, and the Caravan routes through Bokhara and Samarkand; and it opened up new routes across Russia by the great rivers of the Don and Volga, to trade with Scandinavia. In the tenth and eleventh centuries, however, weak Abbasid rulers were unable to maintain their power, and the empire broke apart. The Ummayads in Spain had never recognized the caliphate in Baghdad. Now a large number of new dynasties established themselves throughout the empire—in Tunis and Morocco; in Egypt; in Arabia, Syria, Transoxiana, and northern Persia. For a brief period the glory of Islamic culture sparkled from a galaxy of new capitals: Cordoba, Kairouan, Palermo, Bokhara, Samarkand, Chaznah, Cairo. But this disintegration was ended in large part when the Abbasids became the willing captives of the Seljuk Turks in the mid–eleventh century.

Effects of Islamic Conquests on the West. The influence of this Arab expansion on Western civilization went through two clear phases. The first, from the beginning of the Moslem conquests through the eighth century, was largely negative. The conquest of Syria, Palestine, and Egypt obviously struck an enormous blow to Christianity. When the Arab conquests began, the whole of the Mediterranean basin, north and south, was Christian. When the conquests stopped, the whole of North Africa and the Near East was permanently lost to Christianity. From the Christian point of view at least, this was a tragedy, particularly the loss of Christ's own birthplace to the infidel. Christian hatred of the Moslem acted throughout the Middle Ages as a poison in a religion based on brotherly love. It led to condonement of the slave trade in Moslem captives. It inflamed for eight hundred years the war for the Christian reconquest of Spain. It caused the waste of the Crusades in the eleventh, twelfth, and thirteenth centuries, which diverted the manpower and precariously small resources of Europe to the chimera of reconquering Palestine. During the years of the conquests and immediately afterwards, Mediterranean trade inevitably dwindled, affected by war, Christian and Moslem unwillingness to maintain direct economic contact, Arab piracy, and the Byzantine empire's use of its naval power to isolate the lost provinces of Syria and Egypt from trade with the Franks.

The Cultural Impact of Islam on the West. Once the Arabs had stabilized their empire, and had transformed a state of mounted warriors in constant motion into a settled bureaucratic state, their influence on the West was largely beneficial, even though the Arabs were not interested in what the Europeans might teach them. "The peoples of the north," wrote a tenth-century Arab geographer, "are those for whom the sun is distant from the Zenith. . . . Cold and damp prevail in those regions, and snow and ice follow one another in endless succession. The warm humor is lacking among them; their bodies are large, their natures gross, their manners harsh, their understanding dull and their tongues heavy." The achievements of five hundred years of medieval scholarship made no better impression. "We have heard of late that in the lands of the Franks, that is, the country of Rome and its dependencies on the northern shore of the Mediterranean, the philosophic sciences flourish," wrote a well-informed Arab scholar. "But God knows best what goes on in those parts." The Europeans, however, never lost their interest in the Near or Far East. Trade of Byzantium with its possessions in Italy had never been entirely broken off; and these cities—Venice, Amalfi, Gaeta, Salerno, Bari—after

first profiting from a virtual monopoly of the Byzantine trade, began to
open up a lucrative commerce with Islam itself. The Jews, however, acted
as the main intermediary. A famous passage from an Arab geographer
of the ninth century described Jewish traders from the south of France:

[They] *speak Arabic, Persian, Greek, Frankish, Spanish, and Slavonic. They travel
from west to east and from east to west, by land and by sea. From the west they
bring eunuchs, slave-girls, boys, brocade, castor-skins, marten and other furs,
and swords. They take ship from Frank-land in the western Mediterranean sea
and land at Farama, whence they take their merchandise on camel-back to Qulzum,
a distance of twenty-five parasangs. Then they sail on the eastern [Red] Sea from
Qulzum, to Al-Jar and Jedda, and onward to Sind, India and China. From China
they bring back musk, aloes, camphor, cinnamon, and other products of those
parts, and return to Qulzum. Then they transport them to Farama and sail again
on the western sea. Some sail with their goods to Constantinople and sell them
to the Greeks, and some take them to the king of the Franks and sell them there.*

*Sometimes they bring their goods from Frank-land across the western sea and
unload at Antioch. Then they travel three days' march overland to Al-Jabiya,
whence they sail down the Euphrates to Baghdad, then down the Tigris to Ubulla,
and from Ubulla to Uman, Sind, India and China.*[1]

During the ninth and tenth centuries, therefore, European trade across
the Mediterranean revived, and the European city was soon reborn.

[1] Bernard Lewis, *The Arabs in History* (London: Hutchinson's University Library, 1958), p. 90.

The Giralda of Seville.
Originally a minaret, the
Giralda was preserved as a
belltower when the mosque
of Seville was torn down to
make way for a Gothic
cathedral. Built in 1196, it
displays the delicate tracery
that the Arabs attained by use
of red brick. The top floor,
in Renaissance style, was
added in the sixteenth century.
(Spanish National Tourist
Office photo.)

From the Arabs, a vast range of new products and manufactures entered Europe, mainly through Spain, though the Crusaders also later brought back many things from the Holy Land. The Arabs introduced rice, sugar cane and cotton, oranges and lemons, thus changing the distinctive character of Mediterranean agriculture from its reliance on olives and vines. Paper manufacture came to Spain through Morocco, and made possible the invention of the printing press in Germany in the fifteenth century. Arab handcraft produced the great steel blades of Toledo, the leather of Cordoba, and heavy silks that rivaled those of Byzantium.

In Spain, the Europeans undertook the study of not only the achievements of Islamic culture but the Greek heritage too. The Ummayads established their capital in Spain at the bridgehead on the river Guadalquivir, in the town of Cordoba, which in the ninth and tenth centuries was second only to Constantinople among the cities of Europe. Cordoba had perhaps half a million inhabitants, three thousand mosques, three hundred public baths, great libraries filled with Arabic and Greek manuscripts, numerous hospitals and medical schools, and a great university attached to the mosque that rivaled those of Cairo and Baghdad. Moreover, Christian, Jew and Moslem lived side by side in a toleration enforced by the caliph, thus making fairly easy prolonged residence by Christian students from the northern countries. This tradition of learning was carried on by the smaller Moslem states that succeeded the caliphate: Seville, until its

Air View, Cordoba. The city plan of Arab Cordoba is preserved in the maze of narrow streets that surrounds the vast square of the mosque's outer walls. (Spanish National Tourist Office photo.)

capture by the Christians in 1248; and Granada, the last stronghold of
the Moslems in Spain.

Islamic Philosophy, Science, and Medicine. The transmission of Arab
learning was thus made in the most direct way possible. Christians came
to get it for themselves. And in the state of El-Andalus, or Moslem Spain,
the achievements of the whole Arab world, including those of faraway
Baghdad, were available for study. According to an English chronicler,
Pope Gerbert learned a surprising variety of subjects in Spain:

*Gerbert, coming among these people, satisfied his desires. There he surpassed
Ptolemy with the astrolabe, and Alcandraeus in astronomy, and Julius Firmicus in
judicial astrology; there he learned what the singing and flight of birds portended;
there he acquired the art of calling up spirits from hell: in short, whatever, hurtful
or salutary, human curiosity had discovered.*

The greatest number of Christians came to study classical books that had
been brought from the East, even though many were in Arabic translation.
Cordoba had its center for translation from Greek into Arabic; and later
the city of Toledo, once in Christian hands, became the main center in
Europe for the translation into Latin of Arabic translations from the Greek.
In this indirect way, many of the greatest manuscripts of Athens, including
much of Plato and Aristotle, entered medieval Europe. Christian scholars
were also interested in the philosophical writings of great Arab writers,
especially those who had divorced their philosophy from religion by bas-
ing their writings on classical Greek philosophy. The most important of
all these writers for Christians was Averroës (1126–1198), a protégé of the
caliph of Marrakech. Averroës was admired by Christians for a massive
commentary that he wrote on the works of Aristotle, which was required
reading in the University of Paris. His assertion that religion was an alle-
gorical way of expressing philosophical ideas and the emphasis that he
put on reason as a method of attaining philosophical truth led some of his
admirers into the heresy, called Averroism, of ignoring the truth of revealed
religion. For ignoring the truth of Islam's revealed religion, Averroës's
writings in Arabic were burned by the caliph; in Christendom, Saint
Thomas Aquinas thundered against the Averroists, although he himself
followed many of the writings of Averroës.

The impact of Moslem science and medicine was less controversial.
The greatest medical writer of the Middle Ages was Avicenna, whose text-
book on medicine was the main one studied in European universities for
several hundred years. And it was an Arab physician in Spain who told
the Christians that the Black Death of the fourteenth century was not an
act of God but a disease spread by contagion:

*To those who say, "How can we admit the possibility of infection while the reli-
gious law denies it?" we reply that the existence of contagion is established by
experience, investigation, the evidence of the senses and trustworthy reports. These*

facts constitute a sound argument. The fact of contagion becomes clear to the investigator who notices how he who establishes contact with the afflicted gets the disease, whereas he who is not in contact remains safe, and how transmission is effected through garments, vessels and earrings.[2]

While the Arab contribution to medicine was largely one of saving what was already known, they did make advances in the use of drugs, especially herbs. Many Arabic medical terms have entered the English language, though not always with the original medicinal purpose implied. *Julep, syrup, soda,* and *alcohol* were originally medical terms. From Arab scientists, European scholars took our present system of numerals, which are not Arabic but which had been brought by the Arabs from India; the study of algebra, itself an Arabic word; and the study of astronomy.

Islamic Art and Architecture.   Islamic art and architecture were admired but rarely imitated. It is impossible to mistake a piece of Islamic art. The Court of Lions of the Alhambra, a Persian carpet, Damascus tiles, Baghdad silk, or a Cairo pitcher of rock crystal could not be mistaken for the work of any other culture. The reason for this is that all Islamic art is dominated by the Koran and the Arabic language. The Koran laid down the religious ceremonies that were to be followed by Moslems and hence the primary building in all Moslem architecture, the mosque, was developed in a set pattern to satisfy these functions. Ritual group prayer, including prostration, is prescribed. Hence the house of prayer is a broad, carpeted room where worshippers can assemble in lines; and it has two outstanding architectural features, an empty niche called a *mihrab,* indicating the position of Mecca, and a pulpit on a staircase from which prayer can be led. Since ablution before prayer is required, there is a large open-air court with fountains and washbasins. For the muezzin to call the faithful to prayer, a tower called a minaret was added later. From the simple temple of palm branches that Mohammed constructed to the Taj Mahal, the principles of the mosque remain the same, and can be seen in great splendor at Cordoba.

The entrance to the Cordoba mosque was a wide courtyard, the Patio of the Orange Trees, where the Moslems washed. Rows of orange trees in the court were prolonged inside the building by lines of Roman and Visigothic columns, set in a series of eleven parallel naves crossed by a similar number of aisles. Originally there was no outer wall between the court and the interior, and court and mosque were linked by the lines of trees and columns. As each ruler felt the need for a larger mosque, he simply added a few more aisles, so that the ultimate sense was not of being in a building with a central core but rather of walking through a colorful and somewhat confusing forest of porphyry, jasper, and marble beneath arches composed in alternate bands of red brick and white stone. The tragedy of all Spanish history is symbolized in this mosque. In 1523, the cathedral clergy, with

[2] Philip K. Hitti, *History of the Arabs from the Earliest Times to the Present* (New York: St. Martin's Press, 1964), p. 576.

Entrance Gate, Mosque of Cordoba. This lavishly decorated gateway of the eighth century illustrates the decorative use made by Arab architects of the horseshoe arch. Stylized flower patterns were traced in stucco, while diamond patterns in the square frame are composed of colored tiles and mosaics. (Spanish National Tourist Office photo.)

The Catholic Church within the Mosque of Cordoba. The flamboyant Gothic church erected in the heart of the Arab mosque symbolizes the final triumph of the seven-hundred-year long Spanish Crusade, appears ponderous and overdecorated in comparison with the simplicity of the Moslem arches. (Spanish National Tourist Office photo.)

the permission of Emperor Charles V, hacked out a large space in the center of the mosque, removing sixty columns, and built there a complete Christian church in the shape of a cross. When Charles V saw what they had done, he was appalled. "You have built here what you or anyone else might build," he said, "but you have destroyed what was unique in the world."

It is in the Alhambra palace in Granada, however, that one understands the predominance in all Islamic art of decorative ornament cut in low relief. The Koran and more especially the Sunna forbade the representation of living beings, especially human beings and animals. Although this proscription was later evaded, most Moslem art was based on decoration by use of forms not deriving from nature, and on the use of the Arabic language and especially of quotations from the Koran as the principal form of decoration. The result of this concentration for more than fourteen centuries was to produce an amazing variety of decorative forms in all types of art and handicraft—in leather, steel, ivory, textiles, carpets, wood, stone, stucco, pottery, and glass.

The Alhambra was the fortified palace of the Nazarite dynasty, which ruled Granada from 1232 to 1492. It stands on a tall hill on the edge of the town, commanding broad views in every direction. From the distance it looks like a typical medieval fortress, with bare crenelated walls, rough and primitive, waiting for the Christian invasion that was bound to come across the snowy heights of the Sierra Nevada. The palace was divided into three parts. Administration and justice was carried on in the *mezuar*, the first part a visitor entered. The mezuar led to the Court of Myrtles, a long narrow patio richly decorated at one end with a series of round arches

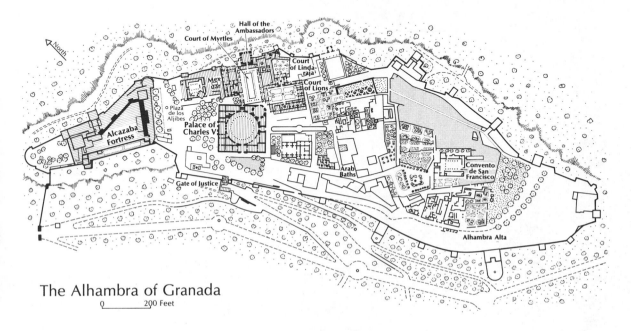

The Alhambra of Granada

0   200 Feet

on delicate columns, with a huge reflecting pool in the center, beyond which was the Hall of the Ambassadors. Here the enthroned sultan received official visitors, amid one of the most beautiful creations of Islamic craftsmanship. Although the room was two stories high and thirty-seven feet square, every flat space on walls, floor, and ceiling was covered with a scintillating pattern of sculptured plaster, tile, or cedarwood. Motifs used by Moslem craftsmen included geometrical designs like squares, circles, ellipses, and cones; more complicated patterns of swirls, scrolls, cusps, and stars; leaves, flowers, birds, animals; and strange stalagmite formations and long borders of Arabic script. In the Patio of Lions, where the harem was situated, the art of decoration fused with the exquisite use of the Moorish arch into an unrivaled composition of colors and shapes. The grey gravel of the courtyard contrasted with the white of the hundred and twenty-four marble columns, the fretwork above them, and the muted red tile of the roof, while from every passageway the tile and stalactite roofs shimmered with the reflected sunshine. Finally in a last cypress-shaded patio

Exterior View, The Alhambra of Granada. In the fifteenth century, the Alhambra was the defense bastion of the last remaining Arab dynasty in Spain. Its vast fortifications give little hint of the delicacy of the interior rooms and courtyards of the red-tiled palace in the foreground. (Spanish National Tourist Office photo.)

The Hall of the Ambassadors, The Alhambra of Granada. The sultan received important visitors in this sumptuously decorated hall. The stucco and tile that covers every space in the 75-foot high room displays all the favorite motifs of Moslem decorative art. (Spanish National Tourist Office photo.)

overlooking the valley of Granada, the Nazarite dynasty inscribed their own farewell to the jewel they had created:

*I am not alone, for a delightful garden can be contemplated
from this spot.
Such a place has never before been seen.
This is the palace of crystal, he who looks on it will believe
he regards the mighty ocean and will be filled with fear.
All this is the work of Imán Ibn Nasar, may God keep his
grandeur for other kings.
His forebears in ancient time were of the most noble, giving
hospitality to the Prophet and his family.*[3]

CHARLEMAGNE AND THE CAROLINGIAN EMPIRE

In the sixth and seventh centuries, many of the states created by the Germanic tribes from fragments of the Roman Empire, such as the Visigothic state in Spain or the Ostrogothic state in Italy, lost the power to control and defend their subjects, and proved easy prey to new invaders. The most important exception was the kingdom of the Franks, which was able to halt the Moslem advance at Tours in 732. Of all the Germanic peoples, the Franks were the most aggressively self-confident. Their tribal law began: ''The illustrious tribe of the Franks, established by God the Creator, brave

---

[3] F. Prieto-Moreno, *Granada,* trans. John Forrester (Barcelona: Noguer, 1957), p. 19.

in war, faithful in peace, wise in their counsels, of noble body, of immaculate purity, of choice physique, courageous, quick and impetuous, converted to the Catholic faith, free of heresy." Many but by no means all of these qualities had been displayed by Clovis, who at the end of the fifth century had brought most of France and the southern part of Germany under his control; but his family, the Merovingians, had proved to be "rois fainéants," do-nothing kings. In the words of Charlemagne's biographer, Einhard, "The wealth and power of the kingdom was in the hands of the Prefects of the Court, who were called Mayors of the Palace, and exercised entire sovereignty. The King, contented with the mere royal title, with long hair and flowing beard, used to sit upon the throne, and act the part of a ruler, listening to ambassadors, whencesoever they came, and giving them at their departure, as though of his own power, answers which he had been instructed or commanded to give." [4] The tough Frankish virtues were exemplified instead by a new family that had built up vast landed estates in the region of eastern Belgium and, through sheer ability in administration, battles, and intrigue, had kept the office of chief minister, or mayor of the palace, in their hands for several generations. The greatest rulers of this family, Charles the Hammer, his son Pepin, and his grandson Charlemagne, all followed a similar policy. They sought to unify the Frankish kingdom by canalizing the warlike energies of the local lords on their own behalf. They tried to extend Christianity in the area that could be exploited for taxes and new fiefs, to the pagan tribes of Frisia and Saxony. They struck an alliance with the Catholic Church, supporting the pope in Italy against the Lombards and granting rich lands in the newly Christianized territories to new bishops, accepting in return the religious sanction of their political authority and the collaboration of the clergy in bureaucracy and educational tasks of the kingdom. And they attempted to drive back the Moslems, first blocking their advance into France, and then beginning the long reconquest of the Iberian peninsula. Pepin abolished Merovingian rule by asking the pope the loaded question, "What should be done with kings who were living in the kingdom of the Franks without exercising royal authority?" The pope had replied, in an equally disingenuous way, that "it was best that those be named king who exercised the highest authority." With this sanction, Pepin had packed the last Merovingian king off into a monastery, and was crowned king of the Franks himself; and he left to Charles, whose exploits soon won him the title of "the Great" (Charlemagne), an adequate treasury, large family estates, effective cavalry and a papal alliance that could be used both to repress internal discontent and to bless external aggression.

Charlemagne's Character and Military Policy. Charlemagne strode uninhibited into the rough Germanic world, determined to dominate it as a new King David. In a society where physical prowess was the basis for

[4] A. J. Grant, ed., *Early Lives of Charlemagne* (London: Chatto and Windus, 1926), p. 8.

prestige, Charlemagne excelled.   In the stylized court of Constantinople, Justinian could get away with being thin and sallow.   According to Einhard, Charlemagne was a warrior's king:

His body was large and strong; his stature tall but not ungainly, for the measure of his height was seven times the length of his own feet.   The top of his head was round; his eyes were very large and piercing.   His nose was rather larger than is usual; he had beautiful white hair, and his expression was brisk and cheerful; so that, whether sitting or standing, his appearance was dignified and impressive. . . .   His step was firm and the whole carriage of his body manly, his voice was clear, but hardly so strong as you would have expected.   He had good health, but for four years before his death was frequently attacked by fevers, and at last was lame on one foot.   Even then, he followed his own opinion rather than the advice of his doctors, whom he almost hated, because they advised him to give up the roast meat to which he was accustomed, and eat boiled instead.[5]

[5] Ibid., pp. 37–38.

The Talisman of Charlemagne.
Carolingian jewelry, like this charm supposedly worn by Charlemagne, favored heavy settings of gold and large gems. (German Information Center photo.)

Sixteenth-century Portrait of Charlemagne by Albrecht Dürer.   (Deutsche Zentrale für Fremdenverkehr.)

Charlemagne was constantly at war. Every year in the spring his army would gather for the annual campaign. He defeated the Lombards in Italy, and took the title of King of the Lombards. After thirty years of fighting the Saxons were finally subdued. The defeat of Bavaria brought his kingdom to the upper Danube, from which he mounted a great campaign against the Hunnish people called the Avars. The campaign was as profitable for Charles as Justinian's attack on the Vandals, and for similar reasons.

He was able to seize from them all the booty they had been accumulating in a century of depredations, especially the large tribute in gold that had been paid by Constantinople. It was said that fifteen wagonloads of gold, silver, and precious clothing were sent back to his capital after the defeat of the Avars; but his armies left a desolation. "How many battles were fought there, and how much blood was shed," wrote Einhard, "is still shown by the uninhibited condition of Pannonia [Hungary], and the district, in which the palace of the Kagans was, is so desolate that there is not so much as a trace of human habitation. All the nobles of the Huns were killed in this war; all their glory passed away. Their money, and all the treasures they had collected for so long were carried away, nor can the memory of man recall any war waged by the Franks by which they were so much enriched, and their wealth so much increased." Charlemagne was unable to win the primary victory he sought against the Moslems in Spain, but he did establish a foothold on the southern slopes of the Pyrenees, from which the reconquest could be continued. By these conquests, he established an empire that ran from the southern Pyrenees, the Mediterranean shore of France, and central Italy, to Hungary in the East and southern Denmark in the North.

Aachen, Charlemagne's New Imperial Capital. Charlemagne could see, after his conquests, only two rulers with whom he could compare—the caliph in Baghdad and the Byzantine emperor in Constantinople. He was aware of how greatly inferior the Franks were in culture to both those empires; and Caliph Harun-el-Raschid helped remind him by sending as presents "monkeys, balsam, nard, unguents of various kinds, spices, scents, and many drugs, all in such profusion that it seemed as if the East had been left bare so that the West might be filled," and an elephant called Abul-Abaz, which became Charlemagne's special delight. Although Charlemagne enjoyed the primitive Frankish life—he disliked luxurious foreign clothes, ate simple food, lived like a clan leader surrounded by his relatives, and refused elaborate ceremonial—he was determined that his own empire should rival that of Constantinople. Like Constantine, he ordered the building at Aachen of a new capital, as a second Rome and a new Athens. (Constantine had already built a second Rome, but Charlemagne was not prepared to call his a third.) Charlemagne picked Aachen because he liked the hot springs, and because of its central position in his dominions. It

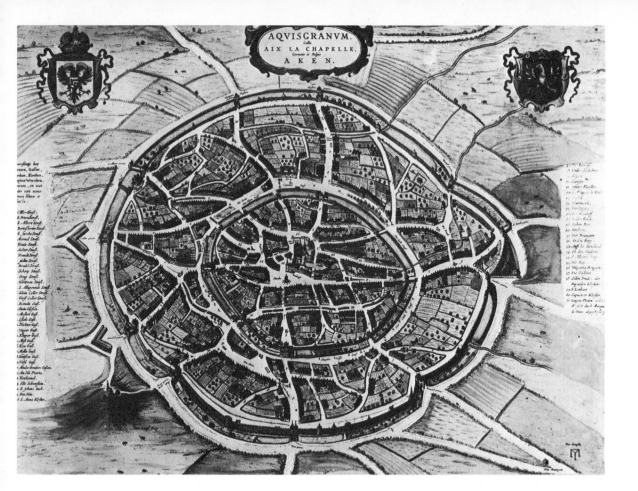

Sixteenth-Century City Plan, Aachen. The successive enlargements of Aachen may be easily distinguished in this sixteenth-century drawing. Charlemagne's small settlement is grouped around the Palatine Chapel, in the very center of town. (German Information Center photo.)

had few other advantages, however, and was abandoned as a capital soon after his death. Like Constantine, however, Charlemagne stood on a high spot, and designated the place for his forum, his senate, the theater, the baths, and the aqueduct. He brought in architects and artisans from his whole kingdom. To obtain antique columns and mosaics, he asked the pope to let him demolish the walls and floors of the palace in Ravenna. But what he created was worlds removed from another Constantinople. In Aachen, there was merely a large palace, surrounded with walls like a country villa, and linked by a long colonnade with an octagonal Palatine Chapel. Around the palace, homes for the officials and scholars of the palace and for the palace clergy were built; and merchants established their warehouses to supply the king.

The most ambitious building was the chapel. Charlemagne had never visited Constantinople but he had asked his ambassadors for exact descriptions of the churches there; and in the lands he had conquered from the Lombards, he possessed the finest church Justinian had built in Italy, San Vitale in Ravenna. He sent his architects to use that church as a model. The contrast between San Vitale and Charlemagne's Palatine Chapel is, however, revealing of the difference in character of the two empires. The octagonal ground plan and the three superimposed colonnades are similar. But Charlemagne's architect simply missed out the curving apses that in San Vitale create a sense of undulation, of eddying motion accentuated by the play of darkness, semidarkness, and light. He also did away with the columns that in San Vitale go from ground to dome, replacing them on the first floor with eight huge base pillars split from the upper floors by a heavy pediment. And yet the marble columns, the alternating colors of the reliefs, and the glimpses of sparkling mosaic behind, give almost a nostalgic reminder of the Byzantine beauty of Ravenna. The church is a Frankish interpretation of the Byzantine style, emphasizing the strength and the solidity rather than lightness and elegance. A value system can be seen in the treatment of space.

The Carolingian Renaissance. Charlemagne pursued his emulation of Constantinople by ordering a rebirth of culture. "Because it is our obligation to improve constantly the condition of our churches," he wrote in one law, "we are anxious to restore with diligent zeal the workshops of letters which are almost deserted because of the negligence of our ancestors, and we invite by our own example all who are able to learn the practice of the liberal arts." He established new schools throughout his kingdom.

Cover of the Ashburnham-Lindau Gospel, 9th Century. This is one of the finest examples of jeweled book covers from the Carolingian period. (The Pierpont Morgan Library, M. 1 front cover.)

He brought the English scholar Alcuin to head the palace school in Aachen; and Alcuin's division of education into the *trivium,* of grammar, rhetoric, and dialectic, and the *quadrivium,* of arithmetic, geometry, music, and astronomy, became the basis for education in the rest of the Middle Ages. Large numbers of manuscripts of the Bible, the Church fathers, and classical writers were copied; and his scholars developed the modern form of handwriting, called Carolingian minuscule. Charlemagne himself labored manfully but in vain to learn how to read and write, and kept his writing tablets under his pillow. For all his efforts, however, Charlemagne's court produced no great writers. If Aachen was not a second Rome, it was even less a new Athens.

Charlemagne's Revival of the Roman Empire. The most important requirement for Charlemagne in his determination to equal Byzantium was, however, to be named Roman emperor. The chance came in 799–800 when the pope had fled from Rome to seek safety with Charlemagne, and the throne in Constantinople was held by a woman. Charlemagne was under pressure from many sides to profit from this situation. Alcuin told him he was now superior to both pope and Byzantine emperor. Representatives of the opposition in Constantinople asked him to become emperor there. The church synod tried to persuade him that a woman could not hold the throne of Constantinople, and that therefore the empire could be re-created in the West. On Christmas Day, 800, while Charlemagne was praying during mass in Saint Peter's, the pope placed a crown on his head and the

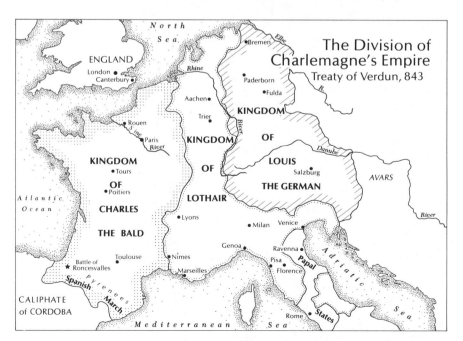

The Division of
Charlemagne's Empire
Treaty of Verdun, 843

people in the church acclaimed him: "To Charles Augustus crowned by God the great and peaceful emperor of the Romans, life and victory!" Nothing was clear about this coronation, either then or now. Einhard said that Charlemagne did not wish to be crowned, but this was probably untrue. He may have been displeased by being crowned by the pope, since it appeared that the Church was naming the emperor. The murky relationship to Byzantium was not cleared when the Franks persuaded the Byzantine emperor to recognize the Frankish king as emperor, but not as Roman emperor, since that left uncertain what he was emperor of. To Charlemagne, however, at the very minimum the title implied that he was the equal of the emperor in Constantinople, and it led to centuries of animosity between the two powers. It also gave the Germanic rulers the title to rule in Italy, and led them into four hundred years of wasted effort in their attempts to hold onto an empire on both sides of the Alps, a goal that brought them into direct conflict with the increasingly ambitious papacy.

The fragility of Charlemagne's achievement was soon revealed. The desire of the local lords to throw off the burdensome controls of the central government were facilitated by the division of the empire at the Treaty of Verdun in 843 among his three grandsons. The western third and eastern third of the empire were later to develop into the modern countries of France and Germany. But the central section, which was taken by the eldest grandson together with the imperial title, lacked all unity, since it consisted of a variegated band of peoples and topography running from Holland in the North to Italy in the South. The central kingdom was divided again and again for the rest of the century, while the eastern and western kingdoms, although nominally united under their kings, were in the control of the feudal lords. This fragmentation of authority made the whole of western Europe an easy prey to new invasions by Moslems, Magyars, and Vikings.

When in the tenth century Gerbert left the glittering cities of Moslem Spain to return to Catholic Europe, the contrast must have been startling. The Europe he was entering was a society of villages. The old cities had decayed, the new towns were still in their infancy. While Cordoba had half a million inhabitants, Paris had only twenty thousand. In England and most of Germany there were no towns at all!

THE MANORIAL ECONOMY OF WESTERN EUROPE

Effects of the Moslem, Magyar, and Viking Invasions. This withdrawal to the village as the basic cell of civilized life in most of Europe, which had begun during the Germanic invasions, was completed by the invasions of the ninth century. The Moslem attacks had been followed by perhaps the most disruptive of all the invasions, those of the Magyars and the Vikings. The Magyars were a nomadic tribe of mounted warriors, possibly related to the Turks, who entered Europe from the East and struck through the Upper Danube valley. For almost half a century they roamed with little resistance

Invasions of the Moslems, Magyars, and Vikings
9th to 11th Centuries

through southern Germany, across Alsace almost to Paris, southwards past the Alps, and in a great loop along both coasts of Italy. They eventually settled in what is now Hungary. Probably driven by overpopulation at home, the Vikings crossed the seas in their long prowed boats, penetrated up the rivers, and even created mounted armies by seizing horses when they landed. Their first attacks came along the North Sea coast of Germany, Holland, and France, and against eastern England and Scotland. But soon expeditions crossed the more dangerous northern waters to Iceland, Greenland, and America, while others struck south from the Faeroe Islands to northern Scotland and to Ireland. They established bases on islands at the mouths of the Thames, Seine, and Loire rivers; but in the ninth century, perhaps because they had already removed all the movable wealth, they came to settle, taking most of northern England, and in 911, accepting the French king's offer of the land at the mouth of the Seine, a province that was renamed Normandy. Their energies were far from exhausted, however. A new invading force made England a Danish kingdom briefly in the early eleventh century; and Duke William made it the principal Norman kingdom by his invasion of 1066. Shortly after, mercenary knights succeeded in conquering Sicily and southern Italy from the Moslems and Byzantines.

Cathedral of Cefalú, Sicily. After overthrowing the Arab rulers of Sicily in the late eleventh century, the Normans erected massive churches in romanesque style, regardless of its unsuitability to the Mediterranean climate. The cathedral at Cefalú on the north coast was begun in 1131 by Roger II, the grandson of the island's conqueror. (Italian State Tourist Office photo.)

Origins of Manorialism. In such conditions of disorder, the majority of Europe's inhabitants could support themselves economically only by agriculture. The peasant was the principal producer, and in most places, the only one, and he had to support the other two classes of medieval society, the warrior and the churchman. In the words of a thirteenth-century poet:

The work of the priest is to pray to God,
And of the knight to do justice.
The farm worker finds bread for them.
One toils in the fields, one prays, and one defends.
In the fields, in the town, in the church,
These three help each other
Through their skills, in a nicely regulated scheme.[6]

Recent historical research has thrown new light on the economic and social forces that shaped the medieval village; and it has shown the great variety of villages that existed in different parts of Europe and the vast changes in population, agricultural technique, and commercial exchange of agricultural products that revolutionized medieval rural society. The older picture of the "typical" and seemingly unchanging medieval village is no longer tenable.

Several theories are offered regarding the origin of the medieval village, which as a unit of production came to be called from the seventh century

---

[6] Cited in Joan Evans, *Life in Medieval France* (London: Oxford University Press, 1925), p. 35. Author's translation.

forward a *mansus,* or manor. One theory assumes that free Germanic tribesmen were compelled to hand over their land to a lord, who became its owner, and in return extended his protection and gave back the land for the peasant's use with certain obligations required. A second theory holds that the manor was the outgrowth of the colonate system of the late Roman Empire, in which the slaves and the tenant farmers had merged into an unfree class that possessed customary rights to the land they worked, under control of the local magnate. Finally, it has been suggested that the great variety of status that existed within the hierarchy of the medieval village, stretching from slave to freeman, was due to the survival of innumerable traditional classifications existing in the different tribal societies that inter-mingled with the Roman society during the invasions. Whatever its origin, the medieval manor possessed certain distinctive features of social struc-ture and land cultivation, which are basic to an understanding of medieval society.

Social Structure of the Manor. The peasant's legal status prescribed the way in which he would support his lord. There were innumerable gradations of peasant status, extending from the slave to the landowning freeman. But by the tenth century, most peasants had become, willingly or unwillingly, serfs. A serf was not a slave; he was not the property of another man. But neither was he free. He was tied to the land that he worked, and could be passed from one lord to another with the land. What made his situation tolerable, however, was that custom or legal contract, usually respected by his lord, laid down the work he must do for the lord and the amount of land that he held for his own use. The estate book of an abbey outside Paris has survived from the ninth century, giving a detailed description of that abbey's holdings and the people who worked them. Among them was a freeman called Bodo:

Bodo a colonus [freeman] and his wife Ermentrude a colona, tenants of Saint-Germain, have with them three children. He holds one free manse containing eight bunaria *and two* antsinga *of arable land, two* aripenni *of vines and seven* aripenni *of meadow. He pays two silver shillings to the army and two hogsheads of wine for the right to pasture his pigs in the woods. Every third year he pays a hundred planks and three poles for fences. He ploughs at the winter sowing four perches and at the spring sowing two perches. Every week he owes two labor services and one handwork. He pays three fowls and fifteen eggs, and carrying service when it is enjoined upon him. And he owns half of a windmill, for which he pays two silver shillings.*[7]

The serfs and the freemen alike, therefore, in return for their land, produced a surplus for others: by giving labor, usually three days a week and more in times of harvest, and by paying directly from their own produce. Charle-

---

[7] Eileen Power, *Medieval People* (Harmondsworth, England: Penguin, 1951), p. 183.

magne had a little island in a Bavarian mountain lake, with several tenants on it, each of whom had to pay him annually eighty-four pecks of grain, four hogs, two pullets, ten eggs, five pints of linseed, and five pints of lentils. Land in a village was divided between that kept for the lord, usually the better land, and that of the peasants. It was also divided according to use. Some was meadow, for grazing the animals; some in vines; some in woodland, where fuel could be gathered and hogs put out to forage, but only with the lord's permission; and most was ploughed. In most of northern Europe this arable land was worked in two, or after the eighth century, three huge fields, cultivated in rotation. The holdings of each man were scattered, in half-acre or one-acre strips, throughout the fields, which ensured that everyone got a fair share of good and badland alike. All the villagers worked together on the fields. They agreed communally what should be planted, and the times of planting and harvest. The harvest was divided up accordingly to the amount of land held by each man. Individual initiative was thus discouraged. Extra work on one's strips, clearing of weeds, or carting in of fertilizer did not enable a man to increase his share of the common harvest.

The Medieval Agricultural Revolution. This system did not, however, prevent extremely important improvements in agricultural productivity between the sixth and ninth centuries. Perhaps the first improvement was the shift in many parts of northern Europe from a primitive scratch-plough, consisting of a conical, or triangular, share that scratched a furrow in light soil to a heavy wheeled plough. The scratch-plough was adequate for the thin soil of most of the Mediterranean region, and was used by the Celtic tribes and the Germanic invaders on the chalky upland soils of northern Europe until the seventh or eighth centuries. Then, however, pressure of population combined with growing evidence of the greater fertility of the heavy, well-watered alluvial soil of the plains and valley made it imperative to open up large stretches of undeveloped clay soils. The heavy plough, equipped with wheels, cut into these heavy soils with a vertical knife called a coulter, a flat ploughshare that sliced the earth horizontally, and a moldboard that turned over the turf to the side. To pull so formidable an instrument, the peasants had to assemble a team of eight oxen; and to use it effectively they had to farm communally. A second improvement was the use of the horse in place of the oxen. The horse can work longer hours and pull heavier weights than an ox; but until the ninth century, it could only be used for light loads because the method of harnessing was a yoke that strangled him under heavy loads. A new horse-collar enabled the animal to pull loads four or five times heavier. When a nailed iron horseshoe was fastened to the horse's brittle hoofs at the end of the ninth century, the peasant had in one animal transport to his field, an animal for ploughing, and driving-power for his wagon, which itself was also improved in design. The third big change was the shift, in the eighth or ninth century in northern Europe, from the two-field system to a three-field system. Under the two-field system, one field was left fallow while the other was planted in winter wheat. When the land was divided into three fields, one field only was left fallow, one was ploughed in the fall and planted with rye or winter wheat, and one was ploughed in the spring and planted with oats, barley, or vegetables. The new system increased productivity by one-half, diversified the crops planted, provided oats as fodder for horses, spread the ploughing through different parts of the year, and lessened the likelihood of famine. Among the great additions to the diet of the medieval peasant was vegetable protein, especially that from peas and beans. "It was not merely the new quantity of food produced by improved agricultural methods," Lynn White, Jr., has concluded, "but the new type of food supply which goes far towards explaining, for northern Europe at least, the startling expansion of population, the growth and multiplication of cities, the rise in industrial production, the outreach of commerce, and the new exuberance of spirits which enlivened that age [after 1000]."[8]

Ploughing in the Late Middle Ages. In this French, illuminated manuscript, several of the technological innovations of the medieval agricultural revolution can be seen—the horse-collar and blinkers, the wheeled plough, the metal coulter, and the mouldboard. (The Pierpont Morgan Library, M. 52 F. 6 enlarged detail.)

Effects of the Agricultural Revolution. The revival of commerce and industry and of city life after 1000 will be considered in Chapter 9. The most immediate result of the improvement in farming methods was an increase in population, which itself compelled the medieval farmer to

[8] Lynn White, Jr., *Medieval Technology and Social Change* (Oxford: Clarendon Press, 1962), p. 76.

bring more land under cultivation. The increase in population was slight until the eleventh century, as there seem to have been long periods of decimation of the population of the villages through disease and especially from the raids of the invaders. But from about 1000 to about 1300 there was a steady increase of the rural population. The only country for which fairly accurate figures are available is England. The population counted by the Norman conquerors in 1086, which was recorded in the Domesday Book, was just over one million. Two hundred years later it had risen to almost four million. Similar growth was probably achieved in most of western Europe during the same period, as more stable political conditions were achieved.

This expanding population fed itself in part by opening up new lands on the edge of the original village settlements, cutting into the surrounding forest or wilderness land for new fields, and turning cattle and sheep loose to graze on the fallow. The most important move was a vast colonization of the forest, marsh, and scrub land through the founding of new villages (often Newton in English, Villeneuve in French, or Neustadt in Germany). The pioneers of this movement of reclamation were not the older monastic orders, like the Benedictines, but the newer orders, like the Cistercians, who deliberately sought solitude in the uninhabited wastes. In addition, speculating lords combined to found new villages, providing money or connections with the land-granting authorities at court and often also the serfs to settle the land. The serfs brought to the new settlements were usually required to render far less in customary dues than those who remained in the older villages, to encourage them to undertake the tough work of forest clearing or of marsh drainage. It is possible that in some of the new villages the serfs were able to throw off their nonfree status completely, and that the existence of such free villages led to a lightening of the burdens on the serfs who remained behind, lest they flee to the wilderness. Serfdom nevertheless remained the normal condition of the peasantry until the great depopulation of the fourteenth century (see Chapter 10) increased their bargaining power with their lords.

Agricultural expansion was at the root of the great economic revival of the eleventh, twelfth, and thirteenth centuries. The landlord class, both clerical and lay, profited greatly from the increase in production, partly by receipt of money rents but mostly by profits taken from provision of mills and from direct appropriation of part of the peasant's harvest. According to Georges Duby, "This explains why so many religious houses flourished, why the aristocracy was so prosperous, civilization and material culture made such vigorous progress." The sale of agricultural surplus in foodstuffs and wine provided work for a large class of commercial middlemen, and of course at the same time supplied the growing cities where they lived. Thus the medieval rural economy came to possess some at least of the characteristics of capitalism—production for the market instead of for subsistence, acquisition of capital in money available for reinvestment to increase future profit, improvement in productivity through greater capitalization per worker, exploitation of technology and of power, and so on. The presence of such factors in the economy of the countryside in the Middle Ages has led medieval historians to deny that a capitalist revolution occurred at the time of the Renaissance in the fifteenth century, and to see instead a gradual transformation of economic practice extending from at least the eleventh century to the seventeeth. The transformation of the village had prepared the way for the revival of the city.

SUGGESTED READING

The life of Mohammed and the history of the early expansion are authoritatively related in the well-illustrated *Muhammed and the Conquest of Islam* (1968) by Francesco Gabrieli, and the whole panorama of Arabic history and civilization is summarized in Bernard Lewis, *The Arabs in History* (1960). The most basic study, and one exceptionally detailed, is Philip K. Hitti, *History of the Arabs from the Earliest Times to the Present* (1964). The West's debt to Islam, especially in architecture, literature, and philosophy is discussed in a series of specialized essays in Thomas Arnold and Alfred Guillaume, eds., *The Legacy of Islam* (1931). David Talbot Rice, *Islamic Art* (1965), is a fine short introduction in English; Georges Marçais, *L'Art musulman* (1962), a historical survey in French, with fine illustrations, and succinct commentary. Moslem Spain receives an overly romantic treatment in Edwyn Hole's *Andalus: Spain under the Muslims* (1958) and a more scholarly treatment in W. Montgomery Watt, *A History of Islamic Spain* (1965).

Contemporary writers still make exciting reading on the history of the Franks. Gregory of Tours, *History of the Franks* (1916), edited by Ernest Brehaut, covers the do-nothing kings. The indispensable life of Charlemagne by Einhard and the dispensable but entertaining life by the Monk of Saint Gall are edited by A. J. Grant, in *Early Lives of Charlemagne* (1905), but many other translations are also available. The best synthesis of the Carolingian achievement is Heinrich Fichtenau, *The Carolingian Empire* (1957); the revival of learning is described with fine illustrations by Donald Bullough, *The Age of Charlemagne* (1965), and in M. L. W. Laistner, *Thought and Letters in Western Europe A.D. 500–900* (1957).

General introductions to the early Middle Ages are given by J. M. Wallace-Hadrill, *The Barbarian West: The Early Middle Ages, A.D. 400–1000* (1962), and in the fresh, lively interpretation of R. W. Southern, *The Making of the Middle Ages* (1953). Christopher Brooke, *Europe in the Central Middle Ages, 962–1154* (1964), has new documentation and is solid in style. The origin and development of manorialism is excellently treated in M. M. Postan, ed., *The Cambridge Economic History of Europe, vol. 1, The Agrarian Life of the Middle Ages* (1966). The technological aspects of the medieval agricultural revolution are detailed, and their effects analyzed, in Lynn White, Jr., *Medieval Technology and Social Change* (1962). The vast recent research on the manor is presented in detail in Georges Duby's challenging *Rural Economy and Country Life in the Medieval West* (1968). The pioneering work of the great French historian Marc Bloch, *Feudal Society* (1961), merits careful reading.

For the Viking invasions, see J. Brondsted, *The Vikings* (1963). Charles H. Haskins, *The Normans in European History* (1915), is still useful, but David C. Douglas, *The Norman Achievement, 1050–1100* (1969), is more up-to-date though still full of admiration.

8
FEUDAL MONARCHY IN THE WEST, 1000-1200

If the manor was the basic economic unit of European society by the tenth century, the fundamental political relationship was of lord and vassal. A system of government, known as feudalism, had been elaborated by the end of the invasions of the ninth century, in which the functions of defense, justice, and even provision of necessary public services were carried out by lords related to each other not by common service of the state but by private, personal ties. In theory, the local lord carried out his administrative duties and military service because he had sworn to his superior lord in the political hierarchy to do so, in return for that lord's aid and protection. In fact, the local lord's political duties were his payment for the land on whose produce he lived. A hierarchy, often called the feudal pyramid, existed, in which in theory at least, all land was granted to the lesser lords by the person at the head of the pyramid, such as the king of France or the king of England or the Holy Roman Emperor. Between the tenth and twelfth centuries, the rulers of England and France were able to solidify their power by use of their feudal rights. By the fourteenth century, the inhabitants of France and those of England had lived so long in their own politically integrated societies and were developing characteristics of behavior so similar within those societies that they thought of themselves as distinct by "nationality." In short, the feudal monarchies had created the French and English nations. The process of definition of the relative position of the lay power and the ecclesiastical, however, brought the German emperor and the pope into a direct conflict that ended with the ruin of the emperor and the consequent fragmentation of political power in Germany. Denied political expression, German nationalism remained a minor force until the nineteenth century.

Knights on Horseback. Stained-Glass Lunette, 1246–1248.
Although this scene illustrates the Book of Judith, the French artist has depicted the knights of his own day, with heavy armor and lances prepared for battle. (Philadelphia Museum of Art. Photograph by A. J. Wyatt, Staff Photographer.)

231

**THE POLITICAL
INSTITUTIONS
OF FEUDALISM**

Consideration of the economic unit of the manor at once raises the question, Who were these lords of the manor who held the demesne and exacted services in labor and kind from the peasants?

The Church as Feudal Lord. Throughout the Middle Ages the Church came to own an increasingly large portion of the land. The pope himself claimed direct ownership of most of central Italy as the result of the Donation of Pepin in 756, a gift of the land to him by the Frankish king Pepin, confirmed by his son Charlemagne. In the rest of Europe, the Church's possessions were the result of vast gifts of land by kings or lords for the foundation of abbeys or churches, of smaller bequests by laymen left in the hope of winning spiritual salvation, of the opening up of new land by the religious orders, and of the voluntary renunciation of land and freedom by free peasants. In the mid-eleventh century, for example, the monastery of Marmoutier in France recorded a renunciation of this kind:

Be it known to all who come after us, that a certain man in our service called William, the brother of Reginald, born of free parents, being moved by the love of God and to the end that God—with whom is no acceptance of persons but reward only for the merits of each—might look favorably on him, gave himself up as a serf to Martin of Marmoutier; and he gave not only himself but all his descendants, so that they should for ever serve the abbot and monks of this place in a servile condition. And in order that this gift might be made more certain and apparent, he put the bell-rope around his neck and placed four pennies from his own head on the altar of St. Martin in recognition of serfdom, and so offered himself to almighty God. [1]

By the thirteenth century, the Church held perhaps one-quarter to one-third of the land of Europe. Its primary function was of course to carry out its religious duties, which encompassed most of the educational and charitable work of the age as well as pastoral and devotional duties. But where the Church held land directly from a lay lord, it had also to fulfill the same obligations as any other lay lord, that is to use the produce of the land to support armed knights for his military service.

The Lay Vassal. The thousands of lay lords living on their manors were the base of the feudal pyramid, a hierarchical political structure by which the main functions of government were assured. The local lord provided justice in his own court, protected the inhabitants of the manor from disorder within or attack from without, and organized the few public services like maintenance of roads. What was unique about this system was the nature of the lord's ties with those above him in the political hierarchy. In theory, every lord was the vassal of another, higher lord, from whom he held his land. The grant of land was at first called a *beneficium*,

[1] R. W. Southern, *The Making of the Middle Ages* (London: Arrow Books, 1962), pp. 98–99.

Ekkehard and Uta, Naumburg Cathedral.
The so-called Naumburg Master transferred to this wonderful secular portrait of the founders of the cathedral the skills he acquired in study of the Gothic sculpture of France. Few statues more beautifully capture the self-assurance of the knightly class at the height of its prestige. (German Information Center photo.)

or benefice, but by about 1100 it was usually called a *feodum,* or fief, from which the word feudalism is derived. In return for his fief, the knight owed his suzerain, who was the person who had granted him the fief, a well-defined number of duties. He had to appear, on horseback and in armor, at his own expense, to fight for his lord—usually for forty days a year. If he had been given a fief so big that it could be subdivided to support several knights, then he had to appear with that specific number of knights and the servants they needed. He owed his lord a financial gift or aid on three occasions: when the lord's eldest son was knighted, when his eldest daughter was married, or if the lord had to be ransomed. He had to offer hospitality to his lord and his retinue as they traveled around the suzerain's possessions and he had to appear at the lord's court when summoned to give council or to share the trial of one of his peers, or equals. In return, the suzerain provided the fief on which his vassal lived, protected him when necessary from outside attack, and provided justice for him in his court. Moreover, the right of the vassal's family to inherit his fief came to be recognized, on the condition that his heirs paid an inheritance tax or relief, and accepted a number of obligations, such as the right of the suzerain to act as ward of a female heiress.

This relationship of lord and holder of the fief was converted into a moral obligation by the ceremony of homage and fealty. The vassal knelt before his lord, put his hands, with palms together, between his lord's hands, and swore to become his man (homage) and to be faithful to him against all men (fealty). This oath established a relationship of mutual trust that was fundamental to feudal society. All the great medieval poems glorified this relationship, especially the most powerful of all, the *Song of Roland,* written about 1100, when the feudal relationship had been fully elaborated. As Roland led a rearguard action for the defense of Charlemagne's main army in the dangerous pass of Roncesvalles in the Pyrenees, the poet has Roland tell his friend Oliver, "For his lord man should suffer great hardships, should endure extremes of heat and cold, should lose his blood and his flesh. Strike with thy lance! And I will strike with Durendal, my good sword which the king gave me. If I die, may he who has it be able to say that it belonged to a noble vassal."[2] And after the action, looking around on the dying warriors who have sacrificed themselves, Charlemagne gives them the highest praise possible. "Lord barons, may God have mercy on you! May he grant all your souls rest in Paradise! May he set them amidst the Holy flowers! Never have I seen better vassals than you."[3]

The ceremonial of knighthood developed rapidly from the eleventh century. It began with the Christianization and the romanticizing of the ceremony of becoming a knight. From early childhood, the son of a lord was put into training for that day. He was apprenticed to another lord, in whose service he moved from duties like helping put on armor and leading the horse, through mock battles with other apprentices, to full-scale charges with armor and lance. Usually at twenty or twenty-one he took a purifying ritual bath, prayed all night in the church, took confession and communion, and was finally admitted to the fraternity of knights by his lord, who presented him with his sword. In one medieval poem, the young man is taking a quick nap after his night's vigil in the church when his uncle arrives.

"Come, Fromondin, get up. You must not sleep too long, good sire. The great tournament ought already to be forming." *The young man leaped from his bed on hearing the voice, and the squires entered to serve him. They quickly booted and clothed him. In the presence of all, Count William of Montclin girded the sword on him with a golden belt. "Dear nephew," he said, "I enjoin thee not to trust false and dissolute men; given a long life thou shalt be a mighty prince. Always be strong, victorious, and redoubtable to all thy enemies. Give the vair and gray to many deserving men. It is the way to attain honor." "Everything is in God's hands," answered Fromondin. Then they led him to a costly horse. He mounted him with an easy bound, and they handed him a shield emblazoned with a lion.*[4]

---

[2] C. Stephenson, *Medieval Feudalism* (Ithaca, N.Y.: Cornell University Press, 1942), p. 22.
[3] Joan Evans, *Life in Medieval France* (London: Oxford University Press, 1925), p. 101.
[4] Cited in A. Luchaire, *Social France at the Time of Philip Augustus* (New York: F. Ungar, 1957), pp. 345–46.

The Rider of Bamberg. One of the few free-standing equestrian statues of the Middle Ages, this figure was completed for the cathedral of the south German city of Bamberg in 1245. (German Tourist Information Office photo.)

Knighthood's high standards were rarely achieved, however. Vassals often deserted their lords, and indeed the practice of permitting a man to hold land from two or more lords often compelled him to decide which of the two he would let down. Many lords oppressed their peasants, and were little better than armed robbers who stole the animals, crops, money, and even the clothes of their neighbors. One French abbey complained that their noble neighbor had broken down their fences, seized eleven cows, cut down their fruit trees, tied up their servants, and at various times helped himself to tunics, capes, cheeses, stockings, and shoes of their servants. Tournaments held in peacetime were vicious bloodlettings, in war the sack of a city was an opening for pillage and murder.

Origins of Feudalism. This system evolved slowly during the six centuries following the breakup of the Roman Empire. Only in the eleventh century, and then only in the several states of northern Europe, did feudalism as a legally organized form of social and political relationships attain the full development just described. Throughout these centuries, one sees the separate appearance of the institutions that were eventually to merge in the fully developed "feudal system." In the Germanic tribes, for example, the chiefs had a band of warriors with whom they consulted, which was similar to the later institution of the comitatus. In the Roman colonate, the lord, or magnate, developed powers of administration over his estates very similar to those exercised by the lord over his manor; and it has been suggested that the idea of a freeman commending himself to a lord in return for protection derived from the bands of clients who waited on the powerful elite in imperial Rome. The concept of doing military service in return for the grant of land may have originated in the eighth century, when the Frankish ruler Charles the Hammer distributed confiscated church lands to endow a number of cavalrymen who were to help him drive back the Moslems from France. At that time he adapted the system of the cataphract, or great horse, which the Byzantines had taken from the Persians, to the conditions of eighth-century Europe. The great horse was just what its name implied, a specially bred animal valued as the equivalent of four oxen or six cows, capable of carrying the knight and his heavy armor, shield, sword, and long iron-tipped lance; and this horse became an even more effective weapon in the eighth century with the use of the foot-stirrup, which enabled the warrior to strike his opponent with the combined weight of his own muscles and his horse's charging body. Only when all the separate institutions—the personal relationship of vassal and lord, the tenure of land in return for service, and the performance of the duties of governmental administration by the warrior class—had been welded into a form of society and government was feudalism complete. It could then become the basis of monarchical power, most notably in the Capetian kingdom of France and the Norman kingdom of England.

**THE CAPETIAN
MONARCHY
IN FRANCE**

In the chaotic ninth century there seemed little chance that France would be united under a strong monarchy. The last Carolingian kings saw France break up into a series of semi-independent feudal principalities. In contrast with the powerful feudal lords, the counts of Paris, who possessed only the Ile de France, a domain about a hundred miles long around Paris, appeared innocuous. Their very weakness, however, worked to their advantage. In 987, reviving the Frankish habit of electing their king, the feudal lords chose Hugh Capet, Count of Paris, as king of France; and paying lip service to their new sovereign, they returned to run their own provinces regardless of him for the next centuries.

The first six Capetian kings (987–1188) worked pragmatically to strengthen their power inside the Ile de France, without attempting any important intereference with their great vassals. They increased their own personal landholdings, and crushed the independence of the lords inside their own domain. They maintained good relations with the Church, with both the pope and the local bishops, and found in the middle classes of their cities a source of financial support and a pool of able administrators. But simply by living long, securing the succession of their eldest son, and receiving the consecration of the Church through the coronation ceremony, they established themselves as the "traditional" monarchs of France, a vitally important factor that set them apart from all other feudal lords, no matter how rich or powerful.

Bust of Philip Augustus. The sculptor of this limestone portrait head was clearly aware of the need to portray Philip as a worthy successor to Charlemagne. Realism had to be sacrificed to regality. (The Metropolitan Museum of Art, Fletcher Fund, 1947.)

Philip Augustus. The position of the Capetian kings was revolutionized by Philip II (reigned 1180–1223), known to his contemporaries as the Conqueror and to posterity as Augustus. Philip was one of those crafty, ambitious medieval kings who respected the feudal bond sufficiently to be able to profit from it and who served the Church with sufficient devotion to enlist it in his own service. By exploiting the moral rules of feudalism and church, he prepared the transformation of the French monarchy from one being held by the supreme lord in a feudal hierarchy to one with an absolute monarch governing by divine right. This condition was achieved during the sixteenth and seventeenth centuries. Philip's father had died when he was fifteen, and during the following ten years he had experienced the most practical political training Europe could offer: a tour of the Italian city-states and a stay with the pope in Rome; a Crusade to the Holy Land; a personal feud with Richard the Lion-Hearted, King of England; and an uprising led by one of his most powerful vassals. From being a high-spirited, active teen-ager with a mop of untidy hair and a love of hunting, he matured into a quiet, self-controlled commander of men, with a parsimony of language and a perhaps overly cynical understanding of the actions of his subjects and his enemies. He impressed his contemporaries as being a worthy successor to Charlemagne, a real king: "A fine man, well proportioned in stature, with a smiling countenance, bald, a rubicund complexion, inclined to eat and drink well, sensual . . . far-sighted, obstinate, rapid and prudent in judgement, fond of taking the advice of lesser people."[5]

[5] Cited in Charles Petit-Dutaillis, *The Feudal Monarchy in France and England: From the Tenth to the Thirteenth Century* (London: K. Paul, Trench, & Trübner, 1936), p. 214.

The Expansion
of the
Capetian Monarchy, 1180–1270

Royal Domain, 1180

Acquisitions of Philip Augustus, 1180–1223

Acquisitions of Louis VIII and Louis IX, 1223–1270

For his whole reign, Philip fought to increase the territory under the direct rule of the kings of France. When he died, he had tripled the royal domain. At the beginning of Philip's reign, as a result mainly of marriage alliances, the king of England ruled a greater area of France than he did: Normandy, Brittany, Maine, Touraine, Anjou, and Aquitaine. Profiting from the psychotic inefficacy of the English king, John, who had quarreled with his own barons and with the pope at the very time that the French were preparing an attack on Normandy, Philip declared that John had broken his feudal vows to him and therefore forfeited all his territories in France to the French king. Philip's cynical use of his feudal rights to justify the invasion of Normandy is illustrated in the letter the pope sent to John in support of Philip's action:

As you have taken away, without justice or reason, the castles and lands of men who consider them as his fief, Philip, as higher suzerain, driven by the complaints of the victims, has demanded, not once but many times, that you make reparation; you have promised but have done nothing and you have crushed the prostrate further. He has borne with you more than a year awaiting the satisfaction he has asked for. With the advice of his barons and subjects he has fixed a certain term for you to appear in his presence to do as the law demands without any withdrawal; although you are his liege subject, you have not appeared on the appointed day

*or sent any representative but have treated his summons with nothing but contempt.
As a result, he has met you in person and warned you in his own words, for he
does not wish to make war if you show yourself what you should be towards him.
You have been unwilling to satisfy him.* [6]

After two years of stiff fighting Philip conquered Normandy, and he took
for himself most of the lands of the English king and of the Norman lords
who remained in England. By 1206, he had taken all the English possessions in France except Aquitaine. After showing how the feudal bond
could be used to justify territorial annexation, at the end of his life Philip
showed how service of the Church through participation in a Crusade could
be equally profitable. In 1223, he sent his son Louis to crush the Albigensian heresy, whose leaders held that the world was a battlefield of the
forces of light and darkness and that the corrupted Catholic Church was a
servant of the latter. After horrible massacres in the name of religion, the
Capetians incorporated the County of Toulouse in their kingdom through
a marriage alliance.

Finally, Philip greatly improved the bureaucratic administration located
in Paris. He began the transformation of his household officers into governmental officials. His chamberlain, seneschal, butler, and constable,
although not yet highly specialized in the tasks assigned them, gathered
round them a staff of civil servants, who formed the nucleus of future governmental ministries. By calling in his greatest barons and bishops to give
him advice and support on important occasions at a meeting of the Curia
Regis, or King's Court, he developed a body with some at least of the characteristics of a legislature. And perhaps most important of all, Philip sent
out paid officials, called baillis, to supervise local administration and justice. Drawn from the poorer nobility, the middle class, and the church,
these professional servants were a direct instrument of the king against
the feudal lords. He even succeeded in putting together a royal income
from a form of taxation, based on the demand for "loans" from groups like
the Jews, special tithes to support crusades, and monetary payment in lieu
of military service. Philip in short succeeded in using his feudal rights
vastly to expand the territories of the kingdom of France and to form a centralized administration to control his kingdom.

For all prehistory, and indeed for a good deal of history, England stood on
the outer fringes of the known world, backward and poverty-stricken. The
four-hundred-year Roman occupation left a superficial veneer of Latin
culture, a few technical advantages like a decent road system, and a population that was unwilling and unable to fight in its own defense. When the
Romans pulled back their garrisons to defend Rome itself from the Visigoths, England was invaded and conquered with relative ease by the Germanic tribes of Angles, Saxons, and Jutes, who drove the unfortunate Celtic

THE NORMAN AND ANGEVIN DYNASTIES IN ENGLAND

[6] Ibid., p. 218.

Tower of London. The Normans kept the defeated Anglo-Saxons submissive by erecting a large number of castles. Rectangular towers, like that in London, were surrounded by earthen ramparts and wooden or stone palisades, and were unassailable with the primitive siege weapons of the eleventh and twelfth centuries. (British Tourist Authority photo.)

inhabitants back to the western edges of the island, to Cornwall, Wales, and Lancashire. The great Anglo-Saxon achievement was the colonization of England, for it was the invaders who cut down the primeval forests and opened up the heavy clay soil of central England to cultivation. In spite of pressure from the Vikings after their invasions in the ninth and tenth centuries and their settlement in the North and East and along the northwestern coast of England, the Anglo-Saxons also gave England several institutions of great importance for its future political and legal development. For purposes of local government, they divided the country into thirty-four shires, administered by a local earl and bishop and by a royal representative called a sheriff (shire-reeve). In the shires and their subdivisions, the hundreds, there were local courts recognizing the king's authority; and there was a central council, called the witan, of all the great landholders, churchmen, and royal officials, and a national militia, called the fyrd. Upon

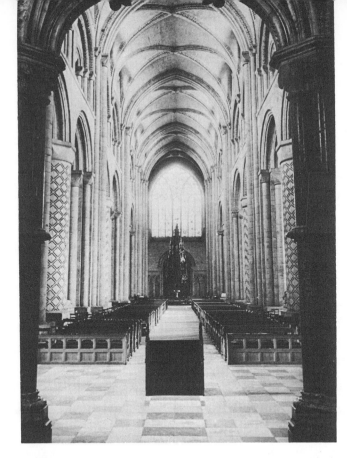

Interior, Durham Cathedral, 1093–1130.
One of the finest Norman cathedrals, Durham displays not only the earliest cross rib vaultings, but great complexity in the patterning of the piers. Each pillar is carved in a different geometrical pattern, while round piers alternate with composite piers on which several ribs have been superimposed. (British Tourist Authority photo.)

these Anglo-Saxon foundations, Duke William of Normandy imposed the most developed form of feudalism, after he had conquered the island in 1066.

The Norman Conquest. The Norman Conquest is graphically portrayed in the famous Bayeux tapestry with its seventy-two scenes embroidered in eight colors of wool on a huge sheet of linen. In this astonishing survival, the whole bloody brutality of the conquest is displayed unflinchingly, and perhaps even with a certain relish. The fleet of Norman ships, with prows like the Viking vessels of the earlier invaders, is seen crossing the Channel to England, with a favoring gale in their sails and the knights' horses lined up, docile, the whole length of the ships. Then, there is the Battle of Hastings (1066), with a seething mass of knights in battle, impaled on spears or lunging with great broadswords through a tumultuous mass of upended horses. Finally, there are the slightly more peaceful scenes of the imposition of Norman rule, with the building of the great castles that were to ensure that the Saxons would never rise again. William brought the whole country under control in five years, shared out the conquered land among the barons who had come with him, the church, and the royal domain, although retaining legal title to the whole country himself. England was thus the only country in which the feudal organization of society was imposed from above at one time, and for that reason it resembled most closely the feudal lawyers' concept of the hierarchy based on vassalage; and through the assessment rolls, known as the Domesday Book, a superb system of state finance was based on accurate tax records of all English landholdings.

Development of Royal Administration and the Common Law.   The Norman kings and their successors, the Angevins, pressed on with the creation of a strong system of central government controlled by the king. Henry I (reigned 1100–1135), William's third son, concentrated on developing a regular monetary income for the crown—from scutage paid instead of military service, rents, tolls, grants from the cities, feudal dues, and fees for nonparticipation in Crusades. To collect and spend the income, he organized a specialized branch of government called the Exchequer, named after the checkerboard table on which the officials rendered their accounts. He also created a Chancery, where royal records were kept, and a small inner council of the Curia Regis to carry on the main decision making from day to day. Henry I thus preceded Philip Augustus by almost a century in creating the instruments of centralized monarchy.

Henry I also developed the king's control over local justice, by sending out officials called itinerant justices to hear pleas throughout the kingdom. But it was his grandson Henry II (reigned 1154–1189) who was most responsible for the development of the modern system of common law. First, Henry greatly increased the use of itinerant justices, whose task was to handle cases brought before the shire courts in a uniform manner throughout the kingdom, thereby establishing a law common to all England. Secondly, to maintain that uniformity, it became necessary to ask what other justices had previously decided on similar cases, what "precedents" existed. A new decision thus created a precedent, and itself became new law. Third, in civil cases, a group of twelve local people were called in to give evidence on which they were supposed to have personal knowledge. They were called a jury, because they were sworn (*juré*) to tell the truth. Finally, a subject could ask the king's chancery for a writ, available at a small fee, requiring that his case be brought to a royal court and that no action be taken that might be harmful to him before the case was heard. These vitally important institutions were basic to the development of the legal system of England and its future colonies.

Conflict of the English Monarchy with the Church and the Feudal Nobility. Henry II, determined to lessen the powers of the separate ecclesiastical courts that claimed the sole right to try clerics, demanded in 1164 that clerics guilty of crimes like murder should be punished in the royal courts. His old friend, Thomas Becket, whom he had named archbishop of Canterbury in the hope of having an ally in the heart of the Church, refused this demand; and after a long trial of strength, Henry, in an unthinking outburst of rage, asked—rhetorically, as he thought—"Who will rid me of this pestilent cleric?" Four knights, taking him at his word, then murdered Becket in front of his altar in Canterbury Cathedral. Becket was made a saint, and Canterbury became the primary goal of English pilgrims, but the final result was a compromise. The Church continued to receive immunity from the royal courts, and the king still exercised the right of picking the principal churchmen in the kingdom.

Henry's younger son, John (reigned 1199–1216), provoked the feudal lords in England to reduce the monarchy's centralized power at the very time that Philip Augustus in France was building up his powers of control. John, a mean, suspicious, and unskillful ruler, infuriated many of his leading vassals by failing to respect his role in the feudal contract. He frequently punished them without respecting their right of trial; and to pay for his constant wars with Philip Augustus, he ruthlessly squeezed every source of income possible from abuse of his rights as suzerain. Perhaps one-third of his barons, accompanied by many leading churchmen, finally took arms against him in 1215, and forced him to accept a long statement of their rights, known as the Magna Carta. Most of the chapters of this famous document were specific limitations on the king's power to abuse his feudal privileges, by his control over heiresses, for example, and his use of scutage and his exorbitant charges for inheritance of fiefs. But several of the clauses, although intended solely to safeguard the rights of the highest ranks of the barons, were to be interpreted, in the constitutional struggles of the sixteenth and seventeenth centuries, as guarantees of the basic rights of all English citizens. The right of a representative parliament to control taxation was held to be contained in the clause: "No scutage or aid, save the customary feudal ones, shall be levied except by the common consent of the realm." And the right of a man to be tried by a jury of his fellow citizens according to the established processes of law was found in the clause: "No freeman shall be taken or imprisoned or dispossessed, or outlawed, or banished, or in any way destroyed, nor will we go against him, nor send upon him, except by the legal judgement of his peers or by the law of the land."

Origins of Parliament. While the Magna Carta was not interpreted in the thirteenth century as anything other than a statement of feudal rights and was largely ignored in the fourteenth and fifteenth centuries, the English created in the thirteenth century the institution that was later to turn that document into a charter of English liberties—Parliament. The idea that the king had the privilege of consulting his principal subjects in a king's council was accepted in the Anglo-Saxon kingdom, with its institution of the witan; it was taken up by the Norman kings in their Great Council; and when the barons revolted against John's successor, Henry III (reigned 1216–1272), in 1256 they required that the Great Council meet three times yearly. What transformed this council into a parliament was the principle

Harlech Castle, Wales, c. 1285. The finest surviving medieval castles were built by Edward I to hold down the newly conquered Welsh. Harlech consists of an inner castle, or donjon, marked by the twin towers on the right of the photo, and an outer wall also strengthened with round towers. (British Tourist Authority photo.)

of representation. In 1265, the leader of the baronial revolt attempted to strengthen his own hand by summoning to a "parliament" the local lords, or "knights of the shire," and representatives of the towns, even though the king refused to recognize this body. Nevertheless, Henry III's son, Edward I (reigned 1272–1307) followed the same principle in 1295, when to make the grant of taxes more efficient, he called to the Great Council not only the upper nobility and clergy but two knights from each shire and two representatives of each large town. For the first time, this council included all the groups later included in parliament, and for that reason it has been called the Model Parliament. The precedent had been set, even though Edward I rarely repeated his gesture. During the following two centuries, the higher clergy and more important vassals separated from the representative members of the council to become the House of Lords, while the knights of the shire and the burgesses joined in the House of Commons. The contest for supremacy between king and parliament did not occur, however, until the seventeenth century (see Chapter 15). Thus, while the French monarchy was gaining ever greater control over its subjects and preparing the institutions of Europe's most centralized monarchy, the English kings had been forced, after creating a powerful state, to admit their subjects to a share in the exercise of that power.

Otto I. This tenth-century
ivory plaque shows the
emperor offering a model of
Magdeburg Cathedral to
Christ. (The Metropolitan
Museum of Art, Gift of George
Blumenthal, 1941.)

**THE CONFLICT
OF EMPERORS
AND POPES**

The Holy Roman Empire under the Saxon Emperors. In Germany during
the ninth century, power and prestige fell to the one dynasty capable of
halting the invasions. In 955 at the battle of Lechfeld, the Saxon king
Otto I (reigned 936–973) decisively defeated the Magyars. Seven years
later he had himself crowned emperor in Saint Peter's in Rome.

The title of emperor had come to mean so little that no one had bothered
with it since 924. The Saxon emperors had, however, a damagingly clear
view of their own place in history: they were the successors of Charlemagne,
in title, prestige, and policy. Otto I, for his coronation as king of the Franks,
had gone to Charlemagne's Palatine Chapel in Aachen; and he had waited
until the pope was ready to crown him before becoming emperor of the
Romans. His grandson, Otto III (reigned 983–1002) was even more direct
in seeking contact with his imperial model. In the year 1000, one chronicler wrote:

St. Michael's Church, Hildesheim. This Benedictine abbey was built in 1001–1033 by the reforming bishop Bernward. The heaviness of the walls is lightened by the four round towers appended to the two transepts, an architectural oddity that was not adopted outside the German-speaking countries. (German Information Center photo.)

He was in doubt where the bones of Charlemagne lay, and so he had the floor [of the Palatine Chapel] breached, and ordered workmen to dig where he thought they were. In due course the bones were found seated on the royal throne. Otto removed the golden cross which hung on Charles' neck, and such of the clothes as had not crumbled to dust, and the rest were reinterred with great devotion.[7]

But under the influence of his mother, a Byzantine princess, he adopted some of the fashions of Constantinople. He lived in a palace on the Aventine Hill in Rome, high above the Tiber, surrounded by ancient Christian basilicas, maintaining punctilious court ceremonial, and served by consuls, senators, prefects, chancellors, and other assorted functionaries. In himself, he saw united the Saxon, the Roman, and the Greek. The burden of his heredity drove him to an early grave, at the age of twenty-two.

The ambitions of the Saxon kings proved double-edged. They did succeed in subduing their feudal nobility, largely by keeping them occupied in profitable wars. They struck an effective alliance with the church, using the clergy in the tasks of secular administration and as leaders of another cultural renaissance ordered from above. They endowed great monasteries like Hildesheim with rich lands, and favored their ambitious building efforts and their patronage of art and of scholarship. They used their power

---

[7] Thietmar of Merseburg, Chronicon, IV, 47: 29, cited in Christopher Brooke, *Europe in the Central Middle Ages, 962–1154* (London: Longman's, 1964), p. 172.

over the papacy occasionally to ensure the election of clerics of high scholarly and moral standards. But the error of the Saxon emperors was to be
deluded by the dreams of reviving Rome. Otto III put on his seal *renovatio
imperii romanorum,* "the revival of the empire of the Romans." Constant
campaigns were necessary to establish German power in Italy, against
Romans, Byzantines, Moslems, and Normans, and they distracted the emperors from the work both of defending the borders of Germany and of
maintaining the obedience of Germany's feudal lords. The emperor's
power was thus extremely vulnerable when, to his surprise, he was challenged by the papacy, which for two centuries had been a docile instrument
of imperial ambitions.

The Reform of the Church. The papacy's determination to reassert the
authority of the Church over the lay power was the sequel to the great reform program carried through in the Church in the ninth century. At the
time of the breakdown of the Carolingian empire, the Church's moral
standards had slumped badly. Monasteries had fallen away from the disciplined simplicity of life laid down by Saint Benedict, partly because of
the riches bequeathed to them, partly because of the nonspiritual duties
given them by the state. Reform was introduced into the Church through
the foundation of new monasteries by the great nobles sincerely concerned
with the decline of its moral standards. The most important, Cluny in Burgundy, was founded by the Duke of Aquitaine, and other reform centers
were created in southern Belgium and Lorraine. In these monasteries reform
implied a return to poverty, though not to manual labor, and a new emphasis
on prayer and liturgical ceremony. Monks from two main centers of reform,
Cluny and Gorze, were invited to reform other monasteries, and in time
these purified monasteries were accepted as daughter houses of the mother
monastery. From the monasteries, reform spread to the papacy itself,
primarily through the intervention of Emperor Henry III. Faced with three
churchmen who all claimed to be the rightful pope, Henry forced the appointment of a fourth, a German reformer, after he had deposed the three
quarreling pontiffs. For the rest of the eleventh century, the papacy
was in the hands of the reformers, who were mostly Germans; and the
emperor was startled to find himself the main object of the pope's reforming
zeal.

Not only did the new popes launch a vigorous attack on the abuses
that the emperor hoped they would control—simony, or the purchase of
church offices, clerical marriage, and clerical concubinage; they also made
the papacy an instrument that could challenge the temporal power—by
ending state interference with the Church and by interfering in, if not dominating, the material sphere. The pope's power lay in a renovated Church
government, from a strengthened college of cardinals through the most
minor offices of the Church bureaucracy; in the skillful use of Church
wealth; in the choice of allies possessing military strength, most notably

the Normans of South Italy and the German feudal nobility; and in the ultimate weapon, excommunication, which enabled the pope to deny any man the support of his peers in this world and of the heavenly host in the next. Even an emperor who would risk damnation was unwilling to chance the consequences of excommunication in this life.

Meeting of Christian and Saracen. In this somewhat anachronistic version, the fifteenth-century artist has portrayed the Crusaders in the puffed doubloon and tight hose of the contemporary courtier. (The Pierpont Morgan Library.)

The Crusades.   The most dramatic expression of the revived prestige of the Church was the Crusades to reconquer the Holy Land. In 1095 at Clermont in central France, Pope Urban II called on the knights of Christendom, and especially those of France, to "enter upon the road to the Holy Sepulcher; wrest that land from the wicked race, and subject it to yourselves." He had been begged for aid by the Byzantine emperor, whose

army had been defeated in Asia Minor by the Seljuk Turks; and he expected
to achieve the submission of the Eastern Orthodox Church to Rome in return for aid to the Byzantine emperor in reconquering Asia Minor. The
Seljuk Turks had also captured Jerusalem in 1071, and were making it
more difficult, though by no means impossible, for pilgrims to visit the
places associated with Christ's life and death in the Holy Land. Nevertheless, pilgrimages to the Holy Land, which brought not only the excitement
of foreign travel, the possibility of commercial transactions, and large-
scale remission of sins, had become so popular by the eleventh century
that even the rumors of Seljuk obstructionism were enough to rouse widespread fury in Europe. To participate in the Crusade, the pope also offered
opportunity for wealth and territorial rule, as well as automatic absolution
of sins to those killed in battle; and to those disturbed by the unruly conduct
of the knights at home, he offered a way of getting them gainfully occupied
in distant lands at the expense of the infidel and of thus securing the Peace
of God at home. The response to his appeal was enthusiastic. After a year's
hectic organization, three large armies set off for Constantinople, from
which they were to attack Syria and Palestine. Most of the knights were
from France and the western parts of Germany, but recruits came from
almost every state of Europe. No kings participated, but several leading
feudal nobles, including Baldwin of Flanders and Duke Robert of Normandy, led large numbers of their personal followers. During the three
years of fighting in Asia Minor and the Holy Land, individual leaders began
to cut out dominions for themselves: Baldwin of Flanders took Edessa;
Prince Bohemond, Antioch; and after the bloody capture of Jerusalem in
1099, the Crusaders handed to Godfrey of Bouillon the hastily created
kingdom of Jerusalem.

It seemed that the First Crusade had thus been a startling success, given
the enormous difficulties of military operations so far from western Europe.
The Crusaders intended to hold the Holy Land by building vast castles even
more elaborate in defenseworks than those in Europe, and they received
a constant reinforcement of knights from newly organized military orders
like the Knights Templar and the Knights Hospitaler. Moreover, they were
determined to make the new possessions a profitable economic concern,
by granting trading privileges to the major Italian cities. Venice, Pisa, and
Genoa were thus encouraged to become the intermediaries who could
sell the products of the Holy Land and the goods brought there from the
East to the ready markets in western Europe.

Within twenty years, however, Moslem power had been revived under
a Syrian prince; and when Edessa fell, Saint Bernard took it on himself to
preach the Second Crusade (1147). Although the French King and the German emperor both took part, the Crusade was a dismal failure. The Crusaders were defeated outside Damascus, and returned home in disarray.
The Third Crusade (1187–1189) was provoked by the military successes
of Saladin, the Moslem ruler of Egypt who succeeded in reconquering the

Jerusalem. When the Crusaders captured Jerusalem in 1099, it was a predominantly Arab city dominated by two seventh-century mosques, el-Aksa and the Dome of the Rock. Today, the skyline is a mixture of Christian, Moslem, and Jewish buildings. (Trans World Airlines photo.)

Holy Land, including Jerusalem itself. This time, the kings of England and France and the Holy Roman Emperor all set off for the Holy Land. The German emperor drowned in a river on the way; the French and English kings bickered constantly, especially when their armies failed to recapture more than a few coastal cities. The English army was finally left alone to conclude a truce with Saladin that gave pilgrims the right to visit Jerusalem. Richard ended his ill-fated journey by being captured for ransom in Austria. This debacle ended the true crusades, that is, the genuine attempt to recapture the Holy Land.

The Fourth Crusade (1202–1204) was a totally different affair. Although its original purpose was supposedly to recapture Jerusalem, the Venetians who provided transport first diverted the expedition to capture the Adriatic island of Zara for them, as payment for their services. Then, heavily in debt, the Crusaders agreed to aid a pretender to the Byzantine throne by conquering Constantinople. Their motives were mixed. The pope still nourished the hope of reuniting the Greek Orthodox and Catholic churches. Unless they took this opportunity of gaining financial and military support promised by the pretender, the Crusaders saw no way of waging a successful campaign against the Moslems. The Venetians wanted a monopoly on Byzantine trade for themselves. The pretender was installed on the throne in 1203, after Constantinople had been taken without much difficulty. But popular resistance to him prevented him from keeping his promises, and in 1204 the Crusaders seized Constantinople a second time. They had agreed in advance on how they would divide up the Byzantine empire among themselves; and they sacked the city mercilessly.

The results of the Fourth Crusade were disastrous. Many of Constantinople's greatest art treasures were destroyed in the looting. Its citizens were confirmed in their conviction that reunion of their Greek Orthodox Church with the Catholic Church was impossible. The Byzantine empire was divided among the city's occupants; and when the emperor installed by the Crusaders was driven out in 1261, the restored empire was a debilitated remnant huddled around the shores of the Aegean Sea and could offer little resistance to the growing attacks of the Ottoman Turks. Finally, the Crusaders had been distracted from the Holy Land, and all future attempts to reconquer it were doomed from the start. Only Frederick II succeeded in gaining possession of Jerusalem, by diplomatic bargaining; and he held it for less than fifteen years. By the end of the thirteenth century, the Crusaders had been ousted from their last foothold in Palestine.

The Crusades were thus notable for their ineffectiveness. They were proof of the extraordinary but ephemeral exploits possible when the Church and feudality combined in a common enterprise. They furthered the taste for eastern luxuries and enriched their supplier. But they did not recapture the Holy Land for more than a short time. They greatly weakened Byzantium as a bulwark of Europe against invasion by the Moslems. They brought little knowledge of Arab culture, which came from Spain instead. And the obvious materialism of the later Crusaders brought discredit on the papacy as the original sponsor of the Crusades.

Confrontation of Pope and Emperor: The Investiture Contest.   The pope's challenge to the emperor reached its most dramatic form during the pontificate of Gregory VII (1073–1085). Gregory believed, with a cutting logic that marked both his character and his intellect, that the pope "alone can depose or reconcile bishops . . . that it is lawful for him to depose emperors . . . that he can absolve from their fealty the subjects of wicked rulers." He thus attacked the power of the emperor Henry IV (reigned 1056–1106) at its most crucial point in the feudal age, the right of a lord to invest every new vassal with his benefice, the symbolic ceremony by which was implied the lord's right to service from his vassal in return for the land. Previously, the Church had willingly supplied men and money in return for their land, and had allowed the emperor to hand each new bishop his ring and staff as proof that they would continue to keep this bargain. When Gregory forbade the bishops to go through with this ceremony, the emperor feared eventual refusal to supply his income and his army.

The conflict was colorful. The German bishops, under Henry's persuasion, wrote to the pope: "Since you have degraded your life and conduct by multifarious infamy, we declare that in the future we shall observe no longer the obedience which we have not promised to you." Henry ordered him to give up the papacy, in a letter that began: "Henry, King not by usurpation, but by pious ordination of God, to Hildebrand, now not Pope, but false monk." The pope's reply was immediate: "I take from King Henry, son of the Emperor Henry, who has risen against your Church with pride unheard of, the government of the whole kingdom of the Germans and the Italians, and I free all Christian people from any oath they have made or shall make to him, and I forbid any to serve the king. . . . I bind him with the chain of anathema."[8] Both his clergy and nobles deserted Henry, on hearing of his excommunication; and to save his throne, Henry rushed across the Alps in midwinter to the papal palace at Canossa where he waited as a penitent in the snow for three days. The pope had no choice but to give him absolution, however unwillingly, for fear of losing his own moral prestige. Gregory's triumph was short-lived. His absorption with political power lost him the support of many of the reformers in the Church; and his reliance on the unscrupulous Normans soon made him their captive— literally, since he died as a virtual prisoner in a Norman castle, after his allies had pillaged Rome itself. He had also weakened the power of the papacy's most effective ally, the emperor himself, by inviting the German lords to revolt against him. The chaotic fighting between nobility, imperial armies, and Normans dragged on for almost fifty years. Only in 1122 was a compromise reached between a new emperor and a less ambitious pope, by a face-saving change in the investiture ceremony.

This struggle between pope and emperor continued throughout the next century. At the end of it, Germany was a misgoverned patchwork of over five hundred feudal principalities; the once flourishing island of Sicily was ruined; the imperial family of the Hohenstaufen was wiped out; and the papacy, which had sacrificed its spiritual prestige in the defeat of the emperor, was about to become the physical captive of the French monarchy. This bloodletting occurred, paradoxically enough, while the civilization of medieval Christendom was reaching its height—not in Rome or in Aachen, but in Paris.

This second phase of the contest of pope and emperor was similar in character to the first. The new dynasty of emperors, the Hohenstaufen family (1137–1268), continued to be swayed by the fascination of Italian rule. At first there seemed to be a real possibility of creating a solid political unit running from north of the papal states through Switzerland to Germany; but the pope succeeded in weakening that scheme by encouraging the northern Italian cities to seek independence of the emperor, the German vassals to revolt, and the Byzantine emperor to send an army to Italy against the Hohenstaufen emperor. In the first half of the thirteenth century, the infatuation of the German emperors with Italy was unfortunately reinforced when they inherited the kingdom of Sicily. The rich, almost semitropical island had never lost its contacts with the trade of the East, as a possession either of Byzantium or of the Arabs; and under the Normans, it had received good government and new wealth from plunder. Sicily was a jewel

[8] Theodor E. Mommsen and Karl F. Morrison, eds., *Imperial Lives and Letters of the Eleventh Century* (New York: Columbia University Press, 1967), pp. 149–50.

North

Sea

Baltic Sea

DENMARK

POMERANIA

Vistula

R.

Hamburg

Elbe

BRANDENBURG

POLAND

SAXONY

R.

THURINGIA

English Channel

LOWER
LORRAINE

BOHEMIA

Rhine

Mainz

FRANCONIA

Nuremberg

Seine

River

River

Strasbourg

Danube

Vienna

River

UPPER
LORRAINE

BAVARIA

SWABIA

Saône R.

HUNGARY

FRANCE

L. Geneva

LOMBARDY

Po

R.

VENICE

KINGDOM
OF
ARLES

Genoa

PAPAL

Rhône R.

Pisa Florence

STATES

COUNTY OF
PROVENCE

TUSCANY

CORSICA

Rome

Castel del Monte

Mediterranean

☐ German Principalities
▥ Kingdom of Italy
▧ Kingdom of the Two Sicilies
(acquired 1186)

SARDINIA

KINGDOM OF
THE TWO SICILIES

Sea

Palermo

Germany and Italy
under the Hohenstaufen Emperors

to bedazzle any northern monarch—with the unspoiled Greek temples
of Agrigento and Selinunte, the Roman theaters of Syracuse and Taormina,
the Byzantine mosaics and the Arab fountains of the great cathedral of
Monreale, the massive Norman churches seemingly transplanted from the
banks of the Seine to the cliffs of the Mediterranean shore—and Emperor
Frederick II (reigned 1216–1250) was peculiarly susceptible to its charms.
He spent little time in Germany, and the only part of the Holy Roman

Empire in which he showed determination to consolidate his power was northern Italy. He ruled Sicily as the descendant of all its past conquerors, speaking all the languages of his island—Italian, Arabic, Greek, and Latin, as well as German and French—continuing the scientific interests of its Moslems, and learning from its multiracial society a tolerance that the pope found close to heresy. He swore to go on a Crusade, but found Crusading methods so repugnant that on his first expedition to the Holy Land he turned back as soon as he was out of sight of land and on the second he took possession of Jerusalem by negotiation instead of battle. His ambition to create a powerful state in Italy, his oblivion to excommunication, and his denial of the supremacy of the papacy brought on him the hatred of almost every pope of his reign. By the 1240s the pope was supporting an anti-emperor in Germany and an alternative king for Sicily; and after Frederick's death, the pope gave the island to Charles of Anjou, the brother of the French king, and excommunicated Frederick's bastard son Manfred, to whom he had bequeathed Sicily. Charles defeated and killed Manfred in 1268, and two years later beheaded in the main square of Naples the last Hohenstaufen, the fifteen-year-old son of Frederick II.

Thus, while the English and French monarchies were successful in creating centralized states within which a sense of national homogeneity could grow, the German emperors, diverted from affairs in Germany by their ambitions in Italy and by their conflict with the papacy, saw their realm break into hundreds of fragments. It was to be in these great feudal monarchies, especially in thirteenth-century Paris, that medieval civilization was to reach its greatest heights.

SUGGESTED READING

The most modern interpretations of feudalism are documented in David Herlihy, ed., *The History of Feudalism* (1971). Older studies that are still useful include F. L. Ganshof, *Feudalism* (1961), C. Seignobos, *The Feudal Regime* (1902), and C. Stephenson, *Feudalism* (1962). Marc Bloch concentrates on economic and social factors in his important *Feudal Society* (1961).

On the French kings, the standard work is R. Fawtier, *The Capetian Kings of France* (1960). The literary sources are entertainingly mined by A. Luchaire, *Social France at the Time of Philip Augustus* (1929) and Joan Evans, *Life in Medieval France* (1925).

G. O. Sayles, *The Medieval Foundations of England* (1948), is a masterly survey of English constitutional history, which comes to life more effectively, however, by a reading of the documents collected in C. Stephenson and F. G. Marcham, eds., *Sources of English Constitutional History* (1937), or D. C. Douglas and G. W. Greenaway, eds., *English Historical Documents, 1042–1189* (1953). Douglas also has a good life of the great Norman, *William the Conqueror and the Norman Impact upon England* (1964). On the later English kings, one should consult C. Petit-Dutaillis, *The Feudal Monarchy in France and England: From the Tenth to the Thirteenth Century* (1964), S. Painter, *The Reign of King John* (1949), and F. M. Powicke, *King Henry III and the Lord Edward* (1947).

Geoffrey Barraclough, *Medieval Germany, 911–1250* (1938), is still the best study of the Holy Roman Empire in the Middle Ages, but it can be supplemented by J. Bryce's classic *The Holy Roman Empire* (1904) and J. W. Thompson's *Feudal Germany* (1928). E. Kantorowicz, *Frederick the Second, 1194–1250* (1931), is a fine life of the most fascinating of the medieval emperors. The growth in the strength of the papacy is analyzed in W. Ullmann, *Growth of Papal Power in the Middle Ages* (1955), and its use in the investiture contest in G. Tellenbach, *Church, State, and Christian Society at the Time of the Investiture Contest* (1940). On the major popes, see A. J. MacDonald, *Hildebrand, A Life of Gregory VII* (1932); Sidney R. Packard, *Europe and the Church Under Innocent III* (1927), and Gregory VII, *Correspondence* (1966). On the Cluniac Revival, see Joan Evans, *Monastic Life at Cluny* (1931). But a vast amount can be learned on the whole monastic movement from David Knowles, *The Monastic Order in England* (1951), in spite of its geographical limitations.

For a new approach to the Crusades, one could begin with the Arab version, presented in Francesco Gabrieli, ed., *Arab Historians of the Crusades* (1969), but the more familiar accounts of Villehardouin and Joinville in Frank Marzials, ed., *Memoirs of the Crusades* (1933), are more exciting. A. C. Krey, ed., *The First Crusade* (1921), quotes eyewitness accounts. More specialized is R. C. Smail, *Crusading Warfare, 1097–1193* (1956), and J. La Monte, *Feudal Monarchy in the Latin Kingdom of Jerusalem* (1932).

9
THE PARIS OF SAINT LOUIS

"I am in Paris," wrote a provincial churchman in 1190, "in this royal city, where the abundance of nature's gifts not only captivates those who live there but invites and attracts those who are far away. Even as the moon surpasses the stars in brightness, so does this city, the seat of royalty, exalt her proud head above all other cities." The charm of Paris, he explained, was the harmony of city and countryside. "She is placed in the bosom of a delicious valley, in the center of a crown of hills enriched with the gifts of Ceres and Bacchus. The Seine, that proud river which comes from the east, flows there through wide banks and with its two arms surrounds an island [the Ile de la Cité] which is the head, the heart, and the marrow of the whole city." Already the quarters of the city were developing a distinctive character according to that aspect of the city's life that had become centered there:

Two suburbs extend to right and left, the smaller of which would be the envy of many another city. These suburbs communicate with the island by two stone bridges; the Grand Pont toward the north in the direction of the English sea, and the Petit Pont which looks toward the Loire. The first, broad, rich, and commercial, is the scene of feverish activity, and innumerable boats surround it laden with merchandise and riches. The Petit Pont belongs to the dialecticians, who pace up and down disputing. In the island adjacent to the king's palace, which dominates the whole town, the palace of philosophy is seen where study reigns alone as sovereign, a citadel of light and immortality. [1]

Medieval Paris was created by the joint efforts of bourgeoisie, monarchy, church, and university. To them it owed the rich variety of its life; to the quality of their achievements in their own spheres of activity, it owed its uniqueness.

[1] Cited in Thomas Okey, *The Story of Paris* (London: Dent, 1906), pp. 69–70.

The Cathedral of Notre Dame, Paris. Flying buttresses give elegance and structural strength to the Gothic apse. (FPG/Mathey.)

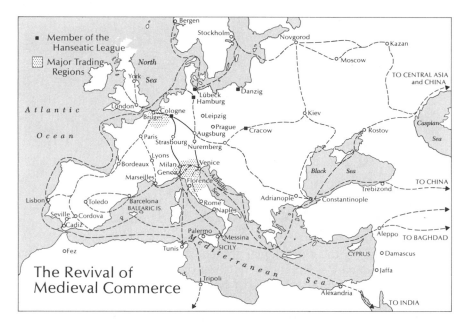

The Revival of Medieval Commerce

BOURGEOIS PARIS   Although Paris never became one of the major commercial or manufacturing centers of Europe in the Middle Ages, it could never have developed to its size and complexity had it not profited from the great revival of commerce and manufacturing in old and new urban centers in Europe from the tenth century on.

Revival of the Mediterranean Cities.   Medieval trade had dwindled to a mere trickle by the end of the Viking invasions of the ninth and tenth centuries; and except for a small nucleus of clerical or lay administrators the great cities had been largely abandoned. From the tenth century on, however, trade revived. The great stimulus came from Constantinople, which, in spite of the Arab conquests in the Mediterranean, continued to trade in the coveted spices of Asia and to ship them into Europe through port cities in Italy, such as Amalfi, Bari, and especially Venice. Built on several hundred tiny islands in the lagoons at the north of the Adriatic Sea, Venice was protected from inland attacks by two miles of water and from the storms of the Adriatic by the reef that formed its lagoons. Although its citizens at first made a small living from salt and fish, it soon profited from its easy access to the growing cities of the Po valley. Over the Brenner Pass its traders reached with relative ease the mineral resources of Austria. Down the valley of the Inn, its merchants joined the trade routes of southern Germany and the shipping of the Rhine valley which led to the Low Countries. The Venetian fleet, constantly increased in size from the tenth century on, was used not only to transport goods but also as an instrument of Venetian expansion. It was used in support of Constantinople's struggle with the Normans of Sicily in the eleventh century, for the conquest of territory down the Dalmatian coast of the Adriatic, and for the transport of Crusaders. After its fleet had brought the knights of the Fourth Crusade to the conquest of Constantinople in 1204, Venice acquired virtually autonomous control of part of the city itself. By the end of the thirteenth century, Venice was second only to Constantinople in wealth. It had a population of at least one hundred twenty thousand. And since power was concentrated in an oligarchy of about two hundred merchant families whose names were listed in the Golden Book, Venice possessed an astonishingly durable and stable form of government. Genoa and Pisa, on the western coast of Italy, broke Venice's monopoly of the Eastern trade by aiding the Crusaders; and they too built up trading routes from Syria and Palestine along the Mediterranean shores and northwards into continental Europe. Pisa's prosperity, however, came to an abrupt halt when it was defeated by Genoa at the end of the thirteenth century; but Genoa in its turn was defeated by Venice in 1380.

St. Mark's Square, Venice. Beyond the five Byzantine domes of St. Mark's Cathedral, begun in 1063, can be seen the three-sided courtyard of the Doge's Palace. (Italian Government Travel Office photo.)

The Commerce of Northern Europe. Trade in the luxury goods of the East such as pepper, ginger, silk, and cotton was certainly the quickest way to make a profit in goods of small bulk. The trading cities of the Mediterranean, however, also supplied more mundane and bulkier items

The Cloth Hall, Ypres. This Hall, constructed in c. 1260–1380, was one of the finest examples of the adaptation of the Gothic style to secular buildings. (Official Belgian Tourist Bureau photo.)

for their own citizens and for the inland cities: wheat, salt, fish, sweet wine of Cyprus, hides, dyestuffs, alum, raw wool, and cloth. In the North of Europe, these bulky items predominated in the trade of the commercial cities. In the Baltic region, furs, timber, salt fish, pitch and tar, hemp, and potash passed through Kiev and Novgorod and through the German cities planted along the Baltic coast, such as Riga, Königsberg, Stettin, and especially Lübeck. The export of wool preoccupied the merchant class of London; the wine of Gascony was the principal item traded in Bordeaux. Increased opportunities in national and international trade led many cities to concentrate on manufacturing specialized goods, for which they became famous throughout the continent. Toledo produced the finest sword blades; Arras, lace and tapestry; and Cordoba, leather goods. But the most important item by far was cloth, whose manufacture was concentrated in two principal regions: the Low Countries, and particularly Flanders, and Florence and the neighboring towns of central Italy.

The Flemish Cloth Trade. The wealth of Flanders was due to a double advantage: its position as the northern terminus of the trade route by which eastern goods were brought north by Italian merchants, and as the manufacturer of the best woolen cloth in the world. The Low Countries, like northern Italy, had a favorable geographical position. Many navigable rivers led into France and Germany—the Rhine, the Maas, the Oise, the Marne. Their ports lay at the midpoint of the North Sea coast, with easy contact with England, northern and western France, and the Baltic. The flat well-watered fields were rich in dairy produce, providing beef, milk and cheese for the city dwellers and more items for export. The fairs of Champagne in France, where most trade between northern and southern merchants took place through the thirteenth century, were only a short overland journey. By the end of the thirteenth century, almost every town of Flanders had mastered the complicated technique of clothmaking, and each was known for its own distinctive brand—for instance, scarlet of Ghent, the lightly woven *rasch* of Arras, and the finely woven *saie* of Bruges. For each stage of the process of manufacture, a specialized group of workers had been formed. First the wool was prepared by sorting, beating, washing, carding, and combing. Then it was spun on a spinning wheel, usually by women. The spun wool was prepared by workers called warpers, who arranged it in threads of the right thickness and length, and it was then woven on a loom by two workers. Finally, it was finished by fulling, a wearisome process of beating and cleaning carried out in a trough with fuller's earth, and by stretching. Dyeing was carried out at any part of the process. Before being sold, it was subjected to further treatment such as raising the nap and shearing. On these processes, the whole social structure of the wool manufacturing towns was founded. The key person in the whole process was the owner of the material, the cloth merchant who brought the raw material and put it out at each step of the process to different groups of workers, establishing his own wages and his own rate of profit. The cloth merchant controlled the city through his powerful guilds and his participation in the city government; and these men, hated by many of their workers, were challenged by the most powerful of the craftsmen, the weavers. Again and again, the weavers rose in bloody but abortive riots, only to be forced back into sullen subjection.

The Economic Function of Paris. Paris had first been settled by a few fishermen who beached their ships upon the three little islands in the center of the river Seine. But it first expanded into a genuine city when the Romans made it the center of their road system in northern Gaul and of their administration. Lutetia, as they called it, was a flourishing city with arena, baths, temples, and palace. But abandoned by the Roman armies in the fifth century, it was preserved from total extinction only by the Catholic Church, which had established a bishopric there in the third century. As elsewhere in Europe, most of the Roman buildings fell into ruin, the arena and baths to the south of the river were covered with grass and bushes, and the major churches were isolated from each other by marshes and fields. After a brief revival under Charlemagne, Paris turned to agriculture for sustenance and to the counts for protection against the Viking invasions. Paris was an easy prey for the black-prowed

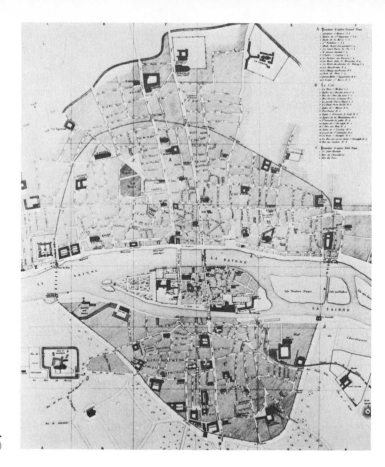

St. Victor Plan of Paris, 1285–1314.
(Préfecture de Paris.)

boats of the Norsemen, who from their island redoubt at Oisselin at the mouth of the Seine would sack it as a mere interlude on their way to invade the richer towns of Burgundy. It was only at the price of a two-year siege in 885–887 followed by the grant of the whole province of Normandy to the invaders that the Counts of Paris were finally able to gain a respite. From this point on, however, Paris reasserted its economic importance.

The settlement of merchants in Paris from the tenth century on illustrates the process of town growth taking place throughout Europe. With the concurrent revival of trade in agricultural produce, local manufactures, and eastern luxuries, merchants in increasing numbers began to travel along the old roads again, especially along the Roman roads, whose superb construction was to preserve them as Europe's main highways for almost two millennia. They settled at fords or bridges, and where principal highways crossed, where important churches or noble and royal households provided a market for their goods, and where a fortress or a city wall provided protection. Paris provided all these advantages. It lay on the Roman road from southern France to Britain and Flanders; its easily navigable river carried goods from eastern France to the Channel. It possessed not only a bishopric but several wealthy monasteries; and from the end of the tenth century, it was the most important seat of the Capetian kings of France. Above all, its walls still survived from Roman days. Merchants attracted by these advantages first settled on the major island, the Ile de la Cité, but soon spread over to the right bank where the river was widest and offered the finest docking facilities, and where by chance no important churches owned property. Thus, very early in Paris's history, the right bank took on the character it has never lost, of the commercial and industrial sector of the city.

At first, the commerce was of a very small scale. The king ordered all trade in basic foodstuffs to be carried on where the main bridge from the Ile de la Cité, the Grand Pont, met the right bank, thus forcing the grouping of the butchers, bakers, and fishmongers next to the money changers whose stalls were already set up along the bridge. But local commerce was soon supplemented with long-distance trading, when the king permitted the holding of a fair, the Foire du Lendit; and with the fair came a great expansion of banking facilities, first run by Jews and then by the Lombard bankers. With the great development of royal power in the twelfth century, the newly wealthy king was joined in Paris by large numbers of feudal lords, while the equally prospering churches and monasteries increased their recruitment and their consumption. Thus the trade in staples dwindled in importance in comparison with the market for luxuries. Many were manufactured in Paris itself. The tailors of linen robes were so swamped with orders that they worked night and day shifts, and were still compelled to recruit foreigners to help them meet their orders. Skilled craftsmen worked to produce jewelry in gold and precious stones, dagger handles, crucifixes in ivory and wood, and crystalware. Others catered to less aesthetic tastes. Barrel makers provided containers for expensive wines and perfumed water; sword and lance makers and saddlers met the needs of the men at arms. Yet again the luxury market was a stimulus to long-distance commerce, in the cloths of Flanders and Tuscany, the silks of Byzantium, or the spices of the Orient. Many of these goods were obtained at the fairs of Champagne, where the Parisian merchants sold their luxury cloths, jewelry, and goldwork; and thus Paris was able to share easily in the great North-South trade of the twelfth and thirteenth centuries.

Parisian Guilds. From the tenth century on, the merchants of the reviving cities had formed themselves into guilds for their own protection, the maintenance of standards, and works of charity and piety. When the towns were still small, most of the merchants in the town tended to join together in one "merchant guild," but from the twelfth century men of the same craft joined together in a "craft guild." In Flanders and Italy, the guilds frequently sought greater independence from their local lord; and in some cases, like Florence, the guilds joined to run the city themselves. But in France the guilds very early struck an alliance of mutual convenience with the king, who regarded them as a reliable source of royal revenue and of support against his feudal nobility, and in return granted them monopolistic trading privileges and the right to elect their own officers. The most important of the early guilds in Paris was the "hansa of the merchants by water," the shipowning guild to which the king gave the monopoly of the carrying trade on the Seine. Other guilds quickly followed—the mercers, the bakers, the dagger makers, the goldsmiths, the fishmongers, and many more. Many received a royal charter, granting a monopoly in Paris. They all enforced strict standards in their craft or trade, controlled the recruitment of apprentices and the employment of journeymen or day laborers, and provided social services for their members. Until the middle of the thirteenth century, this system worked well in Paris. Relative harmony existed between the great mass of artisans and the few extremely wealthy merchants who were already being associated by the king in the work of government. (Philip Augustus entrusted the royal treasury and the royal seal to six bourgeois when he went on a crusade in 1190.) After the death of Louis IX in 1270, however, the tendency of the masters of the guilds to take larger numbers of apprentices and journeymen and to block for many of them the way of advancement into the masters' ranks themselves led to great social friction. The journeymen in particular came to form a class with many of the characteristics of the later industrial proletariat—little prospect of advancement, no personal capital, frequent unemployment, and subsistence wages at best. Throughout the fourteenth and fifteenth centuries, the Parisian working class erupted frequently into riots against the well-to-do bourgeoisie; but they could also be mobilized by bourgeois leaders themselves in movements against the king that were almost revolutionary in character. In 1357–1358, for example, Etienne Marcel, the provost of the merchants of Paris, was able to bring the whole city into insurrection against the dauphin in the hopes of winning important concessions for the representative assembly, the States General, during the Hundred Years' War with England.

During the age of Louis IX, however, these conflicts still seemed distant. Paris congratulated itself on having achieved not only prosperity but social harmony.

THE PALACE: PARIS AS THE CAPETIAN CREATION In spite of its economic importance, Paris has been above everything else a royal city, the capital of "la douce France." It was the presence of the royal government and the determination of the kings to mold the city into a capital worthy of their realm that has made the greatness of Paris.

The Urban Projects of Philip Augustus. The Count of Paris had been chosen king of France in 987. But the first six Capetian kings did not regard Paris as their capital, even though Robert the Pious rebuilt the old Roman palace on the western end of the Ile de la Cité. The court remained peripatetic. Lacking a regular income, it moved around, living off the hospitality of the king's vassals and carrying the government records and treasure with it. It was Philip Augustus who determined to make Paris into a worthy capital of the kingdom he had so vastly expanded by his conquests. At his accession, Paris was a small squat town, of perhaps fifty thousand inhabitants. It had an old wall, built in Roman times but regularly repaired; its streets were thick in mud; sanitation was nonexistent. Although the king's palace on the western end of the Ile de la Cité had been rebuilt less than two centuries before, living conditions for even the king were very primitive. Whenever the king left town for a long trip, one of his usual acts of charity was to bequeath the straw spread on the palace floor to the local hospital. The palace itself had fortified rectangular walls, about a hundred yards in length, with a tall circular tower in the central courtyard where the king kept his armaments. In the living quarters he had only three principal rooms: a large dining hall, used for public meetings of his major vassals, banquets, and reception of important visitors; a private dining room; and an oratory. One chronicler reports that Philip's first idea for the improvement of his city occurred to him one afternoon as he looked out from the palace windows:

He was strolling in the great royal hall thinking over affairs of state and came to the Palace windows from where he often looked out on the River Seine as a diversion. The horse wagons, crossing the city and cutting up the mud, stirred up a stench which he couldn't stand and he decided on a difficult but necessary piece of work which his predecessors had not dared to initiate because of the crushing expense. He summoned the burgesses and the provost of the city and ordered by his royal authority, that all the roads and streets of the city should be paved with strong, hard stone.[2]

[2] Charles Petit-Dutaillis, *The Feudal Monarchy in France and England: From the Tenth to the Thirteenth Century* (London: K. Paul, Trench, and Trübner, 1936), p. 199.

The Ile de la Cité, Paris.
(Interphototèque.)

Only the roads leading to the city gates were paved, however, and the rest of Paris remained glutinous and odoriferous.

Four years later, Philip decided to erect a new city wall. By this act, he shaped the topography of Paris for centuries. The wall ran in two great semicircles, one on the right bank of the Seine and one on the left enclosing an almost circular area about one mile in diameter. The wall was more than ten feet thick and from seven to twenty feet high, broken by sixty-seven round towers and twelve gates. The wall on the right bank, which was built first to protect the business section of the city, took eighteen years to finish; the wall on the left, which safeguarded the intellectual riches of the university, took fifteen. Once completed, the wall influenced the history of the monarchy itself. The strongest fortress of the Capetian kings was now no feudal castle set apart in the countryside, but the capital city itself, defensible only with the aid of the citizens. The alliance of the king and middle classes of Paris led inevitably to the grant of commercial privileges and to a preferential position for Paris over the other cities of France. The wall itself was also a form of real estate development similar in character to the founding of "new towns," the famous *villes neuves*. Philip's wall did not merely surround the populated part of Paris but included large areas of meadow, vineyard, and marsh, whose delighted owners were soon making fortunes by sale of their lands as building lots.

Philip's third building project, erection of a fortress called the Louvre on the right bank just outside the new wall, appeared to be an obvious bastion protecting against attack where the Seine entered the city; a chain was stretched across the river at that point each night. But Philip intended to do more than defend his burghers of Paris. He paid for the fortress himself, kept in it the most important state prisoners, much of the state treasure, and his main supply of weapons. Although he continued to live in the palace on the Cité, he had his own fortress independent of a Parisian population that could turn fickle or even menacing to the monarchy. The Louvre was not only part of the defense of Paris; it could become in time of need the king's refuge from Paris. Already the physical separation of the king from a distrusted people, that led Louis XIV to shift his whole court from Paris to Versailles in the seventeenth century, was glimpsed. Finally, Philip made Paris the center of his improved governmental administration, calling there the barons for the meetings of the Curia Regis and forming from his household offices the nuclei of governmental ministries.

Character of Saint Louis. The achievement of his grandson, Louis IX (reigned 1226–1270), was to make the French monarchy the most admired in Europe for its combination of religious fervor and political astuteness; and as the prestige and power of the monarchy rose, Paris itself experienced a continuing influx of people from all over France and indeed all Christen-

Sire de Joinville Offers His Life of Saint Louis to the King of Navarre.
Joinville's biography was prized in the thirteenth century as a guide to pious living for feudal monarchs. (French Embassy Press and Information Division photo.)

dom, who hoped to benefit in one way or another from the richness of its life.

Both Louis' grandfather Philip and his mother, Blanche of Castile, impressed upon Louis from his early childhood the respect for religion. Blanche trained him in constant devotions and attendance at church sermons, and frequently informed him that she would prefer him to die rather than commit mortal sin. In early youth, Louis was a tall, good-looking gallant with fine blond hair, and at least a moderate interest in the manly pleasures of hunting and female companionship. But ill health that wracked him for his whole life, beginning with erysipelas and compounded by recurrent malaria and anemia, was worsened by his own asceticism, and it played a part in driving him to the consolation of religion. His Crusade to the Holy Land in 1248, which was a disastrous failure and during which he was captured and saw hundreds of his knights and his own brother die, deepened his sense of his own sin and of his responsibility to the Church. "If only I could suffer alone the opprobrium and the adversity," he told a bishop who tried to console him, "and my sins should not recoil on the universal church, then I could bear it with equanimity. But woe is me, by me all Christianity has been covered with confusion."[3] By the age of forty, he was thin, bald, deathly sick, and oc-

[3] Cited in Margaret Wade Labarge, *Saint Louis: Louis IX, Most Christian King of France* (Boston: Little, Brown, 1968), p. 145.

casionally petulant, but suffused with an aura of spirituality. More and more, his devotion reached to extremes. He scourged himself with little iron chains, lost himself in mystical trances for hours prostrate on the stone floor of the palace, personally served meals to lepers, washed the feet of the blind, wore hair shirts next to his skin, and struck without qualm at heresy. For all his kindliness, he declared that "the business of a layman, when he hears the Christian religion defamed, is to defend it with his sharp sword, and thrust his weapon into the miscreant's body as far as it will go." "I have heard him say," his biographer Joinville wrote, "that he would he were marked with a red-hot iron himself if thereby he could banish all oaths and blasphemy from his kingdom." It was evident during his lifetime that France was governed by a saint, a fact that the Church officially corroborated twenty-seven years after his death.

Political Achievements of Saint Louis. What really impressed the thirteenth century was that such accomplishments could be accompanied by solid political achievement. According to Joinville, "the great love that he had for his people appeareth in his saying to my lord Louis, his eldest son, in a dire idleness that he had at Fontainebleau: 'Fair son,' said he, 'I beseech thee to make thyself beloved of the people of thy realm; for in sooth I had liefer have a Scot come from Scotland and govern the people of this realm faithfully and well, than that thou shouldst govern it manifestly ill.'" To Louis, good government implied first of all the extension of impartial justice through the king's powers of legal decision. He dramatized his own interest very effectively. After attending church, he would sit on the foot of his bed with his courtiers around and deal with cases that required his intervention. Or in the summer, with unusual attention to his dress—he wore a coat of camlet, a sleeveless surcoat of linsey-woolsey, a mantle of black silk round his neck, and a coronal of white peacock's feathers on his head—he would sit on carpets in his palace garden by the Seine and pronounce judgment. Of more importance for the future, however, he also had the legal specialists among the members of his Curia Regis devote themselves full time to the study of precedent-making law cases and in giving decisions themselves. These professional lawyers became known as the Parlement de Paris, which developed into the principal law court of France. Moreover, the habit of writing down legal decisions led to the accumulation in the palace of huge quantities of legal documents, whose organization required the recruitment of a large staff of bureaucrats, who helped swell the growing civil service on the island. Many more cases were transferred to Paris for judgment, while Louis's own impartiality was so admired that he was often called to arbitrate cases from outside his own kingdom.

Other members of the Curia Regis began to specialize in financial matters, auditing the accounts of the king's bailiffs, so that also in the palace there appeared the nucleus of the Chambre des Comptes, the king's exchequer. Efficient financial auditing was essential because Louis possessed a large and growing income. The new royal properties seized under Philip, forced loans, taxes on foreigners like Jews or Italian bankers, feudal aids paid by the lords, presents collected from bishops or cities, all had brought the monarchy considerable financial resources. It is characteristic of Saint Louis that, after satisfying the normal functions of government and waging as little war as possible with his Catholic neighbors in Europe, he spent the greater part of his income in the service of religion, especially through his two Crusades, his expensive collecting of relics, and his sponsorship of church building. This was foremost in Joinville's mind as he reported the king's death:

A pitiful thing, and one worthy to be wept over, is the passing of this saintly prince, that kept his kingdom in such holy and righteous fashion, and made such fair almsgiving therein, and instituted therein so many fair ordinances. And even as the scribe that hath made his book illumineth it with gold and blue, so did the said King illumine his realm with the fair abbeys that he there built, and with the great plenty of hospitals and houses of Preaching Friars and Grey Friars and other religious that are named above.[4]

Medieval art and architecture reached their summit in Paris in the thirteenth century because, as has happened at a few rare moments in history, the right patrons appeared at the moment when a new style of art was ready to be born. Or to put it another way, the French king and the leading churchmen of Paris and the Ile de France were prepared and able to spend vast sums of money on art and architecture at the very moment when the principal components of the Gothic style had been invented but not yet combined together into a distinctive form of art.

The early religious history of Paris does not differ much from that of the other great cities of Europe. It had its requisite share of saints and martyrs. The two whose cult exercised the greatest influence on the city were Saint Denis and Saint Germain. Saint Denis, the first bishop of Paris, was tortured by the Roman occupiers in the third century and taken for execution to the hill north of the city which is now called the Mount of Martyrs (Montmartre). His calmness so annoyed his guards that they cut off his head at the bottom of the hill, but the saint picked up his head, washed it in a fountain, and walked on for four miles before he collapsed and was buried. A small pilgrimage church was built to guard his relics; but in the seventh century the Frankish king founded an important Benedictine abbey with vast landholdings and the lucrative right to hold a fair annually. From this time on almost all the kings of France were buried in the monastery of Saint Denis, thus ensuring its continuing importance and prosperity. Another bishop of Paris in the sixth century,

PARIS AND THE GLORIFICATION OF GOD THROUGH ART

[4] Jean Sire de Joinville, *The History of St. Louis,* trans. Joan Evans (London: Oxford University Press, 1938), pp. 227–28.

Saint Germain des Prés, Paris. This fine Romanesque tower survived the destruction of most of the other buildings of the great monastery that occurred during the French revolution. (French Embassy Press and Information Division photo.)

Saint Germain, succeeded in persuading the king to invade Spain to bring back the relics of Saint Victor, and to found a well-endowed Benedictine monastery like that of Saint Denis to hold the relics. When Saint Germain himself was buried in this church just outside Paris, so many miracles occurred among the pilgrims visiting it that he too was canonized, and the church renamed Saint Germain des Prés. In this way two of the richest and most important churches in France were founded. By the time of Charlemagne, Paris possessed a whole galaxy of saints, most of them canonized bishops of Paris, a network of parish churches and largely as a result of the Church's collaboration with the monarchy in the work of government, a large number of highly prosperous abbeys. Rather surprisingly however, during the great period of church building in the tenth and eleventh centuries that followed the reestablishment of relatively peaceful conditions after Norman invasions, Paris and Ile de France achieved very little of real note in art and architecture. The style we call Romanesque was developed by the Normans in Normandy and in England; in Germany; and in most provinces of France except the Ile de France. Since, however, the great style of the Ile de France, Gothic, is a logical progression from the achievements of the Romanesque style, we must glance briefly at what has happened to architecture in the three hundred years that separate the building of Charlemagne's palace church in Aachen and the rebuilding of the abbey of Saint Denis, where the Gothic style began.

Purpose of Medieval Church Building. From the middle of the tenth century, the building of vast new churches became common throughout western Europe, for many reasons. The restored prestige of the Church following the Cluniac reform movement persuaded kings, lords, and townspeople to make large gifts of land or money to the Church, frequently for the specific purpose of improving the house of God and thereby presumably improving their own standing both with the Church and with God. The churchmen too, following the example of Cluny in its extravagant rebuilding as well as its reform program, sincerely believed that the service of God required the erection of ever more grandiose buildings, for the building was a physical representation of the Christian religion. It was in the form of the cross on which Christ had died. Sculptures and stained glass graphically represented, for literate and illiterate alike, the Biblical story and frequently the non-Biblical representation of the punishments of hell and the rewards of paradise. Increasing ritual—the habit of daily mass, the visible presentation of the body and blood of Christ at the high altar, the display of the relics of the patron saint, the complex music of the liturgy, the long processions of richly garbed clergy— all this required a finer and larger house. There were more mundane reasons, however. The central church in town was a meeting place for all townspeople for conversation, business transactions, and even restrained flirtation. It became a theater where visiting players presented morality plays. Competition, too, crept in. Rivalry among cities enabled bishops to draw on huge gifts not only from kings and feudal princes but from guilds or individual artisans and even from the peasantry. The very poorest volunteered their labor where money was lacking. Bishop competed with bishop and abbot with abbot, especially during the building of the Gothic cathedrals of the Ile de France when the competition was simply defined as who could build higher and wider without his church falling down.

The Last Judgment, Facade, Bourges Cathedral. The saved are being separated from the damned by the Archangel Michael, who weighs the souls with his balance. The cauldron of hell is kept boiling by demons with bellows. (French Embassy Press and Information Division photo.)

The Church of the Madeleine, Vézelay.
Founded under the inspiration of Cluny, the abbey of Vézelay was located on the pilgrimage route to St. James's shrine in Spain. (French Embassy and Information Division photo.)

The Romanesque Style. Large size had thus to be achieved by variation on the cruciform ground plan. In the Romanesque cathedral, large size was achieved mainly by bulk of masonry. Walls were immensely thick, and supported by sturdy buttresses built straight against the building. Windows were kept small, to reduce the pressure on the wall. No attempt was made at first to roof with stone, but instead a painted wooden roof was erected. What gave the buildings their beauty was the subtle use of the round arch, which appearing in different forms in the three or four stories of the nave introduced a variety and a sense of movement towards the east that lightened the solidity of the masses of stone. The separation of the bays, by a purely decorative column of stone that ran from floor to ceiling, introduced a vertical drive. But it was in solving the problem of erecting a stone vaulted roof that the early style of Romanesque was transformed. The barrel vault of Vézelay, echoing the pattern of the mosque of Cordoba, was superseded by the far more complex ribbed vaulting of Durham Cathedral in England. The rib vault consisted of two round arches intersecting diagonally. The advantages were already obvious at Durham. It was easier to build; each ribbed vault could be erected separately and the thin masonry filling between the ribs added later when mortar of the ribs had set. This invention made possible that most attractive of all architectural styles, Gothic, which was invented in the building of the Abbey of Saint Denis outside Paris by Abbot Suger in 1133–1144.

The Criticisms of Saint Bernard.   In the years when the great Romanesque churches were building, the Abbey of Saint Denis had not escaped the corruption and preoccupation with worldly goods that had sapped the reforming drive of Cluny; and the two abbeys alike came under the scourging tongue of Saint Bernard, abbot of Clairvaux, the leader of the new reforming order of Cistercians.   The Cistercian order had been founded in Burgundy in 1098 to restore the discipline of the order of Saint Benedict. Its monks had set the example by going into the wilderness to labor, practice celibacy, and live in total simplicity.   But Bernard's overwhelming personality, the power of his preaching, his letters and the example of his own life, made him the self-appointed arbiter of the moral and intellectual standards of Western Europe, and of Paris not least.   He was determined that no breath of heterodoxy should enter the University of Paris, and fought victorious duels with his intellectual superiors like Abelard.   And in monastic affairs, he not only set himself as the disciplinarian but as the judge of artistic taste as well.   He had lampooned the sculptural excesses of Cluny, in a memorable condemnation that showed his understanding as well as his condemnation of the medieval sculptor:

In the cloisters, under the eyes of the brethren engaged in reading, what business has there that ridiculous monstrosity, that amazing mis-shapen shapeliness and shapely mis-shapenness?   Those unclean monkeys?   Those fierce lions?   Those monstrous centaurs?   Those semi-human beings?   Those spotted tigers?   Those

Gargoyles of Notre Dame, Paris. (French Embassy and Information Division photo.)

fighting warriors? Those huntsmen blowing their horns? Here you behold several bodies beneath one head; there again several heads upon one body. Here you see a quadruped with the tail of a serpent; there a fish with the head of a quadruped. There an animal suggests a horse in front and half a goat behind; here a horned beast exhibits the rear part of a horse. In fine, on all sides there appears so rich and amazing a variety of forms that it is more delightful to read the marbles than the manuscripts, and to spend the whole day in admiring these things, piece by piece, rather than in meditating on the Law Divine.[5]

To Saint Bernard, the abbey of Saint Denis seemed in even worse condition. It had become the "workshop of Vulcan" and "a synagogue of Satan"; and this condition he blamed exclusively on its abbot, Suger. "It was at your errors, and not at those of your monks," he wrote to Suger, "that the zeal of the saintly aimed its criticism. It was by your excesses, not by theirs, that they were incensed. It was against you, not against the abbey, that arose the murmurs of your brothers. You alone were the object of their indictments. . . . In fine, if you were to change, all the tumult would subside, all the clamor would be silenced."[6] Although Suger had been the adviser and friend of King Louis VI and King Louis VII and was to be regent of France during the Second Crusade, he could not ignore a direct blast from such a mentor. He reformed his abbey by disciplining its monks and cutting down its extravagant standard of life. But, far from accepting Bernard's artistic stipulations, he challenged them in theory and in practice.

Abbot Suger's Rebuilding of Saint Denis Monastery. Suger loved all the decorative arts of the Middle Ages—the painted frescoes, the cast bronze doors, the exquisite carving in gold, and above all the working of precious stones. In his memoirs on his administration of the abbey, he argued that the contemplation of such works of art brought a man closer to God, and moreover followed Biblical precedent:

Often we contemplate, out of sheer affection for the church our mother, these different ornaments both new and old . . . then I say [quoting Ezekiel], sighing deeply in my heart: "Every precious stone was thy covering, the sardius, the topaz, and the jasper, the chrysolite, and the onyx, and the beryl, the saphire, and the carbuncle, and the emerald.". . . Thus, when—out of my delight in the beauty of the house of God—the loveliness of many-colored gems has called me away from external cares, and worthy meditation has induced me to reflect, transferring that which is material to that which is immaterial, on the diversity of the sacred virtues: then it seems to me that I see myself dwelling, as it were, in some strange region of the universe which neither exists entirely in the slime of the earth nor entirely in the purity of Heaven.[7]

[5] Erwin Panofsky, *Abbot Suger on the Abbey Church of St. Denis and Its Art Treasures* (Princeton: Princeton University Press, 1946), p. 25.
[6] Ibid., p. 10.
[7] Ibid., pp. 63–65.

The Choir and Transept, Basilica of Saint Denis. The originality of Abbot Suger's choir lay in the combination of rib vaults, pointed arches, and flying buttresses. (French Embassy and Information Division photo.)

He obtained his jewels in the most diverse manners. He shamed royal or episcopal visitors into giving him the jewels off their rings to decorate his altar, and he maliciously reported that he was able to buy "an abundance of gems" from monks of three reforming abbeys. He "thanked God and gave four hundred pounds for the lot, though they were worth much more."

Suger's principal work, however, was his rebuilding of the abbey itself. The work, he argued, was made necessary by the vast crowds flocking to see the relics of Saint Denis and the Nail of the Cross. Women, he said, had to walk to the altar on top of the heads of men! He at first intended to send for some of the marvelous marble columns that he had seen in the baths of Diocletian in Rome, but at the last minute the Lord revealed suitable stone in a quarry only twelve miles away. "Whenever the columns were hauled from the bottom of the slope with knotted ropes," he said, illustrating the community involvement in the actual building of the Gothic cathedrals, "both our people and the pious neighbors, nobles and common folk alike, would tie their arms, chests, and shoulders to the ropes, and acting as draft animals, drew the columns up; and on the declivity in the middle of the town the diverse craftsmen laid aside the tools of their trade and came out to meet them, offering their own strength against the difficulty of the road, doing homage as much as they could to God and the Holy Martyrs."[8] To find trees tall enough for the roof,

[8] Ibid., p. 93.

Flying Buttresses, Notre Dame, Paris. The flying buttress transfers the thrust of the stone roof from the thin nave wall downwards and outwards, enabling the architect to open up the walls into huge stained-glass panels. (French Embassy and Information Division photo.)

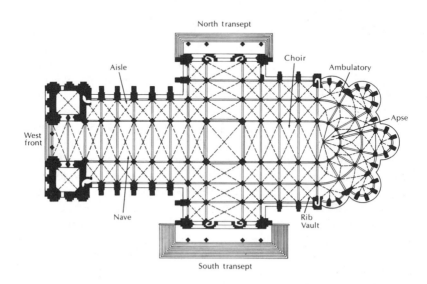

Ground Plan of Chartres Cathedral

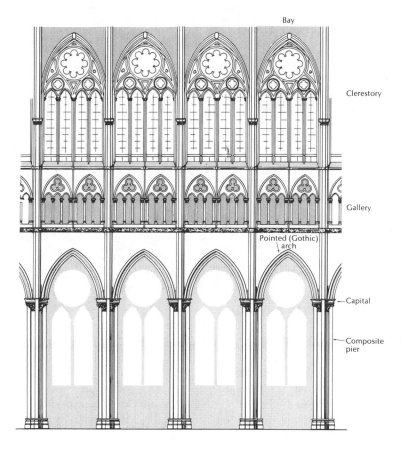

Bay

Clerestory

Gallery

Pointed (Gothic)
arch

Capital

Composite
pier

Nave of Amiens Cathedral

he related that, after a sleepless night of worry, he went himself to one of the abbey's forests, and after searching all day, found twelve trees of the right size, the exact number needed. The work was completed in eleven years, and his new church was consecrated in the presence of the king and twenty bishops in 1144. Immediately, his contemporaries realized that he had revolutionized architecture; and many of those bishops returned home burning with desire to pull down their own cathedrals and erect even finer basilicas than Suger's.

The Invention of Gothic Style. What Suger had done was to combine in a new way three forms already known—the pointed arch, the rib vault, and the flying buttress. The pointed arch created a soaring sense of upward motion in the vertical line of the wall. Construction of the rib vault in the form of a pointed arch allowed roof vaults to be built over any form of

Aerial View, Notre Dame, Paris.
(Interphototeque.)

rectangle, whereas a vault of round arches could be built only over a square. The flying buttress enabled the architect to do away with the thick stonework of the Romanesque wall and to use the space for large windows, which Suger, who loved color and brightness, filled with the first important stained glass windows.

Immediately after the construction of Saint Denis, the powerful archbishop of Sens began his own Gothic cathedral, and shortly after, the cathedral of Canterbury was begun by an architect from Sens. Then the bishop of Noyon, beginning his cathedral fifteen years later, added an extra story to the nave wall, the triforium, and this brought his roof up to eighty-five feet in height. He had reached the height of the side aisle of the Basilica of Maxentius. Then came the cathedral of Senlis, in much the same style, followed by Laon in 1165. Laon marked a big change in Gothic naves, because the architect did away with the composite pier. The ground floor of the nave became a line of identical columns, and the impression was no longer projected of the nave divided into a series of separate bays. For the first time, the spatial sensation of the onward horizontal drive toward the high altar was uninterrupted. This was the point Gothic architecture had reached when the best known of all Gothic cathedrals, Notre Dame de Paris, was begun by Maurice de Sully, bishop of Paris.

Notre Dame de Paris. Maurice, like Suger, was a church-made man, the son of a poor peasant family singled out for tough intellectual training and rapid advancement. Both a scholar and an administrator, he lacked Suger's interest in national politics. For his thirty-six years as bishop,

his chief interest was to build a cathedral worthy of the capital city of
France and of his own ambition. At that time the finest church in Paris
was the monastery of Saint Germain des Prés, an impressive Romanesque
building with a recently completed Gothic choir. But the bishop himself
had only a small dilapidated Carolingian church. Plans for the cathedral
were drawn up in consultation with King Louis VII, whose palace abutted
the site of the new church. Louis, aware that the reputation of the monarchy required that this cathedral exceed any previously built, approved
the extraordinary dimensions Maurice had planned—130 yards long,
with a nave 115 feet high, 30 feet higher than any previous cathedral,
and room for more than ten thousand people inside. The architecture
too was innovative. The transept was moved almost to the middle of the
church, and a double ambulatory was constructed around the nave and
choir. The effect was to unify the whole interior, which no longer appeared
broken into separate units. And at Notre Dame the great program for the
outer decoration of the building brought the art of Gothic sculpture enormously ahead. The sculpture became an integral part of the architecture
of the building and not merely surface embellishment, while the figures
themselves moved from a highly stylized, spiritual form of representation
to ever more appealing realism. The west facade of Notre Dame, planned
and begun under Maurice and completed in 1250, is one of the most
complex and harmonious compositions of the Middle Ages, blending
sculpture and architecture.

The Last Achievements of High Gothic. But even Notre Dame de Paris
could be excelled. When the cathedral of Chartres, a small country town
to the southwest of Paris, burned down in 1194, the bishop sought even
greater height and width: five feet higher and six feet wider. The big
gallery and triforium window that darkened the original nave of Notre
Dame were done away with and huge stained glass windows turned the
nave into a wonderland of light. Here at Chartres, medieval stained glass
presented the whole history and message of the Christian Church. To produce these pictures in glass, the artist built up the window of small pieces
of glass joined together by strips of lead. The glass was colored with metal
oxides in a melting pot, producing color of absolute purity. For variety,
pieces of white glass were fused with pieces of colored glass, producing
the so-called flash glass; and to show figures and faces, a way of applying
a mixture of iron oxide and powdered glass to produce lines and shade was
invented. The artist usually painted a picture, reproduced it in pieces of
glass, joined the pieces in their lead framework, and then put the whole
window inside an iron frame, which could be lifted into place in the stone
tracery. The result was a new art form. The light playing through glass of
different thicknesses and color produced a jewel-like splendor, which
modern artists have been unable to recapture.

The competition continued. Begun in 1211, the cathedral of Rheims,

South Facade, Chartres, c. 1210–1220. The figures of
Saints Paul, John, James the Great, James the Less, and
Bartholemew form one small part of an intricate composition
spreading across three doorways of the south facade. (French
Embassy Press and Information Division photo.)

The Cathedral of Bourges.
Begun in 1192 and completed fifty years later, the nave is 130 feet high and 360 feet long. (French Embassy Press and Information Division photo.)

where the French kings were crowned, reached 125 feet; that of Amiens, begun in 1220, attained 140; and the one at Beauvais, begun in 1247, was 157 feet high. Here at last Saint Bernard's invective against the waste of effort by these cathedral-building bishops seemed justified. The choir of Beauvais fell down the moment it was finished. Rebuilt, it fell again; and although it was repaired, the church was left unfinished, a monument to a style that could advance no further.

At the moment when the building of Beauvais was beginning, Saint Louis created the last of the great Gothic churches of Paris. In 1238, Louis had acquired the Crown of Thorns from the Emperor Baldwin of Constantinople, who had pledged it as security for a loan from a Venetian patrician; and soon after, Louis had bought a piece of the True Cross, a broken fragment of the Holy Lance, the Holy Sponge, the Holy Blood, a piece of the Reed, and even a little stone from Christ's sepulcher. Louis immediately ordered the further expense of a chapel in the palace grounds that would be specially built for the safekeeping and display of the relics. The result

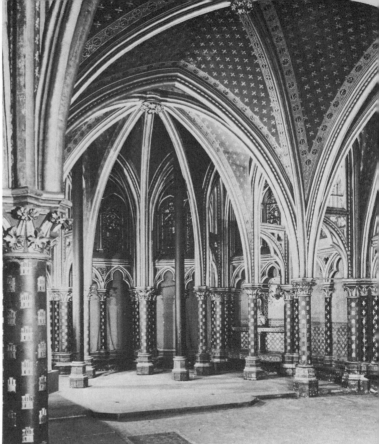

(Left) **The Exterior and** (Right) **the Lower Chapel, Sainte Chapelle, Paris.** Constructed by Louis IX in 1243–1248 to hold the Crown of Thorns and other relics, the chapel stood in the center of the Capetian palace. (French Embassy Press and Information Division photos.)

was the lovely Sainte Chapelle, the Gothic building in which the architect has come closest to achieving the ideal of a wall composed entirely of stained glass.

In the twelfth and thirteenth centuries Paris came to be dominated by the buildings of the Church. As well as the monuments on the Ile de la Cité, there were thirty parish churches, twenty-nine major convents, several huge hospitals, five houses for lepers, and many houses for the orders of mendicant friars. But the most important area in which religion dominated the life of Paris, and Paris dominated the life of Europe, was in the university.

THE UNIVERSITY: PARIS AS THE INTELLECTUAL CAPITAL OF EUROPE

Throughout the twelfth and thirteenth centuries, students from all over Europe swarmed to Paris to enjoy the intellectual excitement of the hard-argued debates between the great masters of its university. Already the student's district, the Latin Quarter, was acquiring that endearing character of boisterous irreverence that it never lost. One visitor from the provinces in the thirteenth century was astounded at their number:

Never before at any time or in any part of the world, whether in Athens or Egypt, had there been such a multitude of students. The reason for this must be sought not only in the beauty of Paris itself, but also in the special privileges which King Philip and his father before him had conferred upon the scholars. In this great city the study of the trivium and the quadrivium, of canon and civil law, as also of medicine, was held in high esteem. But the crowd pressed with special zeal around the professorial Chairs where Holy Scripture was taught or where problems of theology were resolved.[9]

The University of Paris originated in the cathedral school of Notre Dame, and its preeminence in European thought was due, for the next two centuries, to the sparkling intellectual achievement in philosophy and theology of the professors who taught there. During this period every great name in the history of European philosophy appeared on the faculty of the university, among them Abelard, Peter Lombard, Alexander of Hales, Albert the Great, Thomas Aquinas, Bonaventura, Roger Bacon, and William of Occam. And the dramatic evolution of the institutions of the university was directly linked with the equally dramatic development of the philosophical theories of its professors.

The Battle of Realists and Nominalists. At the beginning of the twelfth century, the teachers of the sparsely attended cathedral school were expounding a philosophy established by the Church fathers about the time of the fall of the Roman Empire to which little had been added in the following five centuries. These philosophers, called Realists, taking up a late interpretation of Plato's theory of ideas, held that reality was a series of ideas, or universals, such as justice and humanity, that existed in the mind of God. Particular things, such as an act of justice or an individual person, were only important or real because of the existence of the universals. This theory fitted nicely into the Catholic Church's determination to monopolize truth and to deny reason a primary role in the understanding of truth. Belief was held necessary to an understanding of truth. "I do not try to understand in order to believe, but I believe in order to understand," said the great Realist thinker Anselm. In the period of questioning that began in the early twelfth century, this doctrine came under attack by the Nominalists, who held rather contemptuously that universals were just names, a "breath of the voice," and that individual things were of primary importance and reality. Thus, the Nominalists could argue, somewhat unwisely, that the three parts of the Trinity were real, and that Christians were therefore worshipping three gods rather than one, a doctrine that the Church hurriedly condemned as heretical. This philosophical battle, between Realists and Nominalists, and the later battles of the thirteenth century over the use of Aristotle, were deeply exciting to medieval students and teachers as well as of direct concern to the highest authorities of the Church. Philosophy dealt with matters of faith and thus of salvation, which to the Middle Ages was the supreme form of knowledge. The battles between professors of philosophy in their search for supreme truth attracted large

[9] Guillaume Le Breton, cited in Ernest Barker, ed., *Golden Ages of the Great Cities* (London: Thames and Hudson, 1952), p. 97.

numbers of students. They in turn supported larger teaching faculties, who systematized the curriculum and organized themselves into a self-regulating corporation, or guild, of teachers and degree granters. The guild of teachers or masters created a university.

Peter Abelard.   Paris first became a magnet for that vast horde of students who roamed from city to city in search of someone under whom they could study when Peter Abelard (1079–1142), at the age of twenty-four, challenged the Realistic teaching of the leading professor in the cathedral school, and with a flash of brilliant logic compelled him publicly to change his views. To many students, Abelard was a charismatic figure, a precocious master of the instrument of logic, irreverent to accepted theory and theorists, humorous in his exposure of error—in all, a humane cleric, as shown by his relations with the sixteen-year-old Heloise, whose tutor and lover he became. His students followed him in fascination on the many occasions when his quarrels compelled him to seek new places to teach; and they made the scalpel of his logic, the syllogism, the principal instrument of philosophical surgery for the rest of the Middle Ages. Logic he expressed in a book called *Sic et Non,* in which he laid out 158 problems, with authorities for and against, leaving the reader to come to his own conclusions. In philosophy he sought a midway course between Realism and Nominalism, accepting the Nominalist view that the individual is real and also the Realist view that universals were concepts, not just words, and therefore real too. Abelard's uncompromising use of reason won him the incomprehension and hatred of Saint Bernard, who accused him variously of being tainted with the heresies of Arianism, Pelagianism, and Nestorianism, and had many of Abelard's propositions condemned by church council. Abelard died two years later and was buried in the convent where Heloise had become prioress.

The Organization of the University of Paris.   In the century following the arrival of Abelard, the professors in Paris sought to throw off the controls exercised over them by the cathedral. To do so, they organized themselves into a guild; and in 1229, when the Church and city authorities failed to make redress for the murder of a number of students after a tavern brawl, they suspended their lectures and took jobs in universities elsewhere. (Half of the universities of Europe were formed by similar dispersions of teachers and students. Cambridge, for example, was begun by a dispersion of students and faculty from Oxford.) Neither King Louis IX nor the pope wanted to see the leading Christian university disappear, and they at once confirmed the privileges of masters and students of the university. The papal bull was notable for the effusiveness of its appreciation of the university:

Gregory, the bishop, servant of the servants of God, to his beloved sons, all the masters and students at Paris—greeting and apostolic benediction.

Paris, the mother of sciences, like another Cariath Sepher, a city of letters, stands forth illustrious, great indeed, but concerning herself she causes greater things to be desired, full of favor for the teachers and students. There, as in a special factory of wisdom, she has silver as the beginnings of her veins, and of gold is the spot in which according to law they flow together; from which the prudent mystics of eloquence fabricate golden necklaces inlaid with silver, and making collars orna-mented with precious stones of inestimable value, adorn and decorate the spouse of Christ. . . . Accordingly, it is undoubtedly very displeasing to God and men that any one in the aforesaid city should strive in any way to disturb so illustrious grace.[10]

The chancellor of the cathedral was therefore ordered to grant a license to teach to anyone accepted by the masters' guild, whose claim to run the university was henceforth undisputed by the clergy of Notre Dame. The pope's bull also laid down other recommendations of continuing signi-ficance. The summer vacation was not to exceed one month. Students were not to carry weapons. "Those who call themselves students but do not frequent the schools, or acknowledge any master, are in no way to enjoy the liberties of the students."

By this time, too, the curriculum of the university had been formalized. All students began by spending five or six years in the Faculty of Arts, during which they studied the trivium (grammar, logic, and rhetoric) and the quadrivium (arithmetic, geometry, astronomy, and music), although they devoted most of their time to logic and philosophy. Only about a third of the students completed the arts course, at the end of which they were granted a degree of master of arts and admitted to one of the three higher faculties: theology, canon law, and medicine. A student of theology had many years of exacting study ahead: four years of lectures on the Bible; two years on Lombard's *Sentences,* a summary of theological questions; two years as a lecturer himself on the Bible, and a year on the Sentences; and a final five years of study, before receiving the degree of doctor of theology.

The Franciscan and Dominican Friars.   For many students, the years of study were made tolerable by the corporate life. The arts students were divided into four "nations," France, Picardy, Normandy, and England, to which students from all over Europe were assigned. Most countries of central and eastern Europe were grouped under England. National com-patibility brought students to rent houses together, drink together, and fight together. They go around, wrote one observer, "saying that the English are drunkards and have tails; that the French are proud, soft, and womanish; the Germans mad and indecent in their feasting; the Normans stupid and boastful; the Picards traitors and fair-weather friends. . . . And because of

[10] Cited in David Herlihy, ed., *Medieval Culture and Society* (New York: Walker, 1968), p. 217.

such wrangling they often proceed from words to blows." Their unruliness made them heartily disliked by the law-abiding citizens of Paris, and led to frequent street battles. It was partly to discipline the students as well as to give charity to the deserving poor among them that benefactors in the thirteenth century began to found colleges where students could be lodged and supervised. Robert de Sorbon, whose college developed into the principal school of the university and gave its name, the Sorbonne, to the present school of arts and sciences, reminded his scholars of the advice of Saint Bernard: "There is as much difference between reading and study as there is between an acquaintance and a friend."[11]

Both the organization and the established philosophy of the masters of the university were shaken early in the thirteenth century by the establishment in Paris of houses of the newly founded orders of mendicant friars, the Dominicans and the Franciscans. Both orders were started as yet more attempts to bring the Church back to the primitive ideal of poverty, from which even the Cistercians had fallen. Saint Francis (1182–1226), the son of a wealthy merchant of Assisi in central Italy, had experienced a deep religious conversion after years as a spendthrift and soldier; and on the rocky slopes of the Apennine Mountains of Umbria, he had gathered around him a small group of disciples who followed him in living in total simplicity, begging their food and shelter, and preaching the unadorned gospel of God's love and the brotherhood of all living creatures. To Saint Francis, learning was unimportant; example and eloquence were all. By the time of his death, his order had five thousand members; half a century later, two hundred thousand.

The Dominicans were founded by a Spaniard, Saint Dominic, who was appalled by the spread of heresy through the south of France, and independently reached the same conclusion as Saint Francis: that the corruption in the Church and the heresy without could only be halted by the foundation of a new order devoted to poverty and preaching. But Dominic, challenged by highly educated leaders of the Albigensian heretics, saw from the start that his Dominicans would have to be the masters of theological learning but not of "secular sciences or liberal arts except by dispensation."

Established in Paris, like the Dominicans, in the 1220s, the Franciscan friars ignored their founder's warning against study, and rivaled their black-robed competitors in the pursuit of philosophy and in the acquisition of the professorial chairs that previously had been monopolized by the masters' guild. The masters objected strenuously to the friars' refusal to accept the discipline of their guild and to suspend their lectures in solidarity with the masters during their conflicts with the Paris government. After a long battle involving excommunications, appeals to the pope, muggings of friars in the streets, and the threat of the masters to dissolve the university, a com-

[11] Cited in Joan Evans, *Life in Medieval France* (London: Oxford University Press, 1925), p. 165.

The Meeting of Saint Francis and Saint Dominic by Fra Angelico (1387–1445). The black cape and flowing white vestments of Saint Dominic, on the left, contrast with the rough brown robe of the barefooted Saint Francis, on the right. Fra Angelico painted the altarpiece for a Franciscan monastery. (De Young Museum, San Francisco.)

promise was finally reached, permitting the friars to become professors of theology on condition that they follow the university statutes and the master's oath. The conflict was important in that it recognized the central position of the friars in higher learning, but also strengthened the institutional character of the university.

For these Dominican and Franciscan scholars, the study of philosophy and theology had been transformed by the diffusion in Europe of a vast range of writings of classical Greece, from the Toledo translation school, Sicily, and Constantinople, including most of the works of Aristotle then known and commentaries on them by Arabic and Jewish scholars in Spain. What fascinated thinkers most was the majesty and range of Aristotle's writings, covering everything from biology to poetry. The first reaction of the conservative professors of the university was one of terror at the damage that study of Aristotle's speculations could do to the faith of the students and the reputation of their professors; and in 1210, reading of Aristotle's works on natural philosophy was banned under pain of excommunication. Philosophy was rescued from this impasse and Christianity converted from Plato to Aristotle by the greatest thinker of the Dominican order, Saint Thomas Aquinas.

Saint Thomas Aquinas. Aquinas, the son of an Italian nobleman, had studied in the Benedictine monastery of Monte Cassino and in the University of Naples. He arrived in Paris in 1245 to work through the course of study in the faculty of theology under the fine Aristotelian scholar, Albert the Great. Although he was called to the papal court in 1259, he returned to teach again in the University of Paris from 1269–1272, during which time he composed a good part of his finest book, *Summa Theologica*. In breadth and subtlety, no Catholic thinker has excelled Aquinas, and in the nineteenth century he was officially recognized by the pope as the standard of orthodoxy in Catholic study of philosophy. Aquinas set out to harmonize the writings of Aristotle with the basic dogmas of the Christian Church, by the use of the dialectic. His famous proof of the existence of God begins:

Our consideration of God shall fall into three parts, for we shall consider (1) whether there is a God, (2) how he exists, or rather, how he does not exist, and (3) those things which pertain to his actions, that is, his knowledge, will and power.

Considering the first point, three things will be investigated: (1) whether it is self-evident that God exists, (2) whether his existence can be proved, and (3) whether there is a God. . . .

Aquinas's vast learning stimulated other professors to violent disagreement. Once again, scintillating debate enlivened the lecture halls. The Franciscans in particular challenged his abandonment of Plato and his promotion of reason above a mystical understanding of God; and at the end of the century, Duns Scotus and William of Occam were able to rally most of the professors of Paris to reject Aquinas in favor of a reassertion of Nominalism. Since however they rejected reason rather too enthusiastically, both Scholasticism and probably religion too suffered as a result.

The University of Paris thus represented everything that was most idiosyncratic and typical about medieval culture. It harnessed a vast apparatus of learning in support of doctrines whose truth was taken as self-evident. It rewarded research, but insisted that its results enhance what was already known. It established stiff mental training, but circumscribed it in the study of a fixed group of authoritative texts. It did little or nothing to further an interest in natural science, technology, or the fine arts. It turned higher learning into a predominantly vocational training for three careers, churchman, lawyer, and doctor. And it gave a restricted corporation of teachers so tight a monopoly of stylized learning that innovation outside, and even within, the established fields was only possible after an attack on the institution itself. The University of Paris was thus as unnecessary and as intellectually justifiable—and for roughly the same reasons—as the Cathedral of Notre Dame. They were the supreme achievements of an age of faith.

SUGGESTED READING

Maurice Druon's *The History of Paris from Caesar to Saint Louis* (1969), though slightly romantic, can be consulted for lack of an up-to-date scholarly study of thirteenth-century Paris. Thomas Okey, *The Story of Paris* (1925), and Hilaire Belloc, *Paris* (1923), are useful for some background detail of an anecdotal kind. In French, however, René Héron de Villefosse, *Histoire de Paris* (1948) is very sound; Edmond Faral, *La Vie quotidienne au temps de Saint Louis* (1942) fills in the social history of the period. Roger Dion et al., *Paris: Croissance d'une capitale* (1961) approaches the problem of urban growth from the viewpoint of recent urbanistic studies. The life of Saint Louis is charmingly described in Margaret W. Labarge, *Saint Louis: Louis IX Most Christian King of France* (1968), which contains a good chapter on Paris, pp. 155–68. Jean de Joinville's biography, *The History of St. Louis* (1938) is well translated by Joan Evans.

More general studies on the revival of cities in the Middle Ages include Henri Pirenne's masterly *Medieval Cities* (1925), and his *Belgian Democracy* (1915), which deals fully with the Flemish wool cities. Urban documents are collected in John H. Mundy and Peter Riesenberg, *The Medieval Town* (1958). The pattern of trade is illustrated with documents in Robert S. Lopez and I. W. Raymond, *Medieval Trade in the Mediterranean World* (1955), and synthesized in H. L. Adelson, *Medieval Commerce* (1962).

The art of medieval Paris is exhaustively covered. The ideal way to begin is to let Abbot Suger tell his own story, in Erwin Panofsky, ed., *Abbot Suger on the Abbey Church of St. Denis and Its Art Treasures* (1946). George Henderson, *Gothic* (1967) explains all aspects of Gothic expression in art and architecture. One can then turn to the more specialized studies of Notre Dame Cathedral, especially the evocative description by the architect Allan Temko, *Notre Dame of Paris* (1955) or the beautifully illustrated volumes by Pierre du Colombier, *Notre Dame de Paris: Mémorial de la France* (1966) and Yves Bottineau, *Notre Dame de Paris and the Sainte-Chapelle* (1965). Robert Branner, *St. Louis and the Court Style in Gothic Architecture* (1965) studies the creation of a specifically Parisian style of architecture in the middle of the thirteenth century.

The University of Paris is superbly examined by Gordon Leff, *Paris and Oxford Universities in the Thirteenth and Fourteenth Centuries: An Institutional and Intellectual History* (1968), and the character of student life on the Left Bank can be tasted in Hastings Rashdall, *The Universities of Europe in the Middle Ages* (1936), vol. 1, pp. 269–84. Leff summarizes the course of medieval philosophy in *Medieval Thought: St. Augustine to Ockham* (1958). Other useful surveys are Frederick N. Artz, *The Mind of the Middle Ages* (1962) and Frederick C. Copleston, *Medieval Philosophy* (1952). The story of Abelard is best approached through his *Letters* (1926) or Etienne Gilson's *Heloise and Abelard* (1951).

10
THE TRANSFORMATION OF THE MEDIEVAL SYNTHESIS

In the two centuries following the death of Saint Louis, medieval civilization, which had reached its most sparkling synthesis in thirteenth-century Paris, was slowly transformed. The Middle Ages did not decay and then disintegrate, although many of the forces provoking its transformation, such as disease and war, were destructive. The fascination of the fourteenth and fifteenth centuries is in the reaction of a medieval civilization still intellectually and artistically vigorous and inventive to the impact of man-made and natural disaster, which destroyed more than a third of the continent's population and provoked an economic recession that lasted more than a century.

THE DANCE OF DEATH: FAMINE, PESTILENCE, AND WAR

No image was more common through all the art and literature of the late Middle Ages than that of death. Even if we did not possess clear evidence of population decline from tax records, monastic account books, wills, registers of vital statistics, and studies of town topography and rural depopulation, the new ubiquity of the depiction of bodily decay would lead us to suspect a continuing and catastrophic threat to the people of Europe throughout the fourteenth and fifteenth centuries. The meticulous absorption with the details of human putrefaction would compel us to imagine a society in constant terror.

In the lyric poetry of the Parisian François Villon, there is a recurrent lament for "the snows of yesteryear," for the beauty that passes too soon.

Detail from Virgin and Child, by Master of St. Gudule.
Courtiers stand on the battlements of an imaginary city gazing at the single-masted cogs that carried much of the bulky cargo in the coastal traffic of the fifteenth century.
(Official Belgian Tourist Bureau photo.)

291

Burial of Saint Mary, possibly by Erasmus Grasser (1450–1526). The coffin is carried by the Apostles. The fallen figure in the center is the High Priest, who was reputed to have fallen dead on touching the coffin. (De Young Museum, San Francisco.)

Death makes him tremble, turn pale,
His nose curves, his veins swell,
His neck bursts, his flesh melts,
His joints and tendons grow and swell,
Feminine body, who are so tender,
Smooth, soft, and so precious;
Must all these evils await thee?
Yes, or you must go to heaven alive. [1]

Bishops commissioned tombs in which their own bodies were portrayed being eaten by worms. In the tiny parish churches of Bavaria, the wood carver Tilman Riemenschneider depicted an emaciated Christ writhing in physical agony in the throes of death. And in the widely circulated *danse macabre*, the dance of death, printed on the newly invented woodcut of the late fifteenth century, dancing skeletons carried away men of every character and condition, with robed churchmen and landowners being perhaps the most favored.

Demographic Catastrophe. The facts justify the image. The population of Europe began to decline from the beginning of the fourteenth century, sank rapidly by as much as a third in the second half of the fourteenth century, and only returned to the level of the year 1300 by the early six-

[1] J. Huizinga, *The Waning of the Middle Ages* (London: E. Arnold, 1924), p. 133.

teenth century. The earliest scourge was the elemental fact of starvation. On several occasions, the staple wheat crop was destroyed by summers of abnormally high rainfall, as in 1314–1316. Much of the new land brought under cultivation in previous centuries to meet the needs of the growing population was marginal, and it began to lose its productivity at this time. Deforestation, lack of fertilization, and omission of periods of fallow turned much land to dust, and brought the inevitable consequence of flooding. The first general famine from 1315 to 1317, for example, killed ten percent of the inhabitants of the Flemish city of Ypres; and while localized famines could be mitigated by import of food from unaffected regions, famines affecting most of Europe occurred every few years throughout the fourteenth and fifteenth centuries. In prosperous southern France, there were eleven famines, many of them lasting several years.

In 1347, this weakened population was hit by a second scourge, pestilence—the Black Death, a combination of bubonic and pneumonic plagues that was brought to Europe from Constantinople through fleas on infected rats. Within two years it had spread north from Italy as far as Scotland, striking with seeming capriciousness. In one English village, it killed seventy-four people, in the neighbor village only five. But neither city nor countryside was spared. In Florence, probably fifty thousand died out of a population of eighty thousand; an abbey in the east of England lost half of its tenants. Most historians agree that about one-third of Europe's population perished, and horribly. According to the Florentine writer, Boccaccio (1313–1375), who described in his *Decameron* the flight

The Three Living and the Three Dead, c. 1345. These pages from the psalter and prayer book of the Bonne of Luxembourg reveal the fascination with sudden death that pervaded much of the popular art of the fourteenth century. (The Metropolitan Museum of Art. The Cloisters Collection, 1969.)

of a group of Florentine gentry to the countryside, where they amused themselves relating frequently bawdy tales while waiting for the plague to subside:

In its early stages both men, and women too, acquired certain swellings, either in the groin or under the armpits. Some of these swellings reached the size of a common apple, and others were as big as an egg, some more and some less. . . then the appearance of the disease began to change into black or livid blotches, which showed up in many on the arms or thighs and in every part of the body. And just as the swellings had been at first and still were an infallible indication of approaching death, so also were these blotches to whomever they touched. . . . Oh, how many palaces, how many lovely houses, how many noble mansions once filled with families of lords and ladies remained empty even to the lowliest servant! Alas! how many memorable families, how many ample heritages, how many famous fortunes remained without a lawful heir! [2]

Worse, the plague kept recurring at least once a generation, especially in the big cities. London, which had twenty outbreaks in the fifteenth century, was to suffer its worst epidemic as late as 1665. Fear of plague was perpetually in the background of men's thoughts, and could be played upon by such preachers of repentance as the Florentine monk Savonarola, who threatened, "There will not be enough men left to bury the dead; nor the means to dig enough graves. . . . Men will pass through the streets crying aloud, 'Are there any dead? Are there any dead?'" [3]

Coupled with the scourges of famine and pestilence in medieval litanies was the curse of war. In a sense the whole feudal system had been a preparation for war, or at least for defense; but in the fourteenth and fifteenth centuries men were conscious of war in much the same way that they were conscious of the plague, as a recurring disaster from which no locality was free and whose moment of impact could never be foreseen. In the southeastern part of Europe, the Turks were advancing into the Balkan peninsula, capturing not only the rough lands of the Bulgars and Serbs but the great centers of European culture, Constantinople in 1453 and Athens three years later. In the 1460s their expansionist drive took them into the plains of Hungary, and in 1480 they landed on the heel of Italy itself. Further to the north, the princes of Muscovy were engaged in the campaigns that culminated at the end of the fifteenth century in the throwing off of the yoke of their Tartar overlords. Northern Germany and the eastern shore of the Baltic were ravaged by the continuing crusade of the Teutonic knights for the establishment of Christianity and their own territorial aggrandizement in the lands of the Slavs. Throughout western Europe there was civil strife—in the cities between the lower classes and

[2] Cited in David Herlihy, ed., *Medieval Culture and Society* (New York: Walker, 1968), p. 217. Trans. by David and Patricia Herlihy.
[3] Cited in Margaret Aston, *The Fifteenth Century: The Prospect of Europe* (New York: Harcourt, Brace & World, 1968), p. 15.

the well-to-do patriciate, in the countryside between the peasants and their landlords. Noble family fought with noble family, some of their struggles, like those between the houses of York and Lancaster in England, developing into civil wars for control of whole kingdoms. The effort of the French kings to oust the English from their vast possessions in southwestern France produced the dreadful destruction of the Hundred Years' War. And finally, perhaps affecting the peasantry most of all, there was simple brigandage, by the great mercenary bands employed by the Italian cities, by nobles down on their luck, or peasants in desperation.

War itself did not kill vast numbers of people, although the pitched battles frequently decimated the nobility. (In contrast with later wars, the nobleman in armor actually did the fighting rather than command from a safe distance behind the lines.) War destroyed the productive capacity of city and country alike, and thereby added to the likelihood of famine and the inability of trade to lessen its impact. Marauding armies destroyed livestock, burned fields, pulled down farmhouses and mills; peasants fled, many never returning. Precariously collected surpluses of wheat or wool were commandeered; and the lack of capital, even by lords, made it impossible to restore these depredations. The result was a demoralized society. A contemporary reported on the condition of France in the middle of the Hundred Years' War:

The affairs of the realm went from bad to worse, the public weal came to an end and brigands appeared on every side. The nobles hate and despise the villeins, they care no more for the good of the King or of their vassels; they oppress and despoil the peasants of their villages. They no longer trouble to defend the country: to tread their subjects under foot and to pillage them is their only care. From this day the land of France, hitherto glorious and honored throughout the world, became the laughing-stock of other nations. [4]

Rural Adaptation to Population Decline. Under the pressure of this disastrous population decline, the basic institutions of medieval society changed profoundly; and the change was most palpable in the most fundamental of all medieval institutions, the manorial system. The obligations of serfdom had already been greatly reduced in the twelfth and thirteenth centuries, as serfs were given special privileges in return for their cooperation in opening up new land and as landlords found it more productive to commute labor dues to monetary payments with which they could hire more willing laborers. The institution of serfdom itself was already, in western Europe at least, beginning to disappear. As a result of the fall in population in the fourteenth and fifteenth centuries, this process was accelerated. There was a migration of the peasantry from the land into the cities, which increased the rural depopulation still further and increased

[4] Joan Evans, *Life in Medieval France* (London: Oxford University Press, 1925), p. 188.

the wages the remaining laborers could demand. There was a falling demand for basic foodstuffs, whose price remained stable or declined slightly at a time when the cost of luxuries and manufactured goods was increasing sharply. The landlords' predicament was thus very acute. Many of them made great efforts to avoid making concessions to the peasantry. Some ecclesiastical estates attempted to impose stricter legal ties to prevent their laborers from leaving the land. In England, Parliament passed law after law to keep down wages. In western Europe these efforts provoked three great peasant rebellions in the fourteenth century: in Flanders in 1323–1328; around Paris, in the Jacquerie of 1358; and near London, in the Peasants' Revolt of 1381. In all three, religious reformers inflamed the peasantry against the church; all three were justified by their leaders as attempts to throw off the unjust burdens imposed on the peasant to feed classes who "prayed" and "fought"; and in every case a discontented city—Bruges, Paris, or London—provided leaders and artisan support. All three rural revolts were hopeless from the start, and their repression was bloody. In France alone, twenty thousand peasants were killed. Yet if the immediate revolts failed for lack of leadership, money and weapons, and realizable goals, the transformation of the agrarian system could not be stopped. Only in eastern Europe beyond the Elbe River was the nobility powerful enough to force the peasantry to remain on their lands. In western Europe, the medieval manor was doomed.

The west European landlord was compelled to adjust to market conditions by changing the nature of his farming methods and choice of crops. The most obvious change was a reallotment of land use to the production of crops other than wheat, which would require less farm labor or would fetch a higher price on the market. In England, in particular, much land was devoted to sheep-herding, which was a lucrative agricultural sector as long as the English manufacture of cloth was expanding. In France and Germany, viticulture was expanded to meet greatly increased demand due largely to the fact that the fall of price of breadstuffs left more money available for such luxury items. In England, a similar rise in the consumption of beer made the growing of barley profitable. Barley was also used as fodder for the larger herds of cattle that were raised for meat and for butter and cheese. Not all these stratagems paid off, however. The demand for English wool went through periods of expansion and slump, and the periods of decline provoked considerable social distress. Those, however, who attempted to meet their difficulties by renting out their land found themselves in an even worse position. So much land was available that little income could be obtained from rent. Rents were long-term and fell in real value as money was inflated—and kings were often guilty of debasing the currency and thus reducing the income from leased land. Very frequently nobody was found to lease the land, and it reverted to pasture or to waste. Here in part is the explanation of the abandonment of large numbers of villages; in England alone, perhaps one-fifteenth of all villages were abandoned.

The Papal Monarchy. Nothing more clearly signified the breakdown
of the medieval synthesis than the decline in the prestige of the papacy
and indeed of the whole hierarchy of the Catholic Church. At the end
of the thirteenth century the Church enjoyed a commanding position in
the spiritual and cultural life of Europe, and after its triumph over the
German emperors the pope could even claim a similar predominance
in the political sphere. The papal bull *Unam Sanctam* of 1302 declared that
"both the material and spiritual swords are in the power of the Church. . . .
It is fitting moreover that one sword should be under the other, and the
temporal authority subject to the spiritual power. . . . We, moreover, pro-
claim, declare, and pronounce that it is altogether necessary to salvation
for every human being to be subject to the Roman Pontiff." The means the
Church used to obtain this position of predominance sapped its spiritual
vitality, and even weakened the faith in the importance of the Church to
society.

During the thirteenth and early fourteenth centuries, the popes built
a material power that was the envy of many lay rulers. Increasingly,
they claimed universal powers of judicial administration, and the fees
derived from it. They had a large income from a multitude of sources,
such as feudal dues from their own holdings, tribute from many monasteries,
the first year's income of many newly appointed clergymen, and since
the time of the Crusades a very productive tax on the annual income of
all churches. They maintained large armies, often of mercenary soldiers.
And they constantly interfered in the international relations of the European
states, seeking to arbitrate territorial disputes over inheritances or joining
in national wars of one Catholic king against another. This increase in
the pope's powers had several noxious effects on the Church. First, it
diverted the pope from his religious duties. He found himself spending
his time adjudicating legal cases, many of which were concerned with
squabbles over the financial aspects of church appointments. He was
responsible for the expenditure of vast sums for such nonreligious purposes
as the maintenance of armies at war, the functioning of a luxury-loving
court, and the building of huge palaces as well as ever grander churches.
And he had to recruit and supervise a large centralized bureaucracy.
The attempt to carry out in Rome or Avignon the tasks better left in the
hands of the local clergy alienated the local priesthood as well as their
laity, and encouraged a sense of nationalism among the churchmen of
countries like England, France, and Germany. The popes themselves, of
course, were not alone responsible for the decline in the standards of the
clergy. Church positions had long been regarded as livings for younger
sons of anyone from kings down to impoverished knights. The clergy
had long been guilty of simony, of seeking positions for their relatives
in the hierarchy. Orders devoted to poverty, chasitity, and obedience
had frequently forgotten their vows, and made movements of reform necessary. But in the fourteenth and fifteenth centuries, the decline in the
Church's observance of its spiritual duties, accompanied and worsened

The Palace of the Popes, Avignon. The enormous fortress-like palace was constructed in eighteen years (1334–1352) during the Babylonian captivity of the Papacy. (Samuel Chamberlain photo.)

by an indulgence in its ambition for material power, led to a widespread disgust with the institution and its members.

The Babylonian Captivity and the Great Schism. The so-called Babylonian captivity (1305–1378), during which the popes resided at Avignon on the Rhone river in France rather than in Rome, was a prime factor in creating a chauvinistic dislike of the papacy in every country except France, and perhaps a cynical contempt in France itself. Clement V (1305–1314), although French, attempted to establish his court in Rome, but finding Rome in disorder he settled instead in Avignon, which was a fief of the rulers of Naples. He and the next six popes who lived in Avignon were not prisoners of the French monarchy, as has often been asserted. Some were brilliant men, who helped increase the powers of the papal monarchy by adding to its revenues and its judicial powers, improving its bureaucracy, and building up its armies. But the papacy's ambitions were less tolerable, however, when it appeared that the pope was favoring France at the expense of the rest of Christendom. All seven popes who resided in Avignon were French. All filled the papal bureaucracy and the college of cardinals with Frenchmen. The English and Germans in particular complained about the large sums the Church raised in their countries to spend in France, and found it particularly infuriating that the vast new palace in Avignon was being built by the most extravagant of these popes at the very time that the Black Death was rampant.

The return to Rome in 1378 only worsened matters. Partly out of fear of the Roman mob, who invaded the conclave of cardinals during their election of a new pope, the cardinals elected an Italian, Urban VII, who to their horror started destroying their privileges and their incomes and even created twenty-five new cardinals at once. The French cardinals and one Spanish cardinal then left Rome and elected another pope, Clement VII, who established himself in the papal palace at Avignon. For the next thirty-one years there was a pope and a college of cardinals in Avignon, and another pope and college of cardinals in Rome. The Church dissolved into confusion. Both the popes interfered in local wars as a means of bringing more provinces to recognize the legality of their election, increased their demands for money, and denounced each other as usurpers. This disturbing spectacle even united the English and French for a time in unsuccessfully demanding that both popes abdicate; and the French clergy tried to blackmail the Avignon pope into compliance by refusing him revenues. The faculty of the University of Paris called for a Church council that would settle the disputed succession to the throne of Peter, but when a council in Pisa in 1409 appointed a third pope without being able to persuade the other two popes to resign it merely increased the confusion. Only in 1417 did the Council of Constance put an end to the Great Schism, with the appointment of Martin V, and the deposition or resignation of the other three. But it was too late to save the reputation of the pontiff, at least as long as he clung to the methods of the papal monarchy.

The literature of the fourteenth and fifteenth centuries teems with protest against the state of the Church. To Petrarch, the Avignon papacy was the "whore of Babylon." Dante subjected popes to the punishments of hell—upside down burial, exposure roped and nude. The popular storytellers of France, in their *fabliaux,* or fables, displayed the clergy as seducers and tricksters. But it is in *The Canterbury Tales* of Geoffrey Chaucer (c. 1340–1400), a subtle humorous portrayal of a fourteenth century group of pilgrims journeying to the shrine of Saint Thomas in Canterbury, that we have the most polished condemnation of a clergy guilty not of big misdeeds but of myriad crimes of omission. The Prioress is pretty, well-mannered, and sentimental; but where her rosary should have been, she wore a golden pendant:

And ther-on heng a brooch of gold
    ful sheene,
On which was first i-written a
    crowned A,
And after Amor vincit omnia.

And on it hung a brooch of shin-
    ing gold,
On which was written a crowned A,
And after Amor vincit omnia.

The monk was a handsome horseman,

A manly man, to been an abbot
able.
Ful many a deyntee hors hadde
he in stable;
And whan he rood men myghte
his brydel heere
Gynglen in a whistlynge wynd
als cleere,
And eek as loude, as dooth the
chapel belle,
Ther as this lord was kepere of
the celel.

A manly man, to be an abbot able.
Full many a dainty horse he had
in stable;
And when he rode men might
hear his bridle
Jingling in a whistling wind as clear,
And also as loud, as does the
chapel bell,
There where this lord was keeper
of the cell.

The friar was a jovial fellow, always a success with the ladies.

He knew the tavernes well in
every toun,
And everich hostiler and tappestere
Bet than a lazar or a beggestere.

He knew the taverns well in
every town,
And every inn-keeper and
barmaid
Better than a leper or a beggar.

And already, in the flaxen-haired, smooth-faced Pardoner, with his wallet full of relics and pardons piping hot from Rome, we can see the unscrupulous Tetzel, whose activities two centuries later drove Martin Luther to his first blast against the papacy:

For in his male he hadde a pilwe-
beer,
Which that, he seyde, was oure
lady veyl;
He seyde he hadde a gobet of
the seyl
That Seint Peter hadde, whan that
he wente
Upon the see, til Jhesu Crist
hym hente.
He hadde a croys of latoun, ful
of stones,
And in a glas he hadde pigges
bones. . . .
Upon a day he gat hym moore
moneye
Than that the person gat in
monthes tweye;
And thus with feyned flaterye
and japes

For in his bag he had a pillow-
case
Which was, he said, our Lady's
veil;
He said he had a piece of the
sail
That Saint Peter had, when he
went
On the sea, until Jesus won him
over.
He had a cross of latten, decorated
with stones,
And in a glass he had pig's
bones. . . .
In a day he could make more
money
Than the parson could in two
months.
And thus with feigned flattery and
tricks

He made the person and the
   peple his apes.
But, trewely to tellen atte laste,
He was in chirche a noble
   ecclesiaste.

He made fools of the parson and
   his people.
But last, to tell the truth,
In church he was a noble
   ecclesiastic.[5]

Failure of the Conciliar Movement.   How was the Church to be saved
from this corruption? As at earlier periods of ecclesiastical decline, reformers were not lacking; for the Church's power of survival has been
its capacity to regenerate itself from within. The Church hierarchy proposed
an institutional answer—restrict the papacy's powers by making it subject to the general councils of the Church, to which all Catholic bishops
would be summoned. The justification for this proposal, elaborated in
the University of Paris, was that the doctrines of the early Church had been
worked out in church councils, like that at Nicaea, and that God would
continue to protect such gatherings from error, when they spoke in proper
consideration of the past teaching of the Church. Moreover, the reformers
held, when the council met, one primary task should be the reform of
abuses in the Church that the pope had been unwilling or unable to remedy.
The high point for the supporters of conciliar theory was reached in 1415
at the Council of Constance, when the prelates declared: "The Council
of Constance, an ecumenical council, derives its power direct from God,
and all men, including the Pope, are bound to obey it in matters of faith,
of ending the schism, and of reforming the Church in head and in members." The only achievement of the council, however, was to end the
schism. The popes refused to cooperate in reform measures whose main
purpose appeared to be to reduce papal revenue, and they continually
denied on principle the supremacy over them of Church councils. The
clergy themselves had a vested interest in maintaining the perquisites that
indeed provided the larger portion of the revenues with which to administer their dioceses. The laity, who were not officially represented at the
councils, were unable to pressure the priests; and the councils, lacking
lay members, could hardly claim to be restoring democracy in the Church.
As a result, the conciliar movement got little popular support; and the
Council of Constance, faced by John Huss, a genuine reformer who had
roused the masses of Bohemia to religious frenzy, fell back on repression.
Huss was called to the council on a safe-conduct pass, condemned as
a heretic, and burned at the stake. What really destroyed the conciliar
movement, however, was that everybody present at the councils was
playing politics. The pope concluded a series of agreements with the
governments of the nation-states, without regard to the council's opinions.
The Avignon and Rome factions bargained. Cardinals maneuvered in
their dealings with the pope on one hand and the bishops on the other.

[5] Author's translation.

The popes were then able to ride out the swell of reforming ardor, and thus they failed to channel the vast outpouring of religious emotion that was one result of the miseries of pestilence and war in the late Middle Ages.

Revival of Catholic Mysticism.   This perfervid piety, based on a mystical desire for communion with God, was, however, expressed on an enormous scale throughout Europe, and it found expression in some of the most beautiful pieces of religious literature ever composed.   At times, the furor of religious emotion led directly into heresy condemned by the Church, as with the English reformer John Wycliff and his followers the Lollards, or with John Huss and the Hussites who had to be beaten into submission with large armies.   At times it led to direct abuse of the Church leadership, such as occurred in this denunciation by Catherine of Siena:

They love their subjects for what they can get out of them and nothing more. Their share of the Church they spend entirely on their own garments, loving to go delicately apparelled, not as clerks, and religious, but as lords and courtiers. They take pains to have fine horses, and many vessels of gold and silver for the adornment of their dwellings, possessing that which cannot be ultimately retained, with much vanity of heart; and with the disordinate vanity their heart swells, and they place all desire in food, making of their belly their god, eating and drinking without restraint, so that they promptly fall into an impure and lascivious life.[6]

[6] *The Dialogue of the Seraphic Virgin, Catherine of Siena,* trans. Algar Thorold (London: K. Paul, Trench, Trübner, 1896), p. 264.

French Pilgrims of the Time of Saint Louis.   (French Embassy Press and Information Division photo.)

Peter and Andrew, from the Bad Mergentheim Marienaltar by Tilman Riemenschneider (c. 1460–1531). (German Tourist Information Office photo.)

But most of the mystical leaders remained within the Church, and some, like Catherine herself, in spite of their vituperation against the institutional Church, were made saints after their death. They made so many followers within the Church that many new and influential congregations of monks and friars or of lay people were formed, with such revealing names as the Friends of God or the Brethren of the Common Life. From all parts of the continent and all sections of the Church came the expression of this great desire for the immediate realization of God's presence. From the Franciscans in Italy came the heartbreaking religious poem *Stabat Mater:*

Stabat mater dolorosa	*There his grieving mother stood*
Iuxta crucem lacrymosa,	*Weeping beside the cross*
Dum pendebat filius	*On which her son was hanging.*
Cuius animam gementem	*Through her suffering soul,*
Contristantem et dolentem	*Compassionate and tortured,*
Pertransivit gladius.	*Pain struck like a sword.*[7]

[7] Author's translation.

The German Dominican Eckhart taught of the divine spark in man's mind that united with God: "The eye with which I see God is the eye with which God sees me." From Sweden came Saint Bridget, whose revelations were read all over Europe. But amid the multitude of books of devotion that appeared at this time, the most admired—and the most widely read Christian book after the Bible—was the *Imitation of Christ* by the Flemish monk Thomas à Kempis (1379–1471). Thomas à Kempis had no time for dogma: "What will it profit thee to dispute profoundly of the Trinity, if thou be devoid of humility, and art thereby displeasing to the Trinity?" he asks. And he has no room for the organized Church: "Consider that you and God are alone in the universe and you will have great peace in your heart." The appeal of his book, however, was in the simple, direct prayers he suggests with which the Christian can talk to God.

How can I bear this miserable life unless thy mercy and grace strengthen me? Turn not away thy face from me, delay not thy visitation. Withdraw not thou thy comfort from me, lest my soul "gasp after thee as a thirsty land." Lord, teach me to do thy will, teach me to walk humbly and uprightly before thee, for thou art my wisdom, who knowest me in truth, and knewest me before the world was made and before I was born into the world.[8]

The mystics thus helped preserve the faith in the Christian religion during the period of disenchantment with the institutions of the Christian Church. Because there was no decline in the numbers or enthusiasm of Christian believers, the need for a reform of the institutions of the Church appeared more necessary than ever. This reform took place in the two reformations—the Protestant Reformation of the early sixteenth century and the Catholic Reformation of the second half of the sixteenth century. Seen in this context, the similarity in the writings of Thomas à Kempis, Martin Luther, and Ignatius Loyola is not surprising.

FEUDAL MONARCHY TRANSFORMED INTO THE "NEW" MONARCHY

The crises of the late Middle Ages also transformed the feudal monarchy. By the beginning of the sixteenth century, large parts of western Europe were governed by a very different form of state from that of the thirteenth century, whose ideal we saw in the reign of Saint Louis. Operating under a new set of assumptions of the duties and powers of the government and of the position of the citizen in relation to his government, the rulers of France, England, Spain, Burgundy, and some of the principalities of Germany and Italy had created the modern form of state. The basis of this state was the assumption that *sovereignty* is possessed by the central government—and sovereignty means the right and ability to control the lives and property of the citizens of the state for the purposes of the

[8] Thomas à Kempis, *The Imitation of Christ* (New York: P. F. Collier and Son, 1909), cited in Herlihy, *Medieval Culture*, p. 404.

state, through taxation, law courts, civil servants, diplomacy, and the making of war. This does not imply that by 1500 the exercise of sovereignty by monarchs, rather than by an oligarchy of merchants, or a theocracy of the godly, or even a democracy of all male citizens, had been recognized. The great change was the movement from the feudal conception of the state, in which the power of the king derived from the personal allegiance of a hierarchy of vassals, to a conception of the state in which the political relationship is reduced to one of governor and governed. During the following three centuries, the internal political struggles and the striving of all political theorists was to be devoted to the question of the extent to which the governed can, or should, retain control over the exercise of sovereignty by the governor. But this was only made possible when, as a result of the changes of the late Middle Ages, the feudal concept of political rule was jettisoned.

The Feudal Nobility in Western Europe. The first prerequisite for the transformation of feudal monarchy was, of course, the decline in the power of the feudal lords. Here many factors worked in favor of the king. The value in battle of the armored knight was ended by the long bow, the pike, and gunpowder. In the great battles of the Hundred Years' War, Crécy, Poitiers, and Agincourt, the lines of French knights charged again and again into a hail of arrows from the long bows of the English archers, and fell helpless, pinioned by their writhing mounts and their heavy armor until they were dispatched by the knives of the English foot-soldiers. Sir John Froissart's *Chronicles,* the classic portrayal of the bravery and panache of the feudal knight in these wars, is also a documentation of his anachronism as a warrior:

Poitiers (1356): [*The Prince of Wales*] *addressed his troops as follows: "My gallant men, we are only a few against the might of our enemies, but do not let us be discouraged by that. Victory goes not to the greater number, but where God wishes to send it. If we win the day, we shall gain the greatest honor and glory in the world. If we are killed, there will still be the King my father, and my noble brothers, and all your good friends, to avenge us. I therefore beg of you to fight manfully today; for please God and Saint George, today you will see me act like a true knight."*

Soon afterwards the fighting became general. The battalion under the French marshals advanced before those troops who were intended to break the line of the English archers; and it entered the lane where the hedges on both sides were lined with the archers, who began shooting with such deadly aim from both sides that the horses would not go forward into the hail of bearded arrows, but became unmanageable and threw their riders, who were then unable to rise in the confusion. . . . Seldom can a body of good fighting men have been so totally and speedily defeated as the battalion of the marshals of France, for they fell back on each other so fast that the army could not advance. . . . The English archers were certainly of infinite service to their side, and caused great havoc. For their shooting was so

*accurate and so well concerted that the French did not know which way to turn,
as the archers kept on advancing and gaining ground.*[9]

The use of the pike, a long pole topped by a sharp metal head with point
and curving blade, made it suicidal for a knight to charge at full tilt against
the bristling barbs of a line of pikemen. But above all gunpowder was
eventually to sweep away the great horse. Small guns were probably used
at Crécy, and artillery was quickly developed into a mobile weapon of even
greater use in sieges of castles than in fixed battles.

The Cult of Chivalry. At this very moment when the lord was in economic
difficulties as a landowner and was losing his role as a warrior, the whole
cult of the knight received a curious transfiguration in the most blatant, the
most colorful, and in a sense the most pathetic attempt to perpetuate medieval cultural ideals—*chevalerie,* or chivalry. The less the knight counted
in battle, the more he indulged in the sport of the tournament, which
became a glorious stylized spectacle of gorgeously robed lords and ladies
beneath floating pennants and multicolored awnings watching the combat
of lords whose handcrafted plate armor was in itself a work of art. The
tournament had become a nostalgic entertainment, essential, however, to
the role-playing demanded by society of its new hero, the perfect knight.
The ideal of the virtuous knight, devoted to the unselfish service of God and
his lord and to the worship of some idealized woman, was developed to an
inordinate degree by the poets, storytellers, and historians of this period
because the nobility reveled in it; and it was encouraged for their own purposes by kings and princes, who found in it a method of domesticating the
nobles and of glamorizing the gift of knighthood in the eyes of their middle-
class supporters. The king of England founded the Order of the Knights of
the Garter; the king of France, the Order of the Star; and Philip the Good,
Duke of Burgundy, the most glamorous of all, the Order of the Golden
Fleece. By inheritance, marriage, and conquest, Philip had put together
a rich new state controlling the prosperous towns of Flanders and the fine
agricultural lands of eastern France; and he attempted by the magnificence
of his court's chivalry to make up for his state's lack of a history. Enormous
banquets, elaborate costumes, grandiose tournaments, and above all the
ritual of the Knights of the Golden Fleece gave to his court a fairy-tale
quality. Chivalry became in these two centuries a charming, expensive,
and time-consuming avoidance of reality by a nobility that had lost its
original function.

Yet the pageantry of chivalry should not lead us to dismiss the continuing
importance of the nobility. Great nobles remained a powerful force in the
constitutional development of the western kingdoms. They could still
put large armies into the field, as the noble families who fought the Wars

---

[9] John Froissart, *Chronicles,* trans. J. Jolliffe (London: Collins, 1967), pp. 167–68.

of Roses in England or the great houses who disputed the French throne in the late fifteenth century showed. Many were able to turn from the role of cavalryman to that of professional commander; and indeed it became extremely common for younger sons of the nobility to become professional soldiers. In some European countries, like Germany, the nobility retained control of the officer corps until the twentieth century. The nobility also found a role for themselves in the court of the centralizing monarchies. They not only provided the companionship, and indeed the social setting, against which the new role of kingship could be dramatized. They provided much of the personnel of civil and ecclesiastical administration, such as diplomats, ministers, and abbots. And many were eventually able, in the reviving economy of the late fifteenth and sixteenth centuries, to turn their estates once again into profitable productive enterprises. Chivalry for the nobility was a phase of psychological readjustment to the passing of the great horse and with it their accustomed position on the battlefield.

Ritter Hans von Rodenstein, Tomb in Fränisch-Grumbach and Jörg Truchsess von Waldburg, Tomb in Waldsee. By the fifteenth century, the feudal lord no longer presented the terrifying image of the armored soldier (left) but the glamorous and almost effete figure of the hero of chivalry (right). (German Tourist Information Office photos.)

Continuing Power of the Feudal Nobles in Eastern Europe. In most of eastern Europe, however, the landowners gained a position of supremacy from which they were not ousted until the twentieth century, thus setting all Europe east of the Elbe River on a course completely divergent from that of western Europe. In eastern Germany and Poland, in Bohemia, Hungary, and Rumania, the landowning nobles solved the problem of a declining population by simply tieing the peasant more firmly than ever to the soil and by exploiting their farms for the production of marketable surpluses, especially of wheat. The number of days that a peasant had to work for his lord was vastly increased, in some areas from one day a year to one day a week. The lords forced from weak kings the right to administer their own lands free of any interference from the central government. Poland became the supreme example of noble misrule. Its king was elected by the nobles. The assembly of nobles was responsible for legislation, which it passed by unanimity, and was hence frequently paralyzed by the disagreement of a few lords. The country only survived by the accidental choice of an occasional good king and by the weakness of its neighbors; and in the eighteenth century, it paid the price of centuries of noble misgovernment by being partitioned among Russia, Austria, and Prussia. The prototype of the East European landed gentleman was, however, the East Prussian *Junker,* who controlled the lands of the North German plain to the east of the Elbe until forcibly dispossessed after the Second World War. This group of frugal, self-righteous, caste-conscious martinets added to their landholdings, fought off state interference with the peasantry of their lands, and provided a conservative phalanx of army officers and bureaucrats and occasional government ministers first to the Prussian state and then to a unified Germany. It seemed, however, very possible that western Europe too, with the solitary exception of the city-dominated regions of the Low Countries and north central Italy would follow the same pattern of development, particularly because of the constant wars in which they were engaged.

The Hundred Years' War (1337–1453). Both the French and English monarchies suffered greatly from the Hundred Years' War. The war had begun in 1337, when Edward III of England, who as the ruler of Aquitaine was theoretically a vassal of the king of France, claimed that he was the legal heir to the French throne. He then allied with the townspeople of Flanders against their count, who was a vassal of the French king, and persuaded the Duke of Brittany to revolt. The whole system of feudal relationships was thus thrown into disorder, with every local lord free to choose between the king of England and the king of France, or even the king of Navarre, who later claimed the throne for himself. The English established naval supremacy in the Channel at the battle of Sluys (1340), shot down the French armored knights in the two great land battles of Crécy (1346) and Poitiers (1356), and captured the French king. The suffering in France inflicted by the marauding English (and French) soldiery, coming at the

Entry into Paris of Louis II, Duke of Anjou. The twin towers of Notre Dame dominate the small city of Paris in this fifteenth-century illuminated manuscript by Louis Bruges. (Bibliothèque Nationale.)

same time as the Black Death, caused enormous misery that culminated in a revolt of the Paris bourgeoisie and in the Jacquerie of the French peasantry. Paris itself, which had been the common glory of the French monarchy and of all Christendom a century earlier, was poverty-stricken, plague-ridden, and intellectually isolated. The French king was compelled to buy a brief peace by recognizing the absolute right of the English king to rule Aquitaine and Calais free of any feudal tie and by paying three million gold crowns. After a slight revival under King Charles V (reigned 1364–1380), whose tough General Bertrand du Guesclin succeeded in taking back most French territory except the coastline, the situation of the French monarchy again deteriorated rapidly. His successor, Charles VI (reigned 1380–1422), was periodically insane, and control of his policy was disputed between two great feudal lords, the duke of Burgundy and the duke of Orleans. When the English attacked again in 1415 under King Henry V, the followers of the duke of Burgundy joined him. Henry easily defeated the forces of the French king at the battle of Agincourt (1415), and the Burgundians captured both the mad king and his capital city. His son, the dauphin, however, continued to hold southern and central France and to maintain a royal court at Bourges. A Parisian noted in his journal that year:

Alas, never, I think, since the days of Clovis the first Christian King, has France been as desolate and as divided as it is today. The Dauphin and his people do nothing day or night but lay waste all his father's land with fire and sword and the English on the other side do as much harm as Saracens. . . . And the poor King and Queen have not moved from Troyes since Pontoise was taken, where they are with their poor retinue like fugitives, exiled by their own child, a dreadful thought for any right-minded person. . . . Everything was so dear in Paris that not even the most intelligent of its inhabitants could find enough to live on. Bread especially and firewood were dearer than they had been for two hundred years and so was meat.[10]

Consolidation of the New Monarchy in France   It was at this lowest point in the fortunes of the French monarchy that the foundations of the "new monarchy" were laid. The force that made possible a change in the character of the monarchy was nationalism, a new form of loyalty that transcended the local loyalty of, for example, a Parisian for his city or a Norman for his province. Hatred of the English was transmuted into a love of France to some degree by the mysterious appearance of Joan of Arc, the peasant girl who, after raising the siege of Orleans for the dauphin and persuading him to be crowned in Rheims, was seized by the Burgundians and condemned to death by burning by a court of the Inquisition as a relapsed heretic. Nationalism was far less important as a stimulant to military ardor than as a solvent of the opposition to the more down-to-earth measures that the former dauphin, once he was crowned as King Charles VII, saw it necessary to take to drive the English out of France. In 1439, the king persuaded the Estates General to grant him the *taille,* an annual tax on individual citizens collected by the King's own agents, and with it he created a professional army, the *compagnies d'ordonnances,* composed of cavalry and archers on horseback backed later by mercenary foot soldiers recruited from all over Europe. Charles had taken the crucial steps in creating the new form of state. He had a regular, expandable income and a standing army; and by 1453, he had succeeded in sweeping the English out of all France except the port of Calais.

The consolidation of the powers of the French king was carried much further by Louis XI (reigned 1461–1483), a mean, underhanded, down-to-earth, farsighted ruler. In the account of his reign, *The Memoirs* written by the statesman Philip de Commines, we are fortunate in having what is not only a fine narrative but also an account of the political theory of the new monarchs. In the famous Chapter Ten, "A digression concerning some of the virtues and vices of King Louis XI," Commines stated bluntly

[10] Janet Shirley, ed. and trans., *A Parisian Journal, 1405–1449* (Oxford: Clarendon Press, 1968), pp. 146–48.

the doctrine that Machiavelli was to repeat a generation later, that the virtues and vices of princes should be judged by their contribution to the well-being of the state and not by commonplace morality.

Of all the princes that I ever knew, the wisest and most dexterous at extricating himself out of any danger or difficulty in time of adversity, was our master King Louis XI. He was the humblest in his conversation and dress, and the most painstaking and indefatigable in winning over any man to his side that he thought capable of doing either mischief or service. Though he was often refused, he would never give over a man that he wished to gain, but still pressed and continued his insinuations, promising him largely, and presenting him with such sums and honors as he knew would gratify his ambition. . . . He was naturally kind and indulgent to persons of mean estate, and hostile to all great men who had no need of him. Never prince was so easy to converse with, nor so inquisitive as he, for his desire was to know everybody he could and indeed he knew all persons of any authority or worth in England, Spain, Portugal, and Italy, in the territories of the Dukes of Burgundy and Brittany, and among his own subjects; and by those qualities he preserved the crown upon his head, which was in much danger by the enemies he had created to himself upon his accession to the throne. But above all his great bounty and liberality did him the greatest service.[11]

Louis XI, King of France (reigned 1451–1483). (French Embassy Press and Information Division photo.)

He squeezed higher taxes from his subjects, and by spending as little as possible built up a considerable treasury. He increased the size of the army, and tried not to use it, seeking to defeat his opponents by diplomatic guile and by subsidizing their other enemies rather than by fighting himself. Most of the territories that had been granted to members of the royal family, as semi-independent principalities called appanages, were brought back under the control of the crown. But his most important achievement was to prevent the dukes of Burgundy from achieving their ambition of converting their territories into a new kingdom stretching from the Channel to Switzerland by incorporation of Alsace and Lorraine. The state of Burgundy had known half a century of prosperity under Duke Philip the Good (1419–1467), and its court at Bruges was the most glamorous in Europe. "The subjects of the house of Burgundy were at that time very wealthy," wrote Commines, "by reason of the long peace they had enjoyed, and the goodness of their prince, who laid but few taxes upon them; so that, in my judgment, if any country might then be called the land of promise it was his country, which enjoyed great wealth and repose, more than ever it had since; and it is now probably three and twenty years since their miseries began."[12] This misery had been inflicted on them by the ambitions of Duke Charles the Bold (1467–1477) and the unrelenting enmity of Louis XI. Louis's great stroke was to finance the Swiss confederation's war to prevent Charles from taking the upper Rhine as well as the

[11] Andrew R. Scoble, ed., *The Memoirs of Philip de Commines* (London: G. Bell, 1886), I, 59–60.
[12] Ibid., I, 12–13.

mercenaries of the duke of Lorraine. Thus the three great defeats and Charles's own death were inflicted not by the French army but by Louis's allies; yet when the states of Burgundy were partitioned soon after Charles's death, France took the duchy of Burgundy itself. Looking back on the suffering of the wars and the startling reversal in the fortunes of Burgundy, Commines commented on the role of monarchical power:

The brutishness and ignorance of princes are very dangerous and dreadful because the happiness or misery of their subjects depends wholly upon them. Wherefore, if a prince who is powerful and has a large standing army, by the help of which he can raise money to pay his troops, or to spend in a luxurious way of living, or in anything that does not directly tend to the advancement of the common good, and if he will not retrench his outrageous extravagances himself, and those courtiers that are about him rather endeavor to flatter and applaud him in everything he does, than to dissuade him from doing ill (for fear of incurring his displeasure), who can apply any remedy in this case but God alone? [13]

Establishment of Tudor Rule in England. In two other countries of western Europe, England and Spain, feudal monarchy was also transformed into the "new" monarchy by the end of the fifteenth century. In many ways, English history ran parallel to that of France during the fourteenth and fifteenth centuries. National feeling was stimulated by the Hundred Years' War, first by the great victories and then by the shock of the expulsion from France, and by revulsion from the financial exactions of the pope, especially during the residence in Avignon. The kings sought allies in the local gentry, whose position had been strengthened by the acquisition of new lands at the time of the Black Death, and in the city middle class, both of whom were represented in the lower house of Parliament, the House of Commons. The greater nobility, especially relatives of the royal family, profited from the weakness of young or inefficient kings, to create territorial principalities for themselves, to organize paid, professional armies of their own, and at times to put their own candidate on the throne. At the end of the Hundred Years' War, the great nobility split into two factions, one supporting the claim to the throne of the house of York, the other the house of Lancaster. During the thirty years of the Wars of the Roses (1455–1485), so-called because the emblem of the House of York was a white rose and of Lancaster a red rose, England was in chaos. The nobles built new, heavily fortified castles, increased their private forces by "livery and maintenance," that is, the provision of uniforms and salary, and decimated their numbers in battle and by murder. In a final act of treachery, Henry Stanley in 1485 changed sides at the battle of Bosworth Field, giving the victory over King Richard III to the Lancastrian claimant, Henry Tudor, who, after the crown had been found in a thorn bush, took the title of Henry VII. Henry adopted the thorn bush as an official emblem of the

[13] Ibid., I, 382–83.

new regime, made Stanley first earl of Derby, married the heiress of the House of York, and to everyone's surprise, effectively ended the anarchic independence of the feudal nobility.

Henry VII was the first of the "new" monarchs in England. He profited from the fact that the old noble families had virtually wiped each other out. He formed a new class of career bureaucrats from the middle classes and the Church, and turned over most local administration to the local gentry in their role as justices of the peace. Like Louis XI, whom he resembled in many ways, he built up his treasury by exploiting feudal dues, judicial fines, forced loans, and trade customs, and by seeking peace abroad. While recognizing the importance of Parliament, he consulted it as little as possible, only on rare occasions asking it for money. Henry was typical of the new style of monarch, even in death. He was buried in a tomb of Italian Renaissance style beneath the Gothic vaults of Westminster Abbey.

The Reforms of Ferdinand and Isabella in Spain. In Spain, the transition was carried out by Ferdinand, king of Aragon (1479–1516), and his wife, Isabella, queen of Castile (1474–1504). Their first problem was the disunity of the country. During the long reconquest of the peninsula from the Moors, the territories won back had been divided into several independent kingdoms—Portugal, Castile, Aragon, and Navarre—with the Moors holding on to a last foothold in the southeast in the Kingdom of Granada. Within the kingdoms, the nobility had vast land grants and a tradition of autonomy and bellicosity. The towns had won a limited independence. And racial and religious differences presented a further barrier to national unity; Portuguese, Castilians, Catalans, Basques, and Moors all spoke their own language, while Jews and Moors followed their own religion or a superficial version of the Christianity of the persecuting majority. The war against the Moors, which was completed in 1492 with the conquest of Granada, had, however, given the Christians of the peninsula a sense of common purpose. The marriage of Ferdinand and Isabella in 1469 united the two largest kingdoms permanently; and the "Catholic Monarchs" quite successfully wiped out most religious differences by expelling all Jews and Moors who refused conversion and by turning the Inquisition in search of heresy among Catholics. Moreover, they acquired the two most important prerequisites of new monarchs of the times, a large income and an efficient army. Castile's revenue was expanded thirty times, especially from a ten percent tax on commercial transactions; this eventually, however, did enormous damage to Spanish prosperity. The army was based on a combination of pikemen and soldiers armed with sword and javelin, backed by soldiers with guns called arquebuses, and it was effectively used in curbing the independence of the great nobles. Unauthorized castles were torn down and royal lands taken back, but the nobles were courted with high-sounding titles and ceremonial honors at court.

To Machiavelli, whose book *The Prince* was an accurate summation of the political methods of the new monarchs and whose applicability made the book favored reading of such new monarchs as Henry VIII of England, Ferdinand of Aragon was a model ruler:

Nothing makes a prince so much esteemed as great enterprises and setting a fine example. We have in our time Ferdinand of Aragon, the present King of Spain. He can almost be called a new prince, because he has risen by fame and glory, from being an insignificant king to be the foremost king in Christendom; and if you will consider his deeds you will find them all great and some of them extraordinary. In the beginning of his reign, he attacked Granada, and this enterprise was the foundation of his dominions. He did this quietly at first and without any fear of hindrance, for he held the minds of the barons of Castile occupied in thinking of the war and not anticipating any innovations; thus they did not perceive that by these means he was acquiring power and authority over them. He was able with the money of the Church and of the people to sustain his armies, and by that long war to lay the foundation for the military skill which has since distinguished him. Further, always using religion as a plea, so as to undertake greater schemes, he devoted himself with a pious cruelty to driving out and clearing his kingdom of the Moors. . . . Under this same cloak, he assailed Africa, he came down on Italy, he has finally attacked France; and thus his achievements and designs have always been great and have kept the minds of his people in suspense and admiration and occupied with the issue of them. And his actions have arisen in such a way, one out of the other, that men have never been given time to work steadily against him.[14]

The late Middle Ages had created a new form of state and a new ideal of ruler; and the political and economic, and indeed the cultural leadership of Europe was very quickly to pass to them. Yet during the period when the new monarchies were sharpening their weapons, literally as well as metaphorically, the greatest achievements of Western civilization were to be sought in the cities—those of the northern European seaboard, of western and southern Germany, and especially of Italy.

**THE URBAN
RESPONSE TO
ECONOMIC
RECESSION**

Evidence of Economic Recession. The cities of Europe were even more vulnerable to the impact of famine, plague, and war than the countryside. Much evidence points to a widespread economic recession that struck the cities from the early fourteenth until the mid–fifteenth century. The population of cities, which had been growing rapidly until the early fourteenth century, either stabilized or in most cases dropped considerably. Barcelona's population dropped by two-thirds. Narbonne's was reduced by more than ninety percent. Most cities revived after the Black Death but very few had reached their previous height by the end of the fifteenth century. Physical proof of the concentration of population was provided by the virtual end of construction of city walls in Italy after 1300 and in

[14] Machiavelli, *The Prince,* trans. W. K. Marriott (London: Dent, 1908), pp. 173–74.

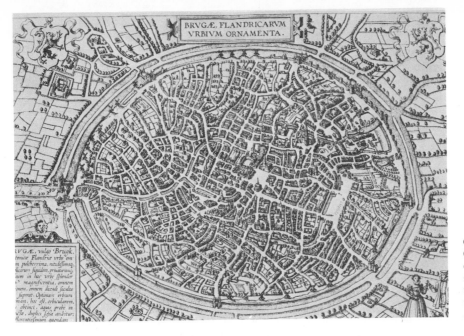

BRVGÆ, FLANDRICARVM
VRBIVM ORNAMENTA.

City Plan of Bruges, 16th Century. Bruges was a canal city like Venice, though on a smaller scale. The waters of the river Zwyn can be seen flowing through the city and around the outer walls.

France and Germany after 1400. The production of the most basic manufacturing industry of the Middle Ages, woolen cloth, had to cut back drastically to take account of the reduction of market. Production of the great Flemish cloth city of Ypres fell from 90,000 pieces annually to 25,000. The sale of raw wool was drastically reduced at the very time that many farmers were converting their land to sheep farming to economize on the use of labor; and the effect of oversupply was to reduce prices from the beginning of the fifteenth century. Competition thus became more cutthroat between the countries producing woolen cloth, and as so often in times of recession, governments fell back on restrictions on imports of manufactured cloth and on exports of raw materials. In Flanders in particular, this form of trade war was clear proof of the sharpness of the recession. The restrictive rules were also applied by the guilds in an attempt to keep down the wages of their workers, as a method of remaining competitive in the smaller market. One cause of the great wave of urban riots that affected all parts of Europe in the late fourteenth and fifteenth centuries was the resentment of the journeyman laborers against these wage regulations; but they were fueled by the determination of the poorer artisan groups, who themselves formed guilds in large numbers in this period, to share in the privileges of the well-to-do guilds, whose members formed the governing patriciate of the cities. Frequently the guilds sought the support of the king, as in France and to some degree in Spain, in winning monopoly positions in their city or their region, so as to limit output and throw competitors out of business. When one looks at patterns of trade, the recession is equally visible. Study of such widely separated ports as Marseilles, Genoa, and Dieppe shows that international trade may have dropped as much as three-fifths from its peak, a far higher percentile drop than that in Europe's population. Clearly, certain areas were more directly affected by the disorder of the wars than others. The great fairs of Champagne, for example, were almost killed by the wars between the Flemish cities and the French king and by the Hundred Years' War.

The indisputable evidence of economic recession that the historian finds in price indexes, parish registers, and company and city archives seems in contradiction with what a visitor to Europe still can see with his own eyes. Throughout the continent, during this period of recession, both large and small cities were being embellished not only with cathedrals and parish churches but with city halls, guildhalls, wool halls, burghers' houses, charity hospitals, and old folks' homes. To take just a few outstanding examples, the citizens of Ulm began to build the tallest spire in Europe only a decade after being hit by the Black Death; the intricate Gothic town hall that dominates the central square of Brussels was begun in 1401; London's elaborate Guildhall, where the Lord Mayor was elected, was started in 1411, in the middle of the Hundred Years' War; and the great patrician palaces of Florence, built by the merchant bankers such as the Rucellai, the Medici, and the Davanzati, were all constructed during the century of economic recession.

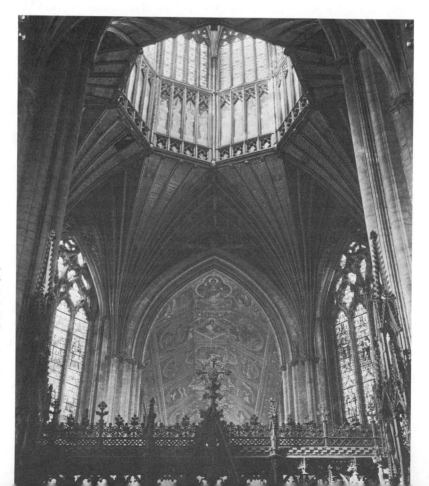

The Octagon, Ely Cathedral. When the cathedral was reconstructed in 1323–1330, the architect broke the right-angle pattern by introducing an octagon of stone over the crossing of nave and transept, which he topped with a lantern tower of wood and glass. (British Tourist Authority photo.)

Spire of Ulm Cathedral. This late Gothic spire, built in 1356, was 630 feet high, and the tallest in Europe. (German Tourist Information Office photo.)

From Russian Novgorod and Norwegian Bergen to Catalan Barcelona and Byzantine Thessalonica, the profits from trade and manufacturing were poured into an urban civilization that is one of the glories of the late Middle Ages, and in this widespread urban vigor, two regions predominated, the Low Countries, with the city of Bruges as its jewel, and northern Italy, with Venice the brightest in a whole galaxy of cities. Bruges, with its soaring church towers, the flamboyant Gothic of law courts and town hall contrasting with the sober rectitude of its brick homes, and its fantastic belfry rising 350 feet above the flat Flemish plain, was an impressive setting for the pageantry of the court of Burgundy. It struck the young English wool merchant John Paston as a fairyland: "I heard never of none like it, save King Arthur's Court." And as for Venice, by the fifteenth century the most romantic city in Europe, it appeared to observers as another Constantinople or a new Rome. The French chronicler Philip de Commines, who visited the city just as the gleaming, white Gothic arcade of the Doge's Palace was being erected beside the lagoon, thought it "the most triumphant city I have ever seen." How then is one to explain the contrast between the statistics of adversity and the physical evidence of prosperity?

One explanation is that in some ways the very demographic decline was profitable to the surviving city dwellers. In areas where there was relative freedom from marauding armies, the reduced city population was able to feed itself from the surrounding countryside, and did not have to seek food supplies from a long distance. Moreover, the decline in grain prices enabled them to satisfy their needs with a smaller proportion of their income, and this in turn gave them more to spend on manufactured products of the towns themselves. Individual manufacturing sectors may have profited from chance consequences of the rural changes. Hides, for example, became cheaper because of the increased number of cattle raised in place of grain growing; and this enabled the tanner to keep a larger number of hides during the process of soaking in oak bark and water. Timber fell in price, and thus increased the profitability of metallurgy. Better sites for location of fulling mills became available as mills were abandoned on the streams. It also appears that one psychological result of the plague was to discourage saving, and to encourage purchase of luxuries in manufactured goods, clothing, and foreign imports. The towns obviously profited, since the reduced number of workers were producing at the same or even a lower level of productivity than before, and thus prices were forced even higher. In England the price level for several basic foodstuffs fell from a level of 100 in the period 1261–1350 to an index of 99 in the following fifty years, while the price index of metals went up to 176, of textiles to 160, and of manufactured agricultural implements to 235. Wages for building craftsmen almost doubled at the same time. There is thus considerable evidence of "temporary, post-plague affluence" in some cities at least.

New Techniques of Business. More far-reaching in its effects was the ability of the merchant class to adapt itself to conditions of recession by inventing far more efficient techniques for carrying on business, by developing new and greatly expanding old sources of wealth, and by profiting from the opening to commerce and manufacturing of new geographical areas.

In the first place, far more effective methods of conducting business were invented, mostly in Italy, from which they were carried north by representatives of Italian companies and eventually adopted by north European merchants too. By the end of the thirteenth century, the typical merchant who traveled himself with the goods he had to sell had been replaced by the merchant who conducted all his business from his home office; and this change involved different organization of the business firm. Previously one of the commonest forms of business partnership had been the *commenda*, a temporary partnership in which several businessmen pooled their capital and sent one of the partners to conduct one trading mission, at the end of which the partnership was dissolved and the profits shared out. The obvious inefficiency of constantly reforming business partnerships was first remedied by associations lasting several years, which employed resident agents in the city in which the firm's goods were to be traded. These agents could be either independent merchants working for a large number of companies or the representative branches of a large home company. Meanwhile, the organization of companies through which capital could be accumulated for reinvestment became more formal. The most successful companies in Italy were family firms in which relatives pooled their savings, appointed a senior partner to run the enterprise and took shares in the company in proportion to the amount they had invested, and often invited outside capital as well. In Florence almost all the major companies were controlled by families, such as the Bardi and the Peruzzi in the fourteenth century and the Medici in the fifteenth. Even self-made millionaires like Francesco Datini of Prato had started out with the aid of the financial backing of their relatives. The collapse of a number of overextended firms after the Black Death, when royal and noble debtors were more than usually tempted to renege on their loans, led most of the larger companies to organize their different commercial and industrial ventures, and their overseas branches, as independent partnerships. In 1455, for example, the Medici set up a partnership for trade in Bruges, and signed a contract to send Angiolo, son of Jacopo Tani, to run it, under strict regulations:

Piero, Giovanni, and Piero Francesco de' Medici are to invest L 1,900 groat; Gierozzi de' Pigli, L 600 groat, and Angiolo Tani, L 500 groat, besides his personal (service). And the latter is bound to conduct (business) and to stay in residence in Bruges and in the neighborhood (in order to attend) faithfully to all (business) that he shall see and understand to be to the honor, advantage, and welfare of the said compagnia *in accordance with mercantile custom, and to all orders and instructions of said Medici and Pigli, engaging in legitimate trade [and in] licit and honest contracts and exchange [dealings]. . . . Said Angiolo promises and obligates himself not to do business for himself or to have business done in his own name or in the name of others, directly or indirectly in the city of Bruges nor in any other place. . . . Further, said Angiolo promises and obligates himself not to have or have [someone else] gamble in any game of zara or cards, with dice or with anything else during the life of this said* compagnia, *under the penalty of L 100 groat for each instance. . . . And let it be understood he will incur the same penalty and disgrace any time he keeps any woman at his quarters at his expense.*[15]

With the conduct of much business by correspondence, and with regulation of far-flung and variegated business enterprises from the home office, written records naturally accumulated. Much of the correspondence was connected directly with business deals. Tommaso Portinari of the Medici office in Bruges, reporting in 1464, had a sorry tale for Cosimo,

[15] Robert S. Lopez and Irving W. Raymond, *Medieval Trade in the Mediterranean World* (New York: Columbia University Press, 1955), pp. 206–208.

the senior partner: "Our profits, as you will see, are very low this year, and expenditures have been high. . . . Let the new year bear the rest of the liabilities. We have made a good start in it and we shall continue in such a way that I hope that, through God's grace, we shall partly recoup the losses of the past. And, besides, we shall make it our care as far as possible to eliminate debtors and to move to a clean slate."[16] Other letters were veritable diplomatic newsletters, indicating how much the profits of the bigger companies were bound up in the political fortunes of the European governments. Where businessmen actually ran the government, as in Florence and Venice, news bearing on business was sent directly through their ambassadors, while the most comprehensive collection of news reports was made by the vast Fugger enterprise in Augsburg. French financier Jacques Coeur was so keen to have immediate political information that he built openings for carrier pigeons into the roof of his great mansion in Bourges. But the most important development in record keeping was also the most down-to-earth, the invention of modern methods of accounting. The replacement of clumsy Roman numerals with Arabic numerals made bookkeeping simpler and faster. The adoption of double-entry bookkeeping, the balancing of debit and credit accounts, became common in the fourteenth century, making possible the immediate establishment of the profitability of any enterprise and of the financial health of one's firm. Accurate bookkeeping made more possible the transfer of large sums of money from place to place without use of currency or bullion. The instrument used was the bill of exchange, by which one branch of a company promised to pay a specific sum of money, often in another currency, through one of its branches or an agent. The letter of exchange could be used by pilgrims, by the Church when collecting its income from other countries, or by merchants settling accounts; and its vast use left the way open for profit making by firms dealing in letters of credit, since there was not only a charge for the service but profiteering on changes in exchange rates or on loaning out the money deposited.

Thus changes in business methods helped the companies diversify their activities by engaging in banking. In their commercial activities they extended and sought credit, on which interest was made, after a certain verbal accommodation with the Church's laws against usury. The deposits of large sums of money for the letters of credit, the profits made from currency exchange, the role of certain companies as tax collectors for the papacy or the monarchies, and many other activities brought huge amounts of capital into the hands of the merchants, enabling them to become moneylenders, especially to princes with urgent needs of large sums of money. The Fuggers loaned Charles of Habsburg 543,000 florins in 1519, so that he could become Holy Roman Emperor by exceeding the bribes being offered to the electors by the kings of France

[16] Ibid., p. 404.

and England. Two of Florence's principal companies, the Bardi and the Peruzzi, however, were ruined in 1343 when the English king refused to pay one and a half million florins he owed them. Banking nevertheless remained a primary source of income for merchant companies throughout Europe, in spite of its risks, and was at the basis of every great fortune put together in the late Middle Ages.

Besides commerce and banking, the merchants also diversified their industrial activities or even shifted into wholly new forms of production. Increased mining of iron ore and other raw materials, in southern Belgium, and in Austria and Hungary, led to foundation of the metallurgical industry, and to investments in armaments and firearms production. Milan, finding its woolen industry in a state of decline, shifted into armaments production, and reached the point where it could outfit a small army in a few days. Liège, in the Low Countries, developed an iron industry, and then specialized in gunmaking. The prosperity of many cities in the Low

Countries, endangered with the growth of woolen industries in Italy and England, was saved by production of new types of cloth, such as linens like the cambric of Cambrai, or by concentration on enterprise hitherto of minor importance, such as the wheat commerce in Ghent. But frequently trade shifted from the old established cities, where guild restrictions crushed out new enterprise and imposed unacceptable financial burdens on commerce, to newer towns. Among the regions of greatest expansion in the fifteenth century were south Germany and Switzerland. They developed new industries like textiles and began to engage in banking, in order to service the growing markets of eastern Germany, Hungary, and Poland. The new wealth paid for the walls and fine middle-class homes of the lovely towns of northern Bavaria, such as Nördlingen and Rothen-

Panorama of Bamberg. Bamberg was an ecclesiastical state, governed by its powerful prince-bishop, whose four-towered cathedral dominates the city. (German Tourist Information Office photo.)

The Grand' Place, Antwerp. The upper floors of these late-Gothic houses are decorated with a triumphal arch covered with elaborate fretwork, a Flemish invention that soon spread throughout northern Europe. (Official Belgian Tourist Bureau.)

burg, and especially Augsburg and Nuremberg. In England, the wool trade brought wealth to the villages of Somerset and East Anglia, where the wool merchants erected parish churches like that of Long Melford, as grandiose as many cathedrals. And in the Low Countries the most significant change was the gradual shift of the role as banking and commercial center for northern Europe from Bruges to the more dynamic city of Antwerp.

Finally, merchants took more drastic measures for ensuring the continuance of their prosperity. Shipping routes were changed to take account of the rise of unfriendly empires, disturbances of war, or changes in maritime technique. The Venetians, for example, began to obtain their spices and other Asian goods from Syria and Egypt rather than from Constantinople and the Black Sea, while the Catalans developed new trade with northwest Africa. From the beginning of the fourteenth century, the Italians adopted new forms of ships, the single-masted cog, suitable for bulky cargoes, and the great galley, operated under sail on the open sea but capable of entering harbor propelled by oarsmen and defended from pirates by bowmen; and annual convoys of these ships were sent from Venice and Genoa to Flanders, calling on the way at the ports of Spain

Sixteenth-Century Galleon. This detail from the "Fall of Icarus" by Pieter Brueghel (c. 1525–1569) depicts the high-sterned galleon developed from the great galley of the fifteenth century. (Royal Museum of Fine Arts, Brussels. Official Belgian Tourist Bureau photo.)

and North Africa. These convoys were so secure that many merchants did not even use the newly invented marine insurance for their cargoes. These great fleets infused new life into the economy of Italy and the Low Countries. Yet perhaps the most important step taken by the cities was to prepare themselves for war and territorial expansion. In the fourteenth century, the Venetians abandoned the tradition of isolation from the mainland that had served them well and began to conquer a land empire that by 1400 included the lower Po valley and the nearby Alpine chain. In this way, they safeguarded their food supply and the control of the passes into south Germany, but only at the expense of long wars and growing dependence on mercenary armies. The Hanseatic League, a union of over seventy cities along the coast of the North and Baltic seas under the leadership of Lübeck and Hamburg, developed a powerful navy, with which they compelled Denmark to open the entrance to the Baltic to Hanseatic ships. In all these ways, the cities preserved their prosperity through recession and boom; and with their wealth they financed the great artistic creations of this period.

The Culture of the Late Middle Ages in Flanders. The cultural achievements were spread throughout Europe—the perpendicular style of late Gothic architecture in England, the burgher houses of the Hanseatic League, the sharply realistic wooden sculpture of south Germany, the illuminated books of Burgundy, the icon-covered cathedrals of the Moscow Kremlin, the songs and masses of the Parisian composers like Guillaume de Machaut. But it was in the cities of Flanders that late Gothic culture reached its highest peak, and it was in Italy that medieval culture gave way to the vibrantly new style of the Renaissance.

In the late fourteenth and fifteenth centuries, the artists of the Low Countries, and especially of Flanders, made great advances in almost every form of aesthetic creation: architecture in the city halls, belfries, and town houses; literature in the works of mystical devotion; music in the masses of Guillaume Dufay of Cambrai; sculpture in the dramatic altarpieces of Claus Sluter and his followers. But it was in painting that Flanders was supreme in the north of Europe, and Bruges was its artistic capital. In Bruges patrons abounded. The most important was the Duke of Burgundy, who moved his court there in 1419. The cloth merchants favored religious paintings with which they endowed the churches, especially triptychs for the high altar which featured the donor amid the groupings of saints and apostles. The foreign colony of resident agents who traded and banked for great Italian companies or the Hanseatic League preferred portraits of themselves, although as the fame of the Flemish artists spread to Italy they occasionally commissioned works for the patrons in Florence or Milan. Two of the finest Flemish paintings are of Italian merchants, Jan van Eyck's *Giovanni Arnolfini and His Wife,* and Hans Memling's *Tommaso Portinari,* whose report to his home office was just quoted. Painters from all over the Low Countries now settled in Bruges, where as members of the painters' guild they ensured that the Flemish style, once created, would remain intact for over a century.

The genius most responsible for the triumph of this style was Jan van Eyck (c. 1380–1441). With Van Eyck, the artist began to enjoy a new and higher status in society. He went on diplomatic missions for the duke, making portraits of possible candidates for the ducal hand. He was proud of his position, had his servants wear ducal livery, and broke with the still prevailing habit of artistic anonymity by signing his paintings. He usually inscribed *Als ich kann* (As best I can), with mock humility; in the Arnolfini portrait, in which he showed himself in the convex mirror, he wrote "Jan van Eyck was here." Van Eyck's technical contribution was in his mastery of oil painting, a technique which for centuries he was considered to have invented. As the Italian writer Vasari explained in the mid-sixteenth century, "To practice this method of painting one must proceed as follows: when one wishes to begin—having coated the panel or other surface with glue and plaster, having polished it and applied four or five layers of mild glue—one grinds the colors with nut oil or linseed oil (nut oil is better, for it yellows less); and having thinned them thus, they need no further treatment before being applied with the brush." The process, however, was much slower and more painstaking than that used today, because Van Eyck had to apply each color like thick glue, and then stroke it with his brush into the right thickness for the modulation of tone he was seeking. The end result, however, was a jewellike sparkle that has endured for five centuries.

Donor with his Patron, St. Peter Martyr, attributed to the Master of the St. Lucy Legend (active 1475–1500). Fifteenth-century artists often depicted the saints in company with the donors of the painting. The spires of Bruges can be seen in the distance. (Los Angeles County Museum of Art, Gift of Anna Bing Arnold.)

Tommaso Portinari, by Hans Memling (c. 1440–1494). Portinari was the Medici agent in Bruges. (The Metropolitan Museum of Art. Bequest of Benjamin Altman, 1913.)

Virgin and Child with Saints and Donor by Jan Van Eyck (c. 1380–1441). To the left of the Virgin is St. Barbara, to the right St. Elizabeth of Hungary. The kneeling donor is Jan Vos, Prior of a Carthusian Charterhouse near Bruges. (Copyright The Frick Collection, New York.)

Giovanni Arnolfini and his Wife by Jan Van Eyck, 1434. (The Granger Collection photo.)

A glance at a couple of Van Eyck's paintings will explain why art historians are divided between those who call him a late medieval painter and those who want to see in him the beginning of the northern Renaissance. The latter find the coming of a new conception of art and of man in Van Eyck's realism, in the portrayal of human beings, of interiors of buildings, and of landscape. In the portrait of Arnolfini, Van Eyck is interested in character. He explores the details of the Italian merchant's face, contrasting its white narrowness with the full, round hat he is wearing, emphasizing the flattened ears, the heavy lids, the heavy skin between the nostrils—a totally competent, self-controlled, perhaps even ruthless leader of the bourgeoisie. Even more striking however is the affection of the painter for the detail of material objects: shoes scattered on the floor, the ermine edging of Arnolfini's gown, fruit ripening in the sun, the intricate bronze candelabra, and the interior scene reflected in the mirror. Then there is the sense of perspective, made palpable by the framework of the window to the left and the bed on the right, a sense of receding space that Van Eyck frequently created by opening up his rooms through windows or porticoes to vast landscapes dotted with ships and towers and tiny people.

But Van Eyck and the Flemish painters who follow him for the next century are not men of the Italian Renaissance, in technique or in thought. The painters of the Italian Renaissance, as we shall see in the next chapter, had a theoretical basis for their work in Neoplatonism—they were out to present the "ideas" of the universe, in the Platonic sense, through pictorial representation. The Flemish artists delighted in the appearance of the things they could see, and presented a visual experience of a given moment in time. They worked instinctively to find the technique necessary; perspective was the result of observation by a craftsman, not of application of a theory of optics. Anatomy was seen from outside the skin, and not, as Italians worked, a presentation of thoroughly understood physiology. As a result, the Flemish paintings still seem stylized, or "primitive," from the way the people stand or move their bodies, and from the treatment of internal space. Their realism is far from photographic. The philosophy of the painters was thoroughly medieval, moreover. Van Eyck saw symbolism in all the material objects he inserted so lovingly in his paintings. In the Arnolfini painting, the little dog represents faithfulness; the fruit, the lost paradise of the garden of Eden; the beads of crystal and the mirror, purity and innocence; and the one lighted candle in the chandelier, Christ as the light of the world. For Van Eyck, the world was a whole. Every scene, the combination of the smallest objects and the broadest landscapes, must be an experience of the overall harmony of God's creation, almost in the same way as a Gothic cathedral. For the Flemish painters, the world of fifteenth-century Flanders was still the world of a living Christian faith. When Van Eyck depicted Prior Jan Vos praying next to the Virgin and Child, or Roger van der Weyden portrayed the Virgin at the foot of the cross as a Flemish matron in a Gothic church, one does not have the feeling, as with many Italian paintings, that the religious story is an excuse for a secular painting. On the contrary, by making the scene contemporary, the Flemish painters emphasized the relevance of the Christian story. It is revealing that when the emperor Charles V retired into the seclusion of a Spanish monastery to devote himself to a life of prayer and contemplation, he took with him only one painting, by Roger van der Weyden.

Throughout the fifteenth century, the artists of Flanders, like Hugo van der Goes, Hans Memling, and Gerard David, continued to produce masterpieces in the tradition established by Van Eyck. The contemporary changes in Italian painting had little influence on them; what interchange there was went from north to south. Hence the swan song of the Middle Ages lasted until the economic decay of Bruges and Ghent could no longer be ignored. From the beginning of the sixteenth century, the cultural life of the Low Countries began to move northward in the wake of its economic prosperity, first to Antwerp and then in the seventeenth century to Holland.

SUGGESTED READING

Among the general surveys of the late Middle Ages, Denys Hay, *Europe in the Fourteenth and Fifteenth Centuries* (1966) avoids narrative in favor of an excellent, original analysis of the nature of society. Wallace K. Ferguson, *Europe in Transition, 1300–1520* (1962) is sound and extensive, and has surveys of music and painting. Louis Halphen and Philippe Sagnac, eds., *La Fin du Moyen Age* (1931) is still useful for its articles by such great French historians as Edouard Perroy and Augustin Renaudet and the Belgian historian Henri Pirenne. Margaret Aston, *The Fifteenth Century: The Prospect of Europe* (1968) is well illustrated, treats Europe as a whole, and is especially useful on the diffusion of knowledge and on travel.

An admirable synthesis of recent research on the economic recession of the late Middle Ages is given by Harry A. Miskimin, *The Economy of the Early Renaissance, 1300–1460* (1969). Fuller and more specialized accounts are provided in the second edition of the *Cambridge Economic History of Europe,* vol. 1 (1966) dealing with agriculture, vol. 2 (1952) with industry and trade, and vol. 3 (1963) with economic organization and policies. The studies of North European trade by M. M. Postan and of southern European trade by R. S. Lopez in vol. 2 are particularly useful. On individual countries, see J. Vicens Vives, *An Economic History of Spain* (1969); Gino Luzzato, *An Economic History of Italy from the Fall of the Roman Empire until the Beginning of the Sixteenth Century* (1961); Sidney Pollard and David W. Crossler, *The Wealth of Britain, 1085–1966* (1968). The great changes in the agrarian economy of Europe during the high Middle Ages and the crisis of the late Middle Ages are described, with great variety of new documentation, by Georges Duby, *Rural Economy and Country Life in the Medieval West* (1968) and by B. H. Slicher van Bath, *The Agrarian History of Western Europe, A.D. 500–1850* (1963).

The changes in political organization that culminate in the "new monarchies" are discussed in Arthur J. Slavin, ed., *The New Monarchies and Representative Assemblies* (1964); but the most graphic account is Philip de Commines, *The Memoirs* (1886).

Among many excellent studies of the medieval city, the German cities receive unusually full treatment in Fritz Rörig, *The Medieval Town* (1967). Henri Pirenne, *Medieval Cities* (1956) is still the standard treatment of the Belgian cities. R. S. Lopez and I. W. Raymond have collected fascinating documents on all aspects of medieval commerce in *Medieval Trade in the Mediterranean World: Illustrative Documents* (1955). First-class monographs on individual cities, especially of Italian cities where documentation is superabundant, are numerous. See especially D. Herlihy's two studies, *Pisa in the Early Renaissance: A Study of Urban Growth* (1958) and *Medieval and Renaissance Pistoia: The Social History of an Italian Town* (1968); William K. Bowsky, *The Finance of the Commune of Siena, 1287–1355* (1970); and J. K. Hyde, *Padua in the Age of Dante* (1966).

The Belgian cities are most usually approached through their art, and up-to-date social and political studies are regrettably rare. William Gaunt, *Flemish Cities: Their History and Art* (1969) is a gorgeously illustrated attempt to link urban influences to style of painting. Joseph van der Elst, *The Last Flowering of the Middle Ages* (1944) is succinct and informative on Flemish painters. Jacques Lassaigne and Giulio Carlo Argan, *The Fifteenth Century, from Van Eyck to Botticelli* (1955) treats Flemish and Italian painting as part of one Renaissance. François Cali, *Bruges: The Cradle of Flemish Painting* (1964) has fine photographs and an evocative account of the development of art in Bruges, with special attention to the influence of folk religion. E. Gilliam-Smith, *The Story of Bruges* (1905) is old-fashioned but rich in detail.

INDEX